FOLLOWING THROUGH

Books by Herbert Warren Wind

The Story of American Golf

*Thirty Years of Championship Golf
(with Gene Sarazen)*

*The Complete Golfer
(Editor)*

*Tips from the Top
(Editor)*

*The Modern Fundamentals of Golf
(with Ben Hogan)*

On the Tour with Harry Sprague

The Gilded Age of American Sport

*Great Stories from the World of Sport
(Co-editor with Peter Schwed)*

*The Realm of Sport
(Editor)*

*The Greatest Game of All
(with Jack Nicklaus)*

The World of P. G. Wodehouse

Game, Set, and Match

Herbert Warren Wind's Golf Book

Following Through

HERBERT WARREN WIND

FOLLOWING
THROUGH

TICKNOR & FIELDS · NEW YORK

Library of Congress Cataloging in Publication Data
Wind, Herbert Warren, date
Following through.
1. Golf – Addresses, essays, lectures. 2. Golf –
United States – Addresses, essays, lectures. 3. Golf –
Great Britain – Addresses, essays, lectures. I. Title.
GV965.W685   1985   796.352'3   85-4781
ISBN 0-89919-398-6
ISBN 0-89919-483-4 (pbk.)

Printed in the United States of America

P 10 9 8 7 6 5 4 3 2 1

All material in this book appeared in *The New Yorker*
in slightly different form.

For Laurie and Bea Auchterlonie

Acknowledgments

I would like to thank William Shawn, the editor of *The New Yorker*, for his help and encouragement over the years. I would also like to thank the members of the magazine's crackerjack staff for their consummate work in making my articles better.

I would also like to acknowledge the assistance of a number of my colleagues on both sides of the Atlantic, who have tramped with me after the players and added so much to the pleasure of the occasion: Peter Ryde, Leonard Crawley, Pat Ward-Thomas, Donald Steel, Mark Wilson, Michael McDonnell, Raymond Jacobs, and Michael Williams, along with Dave Anderson, Robert Sommers, Al Laney, Nick Seitz, Kaye Kessler, Ross Goodner, Bob Green, Dan Jenkins, Dick Taylor, Jim Murray, Mike Hyland, and so many other good companions.

H.W.W.

Contents

Introduction

THEY SAY THAT NOWADAYS MORE THINGS HAPPEN IN A YEAR
than happened in ten years in the nineteenth century or in a score
of years in the eighteenth century. In this revved-up age, many
sports have undergone such drastic alterations that they are
hardly recognizable as the sports they were a mere quarter of a
century ago. In comparison with most games, golf has changed
relatively little over that period of time. Improved strains of grass
have been developed for the fairways and the greens. The graph-
ite shaft and the metal-headed driver and spoon have been introduced. In the 1970s, the United States Golf Association came up
with the ODS (Overall Distance Standard) ball that the top pros,
who generate tremendous clubhead speed at impact, can hit
around two hundred and eighty yards, thus making obsolete
some of the finest holes on some of the best courses in the country, unless those courses have been fortunate enough to have the
land to add new back tees. Prize money has grown by leaps and
bounds, and now many young men and women are able to prepare for careers as touring professionals by going to college on golf
scholarships. Essentially, however, golf has not changed in radical
ways.

The selections in this book were written during the last quarter
of a century. To be more precise, they cover the span from 1962 to
the present time. Why 1962? Well, that happened to be the year
that *The New Yorker* decided to start a new department called "The
Sporting Scene." Many writers have contributed to this department. Roger Angell has produced his brilliant, reflective articles
on baseball. E. J. Kahn, Jr., has covered the Olympic Games, and
Alastair Reid has kept the magazine's readers well informed on

the state of world soccer. For my part, I have written about tennis, football, and other sports but most frequently about golf, the game I know most about and which I have loved since boyhood. This book is a collection of some of my golf articles for "The Sporting Scene."

The New Yorker provides its contributors those two things that enable a writer to delve below the surface of his subject, space and time. Some of the articles reprinted here are very long, such as those on the fiftieth anniversary of the Masters tournament and on the playing of the 1984 British Open on the Old Course in St. Andrews, the lovely seaside town that is "the cradle of golf." They were special occasions. The bulk of my articles are considerably shorter, but since they are sufficiently expansive and wandering many people call them essays. I don't think they are essays in the classic sense, but they do deal with more than just the specific tournament at hand or the kind of golf the winner played.

In putting together this collection, I have taken the liberty of cutting some of the original articles quite severely and using only that section that describes a particular golfer or round or some other aspect of the game that seems worthy of being remembered. In golf on both sides of the Atlantic, the championships have long continued to be played on certain outstanding courses. I mention this since, in writing about a championship, I have often swung back to earlier tournaments played on that particular course, and in preparing this book those excursions proved to be very helpful indeed. When the current championship turned out to be on the dull side — for example, Hale Irwin's victory at Inverness in the 1979 U.S. Open — I thought it far more important to go with the first part of the article, which in this case was largely about Harry Vardon, the first modern golfer, and his adventures at Inverness when the Open was first held there in 1920. The great players of the period between 1962 and the present — Arnold Palmer, Jack Nicklaus, Gary Player, Mickey Wright, Tom Watson, Seve Ballesteros — are, to be sure, dealt with in detail, but because of the frequent use of the flashback, there is considerable space devoted to the giants of earlier eras, such as Vardon, Walter Hagen, Bobby Jones, the irrepressible Gene Sarazen, Byron Nelson, Sam Snead, and Ben Hogan.

I have also included a few articles and chunks of articles that are about people and places not all golfers are familiar with: Bernard Darwin, the best golf writer ever; a journey to Dornoch in northern Scotland, a sterling course that was more or less forgotten for centuries and has recently been "rediscovered" by golf pilgrims; Bing Crosby, the man behind the National Pro-Amateur tournament; Ballybunion, that magnificent Irish links; and the President's Putter tournament, which the members of the Oxford and Cambridge Golfing Society play at Rye, on the English Channel, in the cold of January. The reason for including all these is that they are full of golf.

Golf is a wonderful game. It is the only one played on natural terrain or on grounds made to resemble gently rolling linksland. It is the one outdoor game in which a stationary player hits a stationary ball. The fact that a player must generate his own power is one of the fundamental reasons that golf is perhaps the most difficult of all the major games to play consistently well. For one reason or another, golf seems to provide more fun and humor than any other game, and yet at the same time it has achieved the finest body of literature of any game. And golf has been a lucky game. It has been blessed with admirable champions and, decade after decade, this has renewed the high standards of sportsmanship and the pleasurable atmosphere associated with it.

H.W.W.

January 1985

FOLLOWING THROUGH

The Call of the Masters

Bernard Darwin, the grandson of the famous naturalist, wrote on a wide variety of subjects, but golf permeated his life thoroughly. He was the "golf correspondent" of The Times *of London for forty-five years and contributed regularly to* Country Life *magazine over an even longer period. Sir John Squire considered Darwin one of the six best essayists since Charles Lamb, and there is no question that he is in a class by himself when writing about golf. A great admirer of Bobby Jones, Darwin would have loved the Masters, but he was pushing seventy after the Second World War and never made the journey. Thousands of golfers, however, make it a point to be on hand each April at Augusta. For them it marks the beginning of another spring and another golf season.*

DURING HIS LONG AND REMARKABLE CAREER, BERNARD DARwin, the English golf writer, often had occasion to ruminate on the magic that certain railway junctions had for him — those at Leuchars, Ashford, Minster, Preston, and Birkenhead Park, for example. "Their names," he once wrote, "sound in my ears as chimes, ringing me home to my own country." Leuchars summoned up for Darwin the sound of the porter calling out, "Change for St. Andrews!," and Ashford "Change for Rye!" Minster meant Sandwich; Preston, St. Annes; Birkenhead Park, Hoylake. In this country, travelling to the golf courses where the major championships are held has seldom, even in the days when one bore down on them gently by rail, had anything like the cozy quality that warmed Darwin. The relative size of the two countries has something to do with this, naturally. So has the fact that the top British tournaments are almost always played over the same dozen or so courses, which have long made up what is called the championship "rota," while here it has long been the practice of the United States Golf Association, which conducts the National Open and the National Amateur Championships, and of the Professional Golfers' Association, which handles the P.G.A. Championship, to move these annual events around the country, so that golf fans residing in the various sections have a chance to take them in. Periodically, the National Open returns to a "traditional Open course," such as Oakmont, outside Pittsburgh, where it will be played this June and was last played in 1953. Ordinarily, though, the interval between National Opens at any one course is nearer twenty years than nine, and to hear the chimes ringing you home after an absence of this length requires the historically oriented eardrums of an Arthur Schlesinger, Jr., or a Casey Stengel.

All this comes to mind because another Masters tournament — the twenty-sixth, brilliantly won by Arnold Palmer — has just come to a close at the Augusta National Golf Club, in Augusta, Georgia. It is clearer today than it ever was that this comparatively young event not only is a full-fledged classic but already may have surpassed the United States Open in the hold it has on the imagination of the sports public. Attendance figures are never the whole story, or anything close to it, but this year, for the third time, a total of well over a hundred thousand people watched the four days of play of the tournament proper — more than twice the record turnout for the three days of the U.S. Open. (In addition, twenty million people are estimated to have tuned in to each of the telecasts from Augusta.) The Masters has a great many things going for it, some planned and some fortuitous. It is played on a superb and scenic course that inspires the fine field of players to spectacular feats and offers singularly good vantage points for spectators. It is held at a wonderful time of year, when practically every golfer, after a long hibernation, finds his fancy turning to thoughts of supinating the left forearm or some other such crucial action that will make the season at hand the big one he has been waiting for. It has flavor and innate prestige, since it is permeated with the personality of the founder and president of the Augusta National, Robert T. Jones, Jr., who is that rare sort of hero — in sports or any other field — a man whose actual stature exceeds that of the mythological figure he has been made into. In the judgment of quite a few old golf hands, however, the element that has made the Masters the Masters is that it is played on the same course year after year. For players and galleries alike, the tournament has a familiar, homecoming atmosphere, which none of the peripatetic championships can hope to match. Fewer than a hundred golf enthusiasts, I would guess, regularly follow the National Open from venue to venue, but there must be several thousand persons who, in the manner of Chaucer's pilgrims posting to Canterbury, head for Augusta early each April.

Most of those who come to the Masters from any appreciable distance make the journey by plane. Few flights are scheduled directly from faraway cities to Augusta, for although the sleepy old town has recently been aroused by the establishment of several new industrial plants, there are fifty-one weeks of the year in which travellers can hardly be said to descend on it in substantial numbers. Atlanta, accordingly, serves as a junction. It is not, of course, the sort of junction Darwin had in mind; no porter shouts "Atlanta! Change for Augusta!," and a large air terminal, with its long, hollow corridors and its semi-lost transients, hardly conjures up the feeling that the promised land is at hand. Still, Augusta is only fifty minutes by air from Atlanta, and when you land at Augusta's pleasant little airfield, everything is just as you have remembered. The air is sweet and soft; you never fail to see a few familiar golf faces around the terminal; and the man at the car-rental desk once again can't seem to find a record of your reservation and can't quite fathom how anyone could have written you a confirmation.

The main entranceway to the Augusta National Golf Club is a narrow drive, some three hundred yards long and lined with unbroken rows of magnolia trees, which interlace overhead. A slow progress down this lane to the sunlit white clubhouse is the first of three moves that a very high percentage of the Augusta regulars apparently must make each year before they feel really at home again. The second is a walk around the clubhouse to the terrace at the rear, from which one can gaze down at the eighteen holes, which Jones and Alister MacKenzie, his co-designer, laid out over the slope of a natural amphitheatre. It is the prettiest vista in golf, and the returning regular wants to make certain it's still there. Indeed it is. Rye grass sown with the Bermuda grass is still imbuing the fairways with a distinctive lustre. As befits a property that was once one of the South's leading nurseries, some of the flowering shrubs along the fairways are in full bloom. The pines towering behind the tenth green are just as tall as memory had them. "Yes, it's all intact," the regular says to himself. He is then ready to make the third, and last, move in his annual process of reacclimatization. He watches a twosome of golfers he particularly likes drive off the first tee and follows them out onto the course. After observing the approach shots on the opening hole, a moderate-length par 4, he doesn't bother to find a position near the green but walks directly to a spot at the edge of the rough along the right side of the second hole (555 yards, par 5), about 275 yards out, at just about the point where the fairway begins to tumble downhill to the green. He takes in the two drives. He takes in the two second shots. Somehow this seems to do it — watching one pair of golfers play their tee shots and their long approaches to the second hole. From that moment on, the itinerary of one Augusta regular may have nothing at all in common with that of another. Each man (or small group) plays it by ear. Some go on to the second green, watch their twosome putt out, and perhaps stay with them all the way, if either player happens to be working on a hot round; others wait on the hillside to watch a few more pairs come by, getting their eyes limbered up meanwhile by switching their attention from the putting on the distant green to the second shots played directly in front of them and then back to a new pair driving from the tee; still others head at a brisk trot for the scoreboard near the third green and tune up their arithmetic by studying the scores between quick looks at the action on the third, a short par 4, and side glances at the tee shots on the fourth, a dramatic par 3, 220 yards long, where the pin is usually placed behind a deep key bunker that noses into the heart of the slanting green. Most regulars stay out on the course until late in the afternoon, resting and roving by instinct, and sustaining themselves with pimento-spread sandwiches and the golf itself. The only time they tend to reconvene at a single spot comes when one of the leaders nears the riskiest bend on the course, down by Rae's Creek, for then nearly everyone — as many as fifteen thousand people on some days — perches on a slope that serves as a grandstand for the two make-or-break holes, the twelfth and thirteenth.

This feeling of extraordinary kinship with the Masters is not restricted to those who go to Augusta. In general, golf fans cerebrate and talk about their preoccupation as no other sports group does, and the talk of the returning pilgrims about the Masters — abetted to a considerable degree by the telecasts and by the year-round rhapsodies of the golf-writing press — has created such an inordinate wave of interest in the event that many men who have never set foot on the course have acquired a knowledge of it that really is amazing. You would expect golf fans everywhere in the country to be fairly well acquainted with the last four holes, for these are covered by the television cameras, but somehow they know the terrain and the strategic demands of all eighteen, and can rattle on about "the new green on the eighth," and "that long arm of the creek on the thirteenth that caught Patton's second in '54," and "those gusts of wind that puff up on the short twelfth and give Palmer so much trouble every year," and "the low branches of the pines that kill you on the seventh if you drive it down the right side of the fairway." Only one other course in the long history of golf has ever been comparably familiar to the golfing public at large — the Old Course at St. Andrews. No self-respecting golf club in Britain would think its bar complete unless a print of the famous MacKenzie map of the Old Course hung on the wall, and when you add this handy reference to the decades of chatter about what old So-and-So did on the Road Hole and the trouble young What's-His-Name met up with on the eleventh, it becomes almost understandable — almost, but not quite — that so many Britons know each bunker at St. Andrews by its designated name and could probably walk out blindfolded from the first tee to any one you mentioned.

(1962)

Thunder on the Left

This excerpt from an article about the 1963 British Open is historically important in two respects: it was the last thirty-six-hole playoff ever held, and it marked the only time that a left-handed golfer, Bob Charles, carried off one of the major championships.

GRANTING THAT MOST PLAYOFFS ARE A LETDOWN AND THAT thirty-six-hole playoffs are exactly eighteen holes too long, you could not hope for a more fascinating duel than the one Charles and Rodgers put on. To begin with, the vivid contrast been the two men added a great deal of zest to the long day's journey. Down one side of the fairway walked Charles, a former bank clerk — tall, spare, dark, and aquiline, the proper reserved New Zealander. (As long as there is a New Zealand, there'll always be an England.) He went about his business with scarcely a word or a grimace, acknowledging the gallery's applause with a little upward flick of his forefinger. Down the other side of the fairway rumbled Rodgers, a twenty-five-year-old former Marine who stands a little under five feet eight and packs a hundred and ninety pounds. (His standard evening meal during the tournament, by the way, consisted of some smoked salmon, a double order of filet of sole, a filet mignon, and a triple order of chocolate ice cream.) Blond, freckled, garrulous, and likable, Rodgers has grown up in the television-golf era, which has brought back vaudeville, and on the greens he trots out a wide repertoire of sight gags, comic steps, and patter. He can also play golf — forceful golf — and in the playoff he had to, in order to stay in the game, for Charles went off on the most sensational putting spree I can recall in a major event since Billy Casper's exhibition at

Winged Foot in our 1959 Open. On the morning round, Charles had no less than eleven one-putt greens, and these included twenty-five-footers on the third and thirteenth, a seventeen-foot uphiller on the fifteenth, and a sliding twenty-foot downhiller on the sixteenth. He had a 69 and led by three strokes at lunch. In the afternoon, he dropped only two really sizable putts, but they were the cruelest kind of all. The first, for a birdie, came on the fourth and cancelled out a much longer birdie putt (and an excellent rendition of the old spiked shoe) by Rodgers. The second came on the eighth, a medium-length par 4 where both men were on in two — Charles thirty feet away, and Rodgers, who had fought back admirably to be only a stroke behind at this point, some fifty feet beyond and above the cup. Rodgers holed that monster, and then Charles broke his heart by holing right on top of him again. That was the playoff. Charles' final margin was eight strokes.

As you can see, Bob Charles has the temperament needed in his unnerving profession. It is rooted in his deep confidence that he can play golf as well as anyone in the world. Earlier in his career, when he was new to our pro circuit, he could be as sour as de Gaulle when he felt that he was being viewed more as a curiosity than as a serious candidate for top honors. He has never felt that he was an oddity, possibly because he is naturally right-handed. He started to play golf from the "wrong side" as a boy because his parents were both left-handed golfers and their clubs were the only ones readily available. I don't know where all this leads us, but I have an idea that it will be only a matter of time now before a major title falls to the world's greatest cross-handed golfer — Sewsunker Sewgolum, a South African of Indian descent who is the current Natal Open champion. This is not as farfetched as it might seem. At Lytham, Sewgolum finished a laudable thirteenth with a total of 290, four shots ahead of Palmer. And he wasn't putting at all.

(1963)

North to the Links of Dornoch

The Royal Dornoch Golf Club lies north of the southern Highlands, at about the same latitude as Juneau, Alaska. One of the oldest and most beautiful of the Scottish linksland courses, it had been neglected for many years; it was just too far out of the way. Richard Tufts' enthusiasm for Dornoch — Donald Ross, Pinehurst's golf-course architect, had come from there — led an increasing number of golf pilgrims to make the journey north. In a comparatively short time, it became the "in" course for touring golfers, and it was selected by the R. and A. as the venue for the 1985 British Amateur.

A LITTLE OVER A CENTURY AGO, THE GAME OF GOLF UNDERWENT a change that revolutionized its character and completely redirected its course — the traditional feather-stuffed leather ball, which had been in use for four hundred years, and perhaps longer, was replaced by a ball made of gutta-percha, a rubberlike substance derived from certain sapotaceous trees found in Malaya. Up to that time, golf had been played almost exclusively by Scots living in Scotland, but the new ball, which was harder and more durable, changed all this. Not only was it much easier for the average player to get the gutta-percha ball off the ground and control its general direction but it also flew a thrillingly long distance — yards farther than the old feather ball ever went. In short, the "gutty," as it was known at the time, made golf a better, pleasanter, and far more fascinating game, and started its transformation from an occult Scottish passion into a universal pastime, currently being pursued by some fifteen million devotees wherever grass sprouts, and sometimes where it doesn't. As golf's popularity spread, Scotland's dominance over nearly every phase of the game diminished. By the second decade of this century,

Scots were no longer the only accomplished clubmakers or golf-course architects or teachers, for example. Moreover, Scottish players, who had always dominated competitive golf, were being supplanted by champions produced in the United States and in other countries comparatively new to the game. (It takes some believing, but the last time a Scot residing in Scotland won the British Open was in 1893, when Willie Auchterlonie, of St. Andrews, carried the day.) Scotland has, nevertheless, continued to be regarded as *the* golf country. That this is so is the result neither of a polite gesture toward "the cradle of the game" by the golfers of the world nor of a shrewd conspiracy among them based on an awareness that a great deal of what is romantic and beckoning (and merchandisable) about golf is tied in with its Scottish heritage. The explanation is much more elementary. In the first place, for all the enterprise and enthusiasm of the converts to the game in this country and elsewhere, no one loves golf quite as whole-heartedly as the Scots do, and no one plays it more assiduously. Second, at its best the Scottish golfing milieu remains incomparable, for, in a wonderful way, many of the famous old championship links have proved themselves ageless — as challenging and as enjoyable right now as the Augusta National, Kasumigaseki, Royal Melbourne, or any of the other new-fledged masterpieces. Above all, in no other country is the entire fabric of life threaded so inextricably with golf as it is in Scotland. For instance, there's no need for an enthusiast who finds himself in mixed company to feel that an hour's uninterrupted discussion of golf is perhaps enough and that one must think of the ladies. Most of the ladies either play golf or have played it at one time or another, and the few exceptions are remarkably well versed in the game, or else in acting.

As the venerable but still vigorous home of golf — and in addition one of the earth's most beautiful lands, when the sun is shining — Scotland is annually visited by thousands of golfers from all over the globe. The large majority come as confessed pilgrims and carry long lists, built up since childhood, of the things they must not fail to see or do at the historic shrines. For example, in St. Andrews, the old gray town on the Fifeshire peninsula, these "musts" include a tour of the weather-beaten clubhouse of the Royal and Ancient Golf Club of St. Andrews, the august R. and A., which for over two centuries has been the governing body of the game for all golfers except those in America, where the game is regulated by the United States Golf Association; a visit to the cathedral graveyard in which Old Tom Morris, the beloved nineteenth-century professional, is buried; a call at Laurie Auchterlonie's golf shop, where the son of the 1893 Open champion still turns out magnificent clubs by hand; and, to be sure, at least one round on the Old Course, a heaving sea of dunes, bunkers, and gorse that most golfers despise at first encounter and then grow to love as they become familiar with its strange but functional subtleties. Indeed, I suppose the primary lure that Scotland holds for the modern pilgrim is its celebrated championship courses, on which, as he plays, he can dream his dreams of the old giants and the more recent heroes who performed their unforgettable deeds on that very ground. In Scotland, these championship courses — that is, courses on which British Open and Amateur Championships have been contested — are separated into three geographic clusters; one lies south of Glasgow on the west coast, another east of Edinburgh on the east coast, and the third north of Edinburgh. In the west-coast cluster, bordering the Firth of Clyde, the two most important courses are Prestwick, where the British Open was founded, in 1860, and Troon, where Arnold Palmer established a new record score — 276 — for the Open in 1962. At the risk of irreverence, it might be noted, however, that by contemporary standards Prestwick is a little too short and a shade too quaint to test the most accomplished players, that Troon's holes lack distinction and variety, and that these days the best golf in the area is probably to be found on the remodelled Ailsa course, at Turnberry, twenty-five miles farther south, where the 1963 Walker Cup match was held. The complex of golf links east of Edinburgh, hugging the southern shore of the Firth of Forth, includes Gullane No. 1, Muirfield, and North Berwick. (Strictly speaking, a links is a stretch of seashore made up of sand hills and more gently undulating ground. Golf was first played on links, because the terrain lent itself naturally to use as tees, greens, bunkers, and so on, and also because the sandy soil produced wonderfully crisp, close-knit turf. The British championships have always been held exclusively on linksland courses.) Gullane No. 1, which is where Babe Didrikson Zaharias won the British Ladies Amateur Championship in 1947, and North Berwick, where the in-nine edges along a sharp cliff above the sea, are both very agreeable courses, but the jewel of this area is Muirfield. The finest orthodox layout in Britain, Muirfield is maintained in such splendid condition that it always looks as if a major tournament must be starting there the next day. It is entirely fitting that this classic course should today be the seat of the Honourable Company of Edinburgh Golfers, the oldest club in golf, which was organized in 1744 (ten years before the R. and A.) at Leith and later made its headquarters at Musselburgh before moving down the road to its present site, in 1891. In the third area, to the north of Edinburgh, the outstanding courses are St. Andrews and Carnoustie, which was the scene of Ben Hogan's dramatic victory in the 1953 Open, in which he lowered his score on each successive round — 73, 71, 70, 68 — and eventually won by four shots. Since Scotland is a much smaller country than most people think of it as being — it is only about the size of Maine — all these championship courses are situated within a comfortable three-hour drive from a central point like, say, Gleneagles, and this means that a charged-up pilgrim can, if he wishes, assault a different course every day for a week and still get back to his hotel in time for dinner.

I rank high among the pleasures of a misspent adulthood the dozen trips to Scotland I have been fortunate enough to make during the past twenty-five years — trips that have enabled me to play and study all the championship courses and a number of others. It pleases me greatly that quite a few of my Scottish friends now consider me fairly well acquainted, for a foreigner, with the wine of the country. At the same time, they invariably take pains to point out that the golfer who has visited only the three central clusters of courses has not savored the full range of first-rate Scottish golf, any more than the gourmet travelling in France has exhausted the possibilities for memorable dining once he has eaten at all the restaurants awarded three stars by *Le Guide Michelin*. In the opinion of Sam McKinlay, the editor of the Glasgow *Evening Times* and one of the my most knowledgeable Scottish friends (he is not only a most discerning golf writer but a genuinely gifted player, who represented Britain in the 1934 Walker Cup match), there are at least half a dozen Scottish links of very high rank that have remained comparatively unknown, principally because they are off the golfer tourist's beaten track. These include Cruden Bay, near Aberdeen, to which McKinlay, in the burry version of *Le Guide Michelin* that he occasionally introduces into his golf writings, awards two thistles, the second-highest rating; Blairgowrie, at Rosemount, in the lower Highlands (two thistles); Machrihanish, an old links, with marvellous turf, that sits near the tip of the Kintyre peninsula, west of the Firth of Clyde (two thistles); Nairn, on the southern shore of the Moray Firth, slightly east of Inverness (two thistles); and Dornoch, far up north, well beyond Inverness and, indeed, only seventy miles below John o'Groat's, the northernmost point of Scotland (three thistles, the top rating). Incidentally, in McKinlay's opinion, only St. Andrews, Muirfield, and Ailsa currently deserve three thistles, along with Dornoch. Though he and I had talked for many years about a holiday golfing trip to one or two of these neglected beauties, something or other had always come up, and we didn't manage to pull it off until last spring, when I went over for the Walker Cup match and McKinlay, with local murder cases and soccer fever at a nice low pitch for a change, was able to arrange a short absence from his editorial duties. As an old suscriber to *Le Guide McKinlay*, I was hardly surprised when, on the eve of our expedition, he announced that, all things considered, we could do no better than go up to Dornoch. On the way north, we would definitely play Nairn and maybe Lossiemouth, and perhaps, later on, the little course at Golspie, but Dornoch — that was where we were going.

On an untypically balmy afternoon in late May, three days after the conclusion of the Walker Cup match, I left Glasgow with Mc-Kinlay and his wife, Marian, a non-golfer but a sound, sensitive woman nonetheless. Glasgow is a sprawling place, and when you are heading northeast out of town, as we were, it takes a good forty minutes to get its rampant grime behind you. But then, when you finally do reach the countryside, it arrives with a gorgeous thump. Bluebells and other wild flowers were growing in profusion along the winding roads. In the sunlight, the small lakes and wide fields of the central Lowlands gleamed with their bold primary greens and blues, which, when you see them emblazoned on a postcard, always suggest that an inferior job of color reproduction has been done, even though you may know better. Away in the distance, tying everything together, were the southern ridges of the Grampians, the aggregate designation for the numerous chains of hills and mountains that mark the beginning of the Highlands. It is approximately two hundred miles from Glasgow to Nairn by the main route over the southeastern Highlands, but the roads are excellent and the traffic is light, and a motorist who is in a hurry can knock off the drive in four and a half hours. We took a leisurely six hours, not counting a stop for tea at an inn in Dunkeld, some thirty miles beyond Gleneagles. Tea in Scotland (or anywhere in Britain, for that matter) can, of course, be the best meal of the day, and this tea happened to be a particularly good one, but our stop at Dunkeld stays in my mind for quite another reason. While many of the people I have met through golf have proved to have no other appreciable interests and, accordingly, have on occasion been wearing company, Sam McKinlay has a fine, old-fashioned breadth of knowledge and enthusiasm. Among other things, he has the ability — possessed by many more Britons than Americans — to tap at appropriate moments, with an utter lack of pomposity, a store of quotations from the books we were all subjected to in our youth but now recall only hazily, if at all. At Dunkeld, while we were waiting for our tea, we took a short turn in the garden behind the inn, which backs up on the Tay, the famous salmon river. At this point in its descent from the Highlands to the North Sea, the Tay is only about sixty yards wide — a full, fast-rushing stream shaded by ancient trees and alive with skimming birds. While we were staring at the water, a bird on the far bank broke into song. Marian McKinlay instantly identified it as a thrush. Her husband continued to listen to the bird's song. "Oh, how right Browning was!" he remarked with obvious gratification a moment later. "The thrush does sing each song twice over, infallibly." At my request, since I can never get the passage straight, he recited the pertinent lines from "Home-Thoughts, from Abroad":

> That's the wise thrush; he sings each song twice over,
> Lest you should think he never could recapture
> The first fine careless rapture!

The most scenic route into the southeastern Highlands, and the one that tourists ordinarily take, climbs from Blairgowrie through Braemar to Ballater, the railroad station for Balmoral, where the Royal Family has spent summer holidays since Queen Victoria set the precedent, in 1855. (Victoria, by the way, deserves nearly all the credit for popularizing the Highlands; until she went there, they had been generally regarded, even — or perhaps especially — by the Lowland Scots, as a wild, backward waste.) The route we followed — the through route to the north — runs some twenty miles farther to the west, roughly paralleling the road to

Balmoral and passing through Pitlochry, Blair Atholl, Kingussie, Aviemore, and Grantown-on-Spey, where the main road continues to Inverness and a right fork, which we took, leads to Nairn. Apart from noting that the Highlands are not particularly high — the tallest peaks rise only about four thousand feet above sea level — the only point I wish to make about them is that in late May the heather covering the long, sweeping, rocky slopes is still a wintry dun color, and as a result the vistas, though noble in their contours, are nowhere near as overwhelming as they must be late in June, when the pinkish-purple bell heather bursts into bloom, or late in August, when the real heather, the ling heather, turns the hillsides a vibrant purple. And as for the traveller whose love of the Highlands is based on their rare desolateness, I recommend the Dava Moor, just north of Grantown-on-Spey, for this is an upland desert of unusually dark heather — greenish, blackish brown with a touch of red in it, the fusion of colors that the Scots call "moorit" when they reproduce it in tweed. The road to Nairn cuts slowly across this dour stretch, and, perhaps because I was completely unprepared for any such change, since I had been gazing only minutes earlier at the genial Spey as it purled by Grantown, I found the Dava Moor far more forbidding than any part of the Highlands proper. I was therefore in a suitable mood to twitch a little at the shoulders when, only a few miles beyond the moor, a road sign suddenly announced that the village of Cawdor lay a mile to the west. This, sure enough, is the Cawdor of *Macbeth*, and it is just where it should be. The castle still stands, a minor tourist attraction today. Nairn is six miles farther north, a town of white houses along the blue waters of the Moray Firth.

Probably the first distinguished traveller to visit Nairn was Dr. Samuel Johnson, who passed through with Boswell en route to the Hebrides on their famous journey in 1773. Johnson found the town in "a state of miserable decay" and added, in his best dyspeptic growl, that "we had no motive to stay longer than to breakfast." Nairn has come on quite a bit since then. Having been one of the most popular of the Scottish seaside resorts for many years now, it blandly calls itself the Garden of the North, and not without some justification. It gets more sunshine than nearly any other spot in Scotland, for the rugged mountains along the west coast intercept most of the rain-bearing winds. Nairn has good beaches, and there are some excellent fishing streams close by, but most of the people who vacation there regularly — Harold Macmillan, for one — are attracted by its golf facilities. There are two eighteen-hole courses — Nairn Dunbar, an unexciting layout, and Nairn proper, a splendid test that has several times been the venue of the Scottish Amateur Championship. Catering to the golfers and other visitors are a dozen or so large hotels and numerous guesthouses. We stopped at the Alton Burn, one of the more modest hotels, which looks out on the sixteenth hole of the Nairn course. It was nearly nine o'clock when I met the McKinlays in the bar before dinner, but in Scotland in late spring it stays light until almost midnight, and we watched a steady parade of players moving down the sixteenth fairway. On one wall of the bar was a photograph of Hogan at Carnoustie, and on another was a placard announcing the tournament schedule in the Dundee area, this calendar of events being printed over an action photo of that estimable old Scottish golfer Arnold Palmer. In this setting, we found ourselves warming up to the game, and it was a good thing we did, for after dinner we called on the Kenny Camerons, long-time friends of the McKinlays, and it was like stepping into an inferno of golf. Mrs. Cameron is a perfectly normal Scotswoman, but her husband is the compleat golf fanatic. McKinlay had prepared me for him by telling me that he had a predilection for telephoning in the middle of the night and taking the better part of an hour to replay some exceptionally good recent round of his stroke by stroke and trauma by trauma. Cameron turned out to be a pleasant-looking, baldish fellow, somewhere in his forties, with bright brown eyes and a Scots accent considerably stronger than the McKinlays'. (Theirs is pure, if soft, Glasgow, though when Mrs. McKinlay gets north of Pitlochry her speech recaptures something of the intonation of Banffshire, where she was born.) During the exchange of greetings, the McKinlays happened to mention to Cameron that he looked a little thinner, and with that he was off and running.

"You're right about that," he said, slapping his stomach hard. "I've taken off a full stone in the last two months. Put it on during the winter when the course was frozen solid — a sheet of ice. Mind you, you could have played, but none of the lads would go out with me. They're a soft lot. So I just sat around putting on weight, and then, when the course was finally fit for play, about the end of March, I discovered I had a problem. When I addressed the ball" — and here he leaped to his feet to demonstrate — "I could hardly see it. My stomach blocked out the view." The brown eyes twinkled. "I was scratching around trying to break eighty, and you know, Sam, that's not my usual, is it? I had to either lose the extra pounds or play the ball an inch or two farther away from me, where I could see it, which meant altering my swing. Well, I didn't want to tinker around with my swing, so I just had to lose that extra stone, and now I'm hitting the ball solidly — right in the back, and, more important, dead straight. Not putting, mind you. I can't putt for toffee, never could." Again his eyes twinkled. "But hitting the ball sweetly, that I am. You know our fifth hole, that long two-shotter. Last week, into a nor'wester — nor'nor'west, actually — I hit a switcher off the tee and was up with a spoon, an absolute cracker. The only thing that's bothering me is that if I'd kept that extra stone I might have been up with an iron. There's aye a something, isn't there?"

Cameron paused for a moment to stoke himself with some orange sponge-cake and coffee his wife had produced, but soon he was off again, describing in painstaking detail some of his spring matches against golfers whom McKinlay knew, dissecting Palmer's and Nicklaus's swings, inveighing against the current condition of the greens on the Nairn course, discussing the respective merits of the small British ball and the large American ball, and tirelessly replaying some of the switchers, crackers, thrusters, and screamers he had gallantly dispatched at critical moments over the last three decades. If Cameron were not a first-class golfer — he has been champion of the Nairn Golf Club five times and Nairnshire Amateur champion thirteen times — his monologues might be harder to take, but, on second thought, they might not. He is, as one soon learns, a charming and substantial fellow, yet where golf is concerned he is powerless to control his exuberance. Savonarola could have as easily stopped preaching. It was typical of Cameron that when we finally concluded our visit, well after midnight, and were walking to the car, he should completely transpose a remark I made about his lovely lawn. "Na, na, it's no good at all," he said, shaking his head. "The texture's all wrong. Try practicing a few pitch shots there and it'll ruin your touch. It's nothing like the grass at the club. I think I'll have to rip it up and replant the damn thing."

Just then a bird sang out.

"Hear that?" Cameron asked, his eyes softening. "That's the

wise thrush. Remember the poem? 'He sings his song several times over lest you think he can't capture that rapture again.' Robert Browning."

Three angry voices assaulted him, one on top of another.

"That's *not* the wise thrush," Mrs. McKinlay said.

"Browning wrote no such lines," her husband said, his eyes shut in pain.

"That's enough for tonight, Kenny," Mrs. Cameron said.

The friend of golf and poetry mutely waved an abashed good night.

One of the primary attractions of Scottish golf is its inexpensiveness. The annual dues at the Nairn Golf Club, for example, are six guineas, or less than eighteen dollars; at an American club of comparable quality they would run between four hundred and seven hundred dollars. Similarly, the green fee for a visiting golfer at Nairn comes to only eighty-five cents for a day's play. For a full fortnight's play, the fee is roughly eight dollars — about the same amount a guest must pay for one day's play at many a private club here. Like all but a few of the Scottish courses, Nairn cost next to nothing to build. In 1877, when a group of local sportsmen became convinced that the rudimentary holes of the town's links did not offer a satisfactory test for the new type of golf that the gutta-percha ball had created, they engaged Andrew Simpson, the pro at the Royal Aberdeen Club, to look the situation over and recommend a plan for an up-to-date course. After studying the sandy, whorly, self-draining land that adjoined the original links, Simpson estimated that it would cost between thirty and forty pounds to remove the excess bushes from the new strip and prepare the tees, fairways, and greens of the holes he had plotted. The construction actually came to thirty-six pounds. Nowadays, even in Scotland, it takes that much money to reshape a bunker or put in a new back tee, and the members of Nairn are inclined to think of the nineteenth century as the golden age of golf. They brighten up noticeably when they hear that in America it is nothing unusual for a course to cost more than half a million dollars. Since we have no linksland to speak of, most of our courses are built on clayey soil, and not infrequently the sites selected are fairly rocky or quite heavily wooded. Converting such an area into good golf holes can be a long and expensive operation; the land must be cleared, the contours of the fairways and greens shaped by earth-moving machines, water hazards developed, bunkers excavated, complicated drainage and watering systems installed, and the soil fortified. I might add, however, that one sometimes suspects that a sizable percentage of our modern American golf architects, if they were confronted with an inspiring stretch of linksland, would proceed by reflex to bulldoze the natural contours as flat as an airstrip and then go on to construct a costly succession of trite artificial holes.

McKinlay and I played Nairn for the next three days, for we decided to pass up an excursion to Lossiemouth, thirty miles to the east, when we learned that the Royal Navy had established a jet airbase there, which had set the whole area dinning with noise. We arranged to play our rounds in the afternoon, when Cameron, with his day's business well squared away, was free to join us. He is a fancy-groceries and wine merchant, a sort of Fortnum & Mason of upper Scotland, who supplies many of the fishing and shooting lodges in the Speyside area, and a few as far away as Skye, with the basic delicacies. During our stay in Nairn, the Garden of the North put on a very good show — lots of sunshine and not a drop of rain. There was, however, plenty of wind, and it was piercing enough to force Cameron and McKinlay into two heavy sweaters apiece for golf, and me into two sweaters, a windbreaker, a muffler, and rain trousers. On British seaside courses, where there are no trees enclosing the holes, the wind is the major hazard a golfer must contend with. On the rare windless days, Nairn, for example, is not very much of a problem, for it is a relatively short layout, only 6,342 yards long from the back tees. Set smack beside the Moray Firth, with the peaks of Ross and Cromarty looming grand in the distance, it is an aesthetic treat, but, like a number of Scottish links (among them St. Andrews), it has, to my mind, one serious shortcoming. It is a loop-type course — that is, the first nine holes march more or less in a straight line away from the clubhouse, along the water's edge, and the second nine holes march back, roughly parallel. On most days, as a result of this unimaginative routing, the wind is continuously in the player's face on one nine and continuously at his back on the other — a situation that doesn't make for very interesting golf. An east wind was blowing all three days at Nairn, and we had it with us (and a little across, right to left) on the first nine, and against us (angling across, left to right) coming back. McKinlay and Cameron, consequently, were never over par — 35 — to the turn, and I myself, although I am not at all in their class, experienced only minor difficulties. The second nine was quite another story. On each round, McKinlay and Cameron stood up very well against the blustery wind, playing superb shots that kept the ball low and on a line. They regularly scored only a stroke or two higher coming back than they had going out. I am not a proficient enough player, however, to control the ball when playing into a heavy wind, and at Nairn this was disastrous, for most of the fairways on the second nine are hemmed in tightly on both sides by gorse. In England, gorse is commonly called furze. In Scotland, it is sometimes called whin, pronounced "whun." By any name, it is a thick, spreading, thorny bush that grows from two to five feet high, and generally in clumps. To give it its due, it is, from a safe distance, very lovely to behold, for its flower is the brightest yellow you can conceive of — far more brilliant than forsythia, say. However, a mass of gorse is no place to drive a golf ball into. You can seldom find it, and I am beginning to think that if you can't you are undoubtedly better off, for it is usually wedged so fast among the prickly spines that you need at least two strokes — and often a good many more — to dislodge it and hack it back to the fairway. To be brief, then, each time we tackled the second nine I hooked or pushed at least three tee shots deep into the gorse and slowed the whole parade down. There is nothing much a man can do at such grim moments but play on, accepting his penalty strokes and his general humiliation with what grace he can muster as he broods his way back to the sanctuary of the clubhouse, where, if he is lucky, not too many people will ask him what he scored for his round. I was fortunate in playing with two understanding golfers — though it did take Cameron some time to get used to the fact that an American could be capable of such poor golf. The many spectacular victories in international competitions by our golf teams and our individual stars had bred in him, as in many other Scots, the erroneous idea that all Americans are, *ipso facto*, terrific players. (The corollary is equally false; simply because the top British golfers are not quite in the same class as ours, it does not follow that, as many Americans think, no one in England or Scotland knows how to play the game. In fact, it is my own feeling that the average British golfer is a somewhat better player than his American counterpart.) Cameron, by the way, is only moderately talkative on the links. When he plays a good shot, he follows through with a delighted outburst on the order of "Well done, Kenny, my lad!" or "Ah, Cameron, that's the stuff to give 'em — a real switcher!" but nothing more lavish than that. He is not the facile, Jonesian stylist that McKinlay is, but his method is sound and he is a model of accuracy. He was never once in the gorse during our three rounds, and I could well believe his modest claim that he had lost only one ball all year, and that one in a particularly thick sea mist.

By auto, it is about a hundred miles from Nairn to Dornoch. We made the trip at a leisurely pace, visiting the battlefield on Culloden Moor, where the Duke of Cumberland crushed Bonnie Prince Charlie's Highlanders in 1746, and later stopping for lunch in Inverness, the metropolis of northern Scotland. Actually, we drove on north of Dornoch for about ten miles, to the village of Golspie, where we put up for the next three days at the Sutherland Arms, an old coaching inn, established in 1808 by the first Duke of Sutherland, which evidently lost its old touch with the advent of the internal-combustion engine. That far north in Scotland — we were at about 58° North Latitude, as high up as Juneau — it can be fiercely cold at any time of year, but the sun was out strong as we drove over to Dornoch after breakfast the first morning, and the air was much softer than it had been at Nairn. (*All* of Britain, in fact, was enjoying this same golden weather. It was to last for three weeks, a partial repayment for the island's harshest winter in decades.) Dornoch, the county seat of Sutherland, is an exceptionally trim resort town, with a permanent population of some nine hundred and fifty. The cathedral and most of the other buildings are of a mellowed yellow sandstone, and that morning the whole town absolutely glistened in the sun. The links of the Royal Dornoch Golf Club are only a few hundred yards beyond the main square, and are perched well above the level of the North Sea. Like St. Andrews and Carnoustie and quite a few other celebrated links, Royal Dornoch at first glance is not particularly stirring. A pale brown-green sweep of duneland rolls into the distance, but only two holes are visible, the first and the eighteenth, and they seem to be quite ordinary. While no one expects the pro shop at a Scottish club to resemble our temples of merchandising, the shop at Dornoch, close by the first tee, turned out to be nothing but a glassed-in booth with a roof of corrugated tin painted brownish red. There was no one on duty when we arrived. Indeed, there was no one anywhere in sight. We tried the clubhouse, a small two-story building in which, except for a new bar, everything must be quite as it was in 1904, when the club celebrated the official opening of its extended eighteen holes and Mrs. Andrew Carnegie drove over from Skibo Castle to do the honors. We found the professional, Jimmy MacDonald, in the clubhouse, and he set about rounding up a caddie for me. The only one he could find was his ten-year-old grandson, Michael, and since my bag was much too heavy for a small boy to carry, we strapped it to a golf trolley that he could trundle along. (McKinlay never uses a caddie. He carries a collapsible golf trolley of his own in the trunk of his car, along with his clubs and his spiked shoes.) As we were taking our warmup swings alongside the first tee, I could not help thinking that on such a glorious morning — and a Saturday, too — the Old Course at St. Andrews was probably overrun with golfers, yet here at what one might call the St. Andrews of the North there was not a soul to be seen except a big gray cat with one blind eye. He is called Nelson, and prowls placidly around the first tee from morn to night — the reincarnation, unquestionably, of some old golfer who never got his fill.

It is Dornoch's out-of-the-way location, to be sure, that accounts for the course's relative desertion most of the year. (Only in July and August does it get a fairly brisk play from vacationers on golf holidays.) However, this same remoteness explains the unique position that Dornoch has long held in golf; for over half a century it has been regarded as one of the outstanding courses in the world by men close to the heart of the game, yet very few of them have ever played it. Until last year, the only American of my acquaintance who had was Richard Tufts, of Pinehurst. Tufts' interest had been aroused through his long association with Donald Ross, the eminent golf-course architect, who had emigrated from Dornoch around the turn of the century and designed some six hundred courses in this country, including four at Pinehurst, where he settled. An intense admirer of Ross's talents, Tufts was naturally eager to get to know the course that had shaped the architect's ideas of what constituted a good golf hole and what did not, and he was so impressed by what he saw there that he was constantly singing its glories. Last spring, almost entirely because of Tufts' missionary work, two other Americans I know visited Dornoch — Billy Joe Patton, the Walker Cup star, and Pete Dye, a young golf-course architect from Indianapolis. Dye visited Dornoch just before I did, and when I ran into him later he was raving that it was far and away the finest natural course he had ever seen. "No other links has quite the ageless aura Dornoch does," he said. "When you play it, you get the feeling you could be living just as easily in the eighteen-hundreds, or even the seventeen-hundreds. If an old Scot in a red jacket had popped out from behind a sand dune, beating a feather ball, I wouldn't have blinked an eye."

According to the local records, golf was played in Dornoch as early as 1616, which would make it the third-oldest course in the world, preceded only by St. Andrews and Leith. The first drum-beater for the course, antedating Tufts by three centuries, made his appearance shortly after this. He was Sir Robert Gordon, tutor to the house of Sutherland, and we can assume that he had a reliable golf background, since he had been educated at St. Andrews University. In his history of Sutherland, which he completed in 1630, Sir Robert wrote of Dornoch, "About this town (along the sea coast) there are the fairest and largest links (or green fields) of any pairt of Scotland, fitt for Archery, Golfing, Ryding, and all other exercise; they doe surpasse the fields of Montrose or St. Andrews." Sir Robert also induced King Charles I of England to grant a royal charter to the burgh of Dornoch in 1628, his chief argument being that such recognition might speed up the lagging march of civilization in that part of the northern Highlands. (Dornoch, indeed, was the scene of the last witch-burning in Scotland, in 1722; the charge against the unfortunate woman, one Janet Horne, was that she had turned her daughter into a pony and had her shod by the Devil.) It was not until 1885, however, that the Royal Dornoch Golf Club was founded and Old Tom Morris was commissioned to come up from St. Andrews to lay out nine proper holes. A second nine was added shortly afterward, and then, in 1904, the wholesale changes that transformed Dornoch from just another course into a bona-fide championship layout were carried out under the direction of a remarkable all-round golf man, John Sutherland, who for over fifty years served as the club's secretary. The remodelled Dornoch measured 5,096 yards — a very long course for those days. According to Sutherland's tabulations, these alterations made Dornoch the fifth-longest golf links in Britain — only a hundred and eighty-seven yards shorter than St. Andrews, a hundred and eighty-four yards shorter than Royal St. George's, in Sandwich, a hundred and forty yards shorter than Hoylake, and a hundred and six yards shorter than North Berwick, *and* eleven yards longer than Muirfield, a hundred and fifty-five yards longer than Prestwick, and three hundred and ninety-seven yards longer than Machrihanish (whose popularity was then beginning to wane, because of its shortness and comparative inaccessibility). The leading golf pros of that period regularly took in Dornoch on their exhibition tours — J. H. Taylor, a five-time Open champion, also assisted in revamping a few of the more prosaic holes — but for the amateur cracks the course remained terra incognita until 1909, the year of the so-called "Dornoch invasion." That spring, the British Amateur was held at Muirfield, and two Dornoch players went down for it — T. E. Grant, a baker's apprentice who later became a successful professional, and Sutherland himself. These two unknown northerners proceeded to confound the golf world by eliminating the two greatest British amateurs of that era, Grant accounting for John Ball and Sutherland for Harold Hilton. Ball and Hilton were so taken with the delightful manners of their conquerors that they made a special trip to Dornoch later that season to play an exhibition match and see what the course was like. Soon everyone was "discovering" Dornoch. Immediately before the First World War, it became *the* place for well-to-do golf-oriented English families to rent summer homes. Ernest Holderness, who won the British Amateur in 1922 and 1924, developed his game during summer holidays there as a youngster, and so did Roger Wethered, the 1923 Amateur champion, and his sister Joyce, regarded by many as the finest woman player of all time. After the war, Dornoch enjoyed a second brief period of fashionableness, but by 1930 it was over. Like Machrihanish, it gradually became a place that avid golfers talked of visiting but few actually got to. When the course was remodelled once again, after the Second World War, and lengthened to its present 6,505 yards, the news of these changes created scarcely a ripple of interest south of Dornoch Firth.

What is there so special about Dornoch that it should nurture an exceptional architect like Donald Ross, exceptional players like Holderness and the Wethereds, an exceptional club secretary like John Sutherland, and, I am tempted to add, exceptional admirers like Sam McKinlay, Dick Tufts, and Pete Dye? The answers came fast and clear the morning McKinlay and I played the course. The linksland that at first glance seems so commonplace and even unpromising reveals itself, once you have got two or three holes behind you and are into the heart of the course, to be beautiful golf country. Everything *does* look as if it had been there, untouched, for centuries. In its general topography — its billowing fairways, its deep and shaggy sand bunkers, the eccentric mounding around its greens — Dornoch probably resembles St. Andrews more closely than it does any other well-known course, but there are many basic differences. To begin with, Dornoch has far better turf than does the Old Course, which has been in spotty condition for twenty years. Unlike the Old Course, where a good deal of the trouble is hidden from view, Dornoch presents its hazards frankly, and there are few blind shots. Whereas the Old Course is famed for its huge double greens, which serve both an outgoing and incoming hole, Dornoch's greens are comparatively small and sit atop mesalike rises with unusually steep banks. In the way they are sited and in the severe configurations of their surfaces, Dornoch's greens — and they are the course's most distinctive feature — are quite reminiscent of those at the Augusta National, although Augusta's are much larger. These Dornoch greens demand a good deal of finesse on the approach, for the pitch-and-run shot the Scots customarily play to their unwatered greens will as often as not kick awry off the contours and bounce on over one side or the back of the green. As Holderness has pointed out, the golfer who grows up at Dornoch is forced to learn how to "pitch a ball onto a slippery surface and stop it," and this is a skill that thereafter serves him handsomely wherever he plays. Furthermore, because he is so seldom confronted with a routine chip back to the flag when he misses a green, the Dornoch golfer learns how to improvise delicate little lob-and-run shots. In America, Donald Ross rarely found the kind of terrain that would permit him to reproduce the touchy subtleties of Dornoch's green areas, but their lasting influence on him is visible in the hilltop "crown greens" he built wherever he worked. When he revised the Pinehurst No. 2 course in the mid-thirties, he took special pains to create Dornoch-style mounds, slopes, and runoffs around the greens, and that course is generally acknowledged to offer the most exacting examination in chipping in this country.

Like St. Andrews and Nairn, Dornoch is a loop-type course — in this instance, eight holes out, ten holes back — but the repetitiousness generally inherent in this kind of layout has been avoided with a fine resourcefulness. On the eight outward holes, which are set along a shelf of high land, the tees have been placed so that the fairways do not swing quite the same way on any two holes, and as a result the wind hits the golfer from all directions. The incoming holes manage a similar diversity by rambling up and down between the crusty higher land and the duneland by the sea. The best hole on the course, to my mind, and one that nicely epitomizes Dornoch's originality and appeal, is the fourteenth, which is called Foxy. A complicated double-dogleg par 4, four hundred and fifty yards long, it has an outline resembling the Big Dipper as much as anything else. From the tee, the fairway runs straight out for two hundred and thirty yards, where it breaks sharply to the left and then resumes its old direction, going straight ahead again for a hundred and eighty yards before describing a quick turn to the right and rising to the green, a semiplateau. Actually, the green is dead in line with the opening stretch of the fairway, but the area separating them is a wild upthrust of bush-covered duneland that no sane golfer would attempt to carry without a roaring wind at his back. The ideal way to play this fascinating hole (which, incidentally, does not have a single bunker on it) is to hit your drive with a slight controlled right-to-left draw, so that it swings to the left with the breaking fairway, and to follow this with a slightly cut 3-wood that just shaves the high dunes as it drifts from left to right over the corner of the second dogleg and onto the hidden green. McKinlay played the hole precisely that way, in what was for this part of Scotland a very mild wind. He was around in even par, 72. I wasn't that low, but I played an exceedingly solid round, for me, and that was important to me. Dornoch was one course I wanted very much to like, and, say what you will, you cannot like a course unless you play it reasonably well. I should imagine that Dornoch usually elicits a golfer's best game. It doesn't overawe you with its length. It supplies plenty of gorseless *Lebensraum* to err in. It keeps you on your toes by making it clear from the outset that it rewards only shots that have been well thought out and well executed. And it encourages you to hit decisive shots by providing vigorous, close-cropped turf, on which the ball sits up beautifully, and very true greens, which are a joy to putt. In a word, I found Dornoch all I had hoped it would be — a thoroughly modern old links with that rare equipoise of charm and character that only the great courses possess.

I never did get to play Dornoch again. On the following day, a Sunday, the course was closed to play, for the northern reaches of

Scotland are extremely strict about observing the Sabbath. We spent that day driving the breadth of Sutherland to the mountainous west coast and then back again, and not once, though it was perfect weather for sport, did we see anyone fishing in or boating on any of the sea and inland lochs that abound in that country. One day, I suppose, some high-voltage syndicate will build a Scottish version of our Pebble Beach course along the craggy headlands of the west coast, but up to now the obvious expense of such an undertaking has frightened the developers away. Currently, the only course up north along the west coast is at Gairloch, and that one is a nine-hole billy-goat layout where most of the holes intersect one another and a single cry of "Fore!" can send all the golfers on the course diving flat on the ground. McKinlay rates it at half a thistle. On Monday, there was nothing to prevent our playing Dornoch again, but McKinlay decided that we shouldn't. Relieved and happy that I thought so highly of a course he loved, he felt it was best to leave well enough alone. This proved to be a very prudent decision, for we played the nice little course at Golspie instead, and I was all over the place. McKinlay allowed me to have tea at Dornoch that afternoon, however, and to walk over the links afterward, without a club.

The next day, we made the return trip to Glasgow, and I said goodbye to the McKinlays and went on to St. Andrews, where the British Amateur was in progress.

It is always a pleasure to revisit St. Andrews. Apart from its position in golf, it is, far more than is generally appreciated, a picturesque town, with wide Flemish avenues and old sandstone buildings; it's a lively place, too, largely because of the presence of the hundreds of red-gowned young men and women attending St. Andrews University. The town itself sits atop a considerable hill edged by sharp cliffs, with the four famous courses — the Old, the New, the Eden, and the Jubilee — occupying a large strip of linksland at the foot of the slope. Early last June, during Britain's unusual stretch of balmy weather, the town looked sparkling, but the continuing lack of rain made the courses sere and hard after a while, and during the Amateur the Old Course played as "short" as I can remember it over the past twenty-five years. I was extremely glad of this chance to see and study the Old Course so soon after leaving the far north, for I was anxious to find out how Dornoch stood up against a somewhat surer touchstone than Golspie. It stood up very well, I thought. I quickly learned, though, that those of my British golfing friends who follow the tournament circuit (I had last seen them at the Walker Cup match, twelve days before) were not at all interested in hearing the detailed report on Nairn and Dornoch that I was prepared to give them. I remember with particular vividness an encounter I had with an old friend who has been one of the guiding lights of R. and A. officialdom for the last twenty years. I had always assumed that *he* knew Dornoch, but now I found that he had never been north of Inverness and had no intention of rectifying that omission. "Dornoch's simply too far out of the way," he explained, rather curtly, I felt. "I've no reason to go anyplace near there. I have all the Shetland sweaters I need."

Far from being on the other side of the moon, I reminded him, Dornoch was an easy six hours by auto from St. Andrews. I added, with a little steam, that it was a downright shame for a course of Dornoch's genuine distinction to be so methodically ignored as a venue for an important national or international competition.

"No, we could never risk that," my English friend answered, with a tone of finality. "It's much too cold up there, much too grim. Let's face it. Dornoch went out with the gutta-percha ball."

He had his facts wrong, but I let it go, for I was in exceptionally good humor that day. One thing that I'm sure had contributed to my mood was a letter from Kenny Cameron I had found waiting for me at my hotel. It was exactly the kind of letter I would have expected from him — six tightly packed pages in which he took me through each of the sixty-eight shots he had played in an especially brilliant round at Nairn the previous Saturday. The postscript, too, was completely in character. "The weather continues beautifully warm and sunny," he wrote, "As your James R. Lowell put it, 'What is so rare as a day in June? Then, if ever, the weather is perfect.'"

(1964)

The Third Man
Venturi

Had it not been for his remarkable victory in the United States Open in 1964, Ken Venturi might well have been remembered as the brilliant young player who had three times come tragically close to winning the Masters — in 1956, 1958, and 1960. In the early 1960s, beset by injuries, he almost faded from sight. Just before the 1964 U.S. Open, he suddenly began to look like the Venturi of old. How he won the Open at Congressional is one of the most inspiring stories in American golf.

THERE IS NO QUESTION AT ALL IN MY MIND BUT THAT THE 1964 United States Open Championship, which Ken Venturi won last month at the Congressional Country Club, in Washington, will be remembered as one of the greatest Opens. Such an assertion takes in a good deal of territory, I know, because over the years since 1895, when ten professionals and one amateur teed off in the inaugural U.S. Open, the national championship has, far more often than not, produced climaxes that have outfictioned fiction. Probably no Open can ever match the 1913 championship at the Country Club, in Brookline, Massachusetts, when Francis Ouimet, then an unknown twenty-year-old amateur up from the caddie shack, tied the regal British professionals Harry Vardon and Ted Ray and then went on to defeat them in a three-man playoff, but that is the only Open I would consider more stirring than the one that has just taken place. I am not for a moment forgetting the 1960 Open, at Cherry Hills, near Denver, when Arnold Palmer came dashing out of nowhere to birdie six of the first seven holes on his final round and go driving on to a 65 and victory — or, to cite just one more example, the 1950 Open, at Merion, outside Philadelphia, which Ben Hogan captured only sixteen months after an all but fatal auto accident had made it extremely doubtful whether he would be able to walk again, let alone be a force in competitive golf.

The 1964 Open was notable for much more than a powerful third act. From the morning of the first round, when Sam Snead, the ablest golfer who has never won our national championship, insured his twenty-fourth failure in the event by four-putting the fourth green and then three-putting the sixth (after which he flung his ball in disgust into a convenient water hazard), the tournament was charged with exceptional golf and exceptional human interest, and both kept building until we were presented with the improbable spectacle of a winner emerging from golf's deepest limbo to stagger ashen-faced down the long incline to the final green after beating off not only his last challengers but the threat of heat prostration. To my knowledge, there has never been anything like this in golf history.

A hundred and fifty qualifiers started the Open this year, as usual, but the championship is really the story of three players — Venturi, Palmer, and Tommy Jacobs. Thursday, the day of the first round, belonged almost completely to Palmer. He was a comparatively late starter, going off at twelve-twenty-five, when two-thirds of the field were out on the course or already back at the clubhouse. One of the first men out, Bill Collins, who had the advantage of shooting to greens that hadn't yet been baked hard by the fierce sun, had succeeded in matching par — 70 — but in general the scores were running high, and so was the feeling among the golfers that once again an Open course had been made a bit too severe. For a change, the chief complaint was not that the United States Golf Association, which conducts the Open, had narrowed the fairways too drastically and allowed the rough to grow impossibly high and lush; in fact, it was agreed that the fairways were wide almost to the point of generosity, and that the rough, emaciated by a prolonged dry spell, was eminently playable. Since there was also a minimum of fairway bunkering, Congressional undoubtedly constituted the easiest examination in driving of any Open course in at least a decade. What, then, was giving everyone so much trouble? Well, a number of things. To begin with, Congressional, at 7,053 yards, was the longest course in Open history, and some of the Brobdingnagian par 4s — particularly two holes that are ordinarily played by the club members as par 5s but had been converted into par 4s for the championship — were breeding all kinds of bogeys. On these holes, some of the shorter hitters were unable to reach the greens with two woods, and the longer hitters, who could get home with an iron, found that their low-trajectory approaches were bounding off the greens. Another complaint — and again a legitimate one — was that the greens, a blend of grasses known as Arlington Bent and Congressional Bent, were exceedingly grainy. On long approach putts against the grain, it took a real rap to get the ball up to the hole, and on sidehill putts it was hard to judge how much to allow for the break — sometimes the ball didn't break at all.

Just when the conviction was setting in that, under the existing conditions, no one would be able to score below 70, Palmer went out and brought in a 68. He was not in his most impressive form, either — especially on the first nine, where he hooked several drives badly. Palmer is a resourceful scrambler when he has to be, though, and he bailed himself out of trouble with deft chipping and putting until he got his driving under control. He paced himself shrewdly, picking up his birdies on the short drive-and-pitch par 4s, and coming through with his best tee shots on the long par 4s, where his tremendous power enabled him to play his approaches to the hard greens with lofted medium irons. (For example, on the thirteenth, 448 yards long and with the green lying at the top of a fairly steep rise, he got home with a 5-iron on his second.) Still, his most conspicuous assets were, as usual, his huge confidence and poise. Whereas the awareness of participating in an important championship like the Open rattles most players, even the seasoned ones, Palmer thrives on the pressure, the crowds, the noise — the whole charged-up atmosphere. As he put together his 68, to take a two-shot lead, he seemed more relaxed than a man strolling around his own back yard, and one got the feeling that he might very well be on his way to repeating his classic performance in the Masters last April, when he jumped into a tie for the lead on the first day and then pulled farther and farther away.

Friday, the day of the second round, was humid and breezeless, with the temperature hovering around ninety, but the course played a shade more easily, because, for one thing, a rainstorm shortly after daybreak had taken some of the starch out of the greens. For another thing, a threat of more rain during the day had prompted the officials to place the pins in high spots that would drain well and were less exacting targets. Palmer, one of the earlier starters, reached the turn in 34, one under par. He was playing very well. When he rolled in a curving thirty-five-footer for a birdie 3 on the tough thirteenth, to go two strokes under par for the round and four strokes under par for the tournament, it looked as if he would be holding such a comfortable lead at the end of the first thirty-six holes that on Saturday, when both the third and the fourth rounds would be played, a pair of steady, unfancy 72s would be all he would need to wrap up his second victory in the Open.

Only one other player was making any substantial headway against par. This was Tommy Jacobs, a twenty-nine-year-old Californian who was appearing in his seventh Open. One of the most mature young men on the professional circuit, Jacobs is quite an interesting golfer. Essentially more of a swinger than a hitter, he has a tendency to become a little erratic when the tempo of his swing goes awry, but he can get awfully hot, particularly on long, punishing courses. He plays a much bolder game than most of his all too odds-conscious colleagues, and, in addition, he has streaks when he holes putts from all over the greens. On his first round at Congressional, Jacobs had been two strokes under par after the first eleven holes, only to finish weakly with four bogeys on the remaining seven holes, for a 72. On his second round, playing two threesomes in front of Palmer, he was once again two under par after eleven holes, but this time, instead of faltering, he started to take Congressional apart as if it were a hotel course in Switzerland. Having birdied the thirteenth just before Palmer did, he proceeded to birdie the fourteenth, by planting a 6-iron approach five feet from the cup, and then birdied the par-5 fifteenth with a fourteen-foot putt. This burst put him five shots under par for the first fifteen holes, and spectators from all over the course, including a few Palmer men on detached service from what is known as Arnold's Army, raced to the sixteenth hole to see if Jacobs could hold on the rest of the way. Jacobs occasionally becomes a bit nervous under the strain of competition, but there was not the slightest suggestion of tension about him as he parred the next two holes and then confronted the eighteenth, a par 4 an intimidating 465 yards long, on which the last four hundred yards of the fairway sweep down to a thumb-shaped green that juts well out into a sizable pond. After driving down the left side of the fairway, Jacobs, rejecting a more cautious shot, fired a 5-iron right at the pin. The ball had perfect line, but after plummeting down onto the front edge of the green it stopped dead, a full sixty feet from the cup. Jacobs stepped up and coolly holed that monstrous putt. His 64 did several things. It gave him a halfway-mark total of 136 and catapulted him into the lead, a stroke in front of Palmer, who added a splendid 69 to his opening 68. It equalled the record low score for an Open round, set by Lee Mackey, Jr., at Merion in 1950. (Mackey, incidentally, had an 81 on his next round.) It demonstrated that Congressional, like the first-class course everyone was beginning to realize it was, required excellent golf but would yield to brilliance. Furthermore, as all the facts of Jacobs' round became known — that he had missed the fairway only twice with his tee shots, for example, and that in hitting all but two of the greens on the regulation stroke he had eleven times put his approach twenty feet or less from the pin — there was much speculation as to whether his 64 might not be the finest round ever played by a man in serious contention in a major championship. For my part, I would place it ahead of Palmer's 65 in 1960 at Cherry Hills, Gene Sarazen's 66 in 1932 at Fresh Meadow, on Long Island, and Henry Cotton's 65 in the 1934 British Open at the Royal St. George's, in Sandwich, for all three of those courses were far less demanding than Congressional. Indeed, Hogan's 67 in 1951 at Oakland Hills, near Detroit, is the only round that seems to me to be in a class with Jacobs' 64. (It should, however, be noted that Palmer's 65, Sarazen's 66, and Hogan's 67 all came on the fourth round and carried all three to victory.)

Ever since 1898, when our Open, taking its cue from the older British Open, was extended to seventy-two holes, the final thirty-six have been played in one day. Once, most seventy-two-hole tournaments were set up this way, but in the years after the Second World War there was a trend to a less demanding (and more lucrative) arrangement — one that called for four days of play, with a single round each day. Today, the Open is the only tournament of any consequence in this country that still adheres to the climactic double round. It does so because the United States Golf Association remains convinced that endurance as well as skill should be a requisite of a national champion. Certainly only the soundest swings can stand up under the attrition of thirty-six holes in one day, and that is what the U.S.G.A. has in mind when it speaks of endurance. On Saturday morning at Congressional, however, with the temperature climbing into the nineties, it was apparent that sheer physical endurance would also be necessary. For this reason, most veteran observers felt that Palmer, who is probably the strongest man in golf, would outlast and outplay Jacobs. Another point in Palmer's favor was that the two leaders were paired, as is customary on Open Saturday, and it was thought that Jacobs would find the stress of a head-to-head duel harder to take than Palmer. No other golfer was given more than an outside chance of catching the front-runners. The nearest man, Collins, stood at 141, four shots behind Palmer and five behind Jacobs. Venturi and Charlie Sifford, the outstanding Negro professional, were next, at 142.

The first surprise of the long, scorching day was Palmer's rocky start. Obviously impatient, he went aggressively for the pin on his approaches from the very first hole. Despite the fact that the greens had been soaked by a heavy rain during the night and were holding well, these were questionable tactics — or at least they seemed so after Palmer missed the first five greens. He hit the sixth, but when he then three-putted it, he fell four shots behind Jacobs, who was playing placidly and well. At this point, a third man most unexpectedly entered the picture — Venturi. Paired with Ray Floyd two twosomes in front of Palmer and Jacobs, Venturi had birdied the eighth at about the time Palmer was three-putting the sixth. It was his fourth birdie of the day. He had begun his rush on the first green, when his ten-foot putt for a birdie had hung on the lip of the cup for almost a minute and then toppled in. After that happy augury, he had gone on to birdie the fourth, the sixth, and the eighth and to par the other holes, and so, as he moved with his habitual splay-footed stride down the ninth fairway, wearing his habitual white cap and frown of concentration, he was no longer on the periphery of contention, he was in the thick of it. He had actually overtaken and passed Palmer.

The ninth hole, a par 5 measuring 599 yards, is the longest hole at Congressional. It is called the Ravine Hole, because, about a hundred and ten yards from the green, the fairway, after ascending a gentle hillside, plunges abruptly down some forty feet and then rises as sharply to a relatively small, well-trapped green. It is doubtful if any player in the field could have reached the ninth green in two shots, and, in any event, no one was of a mind to try it; on both banks of the ravine, the fairway had been allowed to grow up into rough, so there was nothing to be gained by taking the gamble. The sensible way to play the ninth, and the way every man in the field attempted to play it, was to lie up short of the ravine on the second shot (usually with a long iron) and hope to put the third shot close enough to the pin to have a crack at a birdie. On his third round, Venturi did precisely this, punching his third, a firm wedge shot, eight feet from the pin. He got the putt down to reach the turn in 30, five shots under par. (His irons to the green had been so accurate that his score could have been even lower; he had missed holeable birdie putts on both the third and the seventh greens.) Venturi kept on going. After getting his pars on the tenth and eleventh holes, he hit what was possibly his best iron shot of the morning on the 188-yard par-3 twelfth — a full-blooded 4-iron, which stopped hole-high about sixteen feet to the left of the pin. He played the sidehill putt to break down some three inches, and it fell into the middle of the cup. That birdie put Venturi six under par for the round and four under par for the tournament. A glance at a nearby scoreboard brought the news that Jacobs had meanwhile bogeyed both the eighth and the ninth and was now only three under par for the distance. It was hard to believe, but it was a fact: Venturi was leading the Open.

If any golfer in the field had swept to the front on Saturday in such a fantastic fashion, his surge would naturally have excited the galleries at Congressional, but the fact that it was Ken Venturi who was working this miracle made the air incalculably more electric. Venturi's rapid rise to fame and subsequent tumble back into obscurity are familiar to all who follow golf. The son of the manager of the pro shop at the Harding Park public course, in San Francisco, he first achieved national recognition in 1953, when, a slim, handsome twenty-two-year-old amateur, he was selected for our Walker Cup team. In 1956, still an amateur after completing a tour of duty in the Army, he confounded the golf world by decisively outplaying the whole field in the first three rounds of the Masters at Augusta and entering the final round with an authoritative four-stroke lead. Then he shot a jittery 80, and lost the tournament by a stroke. It should be remarked, I think, that his play on that last round was not the utter collapse it has since been called, for he hit no really bad shots; rather, he kept missing the greens on his approaches by small margins, and he failed to hole any of the five- and six-foot putts that his chips left him. In two subsequent years, he came very close to winning at Augusta. In 1958, when Palmer first broke through in the Masters, Venturi, who was paired with him on the final round, was only a shot behind as they entered the stretch, but Palmer shook off his challenge by making a memorable eagle on the thirteenth. In the 1960 Masters, Venturi fought his way back into the battle after a spotty first round, and had the tournament apparently won when Palmer, the only man he still had to worry about, caught him by birdieing the seventy-first hole and beat him by birdieing the seventy-second.

After this third disappointment in the Masters, something went out of Venturi's game, and in a relatively short time it was apparent that he was no longer the superb golfer he had been between 1956, when he turned professional, and 1960. In those days, he had been not only one of the leading money-winners on the professional tour but probably the most proficient shotmaker in the country. I believe that the Venturi of that period was the finest iron-player I have ever seen — not excepting Byron Nelson, Venturi's teacher. Venturi's style with the irons was not particularly graceful. He took the club back in an upright arc with three rather distinct segments to it, but he arrived at the top of his backswing with his hands in an ideal position and his body perfectly balanced, and it seemed that all he had to do then in order to come into the ball just as he wanted to was to move his hips a notch to the left at the start of the downswing. Moreover, he possessed a rare instinct for iron play; he adapted his shots not only to the wind and the weather but also to the terrain he was playing from and playing to. For example, he would feather one approach in to the flag with a little left-to-right drift and burn his next approach in low and hard and dead on the target. By 1961, though, as I say, he was no longer playing golf of this calibre, and in the succeeding years his game continued to disintegrate. A succession of physical ailments, ranging from a back injury to walking pneumonia, contributed to this decline, but even when Venturi was feeling fit he played unimpressively. His confidence seemed completely shot. He failed to qualify for the Open in 1961, 1962, and 1963, and last year his total winnings on the professional tour came to less than four thousand dollars. This spring, he suffered the crowning humiliation of having to watch the Masters at home on television, because he had not qualified for an invitation to the 1964 tournament.

Venturi's behavior during his protracted ordeal was exemplary, and it won him the admiration of his fellow-professionals. He never bellyached about his lot, he was not envious of his friends' successes, and he quietly kept trying to put his game together again. This display of character came as a surprise to a number of people around golf. As a young man and one of Hogan's heirs presumptive, he had shown himself to be pleasant and very likable, but, perhaps because his honors had come to him so quickly and easily, there seemed to be large areas in which he lacked perception and tact. After a low round at Augusta, for example, he would come sweeping up the stairs of the clubhouse, the reporters and photographers at his heels, and, sailing by the likes of Hogan and Snead, he would scale his cap halfway across the players' lounge as if he owned the world. He was not arrogant, though; he was simply very young. In adversity, he grew up, and revealed himself as a man of fibre. Late this spring, he suddenly began to play quite well again. In June, in the two weeks preceding the Open, he tied for third in the Thunderbird Open and then tied for sixth in the Buick Open. Though his putting stroke remained somewhat unsound, which it always had been, and though he hit a few wild shots in each round, he was setting himself up far more comfortably before the ball than he had done in years, he was playing with a new vigor, and he was concentrating well.

At Congressional, I watched a good part of Venturi's first two rounds, for, like everyone else, I wanted very much to see him do well. His opening 72 could easily have been several shots higher, for he played a number of holes very loosely. He topped one bunker shot cold, fluffed another bunker shot completely, and, on a hole where his heeled drive wound up deep in the rough, did not even reach the fairway with his recovery. On his second round, he played much more surely, en route to a 70. Early in the round, he sank a few bothersome putts, which did his morale a great deal of good, and he was rifling his irons like the Venturi of old. At the same time, not even his warmest supporters would ever have dreamed that on Saturday he would have the shots, the fire, and the emotional composure to birdie six of the first twelve holes and go out in front.

Venturi did not stay out in front very long. Jacobs, summoning up some fine attacking shots, played the second nine in 34 — one under par — to post a 70 and a fifty-four-hole total of 206. Venturi, after taking a 36 in for a 66, stood at 208. Near the end of the morning round, he had wavered discernibly. On the seventeenth green, he had missed a putt of just eighteen inches, and on the last green he had missed one of thirty inches, in both cases also missing his par. We could only give him all credit for his gallant dash and conclude that apparently he had just run out of gas. Perhaps, after all, that was inevitable for Venturi. Strangely, everyone at Congressional, I think, felt a bit better about things when, shortly after he returned to the clubhouse at the luncheon interval, it was announced that he had been near collapse from the heat on the last five holes. His seemingly imminent failure could at least be attributed to forces beyond his control. On the advice of a doctor, he spent the bulk of the fifty-minute interval resting. He drank some tea but ate no solid food. Then he took some salt tablets and headed for the first tee, accompanied by the doctor, who walked the final round with him.

The leaders had hardly begun the final round when, for the first time in hours, Palmer got back into the picture. In the morning, harried by his wretched putting, he had never really recovered from his poor start and had ended up with a 75, giving him a total of 212 at the three-quarters mark and putting him six shots behind Jacobs and four behind Venturi. All morning long, Palmer had not made a single birdie, but he started his afternoon with a flamboyant one. Jacobs then double-bogeyed the par-3 second, after pulling his tee shot into deep trouble, and Palmer closed to within three shots of him. It now looked very much as if we might be seeing one of Palmer's patented whirlwind finishes. However, when he failed to make even his pars on two of the next four holes it became clear, tardily, that the significant thing about Jacobs' double bogey was that it had thrust Venturi back into a tie for first. Playing two holes ahead of Palmer and Jacobs, Venturi looked drawn and pale, and he was walking slowly on stiff, old man's legs, but he was executing his shots with poise and hitting the ball with an astonishing sharpness. He came to the ninth, the 599-yard Ravine Hole, after parring seven of the first eight, still tied for the lead with Jacobs.

I arrived at the ninth too late to see Venturi play his drive or his second shot. His drive must not have been very long, for, I was told, he played a full 1-iron on his second. What a shot that must have been! There was his ball sitting up in the middle of the fairway a mere five yards from the edge of the ravine. Only an extremely confident golfer would have attempted to lay up so daringly close to the brink, and as I gazed at the ball it occurred to me for the first time that Venturi could win the Open. In any event, that audacious 1-iron put him in position to birdie the hole. The flag was set far to the back of the green, so that there was a menacing trap only about twenty feet directly behind it, but Venturi went for the pin and stopped his wedge nine feet past it. Faced with a delicate downhill putt that broke to the left, he played it exactly right; his ball caught the high corner of the cup and spun in. When it dropped, I felt for the first time that Venturi *would* win the Open. With this beautifully engineered birdie 4, he had regained the undisputed lead, and, as it turned out, he not only held on to it the rest of the way but widened it — eventually to four strokes — for he played par golf in, and both Jacobs and Palmer, forced to gamble at this stage of the game, ran into a succession of bogeys.

Indeed, after the ninth it became increasingly evident that only the possibility of physical collapse stood between Venturi and victory. The sun was still beating down furiously, and on the fourteenth hole, where he had started to wobble in the morning, his slow walk decelerated into a painful trudge and his head began to droop. Into my mind's eye, as I watched him, came a photograph from old sports books showing Dorando Pietri, the little Italian marathon runner, being helped by his countrymen across the finish line in the 1908 Olympic Games after he had crumpled in exhaustion only a few yards from his goal. Venturi hung on tenaciously, however, and while he hit at least one very tired shot on each hole after that, some fortunate bounces and his own tidy work around the greens saw him safely through to the eighteenth hole, the long par 4 sloping gradually down to the peninsula green. He needed only a 7 there to win. His tee shot was weak but straight. He blocked out his 5-iron approach to the right, away from the water, and went into a bunker about forty yards from the pin. He played a much braver recovery than he had to — a beautiful, floating wedge shot that sat down ten feet from the cup. He holed the putt. He had done it.

While I think that the thousands encamped the length of the eighteenth fairway will always treasure that moment when Venturi walked triumphantly off the final green, a champion at last, I am sure they would agree with me that the Open reached its dramatic peak a few moments earlier, when, after hitting his second shot, he came walking shakily down the long slope. He was going to make it now, he knew, and in response to the tumultuous ovation he received as he descended the hill he removed his cap, for the first time that day. A little sun would not hurt now. I shall never forget the expression on his face as he came down the hill. It was taut with fatigue and strain, and yet curiously radiant with pride and happiness. It reminded me of another unforgettable, if entirely different, face — the famous close-up of Charlie Chaplin at the end of *City Lights*, all anguish beneath the attempted smile. Venturi then put his cap back on and hit those two wonderful final shots.

Few things repair a man as quickly as victory. At his press conference back in the air-conditioned clubhouse, Venturi, who has a bright wit, made a number of trenchant remarks. Since we live in an age when every golf hero's band of supporters bears a catchy alliterative name, such as Arnold's Army, Nicklaus's Navy, and Lema's Legions, the new champion got perhaps his biggest laugh when, as he was commenting on how much the cheering of the crowds had helped him all day long, he interrupted himself to say, "For years, all I ever had was Venturi's Vultures." Perhaps he had said this before, but if he had no one was listening.

(1964)

Europe in the Fall
Palmer and Other Visitors

This is an article about four tournaments, each somewhat special, that took place in Europe in 1964. The first was the Seven-Club Tournament at Turnberry, in Scotland. The second was the first Women's World Amateur Team Championship at Saint-Germain-en-Laye, which was won, appropriately, by the French team. In the third, the men's World Amateur Team Championship at Olgiata, in Italy, the team representing Great Britain and Ireland scored an exciting victory. The fourth was the first World Match Play Championship at Wentworth, in England, an event that is still going strong. Arnold Palmer, holing putts left and right, won the final from Neil Coles.

AS FAR AS SPORTS ARE CONCERNED, AUTUMN IS, AS A RULE, A relatively mild and quiet season in Great Britain and on the European continent. Tennis and golf are both about over, after having reached their peaks in early summer — tennis with the Wimbledon championships, golf with the British Open. In England, the cricket stumps have long since been pulled up and stored away. In nearly all countries, the soccer and Rugby league seasons are well advanced, of course, but the significant clashes between the contenders lie months ahead. While some horse racing still goes on, there are few fixtures of consequence. All in all, as the days grow shorter and the sun grows paler and the skies grow grayer and the air grows colder, sports lose a good deal of their intensity, and their devotees begin to translate their energies into longer walks, longer political discussions, and even longer business hours.

This autumn, however, it was a bit different, for in the first two weeks of October golf enjoyed a completely unprecedented Indian summer of importance. Four major events took place: the inaugural Braemar Seven-Club Professional Tournament, over the Ailsa course at Turnberry, in Scotland, from October 1st through October 3rd; the first Women's World Amateur Team Championship, at the Saint-Germain-en-Laye Golf Club, outside Paris, from October 1st through October 4th; the fourth biennial Men's World Amateur Team Championship for the Eisenhower Trophy, at the Circolo Golf Olgiata, fifteen miles north of Rome, from October 7th through October 10th; and the first Piccadilly World Match-Play Tournament, at the Wentworth Golf Club, near London, from October 9th through October 11th. Like any golf fan, my appetite was whetted when I learned of this super-*smorgasbord*, and, reasoning that it might be years before a comparable spread was placed on the table, I made arrangements to go abroad and take in the four tournaments. Their overlapping schedules made it impossible to see any one of the four in its entirety, but I was pleased rather than dismayed by the prospect of looking in on a tournament for two days and then dashing on to the next one, for there is something in all of us that delights in playing the poor man's Phileas Fogg even in this accelerated era when the world has become almost too travellable.

Turnberry stretches alongside the Firth of Clyde, about fifty miles south of Glasgow and fifteen miles south of Prestwick International Airport — and I can think of no pleasanter way to "enter Europe," incidentally, than to disembark at Prestwick, with its unbustling, country pace and lack of confusion, and drive through the scrubbed-down towns and green fields of Ayrshire to the Turnberry Hotel, a large, comfortable place that sits atop an abrupt ridge overlooking the Ailsa links and the sea beyond. I arrived on the morning of the first day of the Seven-Club Tournament, a seventy-two-hole stroke-play event in which, as its title indicates, a player may carry in his bag only seven clubs, instead of the full complement of fourteen he is entitled to in ordinary competitions. To go back a little way, up until 1938, when the fourteen-club rule was passed simultaneously by the game's two governing bodies — the United States Golf Association and the Royal and Ancient Golf Club of St. Andrews — a golfer could carry as many clubs as he wished. Until the nineteen-twenties, however, few players, even among the champions, thought they needed more than ten or twelve — in 1916, for instance, when Chick Evans won the United States Open with a record low total of 286, he did it with only seven clubs — but after Walter Hagen and our other professionals introduced the trunk-size golf bag, around 1924, there was a decided trend toward carrying extra weapons. It soon became fairly commonplace for the serious golfer to supplement his basic set of clubs with such spares as an extra driver that he could resort to when his regular driver was not working too well; a shallow-faced spoon, for tight lies; a spoon with a big pear-shaped head, for gorgeous lies; an all-purpose jigger; a couple of hickory-shafted irons from his old set, for trouble shots; one left-handed club; and an assortment of putters, to suit all types of greens. Lawson Little brought this to its *reductio ad absurdum* in 1934, when, if I remember correctly, he had his caddie lug more than thirty clubs, including eight or nine woods, and after that it was only a matter of time before a limitation on armaments had to be invoked. The main purpose of the fourteen-club rule, apart from insuring the continued existence of able-bodied caddies, was to bring back into the game some measure of the old shotmaking skills that had gradually gone out when, with the increase in the number of clubs carried, it had become unnecessary for a man to be able to play half shots and three-quarter shots, high shots and low shots with each of the clubs in his bag. The rule has proved to be a popular one with most golfers, but, as you might expect, there are two sects of extremists who think it should be revised. On one hand, more than a few of our professional stars, possibly encouraged by golf-club manufacturers, have in recent years been lobbying for upping the limit to sixteen; their contention is that they need, of all things, more pitching clubs. On the other hand, there is, as there always has been, a group of unreconstructed old-timers who remain convinced that fourteen clubs are about five too many to test a golfer's true worth, since, as they are fond of saying, "It allows him to buy too many of his shots in the pro shop." If this is hardly a realistic argument, it is an appealing one, in that it evokes a picture of the golfer as an ingenious improviser, and I know of nobody who plays the game, pro or hacker, who hasn't wondered how he would make out if he had to leave half his clubs in his locker. In any event, it is very much to the credit of the British golf-club manufacturers that when the idea of a seven-club tournament was proposed they didn't sabotage it. Furthermore, it is very much to the credit of the British professionals that they not only agreed to play in such a tournament, at the risk of jeopardizing their reputations by shooting relatively high scores, but also converged on Turnberry as enthusiastic as schoolboys about the novelty of the challenge.

What seven clubs would you pick if you were going to tackle a formidable 7,000-yard seaside links like the Ailsa? Most of us, I think, would settle on a driver, a 4-wood, a 3-iron, a 5-iron, a 7-iron, a pitching wedge, and a putter. At the Seven-Club Tournament, the selection made by each player was posted in the press tent (which in Britain is still literally a tent), and I meant to study these lists closely, but before doing this I went out to the fourteenth hole with some British golf writers I know to watch the parade go by. The first sight that struck my eyes was one for which I was unprepared. George Will and Guy Wolstenholme, two of the best young British professionals, had just driven off the fourteenth, and were walking jauntily up the fairway carrying their own bags — those small canvas sacks that we used to call "Sunday bags" and that the British call "drainpipes." Somehow, I cannot picture Tommy Bolt or Sam Snead doing this. Not long afterward, Neil Coles, the most accomplished British professional at the present time, came off the thirteenth green. Now, this was more like it. He had a caddie, and the caddie was carrying Coles' regular tournament bag, but, with only seven clubs inside, it gaped ludicrously. (About half the players, I later gathered, used a caddie and about half toted their own bags.) Upon closer examination of Coles' bag, I saw that he had brought along only one wood — a brassie, or 2-wood. He hit a screamer with it off the tee on the fourteenth, a par-4 hole, 455 yards long, and then from a very snug lie he smashed another beautiful brassie, fifteen feet from the flag. Today, none of our touring professionals uses a brassie except to drive with occasionally, and I certainly can't remember when I last saw a reputable golfer hit two brassie shots on one hole. It was quite a treat.

I followed Coles in, and he finished with a 75 — four over par, and a very creditable score, but far from the lowest one posted. Then I went to the press tent to look over the lists of clubs that the different golfers had taken. The majority had gone with the orthodox septet — two woods, a 3-iron, a 5-iron, a 7-iron, a wedge, and a putter — but there were several interesting variations. A fairly high percentage, for example, had chosen a 2-iron, a 4-iron, and a

6-iron instead of the odd-numbered clubs. About a fifth of the field had, like Coles, taken only one wood — usually a brassie. At least a quarter of the field had dispensed with the wedge in favor of a 9-iron, and this was one selection I could not understand, for while a 9-iron is at least as serviceable as a wedge for playing pitch shots off firm seaside turf, I would hate to try to blast out of a deep Scottish bunker with so thin a blade. All in all, I gathered, each man had picked the clubs he had the most confidence in, and this conclusion was reinforced on the second day of play, when Tony Fisher, a club professional from suburban London, came in with a wonderful 68 that he had wrought with the unlikely lineup of two woods, a 3-iron, a 5-iron, a 6-iron, a 9-iron, and a putter. He was, as you might imagine, in very good spirits, and claimed he had played only one poor stroke — "a fine attackin' putt from six feet on the seventeenth green, which I left four inches short of the hole."

I spent a good part of that second day, which was my last one at Turnberry, following Arthur Havers, who won the British Open at Troon in 1923, when he nipped Walter Hagen by a stroke. A dignified, white-haired man, now sixty-six, he plays little or no competitive golf these days, but the Seven-Club Tournament fascinated him so much that he mailed in an entry. He wore knickers, carried his own canvas bag, and hit many splendid shots. Partnered with him was another superannuated British Open champion — Fred Daly, a Belfast Irishman, who won the title in 1947 — and there was no question but that they were enjoying themselves hugely. I remember in particular an exchange I overheard as they came off the ninth green after both had gone over par on the hole.

"Yis, yis, yis," Daly groaned with mock heaviness as he wrote the scores down. "They're very keen here on handing out the pencils but not so keen on supplying rubber erasers."

"Seven clubs is no test anyhow, Fred," Havers observed with a gentle smile. "Now, five, that's a proper number."

As I say, the tightness of my schedule made it necessary for me to leave Turnberry before the finish of the tournament, and I had to get the final results from the papers. It was won, I learned, by Lionel Platts, of Wanstead, England, who has been coming up fast for the past four years, with a superb four-round total of 288 (70–74–72–72), only four over par — on a course, mind you, that most people would rank with Muirfield as just about the sternest test in

Scotland. In all, twenty players succeeded in breaking 300. This would seem to indicate that when an experienced golfer is at the top of his game, he can score substantially as low with seven clubs as with fourteen, or thirty-five. It is no trouble at all for him to coax a few more yards from any club when the situation calls for it, or, conversely, to ease up a fraction and float the ball a few yards shorter than he would normally hit it if he were playing a full shot. However, the general complexion of the scoring also made it clear that a golfer whose timing is slightly off will require at least two shots more per course per round, and sometimes as many as seven more, than if he had a full complement of clubs to lean on. And the golfer who is way off his game? Well, he has seven fewer clubs to break over his knee and throw into the nearest water hazard.

I arrived at the Saint-Germain-en-Laye Golf Club on Saturday, October 3rd, in time to watch the last two days of the Women's World Amateur Team Championship, or, as the sign hanging over the driveway to the club proclaimed, "Championnat du Monde par Équipes Dames." Built more than sixty years ago, the course at Saint-Germain was carved out of a lovely old forest of oak, white birch, and spruce. It is what is called in Europe a park course. There is not a great deal of undulation to the terrain, but the holes are well designed, the bunkering around the greens is severe, and the greens are fast and tricky. For this championship, the markers on the tees were placed near the front, so that the course played relatively short — only 5,933 yards. This was an intelligent move, for it meant that the players, instead of having to slug two woods to get home on many of the par-4 holes, could reach them with a drive and a long iron or, sometimes, a medium iron. From the point of view of atmosphere, Saint-Germain was a most felicitous choice. Although golf has been rapidly gaining in popularity in France — there are now about eighty courses — the game has always been the particular province of the upper classes, somewhat like polo in America, and the plant at Saint-Germain, for one, has much more the feeling of a European country estate than of an American country club. By our standards, the club-house is unimposing, but then it was patently intended to be a tasteful French version of a small English clubhouse, and it is. The French have always been very English about their golf. The men like to wear knickers, and the favorite drink of both the men and the women is Scotch. The walls of the lounge and dining room at Saint-Germain are covered, typically, with Cecil Aldin hunting scenes and a heavy thicket of eighteenth-century English sporting prints. At the same time, it is pleasant to report, French golf has some native flavor, and in precisely the ways one would wish. For example, the tournament hostesses at Saint-Germain wore vermilion cashmere sweaters and trim navy-blue stretch pants, and, needless to say, wore them well. More to the point, these were the first tournament hostesses I can remember who not only knew what was going on at their tournament but saw to it — with that attractive assertiveness Frenchwomen have — that everything from the scoreboards to the transportation operated without a hitch. In short, it was a beautifully organized event, and I felt I was attending no new and untried convocation but one that had been held often enough to get all the bugs out of it. It only remains to add, I think, that behind the Championnat's glossy surface lay four years of quiet work by two extremely able and charming ladies — Mrs. Henri Prunaret, of Boston, and the Vicomtesse Lally de Saint-Sauveur, of Paris. Mrs. Prunaret, née Mildred Gardinor, was the captain of our Curtis Cup team in 1960, and it was in that year, at Harlech, in Wales, where the British Ladies' Championship was held after the Cup match in England, that she first got together with the Vicomtesse, who had been the British Ladies' Champion in 1950 and the guiding light of women's golf in France, where a cadre of talented young players was then emerging. At Harlech and in subsequent correspondence, the ladies explored the possibility of an informal match between France and the United States in 1964, when our Curtis Cup team next went to Europe to play the British. Later on, the realization that the autumn of 1964 was when the male amateur golfers of the world would be gathering in Rome for the fourth Eisenhower Trophy match led them to think in terms of creating a tournament of similar scope for the women, and in the late autumn of 1963 the Vicomtesse approached the French Golf Federation with the request that it sponsor a Women's World Amateur Team Championship in 1964. The Federation agreed, and, moreover, wisely placed the Vicomtesse in charge of putting all the parts together. She and Mrs. Prunaret hoped that at least ten nations would agree to participate, but this modest goal was quickly surpassed, and in the end no fewer than twenty-five sent teams of three players each.

Everyone appeared to be entirely happy with the scoring system devised for the new championship: a team's score for each day would be the sum of the two low rounds turned in by its three players, and a team's score for the tournament would be the total of its four daily scores. This is a slight modification of the system used in the Eisenhower Trophy matches, in which the teams are made up of four players and their daily score is arrived at by adding up the three low rounds.

From the first day, the match at Saint-Germain resolved itself into an extraordinarily tight duel between the Americans and the French. Our team was made up of Barbara Fay White, the present Western Amateur Champion; Carol Sorenson, the recently crowned British Amateur Champion; and Barbara McIntire, who has twice been our National Amateur Champion (1959 and 1964) and was British Champion in 1960. Claudine Cros, Catherine Lacoste, and Brigitte Varangot formed the French team. Mlle. Cros, a handsome twenty-four-year-old blonde with a good, compact swing, is the daughter of a well-to-do businessman who has an exceptional talent for teaching golf and has made champions of his two sons as well as of his daughter. Mlle. Lacoste, an easygoing, chubby nineteen-year-old who hits the ball a kilometre, made her way onto the French team by her strong play in this summer's competitions. She has the perfect inheritance for a sportswoman; her mother is the former Simone Thion de la Chaume, who in 1927 became the first Frenchwoman to win the British Ladies' Championship, and her father (whom she looks quite a bit like) is René Lacoste, the great tennis champion of the nineteen-twenties, who won both at Wimbledon and at Forest Hills and led the French to their first Davis Cup triumphs. Mlle. Varangot, blond, athletic, twenty-four, and the daughter of a banker, is a member of Saint-Germain and the 1963 British Ladies' Champion. On most days, she is the best woman golfer on the Continent. During the championship, she was not in anything like her top form, for she was struggling with a swing that had grown too flat, and, besides, she was oppressed by the knowledge that so much was expected of her.

In any event, at the end of the first day of play, France, with a total of 147, compounded from a round of 72 (even par) by Mlle. Lacoste and a 75 by Mlle. Varangot, led the United States by one shot. On the second day, a 71 by Mlle. Lacoste and a 75 by Mlle.

Cros got the French in front by two shots. On the third day, when Mlle. Lacoste soared to a 78, her teammates came through with a 73 and a 75, but the French nevertheless dropped three shots to Miss Sorenson's 72 and Miss White's 73 and began the final day trailing by one. The winning or losing of this tense and dramatic battle ultimately hinged on how the two anchor women, Mlle. Lacoste and Miss McIntire, handled the two closing holes. The young French girl, the longest hitter in the field, finished coolly with par 4s on the 328-yard seventeenth and the tough 405-yard eighteenth. This put matters squarely up to Miss McIntire, playing a hole and a half behind Miss Lacoste and, incidentally, playing so well that an American victory seemed almost a certainty; in fact, a 4 and a 5 on the last two holes would do the trick. At the seventeenth, however, Miss McIntire pulled her approach into a bunker and took a 5. Now she needed a 4 on the eighteenth to win, a 5 to tie. She got neither, I'm afraid. Her tee shot was a good one, but then she hooked a 4-wood into the nest of bunkers guarding the green, misplayed two sand shots, and, after that, just barely failed to sink the twenty-five-foot putt on which everything depended. Final score: France 588, United States 589.

There is no crueler fate in sports than to be the one who loses a team match for one's country, and I cannot tell you how warmly everybody's heart went out to Barbara McIntire, a really superlative sort. She is a first-class shotmaker with a first-class temperament, but even the finest players fail in a crisis now and then, and this, regrettably, is all there is to it. How else can you explain Arnold Palmer's double bogey on the seventy-second hole which cost him the 1961 Masters? Or the way Ben Hogan, of all people, blew a chance to tie for first in the 1946 Masters by three-putting the last green, and then did the same thing again in our Open Championship later that year? The finest players, however, always seem to be able to digest calamity, and I am sure Barbara McIntire is one who will.

After the presentation ceremony, conducted by Jacques Léglise, the president of the French Golf Federation, I was fortunate enough to spot René Lacoste, the father of the tournament's heroine, standing by himself in one corner of the clubhouse dining room. His hands were thrust in the back pockets of his trousers, and as he took in the scene before him his face was lit by a broad, boyish smile. I asked him if his daughter played tennis. "No, but I think she will now," he answered. "I have just finished building a new grass court. It may be the only one on the Continent, I don't know. Anyway, I think she will play tennis now."

One of the aspects of the Women's World Amateur Team Championship that struck me most forcibly was the high quality of the performances turned in by the representatives of the comparatively new-to-golf countries. Whoever it was I was watching — the tall Swedish girls, or the stout Filipino matrons in their blue-and-brown plaids, or the good-natured Austrians, who finished at the bottom in the standings — I saw none of the untutored swings and wayward scrambling I had anticipated, and, in truth, I saw not one topped drive. I mention this because in 1958, when the Men's World Amateur Team Championship, or Eisenhower Trophy tournament, was inaugurated, at St. Andrews, a good many of the players were swatting the ball all over the premises, and a spectator had to be constantly on the alert to dodge errant slices, hooks, smothers, pop flies, shanks, and sclaffs. In 1960, when the second Eisenhower Trophy match was held, at Merion, near Philadelphia, there did not seem to have been much improvement in the general standard of play, but since then there certainly has been. The decline in the dominance of the American golfers over this span of years provides a most effective index. At Merion, our team won in a landslide, finishing an incredible forty-two strokes ahead of the runner-up, Australia, and two hundred and seventy strokes ahead of the last-place team, Ceylon. We won again in 1962, at Kawana, in Japan, but this time our margin of victory — over Canada — was only eight strokes, and the last-place team, Pakistan, was two hundred and two strokes off the pace. In the match this October at the Olgiata Golf Club, outside Rome, we not only failed to win but ended up in fourth place, thirteen strokes behind Great Britain; moreover, our total score for the four days was a mere hundred and fifty-one strokes lower than that of the tail-end team, Uruguay. Some veteran golf observers have remarked that the team we sent to Olgiata — including, as it did, three old fogies in their forties — was not the strongest one we might have selected, but however that may be, I think it is much more to the point to bring out, first, that this American team was favored to win and failed to because it was clearly outplayed by Britain, Canada, and New Zealand, and, second, that the American total was only two strokes lower than Australia's and — note this well — only three shots lower than Italy's and the Republic of China's. Furthermore, the individual scoring honors at Olgiata went to Min-nan Hsieh, of the Chinese team, with a total of 294 (72–77–72–73), and no American was near him. As you can see, the day is gone forever when a fairly competent British or American amateur with a 2 or 3 handicap at his club can descend on a foreign land during its amateur championship and return home the following week with a cup, a title, and a folderful of press clippings describing him as one of the game's greatest artists since Old Tom Morris.

The meeting at Olgiata, in which teams from thirty-three countries took part, produced two sets of heroes. The first, without any question, was the Chinese team, which, in addition to Min-nan Hsieh, consisted of Chi-hsiung Kuo, Sheng-san Hsu, and Chien-chin Chen. They are all slightly built Taiwanese in their early twenties, and they all swing the same way, which is hardly to be wondered at, since they were all taught by Chien-chin Chen's father, Chin-shih Chen, who for the past thirty-five years has been the professional at the Tam-Suei Golf and Country Club, fifteen miles from Taipei. The elder Chen, I gathered in talking with K. U. Dzung, the captain of the Chinese team, is a gifted analyst, who worked out for himself the dynamics of the modern golf swing by studying hundreds of action photographs of the leading American professionals. He has been coaching his son and the other members of the Chinese team for a number of years now, and not only do they have crisp modern styles but they can play all the shots. When you watch them walk into a bunker, for example, you can tell from the way they plant their feet and poise themselves before the ball that they know exactly how an explosion shot should be executed.

The Chinese team's accomplishment in finishing only three strokes behind the American team is all the more notable when you consider the rigors of Olgiata. Situated in the rolling green-brown Roman countryside, it measures a lengthy 6,879 yards from the back tees, and during the championship it played very long. High winds and rain squalls on the last three days militated against comfortable scoring, and so did the soft greens, which became pocked with spike marks and heel prints early each morning. The course, by the way, was opened for play only three years ago, and so it is still a little on the young side. Designed by C. K. Cotton, the well-known English golf architect, it possesses one novel and arresting feature: on several of the holes, he left isolated oaks standing here and there along the edges of the fairway, and they function very much like fairway bunkers in defining the correct route to the green and punishing the player who strays from it. One more thing about Olgiata. The championship course occupies one end of a twelve-hundred-acre estate that has long been the home of the famous Olgiata racing stable, owned by the Marchese Incisa della Rocchetta. The golf area, which is being developed in a frankly American manner, has already acquired a second eighteen-hole course, a score of posh new villas alongside the fairways of both courses, and rambling clubhouse built in a style that might best be described as Italian Palm Springs.

The second set of heroes at Olgiata was, of course, the team representing Great Britain and Ireland, and you can have no idea of just how sweet this triumph was for them, or how popular it was with their rivals, unless you realize that the British amateur golfers had not won a major international competition since the 1938 Walker Cup match. They had come painfully close on several occasions — indeed, in the first Eisenhower Trophy match they finished a single shot behind Australia and the United States — but time after time they somehow always managed to squander their opportunities. I have long marvelled at, and deeply admired, the resilient spirit the British have shown after each succeeding disappointment and the determination they have mustered for each new attempt. (I am not at all sure that we would do as well if, say, we should suddenly find ourselves supplanted by Japan as the world's foremost baseball nation and be repeatedly thwarted in our efforts to regain our leadership in a game we invented.)

At Olgiata, the British team was composed of three Walker Cup veterans — Michael Lunt, Michael Bonallack, and Ronnie Shade — and one newcomer, a young Yorkshireman named Rodney Foster, and it had as its non-playing captain Joe Carr, of Dublin, one of the soundest and most prepossessing men in all of sports. On the first day, the British jumped out in front of the field by four shots. They led by one shot at the halfway mark and by five shots at the end of the third round, and then held on stubbornly in the last round to win by two shots over Canada. At that, the British had to sweat out an absolutely Palmerian closing rush by Keith Alexander, the last Canadian player on the course. With five holes left to go, Alexander was in a position to earn Canada a tie for first if, by some miracle, he could birdie all five holes. He birdied the fourteenth, a short hole. He birdied the fifteenth, a par 5, after

hitting the green with two long wood shots. He birdied the sixteenth by planting a 2-iron next to the pin. He birdied the par-5
seventeenth. On the eighteenth, a 446-yard par 4, he drove well,
but then he hooked his approach into a bunker, and it was —
mercifully for the British — all over. I think two members of the
winning team, Foster and Carr, should be singled out for particular praise. Foster, appearing in his first international match,
turned in four steady and sure rounds. He has an uncomplicated
temperament to go with an uncomplicated swing, and he looks to
be just the sort of player the British have been seeking for years.
Carr was the perfect captain. He was all over the course, urging
his men on, and off the course no detail escaped his attention; for
instance, he would not permit his players to use the swimming
pool at the Cavalieri-Hilton Hotel, where they were staying, for
fear that the chemicals in the water might conceivably irritate their
eyes. He meant business all the way. Two evenings before the
start of play, the British team, like all the others, attended a gala
cocktail party at the Town Hall, on the Campidoglio, and then a
stupendous buffet dinner at the Castel Sant'Angelo, but after this
night on the town Carr cancelled all after-dark leaves, and for the
duration of the tournament the British players spent their evenings at their hotel, dining together, chatting together, planning
together. They let nothing deter them from their purpose until
their mission was accomplished. They really were a team, and
undoubtedly this is why they won.

I missed the last day and a half of play at Olgiata — and also the
British victory banquet, at which, I am told, Captain Carr was
called on for a speech and responded with a robust Irish ballad —
for I had hurried back to Britain in order to catch the last two days
of the Piccadilly World Match-Play Tournament. This is a new
event on the British professional-golf calendar, which has been
badly in need of a shot of imported glamour. Eight golfers were
invited to participate: Neil Coles and Peter Butler, of England;
Bruce Devlin, from Australia; Gary Player, from South Africa; and
Arnold Palmer, Jack Nicklaus, Ken Venturi, and Tony Lema, from
the United States. Professionals are never eager to compete in
match play — it is far less embarrassing to say "I finished twelfth"
than to say "So-and-So beat me 3 and 1" — but the Piccadilly
tournament offered several attractive lures. First, all matches were
over thirty-six holes — a much less precarious route than eighteen

holes, in which anything can happen. Second, everyone approved of the venue — the West Course of the Wentworth Golf Club, which affords a long, tight, arduous test, and which Palmer considers a blend of Pine Valley and Pinehurst No. 2. And, finally, each man was guaranteed a minimum of a thousand pounds, and first-place money was five thousand pounds, or fourteen thousand dollars — the largest purse in the history of British golf. The eventual winner, as everybody knows, was Palmer, who has taken home quite a few quid from Britain over the past few years.

In 1960, 1961, and 1962, when Palmer was working his way to his present exalted position, he brought off so many amazing eleventh-hour rallies that he was generally conceded to possess the finest competitive temperament of any golfer since Hagen. His victory at Wentworth was built on three characteristically brilliant bursts, one in each of his matches. On the first day, when the other Americans were eliminated — Venturi 4 and 2 by Player, Nicklaus 3 and 2 by Devlin, and Lema 4 and 3 by Coles — Palmer, up against Butler, pulled out a match he could easily have lost. After twenty-four holes, he stood 3 down, and he was having a very hard time concentrating, owing chiefly, as luck would have it, to his enormous popularity with British golf fans. This was his first appearance in the London area — Wentworth is twenty-five miles west of London — and he had drawn a large and excited gallery, which, ignoring what little marshalling there was, spilled under the fairway ropes and practically breathed down his neck while he played his shots. He was on the verge of going 4 down on the twenty-fifth hole when he saved himself by holing a difficult ten-footer. Then, as so often happens when Palmer has made a critical putt, he was off and running. He took three of the next five holes (one with a birdie and another with an eagle), to square the match, and he finally won it, 1 up, when he sank another ten-footer to halve the 504-yard home hole with a birdie 4. Against Player in the semifinals, on the second day, Palmer, 4 up after a 69 in the morning on a course with an approximate par of 73, started the afternoon round eagle, par, par, birdie, birdie, birdie, and went on to win, 8 and 6. In the final, against Coles, who had beaten Devlin, 2 and 1, the day before, Palmer stood 2 down at lunchtime after a so-so 73, and his chances did not seem at all bright. For one thing, his putting was way off, and, for another, Coles, who had scored a 69 in the morning, was hitting the ball with conspicuous ease and confidence, as he almost always seems to do at Wentworth, where he has won three big tournaments. Coles, a medium-sized man with flying hair that gives him more the look of a concert pianist than of a golf professional, is the son of a well-to-do shoe merchant, and first came to prominence in 1961, when he gained a place on the British Ryder Cup team. Now thirty, he is a shy fellow of conservative bent who, not too surprisingly, plays with irons that are six years old and woods that are seven. He has a polished swing, marked by one idiosyncrasy: as he addresses the ball, the face of his club is hooded slightly, and it remains so until he opens it as he comes into the ball. His exceptional balance and hand action help him to get away with this slight departure from perfect soundness. The only real weakness in his game is his putting. He tends to push the ball with a pronounced sweep of the arms, and, as is true of many British players, his attitude on the greens could be a lot more positive.

As the afternoon round got under way, Coles and Palmer, after three halves in a row, came to what proved to be the decisive hole — the fourth, or twenty-second, a 505-yard dogleg par 5. Coles reached the back of the large, sliding green with two magnificent wood shots, and needed only to get down in two to win the hole and gain a commanding 3-up lead. He took three putts. Let off the hook, Palmer responded immediately. On the par-3 fifth, he stuck a 4-iron eight feet from the pin and holed the putt for a birdie. One down now. On the sixth, a short par 4, he pinched a wedge approach seven feet from the pin and got that putt. Even. On the seventh, a difficult par 4, his 8-iron approach rolled a few feet down the back of the upper level of the terraced green, and he debated for a moment whether or not to use his putter to run the ball up to the flag, some twenty-five feet away. He decided to pitch it with his wedge, and holed it, for his third birdie in a row. One up. After that, there was very little to choose between Palmer and Coles. If anything, Coles played a shade more consistently from tee to green. The difference lay in their putting. Where Coles wasted his chances, Palmer seized his. On the thirty-first, he had to hole from ten feet to stay 1 up, and he did. On the thirty-third, after slashing a tremendous 4-iron recovery from the rough, he holed for a birdie from eighteen feet to move 2 up. Then, on the thirty-fifth green, he closed out the match, 2 and 1, by banging a six-footer into the back of the cup to match a birdie by Coles. This year, Palmer has not been putting up to his usual standard, but against Coles that afternoon he looked like the Palmer of 1960, who never missed anything. He was seven shots under par for those seventeen holes in the afternoon — prodigious scoring on a long, treacherous layout like Wentworth, and a triumph of will power, I should say, as much as of athletic skill. Incidentally, this was the first match-play tournament that Palmer had competed in since the summer of 1954, when he won our Amateur Championship four months before turning professional.

One of the nice things about Palmer's press conferences at the big tournaments in our country is the easy way he produces the name of whichever reporter is asking a question. I would guess that he knows the names of at least four hundred American sportswriters. To judge by his performance in the press tent at Wentworth after his match with Coles, he has now gained a similar familiarity with the British press corps. It is a treat to watch him in action. A bulky, mustached man rises and asks Palmer, in a Scots accent, why he putted so much better in the afternoon. "Well, Willie," Palmer says, and goes on to explain that he gripped his putter a little lower down the shaft, and that seemed to help. An imposing, bald, blue-eyed chap with an Oxford accent asks if Palmer might care, perhaps, to estimate the size of the galleries, difficult as that sort of thing is, you know. "Well, Peter," Palmer says, and places the attendance at around twenty-five thousand for the three days. And so on, question after question and name after name, infallibly the correct one. I would back him any day against Jim Farley, Jack Dempsey, or John Buchan's Mr. Memory.

With traffic piled up just the way it is on the Long Island Expressway on a Sunday night, the drive in to London from Wentworth was a long one. It took me two hours to creep the twenty-five miles — ample time in which to think about the golf I had seen in Scotland, France, Italy, and England. It was fortunate, in a way, I decided, that Palmer had carried the day at Wentworth, for otherwise, after the glorious victory of the French at Saint-Germain and the British at Olgiata, everyone would surely be concluding that American golfers, professional and amateur, male and female, were on the downgrade. (Some people did conclude that, of course.) The fact of the matter is, I think, that our players are as good as they ever were but that the players in other countries are vastly better than *they* ever were. And this is a most desirable state of affairs. For all the transoceanic amity generated, there would be no good reason to hold international tournaments such as the two World Amateur Team Championships if their outcome were a foregone conclusion. As things now stand, in a competition in which the teams consist of two, three, or four players, the United States is eminently beatable if a rival team manages to produce its maximum performance when the need is at *its* maximum — and that is as it should be. In particular, amateur golf, which the American sports public has all but forgotten, stands to profit from this international bracing. After the British breakthrough at Olgiata, next year's Walker Cup match will have far more interest than usual.

With these thoughts out of the way, I began to mull over some of the fine points of the four tournaments I had attended and to wonder if I had tried to pack too much into the eleven days. In a matter of minutes, I found myself speculating on whom I would back to win if Arnold Palmer and Arthur Havers were to oppose the Vicomtesse de Saint-Sauveur and Min-nan Hsieh in a twenty-seven-hole match-play four-ball tournament with six clubs, and it seemed to me that perhaps I had watched enough golf for the moment and it was time I got back into some street shoes.

(1964)

The Women
Mickey Wright, Babe Zaharias, and Joyce Wethered

Between 1958 and 1964, Mickey Wright won the United States Women's Open four times, and in the early 1960s she broke just about every record on the Ladies' Professional Golf Association tour. Her finest performance may have been in the 1961 U.S. Women's Open, held at the long and arduous Lower Course of the Baltusrol Golf Club. On the third and final day, the golfers who made the cut played two rounds. In the morning Miss Wright had a 69, three under par; in the afternoon she scored a 72, though her golf from tee to green was just as flawless. The difference was that in the afternoon she two-putted every green. In 1965, worn out by the week-to-week demands of the tour, Miss Wright retired from competitive golf. Was she as good or better than Babe Didrikson Zaharias or Joyce Wethered, both peerless in their days? There is no knowing, of course. Each was the best in her era, and that is all one can ask of any athlete.

THIS PAST JULY, MARY KATHRYN (MICKEY) WRIGHT, THE TALL, blond, and handsome Californian who has been by far the most outstanding woman golfer of our day, returned to college after an absence of eleven years. To spell out this unusual sequence in a bit more detail, Miss Wright left Stanford in 1954, at the close of her freshman year, in order to pursue a career in professional golf, and now, having won all the honors there are to be won, she has, at the antediluvian age of thirty, entered the sophomore class of Southern Methodist University, in Dallas, her adopted home town, where for the past several seasons she has been affiliated with the Oak Cliff Country Club. (She has chosen to major in psychology — a decision that is not at all surprising when one stops to reflect on it, for the women's professional golf tour provides some of the country's top preparatory schooling for that field of study.) Miss Wright hopes that she will be able to play a number of tournaments during her summer vacations, but even so her retirement will be all but complete, and it brings to an end an era that began in 1958, when she established herself as something extraordinary by winning both the United States Women's Open and the Ladies' Professional Golf Association Championship — the equivalent of the men's P.G.A. Championship. From that year on, she dominated women's golf absolutely, just as Bobby Jones dominated men's amateur golf in the nineteen-twenties. For four straight seasons (1961 through 1964), she won the most tournaments, collected the most prize money, and produced the lowest scoring average on the women's circuit. She set new L.P.G.A. records in just about all categories: the most tournament victories in one season (thirteen, in 1963), the most prize money won in one season ($31,269.50, in 1963), the lowest score for a four-round tournament (275, with rounds of 68–68–70–69, in the Spokane Open in 1962), the lowest eighteen-hole score (62, with nines of 30 and 32, in the Tall City Open, in Midland, Texas, in 1964), and the lowest average score per round for one season (72.81, in 1963). During her professional career, she won a total of sixty-five tournaments (including two this year, when an injured wrist severely hampered her play) and close to $200,000 in prize money, both of which achievements are also records. In brief, just as it was Jones against the field, so it has been Wright against the field, and I suppose the only question that remains to be answered is whether she deserves to be ranked as the greatest woman golfer of all time. A good many sound golf observers think so. For my part, I would like to have a little more time to think it over, but I do know this much: there has never been a better woman golfer.

The probably obvious reason I am hedging on this matter is that prior to Miss Wright's arrival on the scene it was standard practice to regard Joyce Wethered, the English star of the nineteen-twenties, and the late Babe Didrikson Zaharias as being in a class by themselves among women golfers. Since each was phenomenal in her own way and incomparable in her own time, it seems to me that perhaps it is more judicious to rank Miss Wright alongside them, and not above them, in much the same manner that it has become customary to acknowledge Ben Hogan as the peer but not the superior of the two super-champions of earlier periods, Bobby Jones and Harry Vardon. Indeed, it occurs to me that before returning to Miss Wright we might do well to spend a moment or two talking about Miss Wethered and Mrs. Zaharias, for the passage of time has already rendered them into shadowy figures — Miss Wethered in particular. A slim girl just under six feet tall who learned the game on the links of Dornoch, she came into prominence at the age of eighteen, in 1920, when British golf was starting up again in earnest after the First World War. That year, her brother Roger, who was later to win the British Amateur Championship, was the captain of the Oxford golf team, and it was the unreserved enthusiasm of Roger and his teammates for her golf that led her that summer to enter her first tournament of any importance, the English Ladies' Championship. (Female golfers are always "ladies" in Britain; over here they're sometimes "ladies" and sometimes "women.") Hoping only to perform creditably, she was staggered when she won the tournament by defeating Cecil Leitch, the leading woman golfer of the day. (Miss Wethered subsequently played in four other English Ladies' Championships and swept the lot.) In 1921, emboldened by this success, she entered the British Ladies' Championship and made her way as far as the final, where she lost to Miss Leitch. Over the next four years, she won the British Ladies' three times, and then she decided that she had had her fill of tournament golf. In 1929, however, when an unusually large contingent of foreign stars, headed by Glenna Collett, three times the American champion, invaded Britain, Miss Wethered came out of retirement and scored a fourth victory in the British Ladies' by defeating Miss Collett, 3 and 1, in the thirty-six-hole final at St. Andrews, in what could well be the finest match in the history of women's golf. Then she went into retirement again, emerging only to play in the annual autumn mixed-foursome tournament at Worplesdon, which is essentially a convocation of old golfing friends, and to make a brief exhibition tour of America as a professional in 1935, two years before she became Lady Heathcoat-Amory.

Miss Wethered's reputation rests not only on her record of winning nine of the twelve championships she played in during her abbreviated career — in 1921 she was beaten in the French Ladies', her only appearance in a foreign championship — but also on her abilities as a scorer and as a technician. At a time when

top women golfers were only just beginning to break 80 in competition over difficult courses, she usually went around comfortably
in 73 or 75. For example, when she and Miss Collett first came up
against each other, in the third round of the 1925 British Ladies', at
Troon, the American girl rose to the occasion with the best golf of
her life and was only one over par after fifteen holes, but by then
the match was finished, 4 and 3, Miss Wethered having played the
last ten holes in six under par. In their return match in the famous
final at St. Andrews four years later, Miss Collett, again in marvellous form, went to the turn in the morning in 34 and stood 5 up.
Thereupon Miss Wethered buckled down hard to her task and
played the next eighteen holes — the last nine of the morning
round and the first nine of the afternoon round — in 73, to take
command of the match. The essence of her style, like Jones's, was
fluidity and rhythm. There is no such thing, of course, as a natural
golf swing — the movements must be mastered by practice — but
Joyce Wethered made golf seem as natural and effortless as walking. Her thoughts on what made for a good golf swing were
uncomplicated and well ahead of her time. She believed that the
club should be taken back a shade inside the line of flight, that the
first yard of the backswing set the tempo for the entire swing, that
the hip pivot should be more restricted than the shoulder pivot,
and that the downswing should be inaugurated by a movement of
the hips to the left — all of which, as we now realize much more
clearly than we did forty years ago, are fundamental to the correct
swing. Most of the time, she played her wood shots with a relatively full swing, and, being a tall girl with a big arc, she hit the
ball a long way, averaging about two hundred and twenty-five
yards off the tee. On her iron shots, which flew in a low, drilling
trajectory, like Gene Sarazen's, she took her hands back only
shoulder-high and finished her swing with her hands again no
higher than her shoulders; in fact, this is the picture that remains
fixed in everyone's mind as most characteristic of her style. During her matches, she talked very little to her opponent and gave
the impression of cool detachment, yet actually she was anything
but relaxed, and the wear and tear on her nerves forced her to rest
for two weeks after each tournament and leave the game strictly
alone. This strain was, of course, what underlay her decision to
quit competitive golf so early. "A less active role has always suited
me perfectly," she explained after her final retirement. "I can
[now] enter into the emotions of the game and enjoy them just as I

like without having to preserve a state of elaborate calmness as a player over incidents which are in reality causing me acute excitement and probably no little apprehension and alarm."

As is probably apparent, Miss Wethered was shy and extremely modest. Not long ago, on rereading her book *Golfing Memories and Methods*, I was especially struck by the elaborate circumlocution she devised to conceal the fact that in the final of the 1924 British Ladies' she had routed Mrs. Frank Cautley, 7 and 6. "I came in to lunch three up, and the day ended in a terrible deluge of rain," she wrote. "Neither of us, probably, was very sorry when the game finished on the twelfth green." I mention this aspect of Miss Wethered's nature because it presents such a pronounced contrast to the temperament and demeanor of Babe Didrikson Zaharias. Having grown up in public, as it were, after attracting universal attention as the nineteen-year-old track-and-field sensation of the 1932 Olympic Games, Mrs. Zaharias was a happy extrovert who loved the spotlight. At the end of a round of golf, she would linger at the clubhouse chatting with one and all, and if she felt that things were too sombre, she would grab her harmonica and launch into an impromptu concert. She was, to be sure, a beautifully coordinated athlete, but the attribute that made her so formidable a competitor was her fantastic confidence. Her golfing friend Peggy Kirk Bell once told me a story that nicely illustrates this. Shortly after Mrs. Bell had turned professional, she was invited by Mrs. Zaharias to be her partner in a rather important four-ball event. On the morning of their first match, Mrs. Bell had a bad attack of jitters; all she could think about was that she might play very poorly and drag her illustrious partner down to defeat with her. "Forget it," Mrs. Zaharias told her. "I can beat any two players in this tournament by myself. If I need any help, I'll let you know."

Mrs. Zaharias had what amounted to two separate careers in golf. The first began in 1936, when she barnstormed around the country with Sarazen and other well-established men professionals, playing one-day stands in which she demonstrated that she could regularly drive the ball two hundred and fifty yards and could occasionally hit it where she was aiming. After a while, she got down to the tedious business of really learning how to play golf — a game in which natural athletes have an advantage, but only after they have toiled enough to master a technique that is quite different from anything required in other games. In 1944, she applied for and received reinstatement as an amateur, and her second career began at the close of the Second World War. She won the Women's Amateur Championship in 1946, and the following spring, at Gullane, in Scotland, became the first American ever to win the British Ladies' Championship. Then she turned professional again. Between 1948 and 1955, her last year as a player (she died in 1956), Mrs. Zaharias won thirty-one professional tournaments, including three U.S. Women's Opens — the last one in 1954, at the Salem Country Club, in Massachusetts. That Open may have constituted this amazing and gallant woman's greatest performance in golf. A year earlier, she had undergone an operation for cancer, but she nevertheless came through with four altogether superb rounds (72–71–73–75) to finish twelve strokes ahead of her nearest competitor. Throughout her career, one of her most valuable assets, naturally, was the distance she could clout the ball. To cite just one example, on the fifteenth hole at Gullane, which is five hundred and forty yards long, she reached the green one afternoon, assisted by a slight following breeze, with a drive and a 4-iron. She was only a moderately large woman — she stood five feet seven and weighed a hundred and forty pounds — but she had exceptional strength and timing. While her swing was not an aesthetic treat, like Miss Wethered's, it was grooved and efficient. The best thing about it was that however hard she hit the ball, she could not hook it — just about the most desirable failing a golfer could have. (The explanation was that she took the club back on the outside as she rocked into her swing, and then brought it directly up; as her hands moved down and through the ball from that position, she never allowed her right hand to cross over her left.) There was a good deal more to her golf than mere power, though. What she strove for on all her shots was feel and control, and, as a result, her short game — particularly her wedge play and her chipping — was definitely superior to that of her competition. "Not many people noticed it, but off the golf course Babe was very dainty with her hands," Mrs. Bell, who was very close to her over the years, remarked not long ago. "She would pick up a cigarette as if she were playing jackstraws. When she lifted a fork or a knife or any other small object, she would move it around delicately and feel its weight and balance. I asked her about this once, and she told me, 'It helps my golf.' "

*

By a happy coincidence, in the 1954 U.S. Women's Open, which was Mrs. Zaharias's last championship, she was paired in the double round on the last day with Mickey Wright, a tall (five-foot-nine), slender, exceedingly nice-looking nineteen-year-old amateur who had won the Girls' Junior Championship two years before and was making her début in the Open. Miss Wright was very impressive that day. She kept up with her partner off the tee, broke 80 on both rounds, tied for fourth place, and beat all the other amateurs. This was heady stuff for a young girl, and it had a considerable influence on her decision to leave college and turn professional. At that time, Miss Wright had been playing golf for seven years. The daughter of a well-to-do San Diego lawyer, she had taken her first lessons, at twelve, from John Bellante, the professional at the La Jolla Country Club, who also taught Gene Littler the ABCs of golf. However, the instructor who really developed her swing was Harry Pressler, the pro at the San Gabriel Country Club, outside Los Angeles. Every Saturday for two years — the years she was fourteen and fifteen — Miss Wright drove a hundred and twenty-five miles up to San Gabriel with her mother and took an hour's lesson with Pressler. Basically, he set out to teach her how to hit the ball with the same kind of vigorous hand action that the best men players use; most women tend to sweep the ball away with a swing that is nearly all arms, and are therefore rather short hitters. To this end, he emphasized three points for his young pupil to work on: at the beginning of the downswing her weight should start moving across her right foot to her left foot; on the downswing, also, her right elbow should be tucked in close in front of the right hip; and, third, as her hands moved toward the ball, her wrists should remain cocked as long as possible. Miss Wright adhered faithfully to these three fundamentals throughout her career. At certain periods, when her swing went sour, she sought out various professionals whom she respected — chiefly Harvey Penick, Les Bolstad, Stan Kertes, Paul Runyan, and Earl Stewart, Jr. — and asked them to check on how well she was executing the moves she wanted to make, but at no time was she ever seriously tempted to alter the guiding mechanics of the swing she grew up with.

When Miss Wright joined the women's professional tour in 1955, the goal she set for herself, like any red-blooded American girl, was to become the best woman golfer who ever lived. During her first seasons on the tour, she was quite grim and fretful, beneath an innate politeness, because she was not at all sure she could come anywhere close to her ambition. For one thing, she was reminded daily of how far the veterans of the tour surpassed her in skill. Mrs. Zaharias was gone by then, but the other members of what had come to be known as the Big Four — Patty Berg, Louise Suggs, and Betty Jameson — were still very much in evidence. (By the way, I would without any hesitation name Miss Berg as the most accomplished woman shotmaker — and, for that matter, one of the very best shotmakers, male or female — that I have ever had the pleasure of watching.) For another thing, Miss Wright was having her troubles with her own game. While she hit her full shots farther than any other player on the tour, she was generally erratic, because in trying to achieve the maximum delay in uncocking her wrists she developed a habit of dropping her hands too sharply at the start of the downswing and hitting the ball with a flailing action. On top of this, her short game was very weak. "Mickey had no touch at all on her chip shots, and she was absolutely the worst putter I have ever seen in professional golf," Betsy Rawls, her closest friend on the tour, recalled this summer. "Her mental attitude was all wrong. She was preoccupied with playing flawlessly from tee to green. If she didn't hit fifteen of the eighteen greens in the regulation stroke, she was disgusted with herself. She had complete contempt for scrambling. It took Mickey at least two years to learn to respect the short game, and realize that even the top players have to be able to get down in two from off the green. Then her chipping and putting started to improve, and, of course, her scoring did, too."

In 1956, her second year on the tour, Miss Wright won her first professional tournament — the Jacksonville Open. She won three tournaments in 1957, five in 1958 (including the U.S. Women's Open), four in 1959 (including the Women's Open), and six in 1960. In 1961, she really arrived. She won ten tournaments that season, but it was the quality of her play — especially in the Women's Open, which she won for the third time — that revealed her as a golfer eminently worthy of comparison with Joyce Wethered and Babe Zaharias. That year's Open was held on the Lower Course of the Baltusrol Golf Club, in Springfield, New Jersey — a difficult, heavily bunkered layout over arduous terrain that measured 6,372 yards for the championship and played a good deal longer. Miss Wright began with a 72, even par, but an 80 on her second round, mainly because of poor putting, left her four strokes behind the leaders at the halfway mark. On the third day, when the last thirty-six holes were played, she moved out in front of the field with a spectacular 69 in the morning and then added a very solid 72 to finish six strokes ahead of the runner-up, Miss Rawls. En route to her 69, she had no fewer than six birdies, but, in a way, her closing 72 was every bit as brilliant, for she was on every green except two in the regulation stroke; the difference was that she needed only twenty-eight putts in the morning and took two putts on every green in the afternoon. These figures, eloquent as they are, do not begin to suggest the near perfection of Miss Wright's play on the double round. Throughout a long day of pressure, swinging as fluently as if she were on a practice tee, she boomed one long drive after another down the middle of the narrow fairways. For all her length, she had to use a lot of club to get home on her approaches — 3-irons, 4-irons, 5-irons, and 6-irons, for the most part — but on hole after hole, hitting very pure shots, she put the ball within twenty feet of the pin. Had she been holing putts in the afternoon, she could have been around in 66, easily. It can be stated categorically, I believe, that no other woman has ever played a long, exacting course quite as magnificently as Miss Wright did that last day at Baltusrol. In fact, I can think of only one comparable exhibition of beautifully sustained golf over thirty-six holes in a national championship — Ben Hogan's last two rounds at Oakland Hills in the 1951 Open.

After her remarkable performance at Baltusrol, Miss Wright went on to become an even more proficient golfer. The next three years, she led the L.P.G.A. tour in every department; indeed, her domination was so complete that a tournament became news only when she lost it. Everything considered, her competitive ardor held up well. Whenever she was in contention in a tournament, she was able to summon the shots she needed to carry the day. In the 1964 Women's Open, she had to par the last hole, a tough 395-yard par 4, to gain a tie with Ruth Jessen, and she did it, after pushing her 2-iron approach into a greenside bunker, by exploding six feet from the pin and then rapping the putt into the center of the cup; she won the playoff with a 70, an almost errorless round. During those years, Miss Wright could have made a small fortune if she had wanted to, because golf clubs around the country were clamoring for Mickey Wright personal appearances and would gladly have paid her upward of five hundred dollars for an afternoon's work, but she turned down nearly all these offers. In temperament and general sensibility, she is very much closer to Joyce Wethered than to Babe Zaharias, and the thought of complicating an already punishing schedule just to make money appalled her. A highly self-critical and emotional girl, she masked her feelings so well on the golf course that she presented a picture of unruffled calm, but playing the role of the queen had no attraction for her, and off the course she went her way quietly, as she always had. Her idea of a gala evening was to have dinner with a few friends, preferably of an intellectual bent, who were entertaining talkers. Between rounds and tournaments, she spent a good deal of her spare time listening to music — she always carried a portable record-player on the tour — and, in addition, she read exhaustively, studied French and the guitar, and occasionally went fishing. As far as her golf went, she was not a particularly avid practicer, but, like many of the women professionals, she was fascinated by the theory of the swing, and she loved to articulate her thoughts on it in long, rounded sentences.

Then, during the 1964 season, professional golf quite suddenly began to lose its appeal for Miss Wright. Though she continued to maintain her high standard of play, the constant pressure of knowing that she was expected to win every tournament she entered finally wore her down so badly that she developed ulcers. By 1964, moreover, she had been leading the nomadic life of the tour for ten full years, and she found that she was enjoying the off-season months in Dallas, where she shares an apartment with two girls who are social workers, more than the long, arid stretches on the tournament circuit. There was one other reason for her change of attitude — a most important one. She had done everything she had set out to do in golf, and her enthusiasm was waning. (One day last autumn, she mentioned this to Leonard Wirtz, the tournament director of the L.P.G.A., and he astutely called her attention to the fact that there was one record she didn't hold — the lowest score for eighteen holes. It was in her very next tournament that she shot that incredible 62.) For all these reasons, she had her mind pretty well made up a year ago that she would carry on for one more season and then retire. She would naturally have liked to go out in a blaze of glory, but last winter she was unlucky enough to suffer an injury to her left wrist, which she had sprained the previous autumn, and she had to favor it conspicuously even in the two tournaments she managed to win. In June, a fortnight before the Women's Open, which was the tournament she had been waiting for all year, the injury — a form of tendoni-tis — became so painful that she couldn't hit a ball without winc-ing. She rested her wrist until it was time to go to the Atlantic City Country Club, where the Open was being held, but after her first practice round her hand was in such bad shape that she had no alternative but to withdraw from the championship. It was a very hard way to step down.

After Bobby Jones retired, at twenty-eight, in 1930, following his Grand Slam, he played no tournament golf until he appeared in the first Masters Championship, in 1934. Everyone was wonder-ing, of course, whether he would then be able to take up where he had left off and lead the field, but the best he could do was tie for thirteenth, and in his subsequent appearances in the Masters he was never a threat. He had been out of the crucible of competition too long, and, as he readily acknowledged, had lost the knack of concentrating on his shots under the strain of tournament condi-tions. In Mickey Wright's case, it is difficult to predict what effect her present plan to play serious golf only during her summer vacations will have on her game. One might logically suppose that she would have some trouble regaining her old concentration, but ten months away from the lists is not three years, and I don't think that either her rivals or her devoted following would be exactly bowled over if she won a couple of tournaments next summer. As a matter of fact, I am really less concerned about her golf than about her ability to get back into the swing of college. After all, William James and Erik Erikson can be mighty tough, too, when you've been away from them for a while.

(1965)

The P.G.A. Championship at Laurel Valley

There have been many golfers who have had the ability to win a major championship but who, for one reason or another, never did. Dave Marr would have been a member of this legion had he not held on to his lead as he came down the stretch in the 1965 P.G.A. Championship at Laurel Valley. Marr is a man of exceptional sensibility, and his account of the thoughts that went through his mind on the last five holes is enlightening, to say the least.

PERHAPS THE MOST INTERESTING FEATURE OF THE PROFES-sional Golfers' Association Championship, which was held in mid-August at the Laurel Valley Golf Club, in Ligonier, Pennsylvania, was that it was won by a player — Dave Marr — who had been regarded by most of us as too aware, too sensitive, altogether too intelligent ever to capture a major championship. It is probably an exaggeration to call Marr, as some have done, the Adlai Stevenson of golf, but, unlike most of the players on the tour, he does show marked egghead tendencies. A slim, thirty-one-year-old Texan who rather resembles Pee Wee Reese in appearance and manner, Marr reads hard-cover books and serious periodicals, has a quick and enlightening wit, is remarkably *au courant* with the world outside the locker room, and, all in all, may be the brainiest topflight golfer since Bob Jones. Unfortunately, these attributes are generally more of a handicap than a help to the tournament golfer; indeed, it has long been appreciated that the men who have been able to function best under intense pressure have, with few exceptions, been tough-minded, somewhat impassive, relatively unimaginative fellows who could wrap themselves in a tight cocoon of concentration and move undistractibly toward their goal. An athlete who has a delicately tuned intelligence and learns how to make it work for him does have certain advantages over his rivals, but this ability, of course, is more easily postulated than practiced. In any event, three weeks before the P.G.A. Championship, Marr, who had not won a tournament since 1962 but had been playing well this summer, appeared to have the Insurance City Open, in Hartford, all locked up when he was three strokes out in front with only seven holes to go. He bogeyed the twelfth (or sixty-sixth) hole, however, and when he pushed his tee shot out of bounds on the fourteenth, he lost the rest of his lead. He eventually finished one stroke off the winning score. This was not the first time Marr had faded down the stretch, so when he entered the last eighteen holes of the P.G.A. Championship tied for the lead with Tommy Aaron and standing two strokes ahead of those redoubtable warhorses, Billy Casper and Jack Nicklaus, few people considered him a likely winner.

Marr came through with a really superb performance. In retrospect, his round was divided into two distinct segments: the first thirteen holes, which he played almost flawlessly (a hooked approach to the ninth green was his only error), and the last five, which he weathered with a memorable succession of clutch shots. Going into those five holes, Marr still held his two-stroke lead over Casper, who was playing in the threesome directly in front of him, and he led Nicklaus, who was playing in the same threesome as he was, by three strokes. On the fourteenth, a 190-yard par 3 on which the flag was tucked behind a water hazard guarding the right-hand portion of the green, Marr made his second poor shot of the round. Aiming for the safe left side of the green, he pulled his tee shot onto stubbly ground well to the left of his target. When he took three more shots to get down, his lead over Casper was reduced to a single stroke. The fifteenth at Laurel Valley, a 375-yard par 4, doglegs to the right, with a pond filling the angle of the dogleg. To make sure he did not miss the narrow fairway, Marr used an iron — a 2-iron — off the tee. This left him with a fairly long and very touchy approach. The pond was no bother now, but in order to hit the small green he had to carry a greenside bunker directly on his line, and, moreover, he had to stop the ball quickly to keep it from rolling into the bunker on the far side. He played the perfect shot — a high, floating 4-iron that just did clear the front bunker and stopped fifteen feet past the flag. When he holed that putt for a birdie 3, he again led Casper by two strokes and Nicklaus by three, and he seemed as good as in. Not exactly. Indeed, his perils were only beginning. On the sixteenth, a 448-yard par 4 to another heavily bunkered green, he had a 3-iron shot left after a fine long drive. Since the flag was at the extreme right of the green, the one place that Marr did not want to put his approach, if he misplayed it, was in the bunker on the right; with the flag set so near that hazard, it would take an exquisite, and risky, sand shot to get the ball up close. So if he missed the green on his approach, he wanted to be in the bunker on the left, where he would have plenty of room — fifty feet or so — in which to stop a sand shot. As things turned out, his approach kicked into the bunker on the left, and when he wafted the ball to within twenty inches of the cup with a beautifully executed recovery, his tactics looked brilliant. Then he went and missed the putt. Only one shot ahead of Casper now, two ahead of Nicklaus.

The seventeenth at Laurel Valley is a 230-yard par 3 to a treacherously fast green that tilts from left to right. Marr had played this hole well throughout the tournament, and he did it again, busting a 4-wood onto the high side of the green forty feet to the left of the flag. Nicklaus's tee shot had ended up on the left-hand fringe of the green, and Marr, after watching Nicklaus's chip slide and slide down the slippery grade and finally wind up banked against the opposite fringe, eighteen feet beyond the hole, stroked his approach putt very gently. He just wanted to get it close. Even so, the putt ghosted a full eight feet past the hole. Marr was obviously exasperated with himself, and then, to compound matters, Nicklaus holed out the awkward little stab shot he improvised with his 7-iron, and rescued his par. The only good thing about this from Marr's point of view was that he learned the line on his own eight-footer from the way Nicklaus's chip broke in toward the cup from left to right; he had previously read it to break from right to left. Considering how much was riding on that putt, Marr stepped up to it with uncommon speed and rapped the ball firmly into the center of the cup. His worries seemed over now, for he still led Nicklaus by two shots, and on the eighteenth tee he heard the buoying news that Casper had bogeyed the last hole, so that he now led Casper by two also.

It is no trouble at all to bogey the eighteenth at Laurel Valley. A par 4 measuring 470 yards, it falls gradually downhill from the tee for some three hundred and forty yards, then bends acutely to the right and climbs abruptly to a terraced green; that day, the flag was set on the upper level. In order to reach the green in two shots, a player must hit a very big drive and keep it on the fairway. Nicklaus did precisely this. Marr did not. He pulled his drive into a bunker flanking the fairway — a shallow bunker, but a bunker all the same. Now he would have to play skillful golf to get out of the hole with a 5. A 6 was a definite possibility. So was a 3 by Nicklaus. In this hard corner, Marr produced an excellent shot and then a great shot. The first was his recovery from the bunker; using a 7-iron, he picked the ball cleanly off the sand and lobbed it down the fairway to the foot of the upslope. The second was a full-blooded 9-iron that covered the flagstick all the way, although it had been a partly blind shot for Marr; the ball came down in the middle of the green, hopped up onto the upper level, and rolled dead three feet from the hole. It mattered not at all that Nicklaus finished with a 4. Marr was safely home.

Several weeks after this exhibition of fortitude by Marr, a group of golf enthusiasts were sitting around with him one evening, and it occurred to somebody to ask him what had gone on in that active mind of his during those last five holes. How had he felt on the fourteenth tee, for example?

"You won't believe this," he answered, with a little laugh, "but I was so confident of winning I was actually starting to prepare my acceptance speech. When I missed the green with my tee shot, I stopped that stuff quick."

Did he think he had the tournament won when he birdied the fifteenth?

"I really did," he said. "I began to think of all the people it would mean so much to if I did win — my family, of course; and Robby Williams, a professional in Houston who was like a father to me after my own father died; and Claude Harmon, the professional at Winged Foot, who, with Robby, put the polish on my game; and about a dozen other people. Your mind does funny things out there at times like that."

Why did he blow that short putt on the sixteenth?

"I moved on it — moved my whole body," he replied. "As I was saying, when you're so keyed up, your mind plays strange tricks on you. Short as that putt was — or, more accurately, *because* it was so short — I knew I had to be very careful with it. The moment I said the word 'careful' to myself, I thought of the way my three-year-old son always says 'Careful, Daddy' when I toss him in the air and catch him. Really odd! I couldn't have been concentrating on that putt, but I thought I was. I felt rotten when I missed it. When I was walking off the green heading for the next tee, I noticed that two or three close friends who had been following me all day were leaving the gallery and starting for the clubhouse. They obviously thought they were jinxing me."

Why had he taken so little time with that critical eight-footer on the seventeenth green?

"I was sore," he said. "I had thrown away that stroke on the sixteenth, and now it looked as if I was going to throw away another, because of that poor approach putt. When Nicklaus holed his chip, that really made me mad at myself. There was Jack coming through under pressure and me practically tossing away the championship. I wanted to do something decisive."

That 9-iron on the eighteenth — he had played it with so little hesitation and had looked so relaxed on the shot. How come?

"Well, first, I knew what the right club was," he said. "When I played with Bob Goalby on the opening round, he was in that exact spot, and I remembered he'd hit a 9-iron and had the distance perfectly. Second, I was lucky enough to do the right kind of thinking when I was getting set before the ball. Claude Harmon keeps telling you, 'Trust your swing. Trust your swing.' That's the only thing I thought about when I played the shot. I think that's why my action was so free."

The day after that session with Marr, I went back and reread for the nth time what Bob Jones said about tournament golf back in 1927, in his book *Down the Fairway*. The key to success, Jones wrote, was "the stolid and negative and altogether unromantic attribute of patience." He added, "It is nothing new or original to say that golf is played one stroke at a time. But it took me years to realize it. And it is easy to forget, now. And it won't do to forget, in tournament golf."

(1965)

Honourable Company

The young Jack Nicklaus may have been the most awesome power golfer of all time. What set him apart from the other cannoneers in the 1960s was that he hit the ball with a handsome, correct swing, and his tee shots usually found the fairway. His balance and timing were extraordinary, and when he needed distance, he was able to generate enormous energy and release all of it as he hit through the ball. Ironically, he won his first British Open in 1966 at Muirfield — the home of the Honourable Company of Edinburgh Golfers — on a course specifically set up to keep long hitters in check.

A VERY EASY WAY TO GET INTO AN ARGUMENT WITH A GOLF traditionalist, on either side of the Atlantic, is to suggest that the Old Course at St. Andrews is no longer the finest course in Great Britain. Those who take this controversial stand generally concede that the Old Course, though a little too short and idiosyncratic by the best modern standards, is still a superb test of golf, but they contend that there just happen to be some better courses. The one they usually name first is Muirfield, which lies in East Lothian, along the southern shore of the Firth of Forth, some twenty miles east of Edinburgh, and the one they usually name second is the Ailsa course at Turnberry, in Ayrshire, on the west coast, about fifty miles south of Glasgow. There is something to be said for this bold contention. The Ailsa course, which was turned into an R.A.F. airbase during the Second World War, was remodelled in the nineteen-fifties by the Scottish golf architect Philip Mackenzie Ross with such taste and imagination that it emerged not only as a far sounder course than before but also, in the minds of many well-travelled golfers, as the most vibrant, adventurous seaside layout east of California's Pebble Beach. Muirfield occupies a much flatter and less spectacular stretch of dune land than either Ailsa or St. Andrews — or Prestwick, or Birkdale or Dornoch or Sandwich, for that matter — but between 1891, when the course was established, and the middle nineteen-twenties, when it underwent its last considerable revision, its eighteen holes gradually gained character and distinction, and Muirfield came to be recognized as the outstanding "classical," or "orthodox," course in Britain. The qualifying adjectives were calculated to pacify the adherents of St. Andrews, who have always been the first to point out that the Old Course is a law unto itself, quite unlike any other links.

Muirfield's great quality is its frankness — its honesty. There are no hidden bunkers, no recondite burns, no misleading or capricious terrain. Every hazard is clearly visible. Chiefly for this reason, the course has always been extremely popular with foreign golfers, and especially Americans; it has a sort of "inland" flavor that makes visitors feel much more at home on it than on any other British championship course. Moreover, Muirfield is perhaps the most beautifully conditioned course in Britain. The turf on the fairways is firm and crisp, the greens are remarkably true and of uniform speed, and even the numerous bunkers are assiduously groomed. In recent years, the British Open has regained nearly all its former prestige, and while the list of entrants for the 1966 championship early this July would undoubtedly have been imposing wherever the event was held, the fact that it was Muirfield's turn to act as host to the Open guaranteed attendance by leading golfers from all over the globe. (Indeed, the only one who wasn't on hand was Billy Casper, the new United States Open champion, who earlier this season had committed himself to appear that week in a tournament the Mormon Church — his church — conducts.) The winner at Muirfield, as everyone knows, was Jack Nicklaus, and though he obviously played the best golf and earned his victory honestly, many of the players he defeated made no bones about their disappointment. Each of them was convinced that Muirfield was just *his* cup of tea and that *he* should have won there.

Back in 1892, when the British Open was held at Muirfield for the first time, golfers thought somewhat less kindly of the layout. For example, when Andrew Kirkaldy, the rough-and-ready professional from St. Andrews, was asked at the close of the tournament what he thought of the course, he declared, "Ach, it's an auld water meadie. I'm glad I'm gaun home." (The fact that Harold Hilton, an amateur — and an Englishman to boot — had just won the Open might have had something to do with Kirkaldy's dour judgment.) Then, there's the companion story about the nameless visitor who was foolishly asked his opinion of the course after he had battled it on a cold, rainy weekend. "Muirfield be damned, and this whole benighted area!" he spat out. "I don't call this East Lothian. I call it East Loathsome." The chances are that this golfer, like Kirkaldy, came from the Old Course, for over the years there has been a strong rivalry between Muirfield and St. Andrews, which, as the crow flies, is only twenty miles away across the Firth of Forth, on the Fifeshire Peninsula. Muirfield, you see, is more than just a splendid golf course. It is the home of the Honourable Company of Edinburgh Golfers, the one golfing organization in Scotland that possesses a lustre approaching that of the famed Royal and Ancient Golf Club of St. Andrews. The Honourable Company came into existence at Leith, outside of Edinburgh, in 1744, and thus ranks as the oldest golf club in the world — ten years the senior of the R. and A. Furthermore, although the R. and A. later became the official governing body of British golf, it was the Honourable Company that drew up the game's first set of rules (thirteen in number), for its first competition, in 1744, and this is quite a feather in its cap. From the club's inception, its membership has been composed largely of Edinburgh's top-drawer lawyers, doctors, civil servants, and other professional men. (Sir Henry Raeburn, the artist, was an active member, and his full-length portrait of Alexander Keith, one of the eighteenth-century captains of the Honourable Company, hangs in the bar of the present clubhouse.) Like true sons of Edinburgh, the Honourable Company has always been inclined to look upon all other Scots as country cousins — including, one may be sure, the Fifeshire lairds who have traditionally been the backbone of the R. and A. This attitude has gained the club the reputation of being a rather snobbish outfit, but its members believe that a better word would be "discriminating." In any event, in Colonel Brian Evans-Lombe, a former cavalry officer who served the Honourable Company as secretary from 1948 until 1963, when he retired, Muirfield had the ideal administrator. Evans-Lombe, who was enamored of detail, created a whole new standard for course maintenance. Under his direction, the bunkers became works of art — walled with rectangles of turf fitted together so precisely that a master mason could learn from them. He was openly critical of careless visiting golfers who replaced their fairway divots with the grain going the wrong way. In time, Evans-Lombe, fundamentally a most pleasant man, became, like all high-strung perfectionists, impatient of interruptions in his schedule, as he demonstrated one May morning in 1959 when, only a day or two before the Walker Cup match at Muirfield, John Ames, then the president of the United States Golf Association, arrived at the club and knocked on the secretary's door to pay his respects. "What is your name and what do you want?" Evans-Lombe asked brusquely, without looking up from his desk. "My name is Ames and I'd like a locker," the intruder replied calmly.

The American team won that Walker Cup match, 9–3, defeating what was possibly the strongest British side ever assembled, and, in general, American golfers have fared well at Muirfield. It was there in 1920, for example, that Bob Gardner, an exceptional all-round athlete from Chicago (he was the first pole-vaulter to clear thirteen feet and was twice our Amateur golf champion), came within a whisker of becoming the first American-born challenger to carry off the British Amateur. In the final, against Britain's Cyril Tolley, Gardner, three down with only four holes to play, won three of them (the thirty-sixth with a birdie) to even the match and send it into extra holes. In those days, the first hole at Muirfield was a long one-shotter. Gardner put his tee shot nicely on the green, but Tolley followed with an even better shot, twelve feet from the cup, and after Gardner missed his putt, Tolley holed, and that was that. The next time the British Amateur was held at Muirfield, in 1926, an American finally broke through — Jess Sweetser. The astonishing thing about Sweetser's victory was that he somehow managed to stand up to the exhausting physical demands of the championship despite a severe illness, which he thought at the time was simply a bad case of flu but which proved to be tuberculosis. (He recovered from it completely.) Sweetser's hardest match en route to the final — he won that easily — came against the Honourable W. G. Brownlow (later Lord Lurgan), in the semifinals. Brownlow, whose golf costume included a small peaked cap, a clerk's long coat, and black silk gloves, was two down with two to play, but on the seventeenth green, after changing from a blade-model putter to a wooden-headed putter, he rolled in a twisting forty-five-footer to win the hole. On the eighteenth, he rolled in a thirty-five-footer to win that. Sweetser eventually beat him on the third extra hole. In 1929, Muirfield was the scene of Walter Hagen's fourth, and final, victory in the British Open — a sensational performance in which he finished a record-breaking 67 on his second round by hitting the flapping flag on the home green with his approach shot, and on the final day left the field far behind with two superb 75s in a full gale. As you can gather, Muirfield has been a good place for making history.

The story of the 1966 British Open is, essentially, the story of how Jack Nicklaus, who won our Open in 1962, our Professional Golfers Association championship in 1963, and the Masters in 1963, 1965, and 1966, finally captured the one major championship that had eluded him during his fantastic four-and-a-half-year career as a professional golfer. From beginning to end, the burly, blond twenty-six-year-old Ohioan dominated the tournament, but his road to victory was a bumpy one, and on the last round there were a number of moments when it looked as if the 1966 British Open would go down in history as the championship that Nicklaus lost, much in the same way that our 1966 Open, at Olympic, will probably be remembered as the championship that Arnold Palmer lost. Nicklaus's ultimate victory was as much a triumph of character as of golfing ability. While it has been abundantly clear for some time now that, beneath the warmth and spontaneity of his nature, Nicklaus has the fibre, the persistence, and, in Bobby Jones' memorable phrase, "the sheer delicatessen" to withstand the considerable pressure of modern big-time, big-money golf, Muirfield marked the first occasion on which he was able to marshal these attributes conspicuously well in a tournament played in a foreign country. And — let there be no mistake about it — it is an infinitely harder task for a golfer to win an important event across the water than on his native heath.

This year, Nicklaus was making his fifth attempt to win the British Open — that oldest of all open championships, inaugurated in 1860. On his first try, in 1962, at Troon, he sprayed the ball all over the course, and the British galleries could not understand how he had ever beaten Palmer in the playoff for the United States Open a few weeks before. He was much more impressive the following year at Lytham, seeming to be on his way to victory until he made two disastrous errors on the last two holes, allowing Bob Charles and Phil Rodgers to nip him by a stroke. In 1964, at

St. Andrews, he started so slowly that a 66 and a 68 on the last day were of no real consequence, and last summer, at Birkdale, he ruined his chances with a 77 on the third round. Determined to do better this year, he arrived at the scene of the Open a full week before the start of play. This was the first of many intelligent moves he made, for it enabled him to get thoroughly acquainted with the course, and, considering the way Muirfield was prepared for the championship, it required a lot of knowing. Of the seven courses over which the British Open is regularly rotated, Muirfield is the shortest — it measures 6,887 yards, which seems quite long by American yardage standards but really isn't when you consider the huge distances the smaller British ball can be propelled by players of international class — and, accordingly, the Championship Committee concluded that it would provide a more suitable test if it were toughened up a bit. They accomplished this by giving Muirfield much the same treatment that the United States Golf Association annually gives the course selected for our Open. The fairways were narrowed drastically and the rough allowed to grow high and thick. In truth, I have never seen such tall rough, for the flowering spears of bent grass, going to seed, stood well over a foot high and actually waved in the wind like a field of wheat. The key to scoring respectably at Muirfield, just as at Olympic in our 1966 Open, was to keep out of the rough, no matter how much distance off the tee you had to sacrifice. Nicklaus perceived this clearly on his first practice round, and there and then made the decision to use his driver off the tee on only four or five holes and go with his 1-iron, or sometimes a shorter iron, off the other tees. Not once did he stray from his plan of non-attack, and when you are only twenty-six years old and know you are perhaps the longest driver in the world, this takes restraint of the first order. On the last two days especially, when Nicklaus twice saw a sizable lead melt away, he must have been strongly tempted to call up his long artillery, but he kept to his plan, and in the end it won for him.

On a British seaside links, the wind is always a far more important factor than it is on a tree-lined American course. At Muirfield, the prevailing wind is westerly. However, on Wednesday, the opening day, it shifted around, for the first time in more than a week, and came directly out of the east. It was a soft, light wind — the kind made for low scoring — but the Open contestants, having had no opportunity to practice in an east wind, were up

against what amounted to a new course, and they played tentative, indecisive shots as they felt their way around it. Nicklaus,
like everyone else, experienced some difficulty in selecting the
right club under the new conditions, but on several holes his
elephantine golf memory came to his assistance. For example, on
the fourth, a 187-yard par 3, where he had been using a 6-iron on
his practice rounds, with the west wind behind him, he was pondering how much more club he would need when he suddenly
remembered that in the 1959 Walker Cup match he had played
Muirfield in an east wind and had used a 4-iron off the fourth. He
went with that club, and put the ball five feet from the hole. He
played an even better shot — in fact, one of the most amazing
shots I have seen in a long time — into the wind on the seventeenth, a 528-yard par 5. Here his drive ended on the fairway but
so close to the grassy slope of a bunker that on his second shot he
had to stand with his feet ten or twelve inches below the ball. A
hundred and fifty yards farther down the fairway, his route to the
green was menaced by an abrupt ridge of bunkers. As I saw it, the
only thing for Nicklaus to do from an awkward stance like that,
since he could hardly hope to reach the green, two hundred and
twenty-five yards away, was to lay up short of the ridge with an 8-
iron or a 9. He had another idea — a 1-iron. Somehow, instead of
thumping the turf behind the ball and jerking the shot off to the
left — the almost invariable result even for a first-class golfer
when he tries to do too much from that kind of stance — he maintained both his balance and the tempo of his swing, struck the ball
clean as a whistle, and sent it flying dead on line for the distant
pin. It finished thirty-five feet away, and he had the easiest of
birdies.

The wind was back at its usual stand on the second day, puffing
gently out of the west, and this led to more positive shotmaking
by the field in general and to some extremely low scoring. Peter
Butler, the English professional who was one of the leaders at the
halfway point in the 1966 Masters, was out in 34, two under par,
and back in 31, four under, for a 65, a new course record. Phil
Rodgers, the chunky young professional from La Jolla who has
played so well on our tournament circuit this year, was around in
66. On the green, Rodgers uses a revolutionary putting technique
developed by his friend and neighbor Paul Runyan. He tucks the
butt of his long-shafted (thirty-nine-and-a-half-inch) putter into
his stomach, anchors it there with his left hand, slides his right

hand seven or eight inches down the shaft, and raps the ball with that hand. On his second round at Muirfield, he holed four long putts and needed only twenty-six putts in all, and by the time he had finished his round, to judge by the conversations one over-heard, he had converted at least half his gallery to his method. Five other players broke 70, including Nicklaus, who had a 67 — a handsomely uneventful round, in which he played one sound drive and one sound approach after another, holed a couple of sizable putts, and struck his shots with increasing sharpness as the round progressed. Nicklaus's total of 137 gave him the lead at the 36-hole mark: a stroke in front of Butler; three in front of Rodgers, Harold Henning, of South Africa, and Kel Nagle, of Australia; and four in front of Doug Sanders, another member of the large American contingent. Palmer, eight shots off the pace at 145, seemed virtually out of it. The significant fact at the conclu-sion of Thursday's play was that Nicklaus looked to be in one of those moods, as he was in the 1965 Masters, in which he would draw farther and farther away from his challengers and win in a walk.

Playing conditions were a trifle more difficult on Friday, the day of the third round. For the third day in a row, there was not a drop of rain — a benevolence one doesn't expect in Scotland — but the wind, again out of the west, was rather stiff, blowing at eight or nine knots. Nicklaus, who was paired with Butler in the last two-some, was thinking his shots out with care, and reached the turn in even par. Since he flights the ball in a much higher trajectory than any other player, some observers had predicted that he would have his problems with the wind, but things worked out quite differently. As he strode up the tenth fairway, five under par for the tournament, he had widened his lead over Butler, the nearest man, to four shots and had moved a full seven shots ahead of Rodgers.

I joined the large gallery that went out to watch Nicklaus play the second nine. Just about the only item that had not been pro-vided for in this magnificently produced Open was a nice distribu-tion of up-to-the-minute scoreboards around the course, so that one could keep abreast of developments, but what the other play-ers were up to seemed almost irrelevant when Nicklaus, solemn and painstaking, started home with four good pars. On the four-teenth, he dropped a stroke to par with a loose chip, and on the next hole his approach shot trickled into the rough behind the green and he dropped another stroke when it again took him three to get down. The greens, dried out by the sun and the wind, had become exceedingly fast, and Nicklaus was obviously having trouble coping with them. In any event, on the short sixteenth he took three putts from forty feet (this, incidentally, was his first three-putt green of the tournament), and there went another precious stroke. On the long seventeenth, a logical birdie hole with the helpful following wind, he was lucky to rescue his par 5 with a seven-foot putt after almost missing the ball cold on his third shot — a wedge shot, from a hanging lie in the rough behind the green, which he bobbled barely a yard. On top of this, he failed to get his par on the eighteenth when he pushed his approach into a greenside bunker. That made four bogeys on the last five holes, giving him a 39 back for a wobbly 75 and leaving him only one under par for the distance. And that was only the half of it. While Nicklaus was frittering away stroke after stroke, a number of his rivals had taken the second nine apart. The first intimation I had of this came when a breathless Scotsman rushed up to me, as I was watching Nicklaus botch the seventeenth, and asked if I could verify the report that Rodgers had overtaken and passed Nicklaus and was now three under par for the tournament. I told him this was flatly impossible — Rodgers, by my arithmetic, would have to have played a 30 on the second nine to stand three under. Well, he had, as I learned shortly after I got in. He had ripped home par, birdie, par, birdie, par, birdie, birdie, birdie, par — 40 out, 30 back, if you can believe it. On that second nine, he had picked up no fewer than nine strokes on Nicklaus — an incredible swing. It was a whole new tournament. Palmer, for example, who had been nine shots behind Nicklaus at the turn, was now only two behind, having fired a 32 in for a 69. ("I thought I was the only one those things happened to," Palmer remarked that evening of Nicklaus's misfortune. He was referring, of course, to our 1966 Open, in which he had thrown away a seven-shot lead on the last nine holes of the tournament proper and then, in the playoff, had lost six more shots to Casper on the second nine.) For Nicklaus, the one consolation was that his partial collapse had come not on the final round but on the third. There was still a day's play in front of him. He was fortunate, too, in that this year, for the first time in the century, the British Open was not played as a three-day competition with thirty-six holes on the final day; if Nicklaus had had to go out on the course for another round after his rocky 75, it is quite unlikely that he would have been able to regain his composure. Overnight, he might.

This year, we have had a run of unusually dramatic tournaments, and perhaps we should have anticipated that the climactic fourth round at Muirfield would pack all the suspense of a tale by John Buchan. Five men were in the thick of things: Rodgers, who started the day with a total of 210; Nicklaus, at 212; Sanders, at 213; Palmer, at 214; and Dave Thomas, of Wales, the hope of Britain, also at 214. Paired with Henning, Thomas was off just ahead of Palmer and Sanders, with Rodgers and Nicklaus bringing up the rear. To the minds of the long-suffering British golf fans — they have not been able to celebrate an Open victory by a native son since 1951, when Max Faulkner won — British golfers crumble whenever they find themselves in a contending position on the last round of an important championship. Thomas, a big, strong fellow who can hit the ball about as far as Nicklaus can, began by splitting the nineteen-yard-wide fairway on the first hole, a tough par 4, and then bashed a 4-iron through the brisk west wind to within five feet of the hole and sank his birdie putt. Despite missing a three-footer on the ninth, he was out in 34, functioning as coolly as if he were merely involved in a British circuit tournament, with no Americans to worry about. At this point in his round, Thomas nevertheless stood three strokes behind Nicklaus, who had taken over the lead from Rodgers by rushing to the turn in 33, with six pars and three birdies. His prettiest birdie had come on the 516-yard fifth, where, after finding the bunker to the right of the green on his approach — with the wind behind him, he had used only a 7-iron — he feathered a delicate sand shot two feet from the cup. He appeared to have a firm grip on himself again — and he needed it, for Palmer, Rodgers, and Sanders (who had holed out a short pitch to eagle the ninth) were still definitely in the hunt, along with Thomas. Palmer was the first to go. He went on the tenth, a par 4, where, after hooking his drive into the rough, he decided to risk a herculean recovery from the tall grass and succeeded in advancing the ball only some sixty yards, into taller grass. It took him three more shots to get out of the rough, and when he then rimmed the cup on a shortish putt, that was a 7 — a cruel exit for the man who, far more than any other one person, has been responsible for breathing new life into the British Open.

About half an hour after this, when Nicklaus reached the eleventh green and was lining up a seven-foot birdie putt, he appeared to have the tournament tightly wrapped up again. He still led Thomas by three strokes, though the Welshman was continuing to play very well; he now held a four-stroke margin over Sanders, who had taken a double-bogey 6 on the eleventh after pulling his tee shot into the rough; and he also held a four-stroke margin over Rodgers, whose putter had lost its magic. And, of course, if Nicklaus could hole his seven-footer, he would pull even farther away. (As he bent over his putt, he later confessed, he said to himself, "Well, Jack, you're playing one of the finest rounds of golf you've ever played. Now keep it up.") Seconds before he struck the putt, a swallow, flying low, darted across the green into his line, stopped short, fluttered an instant, then wheeled around and flew back. I doubt if Nicklaus was distracted by the bird, or even noticed it, but he hit a jerky putt that broke off in front of the cup and rolled fifteen inches past it. Then he fluffed that simple tap-in, and, just like that — as fast as a snap of the fingers — he was a different golfer, vastly less assured. He made his par on the twelfth, but only because he pulled his drive so badly that it finished in a patch of rough, along the perimeter of the hole, that had been trodden down by the galleries. Then his round took on the nightmare quality of the previous day. He could do nothing right. He failed to get his par on the short thirteenth, where he missed the green. On the fourteenth, a long par 4 into the wind, he had no chance for his par after driving into a bunker on the right. Now — shades of Palmer at Olympic! — he had completely dissipated a big lead for the second day in a row. Thomas, who was coming off the eighteenth green at this moment, had caught him by playing the second nine in 35, and Sanders, who was teeing off on the eighteenth (which he subsequently parred), had caught him by birdieing the fourteenth and parring the remaining holes. The situation was eminently clear: If Nicklaus could pull himself together and par the last four holes, he would tie Thomas and Sanders. If he could birdie one of the holes — the long seventeenth would be his best bet — he could still win.

Nicklaus managed his par on the fifteenth, a 407-yard par 4, but after leaving his approach forty feet short of the pin, he had to work hard to get down in two putts on the humpy green, which is known as the Camel's Back. On the sixteenth, a 198-yard par 3, he hit a rather indifferent 7-iron thirty feet below the cup, which was cut at the top of an upslope on a very slippery green, but he laid his approach putt absolutely dead. It was the best stroke he had summoned since the eleventh hole, and it seemed to give him a tremendous lift. Where he had been struggling, he was suddenly the lion of old, patently confident that he could now get the birdie and par he needed to win. The par-5 seventeenth, five hundred and twenty-eight yards long, was the crucial hole. Sanders and Thomas had both missed their birdies there — Sanders when his tee shot had bounced into the edge of the rough, Thomas when his approach shot, slightly underclubbed, had stuck on a mound of rough guarding the entrance to the green on the right. Nicklaus made no mistakes. With the wind at his back, he took a 3-iron off the tee and cracked the ball two hundred and eighty yards down the right side of the fairway. He elected to play his 240-yard approach to the half-hidden green with a 5-iron and came through with a beautiful shot that sailed high over the bunkered ridge, carried the mounds in front of the green, and came to rest fifteen feet from the hole. His putt for an eagle hung on the lip, but his birdie was a mere formality. Now a par 4 on the 429-yard eighteenth would do the job. The first imperative here was to hit the narrow fairway off the tee. Playing the right-to-left crosswind expertly, Nicklaus was down the middle with a 1-iron. He then produced another superlative stroke — a 3-iron shot, purposely cut just a fraction so that it would hold its line in the crosswind — which landed in the heart of the green and ended hole-high twenty-five feet to the right of the pin. He was down in two safe putts and, to tremendous applause, walked off the green the 1966 British Open champion.

Nicklaus ended his big day by making a first-class acceptance speech at the presentation ceremony after receiving the Open trophy from the captain of the Honourable Company (with Raeburn's ancient captain looking on through the clubhouse windows). Nicklaus's speech had to be a very good one, for otherwise Sanders, who had been called on for a few words a moment before as one of the two runners-up, would have stolen the show. Sanders delivered a couple of funny one-liners — "If I could have had the periscope, the lost-ball, and the hay concessions, I think I'd be the leading money-winner now" — and he could not have been more charming. In America, where he affects the role of a backwoods Nathan Detroit, his adroit little talk would have caught everyone off balance, but at Muirfield it was simply a continuation of the modulated, pleasant manner in which he had gone about his work all week. He wore his usual collection of gaudy outfits — the lemon-and-lime on Wednesday, the blue on Thursday, the nasturtium on Friday, and the Japanese-bridge magenta on Saturday — but such was his rapport with the crowds that everyone thought his clothes rather nice-looking. Indeed, the golf correspondent of the London *Times*, an august type who is seldom seen in anything flashier than tan, went so far as to declare that deep down in their hearts all golfers want to dress like Sanders but lack the aplomb to carry it off. Thomas, the other runner-up, was naturally accorded an ovation at the presentation ceremony. He had succeeded in doing something no British golfer had done in a decade: he had played a brilliant, aggressively sustained last round, a 69, not when he was hopelessly out of the running but when he was in the thick of the battle the whole long day. No other British golfer finished among the first twelve.

By annexing the British Open, Jack Nicklaus has entered the honourable company of Gene Sarazen, Ben Hogan, and Gary Player, the only other golfers who have won the game's four major championships. His victory was enormously popular in Britain, where he is admired equally for the power and precision of his golf, the sportsmanship he has shown in many awkward corners, and the good nature and politeness that he radiates, whether he is chatting with old friends or dealing with a ring of autograph hunters. The best thing about Nicklaus's victory was that he *won* the championship. He did so by hitting four of the finest irons you will ever see on the last two holes, after weathering the kind of jittery passage from which most golfers never recover. I have an idea that if Nicklaus had blown this British Open, after letting the championship slip away at Lytham three years ago, it might always have escaped him. However, he has won the British Open, and won it, moreover, on a course not truly suited to him, and in doing so he has consolidated his position as the greatest golfer in the world today.

(1966)

Hogan
Something to Remember Him By

This is a short excerpt from the article on the 1967 Masters. On the third round, Ben Hogan, well past his peak years, played the second nine so beautifully that those who were lucky enough to see it will never forget it.

FOR YEARS NOW, GOLF PROMOTERS HAVE DREADED HOLDING tournaments in which the Big Three were not entered, but the relative quiescence of Nicklaus, Palmer, and Player at Augusta demonstrated that dullness is not the inevitable result when they are either absent or not in the thick of things. Five less publicized entrants — six if one includes Tony Jacklin, an engaging young man from Lincolnshire who showed us the best golf a British pro has produced in a big American tournament since the war — made this Masters a lively and stirring event: Gay Brewer, who won it, Bobby Nichols, Bert Yancey, Julius Boros, and, quite unexpectedly, Ben Hogan, the greatest golfer of the steel-shaft era. On Saturday, in the third round, Hogan, after scoring a 74 and a 73 on the first two rounds, which is about what one looks for from a fifty-four-year-old man short on practice and hobbled with an assortment of injuries, burned up the course with a 66 — out in 36, even par, and home in 30, six under. This round of Hogan's really brought the 1967 Masters to life. The fact that it vaulted him to within two shots of the leader, and thus put him in a position to pull off a miracle, was important, of course, but there was more to Hogan's round than that. Years after we had all thought we could never again hope to see this incomparable shotmaker at the peak of his powers, here he was — gray hair edging his teak-colored neck below his old flat white cap — knocking down the pins just as he did two decades ago. Oh, it was something to see! On the fourth round, he faltered early, a victim of the nerves that afflict fifty-four-year-old athletes, and was soon out of the running, but his 66 was a story in itself. I was lucky enough to be standing alongside the tenth green when he started his exciting rush down the back nine by planting a 7-iron pin-high, five and a half feet away, and tapping a touchy downhill putt into the center of the cup. It was a good-looking stroke, that putt; Hogan quickly got himself into a comfortable stance, and, somehow avoiding the long agony of freezing over the ball and finding himself unable to take the putter back (a problem that has plagued him in recent years), he dispatched the ball with little hesitation. As he walked to the eleventh tee and mounted it — it is cut deep in the woods, and few spectators cluster there — three young boys seated on the ground and propped up against a pine tree began to applaud him. Hogan gave them a broad smile that seemed to signify both amusement and appreciation, and, after groping for something to say, simply said, "Attaboy!" Then the smile came off and he got down to his tee shot. He hit a rouser far down the right side of the fairway, Position A. He drew his approach, a 6-iron, artistically. It came in dead on the pin and stopped a foot away. A second straight birdie. A third came on the short twelfth: an arrow of a 6-iron to fourteen feet and another unstuck putt. On the par-5 thirteenth, he made yet another birdie after a 4-wood to within fifteen feet of the stick and a somewhat timorous try for the eagle. A mere par 4 on the fourteenth, but a good one. Here his approach ended up in the deep swale at the front of the green, and his first putt left him a four-and-a-half-footer, but down it went, as firmly as if Billy Casper had tapped it. Then a fifth birdie, on the fifteenth, a par 5, five hundred and twenty yards long — on in two, twenty-five feet from the cup, after a well-positioned drive and a solid 4-wood, and down in two after a strong bid for the eagle. No wavering now. If anything, a crisper gait between shots. Orthodox pars on the sixteenth and the seventeenth, and then a final, masterly birdie on the 420-yard eighteenth, uphill all the way. A drive faded to fit the contour of the fairway was followed by a 5-iron to fifteen feet and another confident putt. 332 444 343 — 30. How that exhibition of flawless golf lifted everyone! Usually, when a long tournament day is over, the galleries plod for the exits tired in eye and limb, but there were no weary steps that evening. Hogan sent us home as exhilarated as schoolboys.

(1966)

Rule 38, Paragraph 3

The saddest moments in golf occur when a scoring error changes the losing and winning of a tournament. There have been two tragic instances of this in our time involving Jackie Pung in the 1957 Women's Open Championship and Roberto de Vicenzo in the 1968 Masters. The circumstances are detailed here. No one wants a golfer to lose or win because of an arithmetic error, and there is less likelihood of this occurring today. Contestants can now enter a large tent close to the final green and carefully check their card and even ask for help before signing it and turning it in.

ABOUT TEN DAYS BEFORE THE START OF THE RECENT MASTERS golf tournament in Augusta, Georgia, Ben Hogan announced that he would have to withdraw, because of a bad knee. This was extremely disappointing news, for the Masters is the only major championship in which one can usually count on seeing Hogan in action — a sight that is still one of the supreme treats in sports. Hogan is now in his middle fifties and has probably won his last championship, but every April, when he punched those meticulous irons to the huge, weaving greens of the Augusta National, time seemed to stand still and one was reminded that he was still the best striker of the ball in the game — a perceptibly finer technician than Arnold Palmer or Jack Nicklaus or any other current hero. Oh, yes, Hogan would be missed — and all the more keenly since it was only last year that he brought the Masters to life on the third round by playing the second nine in a fantastic 30, en route to a 66.

Right on top of this — about a week before the Masters — there came an even more jolting piece of news: it was questionable whether Bob Jones, who founded the tournament, in 1934, would be able to attend. Since 1948 — the last year a worsening spinal condition permitted him to compete in the event — he has been, God knows, a far from well man. For the past ten years, there had been reports every spring that he would be unable to make it to Augusta from his home in Atlanta, but he had always managed to, and, tapping some wonderful wellspring of spirit, had always been in the midst of things — greeting a parade of friends at his cottage off the tenth tee, dining with the old pros and the young amateurs, going out onto the course in his golf cart and scrutinizing the play of the leaders, and wrapping up four days of activity by presiding at the presentation ceremony with his warm, discerning Georgian eloquence. This year, it was different. Jones himself — and he abhors any mention of his invalidism — had written to friends that he might not see them at Augusta, since his health was "not as robust as it was last year." Well, he got there, somehow, but he wasn't up to going out onto the course and watching the play, or even attending the presentation ceremony. What was important, though, is that he was there. Without Jones, the Masters just wouldn't be the Masters.

For quite a few years now, it has been customary for a group of about five of us to pay a visit to Jones at noon on Wednesday, the day before the start of the tournament. It is the highlight of the tournament week for me, because Jones *is* an exceptional man. As the most popular Southerner since Robert E. Lee and the most admired American athlete in the so-called Golden Age of Sport, he knew the best that life has to offer, and over the past twenty years he has known some of the worst. He has stood up to both situations with equal grace. He is the only person I know, in or out of sports, who has the Churchillian quality of being larger than life and at the same time intensely human and intimate. I love to be in his company and listen to him talk golf. On this latest Wednesday visit, at our prodding, he touched on a wide variety of topics, among them his estimate of the great English professional Harry Vardon (whom he partnered in the 1920 United States Open, when Vardon was fifty and Jones a kid of eighteen), his almost perfect round of 66 at Sunningdale in 1926 (when he hit the green on all the par 4s and par 5s in two), why he has always felt that it is easier to win a major championship than a run-of-the-mill tournament (the pressure is so overwhelming in the championships that it kills off all but five or six players in the field), and the good points and shortcomings of televised golf (he has had his fill of the word "prestigious," for one thing). I particularly remember Jones's account of how he and Cyril Tolley played the short eleventh at St. Andrews in their celebrated match in the 1930 British Amateur. Jones had been talking about the lush condition of the fairways at Augusta, and how the course in general was much heavier and slower than he would like it to be, and from that he slid into an appraisal of the classic British seaside courses and how wonderfully racy they were in his day. "Those greens on St. Andrews used to be so crisp that you could hear the crunch your spikes made when they cut into the turf," he said. "Oh, they were fast! It was quite a different kind of golf, really. You had to invent all sorts of approach shots to get the ball near the hole, and when you were playing in a stiff wind — and you did very often — this doubled the difficulty. For example, when the wind was blowing out of the northwest, at your back, there was no way you could hold the ball on the green on the eighth, the first of the two short holes. At St. Andrews, of course, the wind can shift a hundred and eighty degrees in a half hour, and sometimes when you came to the eleventh, the second short hole, it might be blowing behind you again — out of the southeast this time. The eleventh played hardest, though, when the wind was directly in your face, which it was the day of my match with Tolley. As you probably know, the hole is about a hundred and sixty yards long and the green slopes down from the back at a very steep angle. You don't want to be short, because the pin is usually positioned behind the Strath bunker, and you don't want to be long, either, because you want to avoid that downhill chip at any cost — and, besides, the Eden River lies just beyond the green. Cyril had the honor. He took a long iron and hit a very strong shot that was heading right for the pin. Then the wind began to push it back, and I thought to myself, 'That could end up in the Strath.' Well, the wind blew that ball so far back it landed in the fairway forty yards short of the bunker. After observing this, I took a 3-iron and hit a low-trajectory shot that finished on the bank at the back of the green. When I was walking up, I had a chance to look at Cyril's lie. The wind had whipped so much sand out of the Strath that there must have been a good half inch of it under his ball. He fluffed his second short of the bunker and he fluffed his third into it. He played an excellent explosion next to the pin then, but that meant the best score he could make was a 5 and that all I had to do was get down in three to win the hole. I managed to keep that downhill chip of mine on the green — that was about all I did — and I got down in two struggling putts.

"When you win a par-3 hole from a golfer like Cyril Tolley with a dashing 4, you remember it, as you can see — but I've allowed myself to get sidetracked. The point I set out to make was that on the old hard, fast courses golf was a more exacting game and, in a way, a more fascinating one. I was discussing this with Arnold Palmer the other evening, and my position was that we've permitted ourselves to go too far in the other direction. With our soft, holding greens today, golf has become almost entirely target golf. You fly your shot right to your target and it settles where it lands. Of course, mine may be an old-fashioned view, but I believe that the bounce of the ball should be a part of the game, and when you play a fast, resilient course it is. Then, as I said, you must improvise all sorts of shots to cope with the terrain. I know that some of those little pitches and pitch-and-runs — the ones that came off successfully — gave me as much satisfaction as any shots I ever played."

I could listen to Jones all day.

They say that if a man builds anything really well, whether it is an empire or a business or a golf tournament, it will continue to function almost as efficiently in his absence. My guess would be that in 1990, when Jones and his gifted associate Clifford Roberts, the perennial chairman of the tournament, will both have long since ceased to make it to Augusta in the spring, the Masters will still be the most flavorful, evocative golf event in the world. We had a sort of glimpse of this prospect this year. Not only was Jones confined to the sidelines and Hogan absent but on the eve of the first round Gene Sarazen, who has always added so much to the occasion, had to withdraw because of a torn leg muscle, and at the halfway mark the tournament was deprived of its most idolized contemporary champion, Arnold Palmer, who failed to survive the thirty-six-hole cut after a second round of 79. Yet, for all these losses, it turned out to be one of the best Masters tournaments ever — indeed, one of the most genuinely thrilling championships of modern times. For one thing, it is hard to remember a championship in which so many golfers were in a position to win throughout the full seventy-two holes. On Friday, the day of the second round, six different players held the lead at one time or another, and at the close of the day only four strokes separated the top nineteen players. On the third round, there was a chaotic logjam all afternoon long, and it looked as though we would end up with six co-leaders at 211 — Don January, Bob Goalby, Bruce Devlin, Ray Floyd, Frank Beard, and Gary Player — until Player, the last of them to come in, holed a sinuous thirty-foot birdie putt on the last green to stand at 210, six under par. We had a leader, finally, but no fewer than sixteen golfers were bunched within four strokes of his fifty-four-hole total. What with this unprecedented congestion, Sunday, the day of the final round, promised to be a day to remember. It was, but not in the way that had been anticipated.

The first thing that aroused the immense, expectant crowd on Sunday afternoon was an amazing opening charge by Roberto de Vicenzo. In the Masters, as in most stroke-play events these days, the players with the lowest scores go out at the end of the field. De Vicenzo, a veteran from the Argentine, standing at 212, two strokes off Player's pace, and Tommy Aaron, a young Georgian, three strokes off the pace, teed off at one o'clock, in the fifth-from-the-last twosome. On the first hole, a 400-yard par 4, the pin was positioned on the extreme left, about twenty feet from the front edge and directly behind the green's solitary bunker. De Vicenzo, after a long right-to-left drive (he plays everything with draw), had only a 9-iron left. He hit a gorgeous shot. The ball cleared the bunker by about three yards, hopped for the cup, and rolled in — an eagle 2. As quickly as that, de Vicenzo had jumped into a tie for the lead. He went out in front by a stroke when he birdied the second hole, then in front by two when he birdied the third. (Actually, he came within a foot of holing his approach for a second eagle.) By this time, de Vicenzo had collected a fervid gallery of rooters, which continued to swell as he made his way to the turn in 31, adding a birdie on the eighth to go five under par for the round. He is an easy man to root for, Roberto de Vicenzo, the ex-caddy from Buenos Aires. By far the most accomplished golfer ever developed in South America, this strong, handsome, baldish man, who has a droll sense of humor and a congenial nature, has travelled the world the last thirty years like the golfing equivalent of a Guiomar Novaes or a Claudio Arrau. One week he is in Nairobi for a television golf match, the next week in Le Zoute for the Belgian Open, the next in Bogotá winning his umpteenth Colombian title. All told, he has won a hundred and forty tournaments, but until last July, when he captured the British Open at

Hoylake after twenty years of trying and half a dozen near-misses, he had never won a major championship. The British adore him, and if even an English or a Scottish golfer had presumed to overtake de Vicenzo at Hoylake with an eleventh-hour rally the spectators would probably have chased the upstart off the course. In our country, he has won a fair number of tournaments — his first the Palm Beach Round-Robin in 1951 — but he had never been a force in our big events. His best finish in our Open was a tie for eighth in 1957, and his best at Augusta a tie for tenth last year. On this latest Sunday at Augusta, the old campaigner was celebrating his forty-fifth birthday. I should have said it was at least his forty-fifth; de Vicenzo is not the kind of fellow who aspires to be a senior golf champion.

That great burst on the front nine placed de Vicenzo nine under par for the tournament. This is the language in which one always converses at the Masters, for on the scoreboards around the course the progress of the ten leaders is posted hole by hole not in terms of that day's round but in terms of a player's composite score in relation to par; green numerals denote the number of strokes a player is over par, red numerals the number of strokes he is under par. De Vicenzo's red 9, however, gave him only a one-shot lead over Devlin, who was playing four twosomes behind him and had gone eight under after birdieing the first three holes, and it gave him only a two-shot lead over Goalby, two twosomes behind him, who stood seven under after birdieing the fifth and the sixth. Nine holes are a long, long way to go in golf, and especially at the Augusta National, where on no fewer than five of the last nine the green is protected by a water hazard, and disaster can be instant and final. There was nothing defensive about de Vicenzo's golf as he started home, however. He saved his par on the tenth with a beautiful explosion shot that ended up four feet from the hole. On the 445-yard eleventh, he took the bold line over the water and fired a 4-iron nine feet from the flag, only to miss the putt. On the short twelfth, with the flag tucked dangerously close to Rae's Creek, he put his tee shot, a 6-iron, eleven feet from the flag, and this time he made his birdie putt. Six under par now for the round, ten under for the tournament. Ordinarily, that kind of scoring would have shaken off the rest of the field, and the concluding holes would have been a comfortable, triumphant march, but not this day. Goalby was still coming. After a birdie on the eighth and pars on the ninth and tenth, he was still only two strokes behind. As the steamed-up spectators began to realize, the outcome of the tournament could very well hinge on how the two men fared on the two par-5 holes on the second nine — the thirteenth and the fifteenth. The thirteenth, 475 yards to a green guarded by a creek, and the fifteenth, 520 yards to a green guarded by a pond, are the logical birdie holes down the stretch; they are, you might say, par-4½ holes, since each can be reached with two long, accurate shots. On the thirteenth, de Vicenzo, after finding a greenside bunker with his second, had to be satisfied with a 5. On the fifteenth, he bunkered his second again, but this time he got his 4, with a nice sand shot and a ten-foot putt. He wanted that putt so badly that when the ball fell he did something — quite unconsciously, I'm sure — that I had never seen him do before: he punched the air forcefully with his right hand, the way younger and showier players do. Eleven under. That could do it.

Not at all. At about this same moment, Goalby, on the thirteenth green, holed for a birdie 4. Ten minutes or so later, he rammed in a twenty-footer from just off the back edge of the fourteenth for yet another birdie. He was ten under par now, with the eminently birdieable fifteenth coming up. He could catch de Vicenzo there. Goalby's stirring countercharge, it must be said, came as rather a surprise. It is not that Goalby isn't capable of very hot golf. During his eleven years as a touring professional, he has put together a lot of brilliant passages — including a run of eight consecutive birdies in the 1961 St. Petersburg Open — but most of these have come in comparatively minor tournaments. In seven previous starts in the Masters, he had never placed among the first twenty-four finishers. The main reason he has had to be content with second-echelon status among the pros has been his chronic wildness off the tee. Like de Vicenzo, he has long had to battle a hook, and often the correction is an overcorrection — a lavish slice. He is a good iron player, however, very adept with the wedge, and he is also a sound putter, but perhaps his most valuable asset is his flair for competition. A husky six-footer, now thirty-seven, he was the best all-round athlete that Belleville (Illinois) High had ever produced, and, after that, a quarterback for the University of Illinois, and although his temper has given him trouble at times, the drive and resourcefulness that made him a star in team sports have been a great help to him in professional golf. He had certainly shown his stuff in his pursuit of de Vicenzo, and he showed it again on the long fifteenth — *the* critical hole. After a fine drive far down the fairway, he settled on a 3-iron. He played an almost perfect shot. On the flag all the way, the ball carried the pond with plenty to spare, pitched softly on the front part of the green, and finished eight feet from the hole. This "career shot" of Goalby's prefaced what must surely stand as five of the most dramatic minutes in the history of tournament golf. Playing the seventeenth, a 400-yard par 4, which parallels the fifteenth, de Vicenzo answered Goalby's challenge almost immediately by planting his approach — a pitching wedge — three feet from the hole. Moments later, three hundred yards apart, de Vicenzo bent over the putt for his birdie as Goalby simultaneously bent over the putt for his eagle. If either missed, the other would be in the lead. Both putts were struck at almost the same instant. Goalby's went in. De Vicenzo's went in. Two tremendous roars cut the air and two red 12s went up on the scoreboard.

After that, both men wavered slightly, for the first time. On the eighteenth, a 420-yard 4 that climbs uphill all the way, de Vicenzo, after pulling his 4-iron approach to the bottom of the bank at the left of the green, eventually missed the eight-footer he needed for his 4. Goalby, with two pars to win, three-putted the seventeenth from forty-five feet. Now he needed a 4 on the eighteenth to tie. He sliced his tee shot badly into the trees on the right but got an enormous break when the ball ricocheted back onto the fairway; he reached the back of the green with a superb 2-iron, and got down in two putts from fifty feet. Two red 11s on the scoreboard. A mood of happy exhaustion among the spectators. A playoff on the morrow.

I have gone into this detail about the de Vicenzo–Goalby duel for two reasons. First, golf of this surpassing quality — a 65 and a 66 under the harshest strain — deserves to be described, for, as far as I know, never before have two men, thrusting and parrying on the last round of a major championship, both scored as low. (The pace they set was so fast that a closing 69 by Devlin, a 67 by Nicklaus, and a 65 by Bert Yancey, which might normally have won for any one of them, were rendered irrelevant.) Second, I think it is important to record the golf that Goalby and de Vicenzo played, because it is almost bound to be forgotten in the cruel, depressing aftermath of that memorable afternoon. It was discovered soon after de Vicenzo had completed his round that he had signed an incorrect scorecard. Aaron, his playing partner and "marker," had put down a 4 for de Vicenzo on the seventeenth, instead of the 3 he had made. De Vicenzo had not detected the error. Under Rule 38, Paragraph 3, of the Rules of Golf, "A score higher than actually played must stand as returned." This changed de Vicenzo's score for the last round from a 65 to a 66 and made his four-round total a stroke higher than Goalby's. The tournament was over. There was no need for a playoff. The 1968 Masters champion was Bob Goalby.

I don't think there is much to be gained from discussing the way the error was discovered, or de Vicenzo's sportsmanship in his hour of misfortune, or Goalby's graciousness. (De Vicenzo, despite his halting English, made a thumping good speech at the presentation ceremony, in which he blamed the scorecard error entirely on himself and went as far as to say that the pressure that Goalby had put on him perhaps accounted for his making the error. Goalby was direct and unmistakably genuine in declaring his sympathy for de Vicenzo, an old friend, and in stating that he would have much preferred to win the Masters in a playoff.) What had been a glorious day of golf and the climax of an extraordinarily exciting tournament had been turned to ashes by an arithmetical technicality. I know that the moment I heard the official announcement I was struck numb. All of a sudden, it was "Alice in Wonderland" time. The minute before, we had been talking apples, and now we weren't even talking grapes — we were talking one-horse shays. I had felt like that once before in golf — in 1957, at Winged Foot, when, forty minutes after Jackie Pung won the United States Women's Open Championship, a voice over the loudspeaker system informed us that she hadn't; her winning total was correct but she had been disqualified for signing a scorecard on which her playing partner had put her down for a 5, and not a 6, on the fourth hole. (Under Rule 38, a golfer is responsible for the correctness of his score for each hole but not for the total. A scorecard cannot be altered once the golfer has turned it in to the tournament scoring committee. Disqualification is the penalty if the player returns a score for any hole *lower* than the one he made — as in Mrs. Pung's case. If a higher score is erroneously returned for any hole, it stays — as in de Vicenzo's case.) I had hoped never to see another day like that one at Winged Foot, and here we were again.

Inevitably, the main point debated that evening at Augusta — and it has been debated ever since — was whether Rule 38 is a good rule or a bad one. For my part, I consider it a very bad rule, and have felt this way from the moment in 1957 when the Mock Turtle and the Mad Hatter invaded Winged Foot. Any rule that can create a situation that hurts the winner as well as the loser and makes nonsense of a significant championship must be a bad rule. The main trouble, it seems to me, is that the philosophy behind the rule is seriously anachronistic where modern *tournament* golf is concerned. Golf grew up as "the gentleman's game" because of the unique dimensions and character of the playing area. Eighteen holes cover a hundred and thirty acres or more of fairway, rough, green, and hazard, and since the play of each golfer could not be superintended, it was up to each man to obey the rules. When you and I were playing a friendly match, I did not sprint across the fairway to make sure you didn't ground your club in a bunker, and you did not come pounding into the woods to see that I didn't improve my lie. In a stroke-play tournament, the same code obtained. When you and I disappeared around the bend to play the eighth and ninth holes, where there was no one to watch us, it was up to us not to cheat; if we gave each other lower scores than we made, this would affect every player in the field. The scorecard became the badge of honor, and, with so much depending on the return of correct scores, drastic penalties were written into the rules for errors in scoring, and the penalties were strictly enforced. However, modern tournament golf takes place under totally different conditions. In an event like the Masters, for instance, with hundreds of spectators lining each hole (and millions more watching on television), no one is going to "win with the pencil." Everybody knows the score. The problem today, when professional golf has become so popular, so high-powered, so rich, and so heavy with pressure, is to see to it that no one loses with the pencil.

Some people defend Rule 38 by arguing that it is not putting an unreasonable burden on the golfer to require him to be responsible for the correctness of his scorecard, but — since accidents do happen — it is possible that they underrate the stress a player is under. (When de Vicenzo, after four gruelling hours on the course, went over the figures Aaron had marked down on his card, the one thing on his mind was the probability that he had lost the tournament by failing to make his par on the last hole. "I look over the card three times, four times," he said, "and all I see is the 5 for the eighteenth. I see nothing else.") Other people who want the rule to stand believe that the way to insure that nothing goes wrong is to set up, off the last green, some enclosure — say, a large tent — in which a player can go over his card in peace and privacy. This would assuredly be a step in the right direction, but I do not think it goes to the heart of the matter, which is this: The score that the player makes on the course is the score that he should be credited with. It should be the responsibility of the tournament officials as well as of the golfer to see that the score he returns is the right score. If an error is discovered, the important thing is to see that it is corrected. No penalty should be imposed. Golf, like every other sport, is meant to be a test of athletic ability and not of bookkeeping. Granted, it will take many, many sessions for our rules-making body, the United States Golf Association, even to begin to develop the machinery necessary to take into account both the game's traditions and the realities of present-day tournament golf, but I trust that this matter is on the current agenda. Nobody wants ever again to have to go through another such Sunday as the one at Augusta, when legality is served, but justice, as golfers understand it, isn't. It is really an indignity to the game.

As the head of the Masters, Bob Jones always wants to be kept informed of any and all problems. He was watching the concluding stages of the tournament on television in his cottage with his son, Robert T. Jones III, when word was brought to him that de Vicenzo had signed an incorrect card. Before taking any action, the four co-chairmen of the tournament rules committee wanted to have Jones's opinion, and, along with Clifford Roberts, they quickly assembled at his cottage. Jones made it very clear that his primary concern was to find some way, if there was a way, of waiving the rule that would cost de Vicenzo a tie and the chance to win in a playoff. In the opinion of Isaac Grainger, a former president of the United States Golf Association and the most experienced rules man present, the only avenue was to make the freest interpretation possible of what constituted an official return of a scorecard by a player to the scoring committee. However, the precedent, he said, was that once a player had left the roped-off area around the last green — as de Vicenzo had, to go to the television room — the card must be regarded as officially returned. Jones then asked the group if there was any other loop-hole they could think of. There wasn't, he was told — not without violating the rules.

"That's all I want to know," Jones said.

When I spoke with Grainger the other day, he remarked that he had never seen a more tragic look on a man's face than the one on Jones's when they left the cottage. It is easy to understand. The only way that Jones could have done what he wanted to do was to place himself above the rules of golf, and he would be the last man to do that. I should think this must have been the unhappiest hour of his sixty years in golf.

(1968)

Ballybunion

If there is a land that compares with Scotland in the quality of its best courses, it is Ireland. Some years ago I circled the island to play its most celebrated links: Portmarnock, Royal County Down, Royal Portrush, Rosses Point in Sligo, Lahinch, and Ballybunion. Portmarnock and Royal County Down deserve consideration in any golfer's list of the dozen finest courses in the world, but it is Ballybunion that really bowls over the visiting golfer. I went to Ballybunion from Killarney with a small party headed up by Dr. Billy O'Sullivan and was awed by the course. It is something like a Gaelic version of Pebble Beach.

I should make three points to bring matters up to date. First, about a decade ago, a new clubhouse was built next to the thirteenth, and that hole now is the opening hole. The old eighteenth is now the fifth, the old first is now the sixth, and so on. It makes for a much better routing. Second, the old green on the old second was lost because of erosion, but the new green, nicely situated behind the large sand hill, makes it a very good hole if not quite the test it was when the old green stood at the edge of the cliffs. And third, Ballybunion now has a fine second eighteen-hole course laid out by Robert Trent Jones in the sturdy duneland contiguous to the first eighteen.

MY SCHEDULE FOR SUNDAY CALLED FOR ME TO DRIVE TO BALLY-bunion, an hour and a half away, and return to Killarney in the evening. Ballybunion was the last course on the itinerary that MacWeeney had prepared for me, and, in a way, I was glad that it was. I had been moving at a pretty fast clip, and the succession of long days and late nights was beginning to get to me. Accordingly, I planned to take it easy on Sunday: I would sleep until ten, wrap up Ballybunion as quickly as possible, and get to bed back in Killarney no later than ten that evening.

The day worked out very well, but somewhat differently from what I had planned. At eight o'clock, I was awakened by a telephone call from Dr. O'Sullivan. Wouldn't it be pleasanter for me if I had some company on my trip to Ballybunion? Indeed it would, I told him. Very well, then — he and Finbarr Slattery would come by my hotel and collect me at nine-thirty. I had no sooner hung up, it seemed, than the phone rang again. It was Slattery, announcing that he was looking forward eagerly to the day's excursion.

Ballybunion is a small gray seaside resort in northern Kerry, fifty miles west of Limerick and twenty miles due north of Tralee. A far less prepossessing village than Lahinch, it stands on the south shore of the Shannon estuary, facing the Atlantic. Though it was thick with holiday people this Sunday, I gathered from Dr. O'Sullivan that it had never been very prosperous. The golf links, he said, had suffered down through the years from lack of funds. In his opinion, the course was potentially the equal of any in Ireland, but the club had never had the wherewithal to maintain it in first-class condition or to develop it as a richer club might have. On top of this, there was now the problem of erosion to cope with. Some sections of the high, steep cliffs along the shore were slipping into the ocean, and not at a geological rate, either; in fact, one or two greens might be lost in a matter of years. The principal point he wished to stress, however, was the quality of the course. One Irish Professional Championship, two Irish Amateurs, and two Irish Ladies' Championships had been held there, and he had yet to meet the golfer who had not been both charmed and awed by Ballybunion. "On the other hand, it's virtually unknown," he added. "Very few tourists from Britain or America — or, for that matter, from other parts of Ireland — bother to visit it. They know about Ballybunion, but it's stuck off by itself on the road to nowhere, so in the end they pass it by. They make a tremendous mistake."

At first glance, even the most distinguished linksland courses look utterly ordinary to the man who has never played them before. If a golfer stands on the terrace at the Augusta National Golf Club, say, and takes in the wide panorama of lush fairways swinging through tall pines, he senses at once that an authentic championship layout awaits him — an experience that also occurs at most of the world's renowned inland courses. But let him stand on the first tee at St. Andrews or Ballybunion, and all he sees is a treeless sweep of billowing pale-green land with a few dun-colored sand hills in the distance — a most unpromising vista. A fragment of fairway is visible here and another fragment there, and a few numbered flags are blowing in the breeze, so what he is looking at is evidently a golf course, but it might as easily be pastureland. It is only when the golfer gets out onto a linksland course that he discovers, to his amazement, that it is filled with great golf holes, all the more appealing since their strategic features were molded by nature instead of by the bulldozer. I should state before going any farther that I did not play Ballybunion. In retrospect, I regret this, but when we arrived that morning a chilly, moisture-laden twenty-knot wind was busting in off the ocean, and it completely doused what little desire I had to play golf. I could picture myself having one of my sparkling rounds, in which I would be standing deep in the alien corn on shot after shot while Dr. O'Sullivan patiently studied some adjacent par-3 hole and Slattery ruminated over the stubborn refusal of the local farmers to give up their traditional potatoes and raise dairy cattle instead, as he had been urging them to. Instead, we walked the eighteen holes. At the start, there were just the three of us up from Killarney, but on the second hole we were joined by Paddy Allen, a dedicated Ballybunion man in his sixties, who had long been one of the club's best players and was now a club trustee. (Allen had been waiting at the small, plain clubhouse to greet us on our arrival, along with his brother Tom, the club steward upward of fifty years, and both had been openly delighted at seeing Dr. O'Sullivan. Allen had then phoned the captain and a few other members about our plans for the day before catching up with us.) By the time we reached the fifth tee, our walking party had been supplemented by a dozen Ballybunion men, among them the captain, J. D. Mahony; the secretary, Michael Handrahan; and a Dr. Walsh, who was forced to leave us at the fifteenth hole when a young boy raced out to inform him he was urgently needed to deliver a baby. In its general pattern, this walk was similar to the shorter one I had made with Mixie Murphy's band at County Sligo; groups of two or three went off by themselves and then converged at some natural collecting point, like a bunker, where new clusters broke off. Despite the ripping wind and some intermittent rain, the walk, which took two hours, was profoundly exciting. To put it simply, Ballybunion revealed itself to be nothing less than the finest seaside course I have ever seen. It shows its quality on the very first hole, a par 4 that doglegs to the left and seems a good bit longer than 372 yards — its length on the scorecard. From the tee, the hole appears to be a rather banal par 4, but when, upon reaching that point in the fairway where an adequate drive would finish, you study the long, narrow green, a medium-iron away, and the fanciful convolutions of the land in the green area, your assessment changes radically. It is, you perceive, a formidable, arresting hole. When I expressed these thoughts to Dr. O'Sullivan, he agreed completely. He went on to observe that he had never seen Ballybunion in such excellent condition. "Usually, it's all kind of shaggy and spotty, but everything's cut so crisp today. Maybe it's because they knew we were coming. Whatever the reason, the course looks grand, doesn't it?"

The second hole certainly did. It is a 413-yard par 4 running roughly parallel to the seventy-foot-high cliffs that plunge down to the beach and the water. Actually, the hole plays as a slight dogleg, to the right. The correct line on the tee shot is down the left side of the fairway, for this opens up the entrance to the green, which is flanked on the left by a massive sand hill and on the right by the cliffs. From the tee, the entire hole is visible, and, as if this were not an exhilarating enough prospect, farther in the distance, at the end of a tight valley between two rows of sand hills, the eye takes in the minute green of another dazzling cliffside hole, the sixth. I breathed it all in slowly, wondering first to myself and then aloud who the architect was who had had the genius to use the duneland in such a thrilling way. Dr. O'Sullivan didn't know, but when I later asked Paddy Allen he told me that the credit for both holes belonged to the late Tom Simpson, a much admired English architect; they were two of four holes that Simpson had substantially improved when he remodelled the course in the nineteen-thirties. Allen said this with a dour matter-of-factness that didn't tally with the pleasure a dedicated Ballybunion man would normally take in showing these superior holes to visitors. His voice and his countenance became noticeably grimmer a moment later, when, after we had walked behind the second green, he pointed out some rude wooden props that had been rigged against the face of the cliff. This was one of the places where erosion was proceeding at alarming speed. He shook his head sadly as we walked back to a sheltered basin on the inland side of the large sand hill flanking the green. "If we lose the second green," he said, "this is where the new green will probably go."

"It will ruin the hole, Paddy," Dr. O'Sullivan expostulated.

Allen opened his palms in a gesture of resignation. "Yes, Billy," he said. "It will be just another golf hole." He walked away to commune with himself.

A tourist driving through Switzerland is staggered by its prodigal beauty; around the bend from the most wondrous view he has ever beheld he comes upon a view that surpasses it — and so on and on, endlessly. Ballybunion is something like that. I do not mean to suggest that there are vistas that put the one from the second tee to shame — there aren't — but there is a correspondence in the way one stirring hole is followed by another and another. The third, for example, is a 145-yarder that moves through the sand hills to a devilish little green that tips into an abrupt downslope on the right and is bunkered on the left and in front. On the fourth, a 451-yard par 4 on the inland side of the sand-hill belt, the key hazard is a deep bunker carved in the face of a rise in the middle of the fairway about twenty yards in front of the plateau green; anything less than a perfectly struck second shot will end up in it. (A sign at the edge of the bunker informs the golfer that it is called the Crow's Nest. There are similar signs at the other major hazards on the course — an original touch and a flavorsome one.) The fifth hole, which curves back toward the ocean through another twisting valley, is a very attractive drive-and-pitch par 4, 343 yards long, a dogleg to the left this time. The sixth, which I've already mentioned, is a perfect beauty — a 450-yard par 4 that tumbles downhill along the cliffs to an inviting green. And that is the way it keeps going at Ballybunion. There is not one prosaic hole — not one single "breather" — in the whole eighteen. If the course has a weakness, I suppose it is the comparative plainness of the last two holes — a pair of par 5s stretching over the somewhat featureless interior ground. They are not trite holes, for they are imaginatively bunkered, but they do lack the beauty of the rest of the course, and as a result they are somewhat anticlimactic.

At the conclusion of our walk, I found I could remember each of the eighteen holes without much trouble. This is probably the oldest and soundest rule of thumb for judging the merits of a course that a golfer has just seen for the first time. Apart from the first six holes, three others remained especially distinct: the tenth, a 210-yarder over difficult duneland, where the prevailing wind, from the west, sweeps across from left to right; the 368-yard thirteenth, where the sand in a fifty-yard-wide bunker called the Sahara is strewn with deer bones, shells, stones, and ashes deposited in the fifteenth century by a tribe that used the cavity as a midden, or dump; and the fourteenth, a 376-yard par 4 that Simpson enlivened by placing in the drive zone a mounded double bunker, which the members immediately dubbed Mrs. Simpson. Ballybunion is a moderate 6,317 yards in length, par is 71 (34-37), the course record is 65, and, as I say, no other links, in my opinion, presents such a satisfying adventure in golf. The course has two endowments that I believe to be unique. First, it is the only links I know of where most of the oceanside holes are perched atop spectacular cliffs, in the manner of Pebble Beach (which is not a true links). Second — and this is undoubtedly the secret of its character and charm — it is the only links I know of where the sand-hill ridges do not run parallel to the shore but at a decided traverse. This opens all sorts of possibilities — dogleg holes of every description sculptured through the choppy land, and straightaway holes where the sand hills patrol the entrance to the green like the Pillars of Hercules. One more point: Unlike most links, Ballybunion challenges you with target golf. There is none of that bouncing your iron approach short of the green and letting it bobble toward the flag, as you do on most courses in the British Isles. No, you aim for the flag, and if your shot lands on the green the green is sufficiently receptive to hold it.

The miracle is that every one of the several golf architects who had a hand in creating Ballybunion recognized how the terrain should be handled. During lunch, at the Castle Hotel, Paddy Allen, having pored over the club records at the finish of our walk, supplied some information on these architects. The man who took care of the course when Ballybunion was founded, in 1896, was one P. Murphy, who was paid nine shillings a week. Financial woes brought the original organization down, and the club was re-formed in 1906, at which time Captain Lionel Hewson, for many years the editor of the magazine *Irish Golf*, built the nine holes that became the basis of the present layout. In 1926, when the course was extended to eighteen holes, the work was directed by a man named Smyth, who was a designer on the staff of Carter

& Sons, a London firm specializing in the construction of sports grounds. Then, in 1936, Simpson was brought in to remodel the course. He was given carte blanche, but, recognizing the unusual worth of the existing layout — something that few architects would have managed to do, in their eagerness to edit their predecessors — he made only four changes: he re-sited the second, fourth, and eighth greens and introduced the Mrs. Simpson double bunker on the fourteenth. Finally, the course reflects the devotion of William J. McCarthy, a local solicitor and hotel owner, whose father was one of the club's founders. McCarthy, who is still active in the club, served for more than two decades as Ballybunion's honorary secretary and also performed the duties of a kind of resident architect. In the early nineteen-fifties, he built two first-class new holes to replace the old eleventh and twelfth, but, in truth, there is hardly a hole that McCarthy has not enhanced by some skillful little touch, like recontouring a bunker or relocating a tee.

During lunch, Dr. O'Sullivan, both as a regional hero and as the representative of a more thriving and worldly golf club, was kept busy answering a stream of questions from the Ballybunion men about how they might go about improving their hard-pressed operation. The Doctor strongly recommended that the members, if they were in a position to do so, acquire the seashore property adjacent to the course, as a safeguard against invasion by get-rich-quick realtors. He emphatically supported the proposal that a new clubhouse, however modest, be built as soon as possible at the edge of the sea, close by either the sixth or the tenth green. (One of the incidental advantages of such a move would be that the order of the holes would necessarily be changed for the better if either the seventh or eleventh became the first hole, for then the present seventeenth and eighteenth would be played in the middle of a round, and the course would surge to a much more stirring finish.) He also suggested that the club seek professional guidance in dealing with the erosion problem. He was listened to most attentively. In fact, there were only a few light moments during the lunch. One of them came when Dr. Walsh, the delivery completed, rejoined the party. Was it a boy, he was asked. "No," he said. "Only a child."

My overriding memory of the lunch, however, is the unbroken gravity of the Ballybunion men as they discussed with Dr. O'Sullivan the steps they should take to make the golf world more conscious of their course. Paddy Allen was still wrestling with that problem when I said goodbye to him. "We can't expect anything like the number of tourists Portmarnock gets," he told me, in a small voice that grew emotional despite his efforts to speak calmly. "But we need a better bite off the plum — a much better bite. As you saw for yourself, Ballybunion is a fine, fine course. And that champagne air off the ocean — " He broke off, then continued, "The course means everything here. Take away the golf course and you take away Ballybunion."

(1971)

An Entirely Different World
The President's Putter

The Oxford and Cambridge Golfing Society was established by graduates of the two universities in 1898, but it wasn't until 1920 that the Society's annual tournament, the President's Putter, was inaugurated. It was played, as it continues to be, at the Rye Golf Club, smack on the English Channel, in early January. There was a sensible reason for selecting such a date: it is the one time during the year when both graduates and under-graduates are free to get together for a few days of golf in the convivial atmosphere that marks the Putter, as the tournament is usually called. There is a second reason for holding the event when the weather, as often as not, is bitterly cold and windy. The possibility of having to battle the elements holds a strong appeal for the eccentric side of the English character.

ON THE SIXTH OF JANUARY, THE DAY WHEN THE HUNDRED-AND-twenty-five-thousand-dollar Los Angeles Open, the first event on the 1972 American professional golf tour, got under way, a tournament of considerably less surface glitter was beginning at the Rye Golf Club, a few miles to the east of that ancient Cinque Ports town on the English Channel. This was the President's Putter, a four-day match-play affair that the Oxford and Cambridge Golfing Society annually holds early in January. It would be hard to imagine a more amateur occasion. As a rule, the galleries are very small, rarely exceeding three or four hundred spectators — and an equal number of dogs — even on the day of the final. And whereas first place in the Los Angeles Open is worth twenty-five thousand dollars nowadays, all that the winner of the President's

Putter gets to take home is a silver medal with the inscription *"Primus inter pares."* Literally translated, this means "First among equals," but most of the members prefer the freer translation proposed decades ago by Arthur Croome, a famous secretary of the Society: "He was lucky to win."

It is precisely this low-key amateur ambience that makes the President's Putter special and significant. In our country, amateur golf — the authentic article — has almost died out; just about all our amateur competitions are dominated by players who are attending college on golf scholarships in preparation for a career in professional golf. (Over the last twenty years, no fewer than fifty-five young men from the University of Houston — the Notre Dame of golf — have gone on to seek their fortune on the pro tour.) However, what really sets the President's Putter apart is that it is played under the worst conditions of any golf tournament in the world, southern England in January being somewhat less balmy than southern California. Gale-force winds and cold, sluicing rains from off the Channel frequently rip over the links. As often as not, the fairways and greens are frozen bone-hard. Every now and then, for good measure, there is snow to contend with. In 1960, for instance, with the links coated white on the final day, the players were provided with red golf balls and forecaddies were stationed along the fairways, and the tournament was able to finish on schedule. Two years after that, when the President's Putter was beset by perishingly cold weather, David Phiri, a black Zambian who was on the Oxford team, appeared for his first match wearing three pairs of socks, underwear, pajamas, a pair of rain trousers over his regular trousers, a heavy shirt, six sweaters, two scarves, two pairs of gloves, a woollen hat, and the kind of face-protecting hood called a balaclava. Somehow or other, he won that match.

Why, you might ask, have the members of the Society not chosen to come in from the cold, like sensible men, and shift their tournament to a more reasonable time of the year? Because they are English, by and large, and, *ipso facto,* born eccentrics — this, I suppose, would be the best answer. In no other people do you find that streak of masochism which sneers at the uncomfortable and revels in the hazardous. It was this wonderful madness that planted the Union Jack in every corner of the globe and drove Burton toward the source of the Nile, Shackleton toward the South Pole, and Whymper toward the summit of the Matterhorn.

Shift the President's Putter to July? My good man, you must be out of your mind! That would spoil all the fun.

After several false starts toward Rye in previous winters, I finally made it to the President's Putter this year. I came well prepared, with several sets of long woollen underwear and the type of quilted goosedown trail jacket that trappers in British Columbia swear by. I was "up" for the tournament in another sense as well, having carefully read everything I could find about it. To begin at the beginning, Oxford and Cambridge first met at golf in 1878, at the London Scottish Golf Club, in Wimbledon. The university match became an annual fixture and, historically, an important one — the oldest amateur golf event in the world, seven years older than the British Amateur Championship. The Oxford and Cambridge Golfing Society was founded in 1898, an amalgam of old Dark Blues from Oxford and old Light Blues from Cambridge who enjoyed one another's company and thought it would be a good idea to play some weekend golf together on a regular basis. By the following year, things were fairly well organized, and the Society played eight matches. Two of them, naturally, were against Oxford and Cambridge. Also included in the schedule was a swing through Cheshire and Lancashire for matches against such prominent clubs as Royal Liverpool, Formby, and Royal Lytham & St. Annes, and this set a precedent for an annual golf tour — of Scotland, Ireland, or the Cheshire-Lancashire area. In 1903, the Society made a tour of the United States. It was never repeated, though it was a most successful thirty-nine-day junket, in which the visitors lost only two of their ten matches and — what was even more remarkable — not a single trunk or valise, thanks to the foresight of Mansfield Hunter, one of their top players, who took his valet along and assigned him to look after the baggage.

In those early days, the top office in the Society, that of president, was held by the Right Honourable A. J. Balfour, a very keen golfer. However, affairs of state generally kept Balfour busy, and the actual guiding spirits were John Low, the perennial captain, and Arthur Croome, the perennial secretary. Low, a Scotsman of independent means who did some occasional writing on golf, was a proficient enough player to reach the semifinals of the British Amateur in 1897 and 1898 and the final in 1901. He is credited with being the first golfer to take a favorite iron of his to a clubmaker and have a matched set, from driving iron through niblick, made from it. A clubbable man, Low is also credited with setting the Society's appealing tone, wherein a proper seriousness about one's golf is blended with a fundamental conviviality. Croome, a tall, lean, punctilious man, who, in the best English-public-school-nickname tradition, was called Crumbo by his friends, was a classics master at Radley for many years and later wrote about golf for the London *Morning Post* and about cricket for the *Times*. In his opinion, a feeling for dance tempo was the key to the golf swing, and to make sure he had the right timing going, when he was playing a shot he would say to himself, "One, two, deliver the cue." Croome was far from being the Society's only curiosity. There was Guy Ellis, who during the summer regularly played three rounds daily at St. Andrews using a different set of clubs on each round. He believed he would grow stale if he didn't. There was the Honourable Denys Finch-Hatton, who at Oxford adopted the practice of wearing a violently checked sports jacket along with knickers of a different and even more violent check, and topping off the ensemble with a deerstalker hat. Finch-Hatton was extremely generous about conceding putts, and there is a story that in one match against Cambridge an Oxford partisan, upset by this, said to him, "Do remember, Finch-Hatton, that you are playing for your side, and *not* for yourself," to which Finch-Hatton replied, "And do remember that you are playing for neither." He became a celebrated white hunter in Kenya and figured memorably in Isak Dinesen's *Out of Africa*. And there was Sir Harold Gillies, a famous plastic surgeon, who, having previously rigged up a complicated apparatus, left the room during a speech by Croome at the Annual Dinner at Rye and, unobserved in the wings, lowered a chamber pot inches above the speaker's head. Finally, there was Bernard Darwin, the great golf writer, who, though he was indeed a character of the first pith and a very able golfer, contributed most valuably to the Society by writing about the charms it held for him. He was especially devoted to the President's Putter, which he once described as "a little red glowing jewel set in the cold waste of winter" and as having "something of that defensive, almost defiant quality which Chesterton called, in a fine phrase, 'making merry in the belly of a fort.' "

The Putter, as the tournament is usually called, was inaugurated at Rye in 1920. It was given its name because Low, who had become president the year before, made a gift to the Society of the old wooden-headed putter that Hughie Kirkaldy had used in winning the 1891 British Open and that he himself had used in going to the final of the 1901 British Amateur; the idea was that the golf ball the winner had played with in the final should be attached to the putter by a silver band and chain. From the outset, the tournament had a certain stature. As it happened, the three top amateur golfers in Britain in the nineteen-twenties — Ernest Holderness, Roger Wethered, and Cyril Tolley — were Oxford men, and their prestige rubbed off on the Putter. Holderness, the winner of the British Amateur in 1922 and 1924, swept the first four Putters, and after a hiatus of six years he won for a fifth time. A reserved, hard-to-reach man who inherited a baronetcy from his father and had a long career in the Home Office, he had precious little to say on the links, and one young opponent of his in the Putter reported that Holderness addressed only three sentences to him during their match: "I think that's three up" and "Thank you very much. That's five and four." Wethered, who, in addition to capturing the British Amateur in 1923, tied for first in the British Open in 1921 only to lose in a playoff to Jock Hutchison, also won the Putter five times. Talented though he was, his sister Joyce was a good cut above him, and many consider her the finest woman player of all time. As for Tolley, a power hitter, who was the Jack Nicklaus of his era, he had won two British Amateurs and two French Opens long before he managed to win the Putter — in 1938, when he reached the final for the fourth time. In 1924, one of the few years in which the Big Three were stopped cold, the victor, to everyone's extreme pleasure, was Bernard Darwin.

In the period following the Second World War, the membership of the O. & C.G.S. grew to six hundred, and lately the Society has made it a policy to schedule more than twenty team matches a year. On the other hand, the Putter lost a little of its eminence, for the simple reason that only a sprinkling of the country's leading amateurs in the postwar years had attended Oxford or Cambridge. For all that, the quality of the golf in the Putter remained quite high. During the late nineteen-forties and the fifties, four men dominated the event — Leonard Crawley, P. B. (Laddie) Lucas, Tony Duncan, and Gerald Micklem — and they were all players of the top international class. (Incidentally, all of them except Crawley served as captain of the British Walker Cup team, and that distinction would have undoubtedly gone to Crawley as well had his job as golf correspondent of the London *Daily Telegraph* permitted him the time to take on outside duties.) From a different point of view, the significant year was 1954. Undergraduates had been encouraged to play in the Putter from its earlist days, but that winter, for the first time, an undergraduate — Gordon Huddy, of Cambridge — succeeded in winning it. Then, as so often happens once a barrier has been broken, the whole complexion of things changed, and in the eighteen years since Huddy's victory the tournament has been carried off six times by undergraduates and three times by players who had "gone down" from their university only the previous June.

Another major change in the Putter in recent times has been a dramatic increase in the extent and variety of the bad weather it has been obliged to endure. More often than not, the week after Christmas has brought a heavy blizzard, which has left the links at Rye caked with snow on the eve of the tournament. Almost invariably, as if some kindly, golf-oriented Providence were watching over the Society, the snow has melted away at the eleventh hour. In 1963, though, the usual miracle was not forthcoming: on the day of the opening round the course still lay under a cover of snow. Just when it looked as if the Putter would have to be abandoned, for the first time ever, except during war years, the Society learned that the Littlestone Golf Club, nine miles away, on the southeastern edge of Romney Marsh, was practically free of snow and would be delighted to put its course at the disposal of the Society, few of the local golfers having planned to go out on the ice-patched fairways and rifle some 1-irons into the teeth of the biting wind. The surprising winner that year was John Blackwell, a middle-aged, silver-haired member of the Blackwells of Crosse & Blackwell, who runs a boys' school called Selwyn House, near Sandwich. A promising eccentric in the best Finch-Hatton tradition, Blackwell always equips his automobile with a record-player, for he finds that when he is on his way to take part in a golf match it calms him to listen to a few sides by Billie Holiday or Ella Fitzgerald. At Littlestone, he combatted the elements by carrying gas-fuelled hand warmers in his pockets and by refuelling himself periodically during the round with nips of a "putting mixture" compounded of orange juice and vodka. Five months later, Blackwell demonstrated that his victory at Littlestone was no fluke, when he went to the final of the British Amateur at St. Andrews and lost only on the thirty-sixth green.

Except for that one switch to Littlestone, the Putter has been held at Rye each winter, somehow or other, although in 1964 it was not completed until two months after it began. That year, a fall of sticky snow on the Saturday made the course unfit for play, and the last three rounds had to be postponed until the day after the Varsity golf match in March — the first time all the players involved were free. Donald Steel, the eventual winner, had both the shots and the necessary stamina: in the morning he won a twelve-hole quarter-final match and a twelve-hole semifinal match, and then he went out in the afternoon and won a regulation eighteen-hole final on the last green.

It was cold and windy but a dim sun was doing its best when I arrived at Rye on the Thursday that the first-round matches in the Putter were being played. Before going out to the links, I took a turn around the town, which lies atop a rather sudden hill. At one time, the hill was right on the water — in fact, there is a good possibility that it was an island — but over the centuries the sea has receded, and today Rye Harbour lies a good two miles away. In summertime, the town is overrun with tourists, and it is easy to see why. The main entrance is from the north, through the Land Gate, which dates from the fourteenth century, when Rye was a walled town, and the gate proper is flanked by two round towers forty feet high. At the crest of the hill stands the Church of St. Mary the Virgin, a combination of late Norman, Perpendicular Gothic, and other styles, which was originally built in the twelfth century and was almost completely rebuilt after the French sacked the town in 1377. Narrow cobbled streets run past such later landmarks as Lamb House, where Henry James made his home during his last twenty years, and past numerous tearooms and shoppes neatly framed with timber or featuring the small-paned windows and the precise tile facing of the Georgian period. The only trouble is that Rye comes off as being a bit too self-consciously picturesque, and you get the feeling as you walk down Mermaid Street or Watchbell Street that when you turn the next corner you may stumble upon an array of movie cameras, trained on Freddie Bartholomew.

To get to the Rye Golf Club, you turn east at the foot of the town onto the road to Camber and drive three miles or so alongside flocks of sheep grazing on Romney Marsh (on your left) until you spot, nestled among the sand hills (on your right), a white stucco clubhouse with a maroon metal roof. While Britain has never been celebrated for the subtle beauty of its clubhouse architecture, the structure at Rye functions well. It has, on its single floor, a commodious changing room (with pegs, not lockers), a room for women (who in Britain are generally not given the run of the clubhouse), a dining room, and a big room with a friendly bar and wide windows looking out on the eighteenth hole. In one corner of the big room, the President's Putter and a second putter, just like it, both dripping with the golf balls of former winners, are on view in a mahogany case. When I entered the big room, shortly after one o'clock, perhaps thirty members of the Society were clustered there, drinking and talking and watching, all of them wearing the club tie — two narrow stripes of light blue bordering a wider stripe of dark blue on a field of grass green. Everyone seemed to be in a merry, chaffing mood. For example, I heard a man near me say to a friend, "I gather you putted very frequently this morning." The rejoinder went: "I'm lying doggo. Watch me when it counts." I was digesting this animated scene when Gerald Micklem, the current president of the O. & C.G.S. and one of my oldest friends in British golf, came striding into the room en route from the ninth green to the tenth tee, and threw down a fast kümmel. (Kümmel has long been a favorite drink of English golfers, because there is an old wives' tale to the effect that it is the best antidote in the world for shaky putting.) Before hurrying out to continue his match, Micklem greeted me with his invariable hospitality, barking out his welcome in quick, peremptory phrases. Then, just as I noticed that he was wearing only a medium-weight sweater and no hat, he surveyed my goosedown trail jacket and the rest of my sub-Arctic outfit. "Think you'll be warm enough?" he asked, and, with a little laugh, strode out into the cold.

I got into the swing of things rapidly. I tossed off a kümmel and went into the dining room, where I had some scrambled eggs and cold ham, the traditional luncheon dish at the Putter for those who bypass the buffet table. John Blackwell, the old Billie Holiday and Ella Fitzgerald fan, came by carrying a tray loaded with a dozen glasses of port and kindly dropped one off for me. (I noticed on subsequent days that, wherever they were, John Blackwell and his brother Tom seemed to be doling out endless rounds of port, and I concluded that a new Putter tradition was in the making.) Then, feeling good and warm, I went out onto the course. Early that morning, I was told, the fairways had been white with frost, but the frost had disappeared hours ago, and now the course was green — unusually green for this time of year. It was also fairly soft underfoot, for, as English winters go, this was a mild one. The run of good weather had had something to do with the fact that a record field of ninety-six golfers had assembled for the Putter. Seven were undergraduates — about the average representation — but what hit me was the number of men of rather advanced years who had turned out. These included R. Salisbury Woods, an eighty-year-old doctor, and a gray-haired gentleman with the soft, genial smile of a rural vicar, who — wouldn't you know it! — proved to be Sir Roger Hollis, recently retired as head of MI-5, the storied counterintelligence bureau. I was also very much impressed by the course, which occupies a superb stretch of linksland, replete with the whorls and dips and slippery plateaus that one finds only on certain seaside stretches of the British Isles. Rye measures a mere sixty-five hundred yards, but except in the hot months when the fairways and greens get baked out it is a splendid test of golf. No fewer than ten of its par-4 holes are four hundred and thirty yards long or longer, and three of its five par 3s demand accuracy of the first order, wind or no wind. The course, which was opened in 1894, is essentially the work of Harry Colt, although Sir Guy Campbell and H. C. Tippett revised many of its holes. When the idea of building a course was first considered by the townspeople, Colt, who had been an outstanding university golfer at Cambridge, was working in a solicitor's office in Hastings — another of the Cinque Ports — nine miles away. His ambition all along had been to design golf courses, and when he was asked to look over the land in the sand dunes and, subsequently, to lay out eighteen holes there, he jumped at the chance. The course at Rye was such a success that it enabled Colt to change professions. He went on to become the premier British golf architect of his day — the designer of such illustrious courses as Sunningdale, Swinley Forest, Stoke Poges, and Portrush, the co-designer of Wentworth, and the consultant whom George Crump called in to help him create the wonderland of Pine Valley.

When I returned to the clubhouse late in the afternoon, I found Micklem — he had that day extended his record for most-consecutive-Putters-played-in to thirty-two — in the big room sorting out a few executive details. A fairly large, very intense man with an outdoor complexion, graying hair, and round, pondering gray-green eyes, Micklem, who graduated from Oxford in 1933 and fought with the Grenadier Guards during the war, has been far and away the most influential individual in British golf over the last quarter of a century. His father having been a wealthy merchant banker, he has had the wherewithal and the time to make the game his primary interest. He made his first indentation as a player, winning the English Amateur twice and earning a place on four British Walker Cup teams. Perhaps his best showing in Cup competition came in 1953, at Kittansett, in Marion, Massachusetts, when he held Gene Littler even over the first eighteen holes of their match. He was the nonplaying captain of the British team in 1957 and 1959, and since moving into the administrative end of the game he has served as, among other things, president of the English Golf Union and the European Golf Association, captain of the Royal and Ancient Golf Club of St. Andrews, and chairman of most of the important R. and A. committees. His ex-officio activities have been at least as valuable. He has travelled to all parts of the country to look over promising young amateur golfers and to see to it that they receive proper encouragement, instruction, and tournament experience; when they have been in the London area, they have enjoyed the hospitality of his home, Titlarks Hill House, which abuts the sixteenth hole of Sunningdale's New Course. In 1969, the Queen made him a Commander of the Order of the British Empire for his contributions to amateur golf, which was in a very bad way when he took over, in the middle nineteen-fifties, but which has been so thoroughly revitalized that last May Great Britain defeated the United States in the Walker Cup for the first time in thirty-three years.

A popular pastime among Micklem's friends is imitating his highly individual way of talking. Part of his voice seems to come from the nasal passages and the other part from his trachea, and since his words pour out at great speed, like a sort of gruff waterfall, he is not easy to understand until you have been around him for a while and your ear has got adjusted. When, as the visiting captain, he spoke to the American press the day before the 1957 Walker Cup match at Minikahda, in Minneapolis, I remember how one local reporter threw his hands up at the end of the talk and wailed, "I didn't get one word that Limey said!" In recent years, Micklem has developed a serviceable transatlantic voice, which he uses on appropriate occasions, and he was thoughtful enough to turn it on as we sat chatting. "I suppose you want to know why

we persist in holding this event at this impossible time of year,"
he said. "Three reasons, really. (A) The golf course is no good in
summer — it plays too short then. (B) Early January is one of the
few times everyone is available. The undergraduates haven't yet
returned to university from Christmas vacation. Same thing with
the schoolmasters. Offhand, we must have ten or eleven schoolmasters in this year's tournament. On top of that, the older chaps
tend to stay around home at Christmas. They haven't rushed off
yet to the Caribbean or Portugal or the other warm places. (C)
Everyone looks forward to the Putter as a sort of winter holiday.
What it really is is a reunion — a chance to see old friends and
enjoy their company. It seems to be precisely what one needs at
this bleak time of year."

A young man stopped for a brief word with Micklem. I got the
idea he was a Cambridge undergraduate, but after introducing us
Micklem shifted from his transatlantic voice into his Thames-side
voice and I couldn't follow him. "Not a bad striker of the ball, that
chap," he said, speaking slowly and clearly again, after the young
man had left. "The difficult thing is to get people to come to the
Putter at an early age — they have so many other things they can
do." He paused for a moment. "Of course, the only way you can
preserve something like the Putter is to get the young fellows into
the spirit of it."

I found the President's Putter a world of its own, an entirely
different world from anything I had ever before encountered in
golf. During my four days at Rye, I lost all track of what was going
on anywhere else. The daylight hours were spent at the golf club
in the company of the stalwarts of the O. & C.G.S., and at night,
since the residents turned in early and there were no other visitors, they were the only people you encountered as you made
your way around the cobbled streets. Rarely did a subject other
than golf command a conversation for long. On Thursday night,
for example, a number of us who were staying at the Hope Anchor Hotel settled in the bar after dinner, where, supplemented by
visiting friends, we talked golf solidly for the next four hours. The
star turn was provided by Tony Duncan, one of the Society's old
lions (he was the winner of the Putter in 1948 and 1958), who told
a series of Bernard Darwin stories. While Darwin the writer was
the soul of serenity and balance, Darwin the golfer had one of the
shortest fuses in history, and this is what Duncan's stories were

about. One incident he related had taken place at the Putter. Darwin, it seems, was playing a man named Speakman, a rather ordinary golfer, but as they came to the twelfth it was still anybody's match. On that hole, Darwin hit a magnificent approach shot that barely missed the pin, but, unluckily, it was a shade too strong and just slid over the green, where it caught a downslope that plunged it into deep rough. Speakman followed with a terrible half-topped approach that hopped through a bunker and onto the green, where it finished close to the pin. The injustice of all this was too much for Darwin. Hurling his club to the ground, he roared, "God damn this blasted course! God damn this blasted hole! And you, Speakman, God damn you!" Another Darwin story that Duncan told had as its setting the annual Medal Day at Woking — a competition that Darwin took very seriously. On the first green, after a fine approach, he missed a five-foot putt. On the second, he missed an eight-footer. After another perfect iron to the third, he missed from six feet. Now he was seething. On the fourth hole at Woking, a tight par 4, the place to be on your drive is between the principal fairway bunker and a railroad track on the right. Darwin threaded the needle with his tee shot, nursed a delicate pitch-and-run three feet from the pin, but then blew the putt, whereupon he sank down on his hands and knees, bit a huge piece of turf from the green, and, lifting his hands toward the heavens, said in a voice that trembled with emotion, "O God, are you satisfied now?"

The following evening, at around six, I attended the Society's Annual Meeting, which was held, according to custom, at the Dormy House, an old private residence just inside the Land Gate. Since 1897, the Dormy House, a quite separate institution from the Rye Golf Club, although their memberships overlap, has served as a social club at which out-of-town members can stay when they come down to play some golf. In recent times, five or six fairly elderly men have lived there on a more or less permanent basis; near the end of his life, Darwin did. All told, the Dormy House has about fifteen rooms, one of them the Darwin Room, which contains a part of his golf library and other memorabilia. The largest room is the billiard room, and it is there that the Annual Meeting takes place. This year, about sixty members turned out for it, the old-timers collecting around the fireplace — a huge one, in which a big fire was leaping — and six or seven of the young bloods perched fashionably on the beige cloth covering the billiard table. The officers were seated on red leather chairs at one end of the room. The proceedings were most informal. When it was time to begin, Micklem got to his feet almost indolently and said, as far as I could make out, "Gentlemen, I'll ask the secretary to read the minutes of the last Annual Meeting." Mungo Swanston, the secretary, did this, then moved on to the presentation of accounts. It is generally recognized, I think, that one of the highest aspirations of every well-bred and well-schooled Englishman is to come up with a witty ad lib when someone he knows is making a formal speech or some serious remarks. I was reminded of this that evening, for when one of the members queried Swanston about an apparent contradiction in the amount of certain entrance fees a droll voice from a shadow-filled corner piped up, "Good question." A wave of appreciative laughter rolled through the room. When Swanston proceeded to clear up the matter with dispatch, another voice sang out, "Good answer," and that broke up the house again. The names of the incoming captain and the new committeemen were then presented, the members voted to hold a dinner in London next year to celebrate the Society's seventy-fifth anniversary, and then all that remained to be done was to conduct the draw for partners in the Secretary's Niblick. This is an alternate-shot foursomes competition at match play that is held during the last two days of the Putter for players who were eliminated from the Putter itself during the first two days. (Everyone gets enough golf at Rye, particularly the hearty types who arrive on Tuesday and warm up for the main event by entering the Croome Shield, an alternate-shot foursomes competition at stroke play, over eighteen holes, in which the two members of each team must have attended the same college. This year, the winners, with a score of 75, were John Uzielli and Robin Burleigh, of Trinity College, Oxford.)

Later that evening, I returned to the Dormy House to attend the President's Dinner, after which, back in the bar of the Hope Anchor, I tapered off by talking golf for two hours more. This time, the stars were the incoming captain, Peter Bathurst, and a friend of his named Roger Hedley-Miller. Both of them seemed to know everything about American golf, and when I at length took my departure they were trying to straighten out who had finished second to Ben Hogan in the 1951 U.S. Open at Oakland Hills — Clayton Heafner or Bobby Locke.

The Annual Dinner (black tie) took place the next night, Saturday — the eve of the semifinal and final rounds, and, as such, the last night when everyone would be on hand. At seven-thirty or thereabouts, groups started to make their way down the narrow streets to the George Hotel. Dinner, in the banquet room, began at eight, and after dinner there were four speeches: the retiring captain proposed the health of the new captain; the new captain responded; a member of the Society proposed the health of the guests; and the vice-captain of the Rye Golf Club replied for the guests. As is usually the case in Britain, all four men had worked hard on their talks, which were full of funny stuff and were very well delivered, but the high point of the evening was unquestionably an ad lib from the audience during Bathurst's speech. The new captain's oratorical style bears a definite resemblance to the rush of a rhino, and when he was charging full tilt into a complicated sentence that included several dependent clauses and two gerundial constructions, he may, in his haste to punch home a climactic series of colorful zeugmas, have neglected to supply the sentence with a subject and a predicate.

"Could we have that one again?" one of the frontbenchers asked in a dry voice. Pandemonium. At the conclusion of the speeches, most of the people made their way to the Dormy House to talk a little golf, for a change, and to end the evening in the kitchen, over a traditional post-Dinner plate of bacon and eggs. When I saw Micklem and the Blackwell brothers happily ensconced at the kitchen table, all I could think of was Low, Croome, and Darwin sitting there fifty years before.

To get on to the golf. While I have been aware for some time now of the vast glamour that the homely virtues of amateur sport hold for the British, the informality and the studied lack of production at the President's Putter went far beyond my expectations. With only a handful of caddies available, nearly everyone carried his own bag or trundled it along in the type of cart that the British call a trolley. The pace of play was nevertheless remarkably fast, the average twosome taking no more than three hours to complete a full round. No officials were posted on the course, for the players are supposed to settle any rules problems among themselves. In the Old School Tie code of sportsmanship that pervades the Putter, it is good form to make little of your own achievements, and several players who I knew had won matches by decisive margins, like 5 and 4 or 4 and 3, told friends who had asked about the outcome, "I think I won by a hole." Being so accustomed to our professional scene, I was struck by these things. I was also struck by the excellent level of the golf. On Friday, I spent part of the morning watching a match in which Ted Dexter, a finalist in the Putter in 1969, defeated a left-hander named David Physick, who carries ten clubs in his bag — a Ping putter, a conventional sand wedge, and eight woods. Dexter is an extremely interesting fellow. The son of the Milan representative of Lloyd's of London, he came into the spotlight early, as captain of both the cricket team and the golf team at Cambridge. He became a national celebrity when he went on to play cricket for England for nine seasons, serving for one year as captain. It is said that some of the men on the team felt that Dexter's manner was rather lofty, and took to calling him Lord Ted. In any event, as an individualist and a fairly outspoken one, Dexter remains a controversial figure. Now thirty-seven, a tall, dark, dashing-looking man with a jutting Sherlock Holmes profile, he works for the B.B.C. as a cricket commentator. This prevents him from playing much tournament golf, so no one really knows how good a player he is, or might become if he were able to devote more time to the game. One thing is sure: he is far and away the longest hitter in British amateur golf and has a most impressive hitting action, somewhat reminiscent of Bobby Nichols' in his prime.

That afternoon, I watched a wonderful match between two old rivals, Peter Moody and David Baxter, who captained Cambridge and Oxford, respectively, in 1969. There was little to choose between them. Baxter, a beautiful player, is the better technician, but Moody, a tall, quiet young man, who was a semifinalist in the British Amateur last spring, is a determined competitor who has learned how to maintain the fine legato tempo of his swing under pressure. Their match, played in intermittent rain and a flapping east wind, went to the eighteenth green, where Moody won it by holing a good, firm four-footer. He was around in 70.

Both Moody and Dexter survived their two matches on Saturday, when the round of sixteen and the quarterfinals were played, and this helped to set up a very attractive card for the semifinals on Sunday morning. In the top half of the draw, Moody, who now teaches school in Dorsetshire, was up against John Turnbull, who is the present Oxford captain and a promising Russian scholar. In the lower half, Dexter faced Dr. David Marsh, a general practitioner of great personal charm, who earned himself a small chunk of immortality last May when he hit the shot that won the Walker

Cup for Britain — a picture-postcard 3-iron to the seventeenth green that covered the flag every yard of the way. I was only hoping that the weather would not turn colder. On Saturday, the temperature couldn't have been below thirty degrees, but a bitter east wind was blowing, and it felt like fifteen — definitely a four-kümmel day.

It worked out just the other way. Sunday dawned clear, mild, and still, and by noon, when a pale sun came out to stay, it was almost like southern California, and I began to wonder if they were having as good a day for the final round of the Los Angeles Open. By that time, the Putter semifinals had been decided. Neither match had caught fire. Moody had built up an early lead over young Turnbull and had methodically closed him out. Marsh had been in nothing like his best form against Dexter, and some erratic putting on the second nine finished him off. After a brief break for lunch, the final, a rerun of the 1969 final between Dexter and Moody, got under way. A friend of Moody's was caddying for him, but Dexter was pulling his own clubs along on a trolley, as he had been doing all week. On this gentle, bright day, Dexter was wearing a mustard-colored visor instead of the woollen stocking cap he had worn in all his earlier matches. He made one other change. In the morning, after hitting two wild tee shots with his driver, he switched to his 4-wood, for safety's sake, and in the final he drove with that club all the way. This decision to forfeit the advantage, both real and psychological, that redounds from outdriving one's opponent by a large margin might have been a mistake. At least, it seemed that way in retrospect, for Dexter never did get winging in full flight, and Moody's superior steadiness prevailed, the match ending on the seventeenth. There was no presentation ceremony — that would have been too flashy for the Putter. As Moody came off the seventeenth green, the captain handed him the winner's medal as unobtrusively as possible, and that was it.

One reason Gene Sarazen, Roberto de Vicenzo, and other veterans regularly return to play in Britain is that the people there never forget the old champions, and welcome them warmly. The British also have a talent for perpetuating their sports institutions. You might expect an archaism like the President's Putter to have vanished decades ago, but it continues to flourish because it still has meaning and substance for the members of the O. & C.G.S. —

those spiritual descendants of Samuel Pickwick and his friends, of Stalky & Co., and of the chaps at the Drones Club. Those were my thoughts, anyway, as I walked back to the clubhouse from the seventeenth. In the crowded big room, I spotted Micklem in a far corner talking nineteen to the dozen, and went over. I told him how much I had enjoyed myself, but added that I felt I had been lured to the Putter under false pretenses. "I know what you mean," Micklem said, in his cordial growl. "Very disappointing weather. Warmest day we've had for the Putter since '58. A few quick reflections: (A) We must all learn to take the bitter with the sweet. (B) In stormy weather, on a frozen course, some of us older players would have been much tougher to beat. No question. And (C) I imagine we'll pay for this tropical weather *next* January. That augurs well, I'd say."

(1972)

Robert Tyre Jones, Jr.

Bobby Jones (as he was known during his playing career) or Bob Jones (as he preferred to be called by his friends) was a most exceptional man. Golfers throughout the world know that he won thirteen major championships between 1923 and 1930, when he retired from competitive golf after sweeping the four major tournaments that he, as an amateur, was eligible to play in: the British Amateur, the British Open, the United States Open, and the United States Amateur. They also know that shortly after his retirement, working in collaboration with Alister MacKenzie, he built his "dream course," the Augusta National. In 1934 the club held an informal spring invitational tournament for Jones's old friends, professionals and amateurs, that grew, almost as if it had been foreordained, into one of the world's four major events: the Masters. Jones was a man of principle with a warm heart and a remarkable mind. There was something magical about his personality: he came across to everyone as the man he was. The people of St. Andrews cherished him so deeply that they made him an Honorary Burgess of the Borough. It is interesting that St. Andrews has accorded this honor to only one other American. He was a fitting running mate for Jones: Benjamin Franklin.

THE 1972 MASTERS, BESIDES LACKING THE DRAMA AND EXCITE-ment that usually accompany the event, was different from its predecessors in another way. The tournament is inextricably bound up with Robert Tyre Jones, Jr. — Bobby to sports historians, Bob to his friends — who, after his retirement from competition, in 1930, helped to found the Augusta National Gulf Club, became its one and only president, designed its superb course in conjunction with Alister MacKenzie, the Scottish golf architect, and served as host of the Masters from its beginnings, in 1934, as an informal spring get-togther, until 1969, when the severe illness he had borne quietly for twenty years became so incapacitating that he couldn't make the journey to Augusta from his home in Atlanta. Jones died last December 18th, at the age of sixty-nine, and at Augusta this April everyone felt his absence sharply and continually. I think this was to be expected. What was surprising was the sense of shock and grief that so many people in golf experienced when word came of his death. After all, we had been prepared for this news for years, and, in addition, in a corner of our hearts we knew it would be a blessing, since the spinal disease that Jones was afflicted with — syringomyelia — was inordinately cruel and crippling. And yet, how hard the news hit when it came! In another corner of our hearts we had been nursing the faint hope that somehow or other Jones would make it back to Augusta one of these springs and we would be seeing him again and talking with him again, and now we knew we wouldn't.

Of the people I have met in sports — or out — Jones came the closest to being what we call a great man. Like Winston Churchill, he had the quality of being at the same time much larger than life and exceedingly human. Jones had a remarkably fine mind, with an astonishing range. As a young man, he first thought that he would like to become a mechanical engineer, and he earned a B.S. degree at Georgia Tech, completing the four-year course of study in three years. During his last semester at Tech, however, he decided that he didn't want to be an engineer after all. He enrolled at Harvard, where he took a variety of courses, mainly in English literature, and received another B.S. degree, at the end of two years. (In one of his literature courses, he was introduced to Henry Fielding, who remained his favorite author; he was very fond of *Tom Jones* but thought that *Joseph Andrews* was a touch better.) Then Jones, who was the son of a lawyer, went to Emory University Law School, in Atlanta. Halfway through his second year, he passed the Georgia State bar exams and entered practice. There was very little he couldn't do if he set his mind to it. His first book, *Down the Fairway*, which was published by Minton, Balch in 1927, was written in colaboration with O. B. Keeler, the celebrated sports chronicler of the Atlanta *Journal*, but Jones loved good writing, and the desire to be a competent writer was strong in him, and from that time on he personally wrote everything that appeared under his name — one of the few sports figures of whom this can be said. I really wonder if anyone has ever written about the business of playing golf better than Jones. Here, from a collection entitled *Bobby Jones on Golf*, is a typical example of the clarity and flavor that marked his writing:

Long ago Tommy Armour asked me which I considered to have been the greatest shot I ever played. "When it meant something," he added. It did not take me long to nominate the iron shot from the bunker on the seventeenth hole at St. Annes that enabled me to nose out Al Watrous in the British Open of 1926. The shot was about 175 yards across a number of other bunkers and dunes. I had a clean lie in the sand, and the shot was hardly more difficult than any blind second of the same length; but I did get a thrill out of it because it would have made such a lot of difference if the blade of my iron had taken the smallest speck of sand before it struck the ball.

"I rather expected you to name that one," said Tommy. "You know, I asked Hagen the same question, and he also named a bunker shot, out of the cross bunker on the fifteenth at Sandwich." I remember the bunker perfectly, having been in it a number of times, and the shot almost as well, although I did not see it.

When Hagen put his second in that bunker in the last round [of the 1928 British Open], he needed a five there, and three pars to finish, to beat the lowest total already in, and, apparently, to win the championship. He found his ball lying cleanly in the middle of the bunker, with the pin perhaps thirty yards away, about in the middle of the green. But the bunker is a formidable one; it is not so very large nor so awfully deep, but the front bank overhangs so that a ball close underneath it is scarcely playable.

The option for Hagen here was to play a safe blast, get his five, and still have to play the last three holes in par, or to take a desperate chance in the hope of getting a four, thus providing a marginal stroke that might well be needed on the finishing holes. He studied the shot with the utmost care, changed clubs at least twice, and ended by playing the most perfect chip imaginable; the ball stopped a foot from the hole, and he finished in par to win. . . .

The short shots off clean sand, like Hagen's, are the most treacherous in golf. The long ones, like mine, are not so bad, for then the main thing is to strike a descending blow, as you would from the fairway — and if you take it heavy, you are hitting hard enough to get out of the bunker anyway. But the delicate stroke, if it fails, fails completely. . . .

Jones had other exceptional gifts. He had a sense of proportion uncommon in a man with a vigorously perfectionist side to his nature. His family — his wife, Mary, and their three children — came first; his work as a member of his Atlanta law firm came second; his golf came third. He had incredible strength of character. As a young man, he was able to stand up to just about the best that life can offer, which is not easy, and later he stood up with equal grace to just about the worst. On top of everything else, he had tremendous personal magnetism. In the nineteen-twenties, golf, though very much on the rise, had not become the major game it is today in this country, yet no other hero of the Golden Age of Sport had quite the hold on the affections of the American public that Jones had. Everybody adored him — not just dyed-in-the-wool golfers but people who had never struck a golf ball or had the least desire to. They admired the ingrained modesty, the humor, and the generosity of spirit that were evident in Jones's remarks and deportment. They liked the way he looked, this handsome, clean-cut young man whose eyes gleamed with both a frank boyishness and a perceptiveness far beyond his years. (This was one time when a person's appearance perfectly matched his substance and charm.) Jones, in short, was the model American athlete come to life, and it is to the credit of the American public that they recognized this almost instantly. His presence was enough to guarantee the success of any tournament. More than eighteen thousand spectators wedged themselves onto Merion's famous East Course, outside Philadelphia, for the final of the 1930 United States Amateur to see their hero complete his Grand Slam of the four major championships — the British Amateur, the British Open, the United States Open, and the United States Amateur. Jones's appeal crossed oceans. For the Scots, he was the dream golfer they had been waiting for all their lives. This was particularly true of the natives of St. Andrews, and on several occasions when Jones was involved in a match on the Old Course, or was just playing an informal round, the whole town poured onto the links to watch him. (The Royal and Ancient Golf Club of St. Andrews, of which Jones was an honorary member, will hold a memorial service for him on May 4th, at the end of the club's spring meeting.) To protect himself from his frenzied idolaters during a championship, Jones at times took the precaution of having two friends convoy him down the fairways, one walking on each side of him, but inevitably tournament play — trying to live up to everything that was expected of him, trying to maintain his concentration and timing under prolonged pressure — took a great deal out of him. Many people missed this, for he somehow managed to appear unfrazzled, and when he spoke, even under stress, his words still oozed out in that slow, thick Georgia drawl, like Karo syrup. But Jones felt the strain, all right. During one Open championship, he lost eighteen poinds. During another, he was so exhausted and numbed at the finish that he couldn't get his fingers to unknot his sweat-soaked tie, and his friend Keeler had to cut it off with a pocketknife. Jones loved to compete — beneath the controlled exterior beat a heart every bit as fiery and determined as Ben Hogan's — but there was no way he could escape the punishment that the championships brought on, and this, as much as any other single factor, prompted his decision to retire from competitive golf in 1930 following his Grand Slam.

When he retired, Jones was only twenty-eight. It seemed that he had been around much longer than that, though, because he had been in the spotlight practically all his life. At the age of nine, he won the junior championship of the East Lake Golf Club, outside Atlanta, by beating a boy seven years older. At thirteen, he won the club championship at East Lake and also at nearby Druid Hills. The next year, he won the Georgia Amateur Championship and made his début in national competition in the U.S. Amateur. A chunky youngster, as cocky as they came, Jones was the sensation of the tournament; he defeated two good players, Eben Byers and Frank Dyer, before going down in the next round to the defending champion, Bob Gardner. At this period, Jones was notorious for throwing clubs after he had hit bad shots, and in later years, when he described his match with Byers, another high-ranking club-thrower, he liked to explain that he won because Byers ran out of clubs first. Temperamental outbursts, always directed at himself, continued to mar Jones's performances until 1921 — he was nineteen then — when a critical incident took place in the British Open. He had started off well in that championship, but on the third round, played in wind and rain, he took forty-six shots on the first nine, and after starting back with a double bogey on the tenth he picked up his ball on the short eleventh, where he was facing the prospect of a triple bogey. Instantly, he was appalled by what he had done. As he saw it, he had quit under pressure — an unpardonable act. Right there, Jones grew up. Indeed, the ever-rankling memory of this petulant gesture in the 1921 British Open led him to set an incredibly high standard of sportsmanship throughout the rest of his career.

Almost invariably when the subject of Jones's sportsmanship comes up in a discussion, someone will mention how he twice called penalty strokes on himself in our Open — once in the second round of the 1925 championship, at the Worcester Country Club, in Massachusetts, when, after he had addressed the ball, it moved slightly in high grass as he was preparing to play a recovery from the rough on the eleventh hole, and once in the second round the next year, at Scioto, in Columbus, Ohio, when his ball moved the tiniest fraction as he was addressing it with his putter on the fifteenth green. Both times, no one else saw his ball move. In 1926, as it happened, Jones went on to win the Open, but in 1925 he finished in a tie for first with Willie MacFarlane, to whom he subsequently lost in an extended playoff, so it is often argued that the penalty stroke Jones called on himself cost him the championship. Maybe yes and maybe no. One can't alter one fact and presume that all the others would have remained unchanged. In any event, I think there is a certain danger of missing the point about Jones's sportsmanship if one places the primary emphasis on those two instances. They are better viewed, I believe, as dramatic examples of Jones's tenet that there is only one way to play golf, and that is by the rules. As for his sportsmanship, it was essentially embodied in the conviction that a man could go all out to win and at the same time have a genuinely friendly regard for his opponent or opponents. (One of the most appealing scenes in golf history is the one in which Jones and Al Watrous, who were paired on the final day of the 1926 British Open, stretched out on cots in a room at the Majestic Hotel in St. Anne's-on-the-Sea and shared some tea and cold ham in the brief interval between the morning and afternoon rounds.) When Tommy Armour once was asked to describe Jones, the first word that came to his mind was "considerate." Gene Sarazen put it this way: "Bob was a fine man to be partnered with in a tournament. . . . He made you feel that you were playing with a friend, and you were."

It can also be said that Jones, more than any other athlete, is responsible for inventing the graceful sort of acceptance speech that has become standard in sports today. Of course, he had a lot more practice than anybody else. Anyhow, if it was a match-play tournament he had won, he made it a habit to include the runner-up in his comments. It was always "As Alec and I were walking down the back nine today," and not "As I was walking down the back nine today." He might have creamed old Alec 10 and 9, but when he spoke of him it was as a co-finalist, as a peer. It was the same thing, with minor variations, after a stroke-play tournament. And he was no less respectful toward his rivals in private conversation. While one certainly couldn't accept as gospel everything one heard about Jones, I have always believed the story that when a friend asked him if there was any golfer he ever wanted to beat for personal reasons, Jones replied, "Just one," named the player, and explained, "We were in the final of an important championship, and just before we were to tee off he came over and said, 'I really don't care who wins this thing, you or I. Let's just go out there and have a nice, pleasant, enjoyable round.' I didn't appreciate that. I knew he wanted to win that championship just as much as I did."

After losing in the final of our Amateur Championship in 1919 and finishing a stroke behind the winner in our Open in 1922, Jones broke through in 1923, capturing the Open at Inwood, on Long Island, after a tense playoff with Bobby Cruickshank. Thereafter, he was almost unstoppable. When one looks back at the record he compiled, it is hard to believe that any man could have risen to the occasion so regularly. Briefly, Jones appeared in four British Opens and won the last three (in 1926, 1927, and 1930). In his last eight starts in the U.S. Open, he won four times (in 1923, 1926, 1929, and 1930), lost twice after a playoff (in 1925 and 1928), and finished second another time without a playoff (in 1924); in 1927, the one year in that stretch when he was neither first nor second, he tied for eleventh. He won the U.S. Amateur five times in his last seven attempts, losing to George Von Elm in the final in 1926 and to Johnny Goodman in the first round in 1929. In 1930, after two failures, he won the British Amateur, and this triumph was doubly sweet inasmuch as it set up the Grand Slam. All told, Jones won thirteen major championships — the greatest number of any golfer (Nicklaus, by the way, has now won twelve.)

Most people who follow sports are fairly well aware of Jones's fantastic record, yet in a curious way many of them do not properly understand what a magnificent golfer he was. In the back of their minds the idea persists that in the nineteen-twenties the game was so primitive and the field so seedy that all a man had to do to win a golf tournament was to slop around in a 74 or a 76. Nothing could be wronger. The field that Jones competed against was an extremely strong one, and, considering that the golfers then were still playing with wooden-shafted clubs and relatively "short" golf balls on courses with slower fairways, heavier roughs, and infinitely less uniform greens than are standard now, the quality of their golf and scoring was proportionately just as good as it is today, if not better. The example that always leaps to mind is the 66 that Jones shot in the qualifying round of the 1926 British Open, at Sunningdale, outside London — a course that measured something over 6,600 yards and played to a par of 72. It was how Jones fashioned that 66, not the score itself, that was arresting. Most low rounds are the result of a streak of red-hot putting, but en route to his 66 Jones holed only one putt of any length — a twenty-five-footer on the fifth hole — and in all he took thirty-three putts, which is a lot. Rather, what was extraordinary was his almost flawless shotmaking from tee to green. In fact, he mis-hit only one shot. On the thirteenth, a 175-yard par 3, he struck a 4-iron a trifle thin and dumped the ball into a greenside bunker, but he got down in two and saved his par. (In the set of clubs Jones assembled, there was a 1-iron, a 2-iron, and a 4-iron. The rest were called by their old Scottish names.) Otherwise, he was putting for his birdie on every green; in fact, on the four par 5s he was putting for his eagle. Perhaps the only way one can begin to appreciate the supernal character of this round is to know the various clubs that Jones used to hit the greens, for Sunningdale gave a golfer few chances to toss up short pitches with the lofted irons and demanded that he play most of his approaches with the comparatively straight-faced irons — the hardest clubs in the bag to hit precisely and accurately. The breakdown he presented in *Down the Fairway* is not quite complete, but, filling in the blanks as best one can, one arrives at the following tabulation: on the three short par-4 holes, he almost drove the green and left himself with only a chip shot, but on the seven other par 4s he used his mashie iron (a variation of the 4-iron) on two of his approach shots, his 4-iron on four, and his mashie (or 5-iron) once; on the three par 3s that he hit in the regulation stroke, he used his driving mashie (a relative of a 1-iron) once, his 4-iron once, and his mashie once; in getting home in two on each of the four par 5s, he used his 2-iron once, and his 1-iron once, and his brassie (or 2-wood) twice. That's not bad, is it?

Jones accomplished his prodigies of shotmaking with what was far and away the best swing of his time — and one of the best swings of all time. In the wooden-shaft era, because of the inherent torque and torsion of the clubs, all golfers worked on being smooth and not rushing their swing, since a minute flaw in timing might be magnified into a disastrous error, but no one was close to Jones when it came to executing the correct movements rhythmically, fluidly — almost lyrically. This helps to explain why *How I Play Golf*, a series of short instructional films that he made for Warner Brothers after his retirement, went down extremely well with the largely non-golfing audiences at our movie houses: watching Jones hit a golf ball was an aesthetic treat, even if you couldn't tell a duck hook from a double eagle. When one studies his swing in slow motion today, it looks a trifle looser, particularly on the backswing, than it did back in the nineteen-twenties, but it is still very, very impressive. He deviated hardly at all from the perfect copybook form, but he did stand with his feet closer together than any champion before or after him, for he believed that one of the key elements in a sound golf swing was a full, free hip turn on the backswing and that a narrow stance helped a player to achieve this. Jones was a man of only medium size, but because of the fullness of his arc, his excellent balance, and his really extraordinary timing he was one of the longest hitters of his day and quite possibly the finest wooden-club player ever. Most of the time, he was content to get his drives out between two hundred and twenty-five and two hundred and fifty yards and to make certain he kept the ball on the fairway, but when he wanted to open up he could really move that ball. For example, on the last hole of the 1926 U.S. Open, when he was leading the tournament by a single stroke and naturally was keyed up high, he smashed his drive a full three hundred yards down the fairway. His shots had a distinctive flight, much higher than most golfers'. I remember standing with a group that included Walter Hagen behind a green on the Meadowbrook course, near Detroit, during the 1955 P.G.A. Championship, when Jack Burke, Jr., hit a towering 5-iron approach that was dead on line and coasted down right over the top of the flagstick. "That's how Jones's irons used to look," Hagen said. "The ball came in as big as a grapefruit."

Jones understood the dynamics of the golf swing exceedingly well, and he knew what he was doing every step of the way. He preferred to play his shots so that the ball moved from right to left, and most of the time he did "draw" the ball in this fashion, but in 1926 he won both the British Open and our Open fading the ball from left to right. On the greens, he was a lovely putter. He couldn't compare with Hagen as a holer of putts (who could?), but he had a marvellous touch on his long approach putts, and in a critical situation he never missed a short one. This was true of Jones's whole game: he was wonderful in the clutch. In at least one big championship each year, he would be marching to victory, cool and assured, when, to the complete confoundment of his gallery, he would suddenly lose his concentration and throw away three or four or five strokes. However, with his back then to the wall, he could almost always summon the great shot he needed to extricate himself: the 2-iron on the eighteenth hole of the playoff of the 1923 Open, against Cruickshank, which he rifled across a lagoon and put six feet from the flag; the mashie iron from the sand on the seventy-first hole at St. Annes in the 1926 British Open, against Watrous; the slippery twelve-foot sidehill putt on the seventy-second green in the 1929 Open, at Winged Foot, in Westchester, which he had to hole to tie Al Espinosa; the thirteen-foot putt he needed to halve the seventeenth hole at St. Andrews with George Voigt and stay even with him in their semifinal match in the 1930 British Amateur. One could go on and on. In top form, Jones could be devastating. Early in 1930, when he faced the full professional pack in the Southeastern Open, in Augusta, he finished thirteen strokes ahead of the second man, Horton Smith. In our Amateur, he fairly triturated his opposition. In 1925, at Oakmont, near Pittsburgh, he won his four matches — all of them thirty-six holes — 11 and 10, 6 and 5, 7 and 6, and 8 and 7; in 1928, at Brae Burn, outside Boston, he won his last three matches 14 and 13, 13 and 12, and 10 and 9. Once, when I was talking with Francis Ouimet, an altogether modest and gracious man, about the long interval between his first victory in the Amateur, in 1914, and his second victory, in 1931, he raised his voice to a dramatically emotional level, which was most unlike him, and said, "Don't get me wrong, but I played some pretty darn creditable golf in the Amateur in the twenties. Then I'd run into Bobby, and he would absolutely annihilate me. You have no idea how good Bobby was!"

It is doubtful whether the Masters, for all its multiple virtues, could have risen to prominence practically overnight and become accepted in hardly more than a decade as the peer of the U.S. Open, the British Open, and our P.G.A. Championship if anybody other than Bob Jones had created the event and watched over its development. From the outset, the tournament reflected his personality: its atmosphere was both dignified and informal, and it was pervaded by the spirit of golf at its best. Jones broke his retirement to play in the Masters. He made his final appearance in 1948, when pain in his neck and shoulders, which had been bothering him for some time, became so intense that he underwent surgery to relieve pressure on his spine. Two years later, another operation was necessary. It was finally discovered that he was suffering from a rare disease of the spinal cord that might gradually bring about almost total muscular paralysis. By this time, Jones had to walk with a cane and was in constant pain, but he made it a practice, as he continued to until a year or so before his death, to go to the office daily and to keep busy in golf. In 1953, for example, he flew to New York to attend the dinner honoring Ben Hogan, on Hogan's return from Britain, for his sweep that year of the Masters, the U.S. Open, and the British Open — the greatest golfing feat since Jones's Grand Slam. In 1954, he made it up to Winged Foot for the celebration of the twenty-fifth anniversary of his victory in the 1929 Open. As part of that program, Sarazen, Armour, and other notable golfers gathered at the eighteenth green to see if they could hole the subtle twelve-foot sidehiller that Jones had made to tie Espinosa (whom he proceeded to beat by *twenty-three* strokes in their playoff). When this was over, Jones was called on to say a few words. Through some oversight, the microphone on the green had been set up fifteen or twenty feet from the golf cart in which Jones had been seated. It took him almost two minutes to climb to the microphone up the mild incline, which must have seemed like a mountainside to him. He then made one of the nicest and wisest golf talks you've ever heard. When the first World Amateur Team Championship for the Eisenhower Trophy was scheduled for October, 1958, at St. Andrews, Jones, a close friend of the General's, was asked to serve as captain of the American team, and accepted. It is hard to know how much this trip took out of him. (I remember thinking when I saw him in his golf cart out on the links at the St. Andrews he loved so deeply that if it were not for his illness he might have been spending this period in Britain as Eisenhower's Ambassador to the Court of St. James's. He would have been ideal for the post.) During his 1958 visit, St. Andrews seized the opportunity to make him an Honorary Burgess of the Borough — the first American so honored since Benjamin Franklin, a hundred and ninety-nine years before. The ceremony took place one evening in Younger Hall, the largest auditorium in town. Seventeen hundred fervent St. Andreans crammed it to the rafters, literally. Jones spoke without notes that evening, and the occasion and the warmth of the audience fired him to a high pitch of eloquence. (I remember that he said of the Old Course, "The more you study it the more you love it, and the more you love it the more you study it," and also, "I could take out of my life everything except my experiences at St. Andrews and I would still have a rich, full life.") At the end of his talk, he was helped from the stage to his electric golf cart, and as he directed it down the center aisle toward the door the whole hall suddenly burst into the old Scottish song "Will Ye No' Come Back Again?," and it came pouring out with all the wild, overwhelming emotion of a pibroch wailed in some lonesome glen.

In the nineteen-sixties, when Jones was confined to a wheelchair, the word went round each winter that his condition had become worse, and everyone in golf speculated on whether he would be able to attend that year's Masters. He had suffered from heart trouble since 1952, and now that, too, became increasingly debilitating. Somehow he got to Augusta each April, though by then his body had so wasted away that he weighed scarcely ninety pounds. His arms were no bigger around than a broomstick, and he could no longer open his fingers to shake hands or grasp a pen. Yet this indomitable man kept going. For many years on the day before the start of the Masters, I called in on him in company with Ed Miles, of the Atlanta *Journal,* and Al Laney, of the New York *Herald Tribune,* who was one of his oldest and closest friends. We would walk over to Jones's cottage, near the tenth tee, torn by mixed feelings — the prospect of pleasure and the prospect of sorrow. Mrs. Jones or their son Bob or his wife, Frances, would be there to greet us. There would be a few cordially jumbled minutes during which personal news was exchanged and it was computed how many people wanted Coca-Cola and whether they wanted it in a glass or out of the bottle. By this time, Jones would have appeared and would be contriving a seating arrangement that enabled him to see everyone. He never looked as bad as you dreaded he might. While his body had withered to nothing, his handsome head and features remained relatively untouched, and his mind was as good as ever. We would ask him all sorts of questions we had stored up about new golfers and old tournaments, and he would answer them with amusement and flair. You could listen to him all day. He had the same feeling for words as Adlai Stevenson, and the same wonderful self-depreciatory sense of humor. Inevitably, as the session continued you became aware that you and your friends were doing all the talking — telling Jones what you had been up to and what you thought about this and that. Jones did not bring this about by any conscious technique; he simply was extremely interested in what his friends were doing, and you felt this interest. Leaving was always hard. When he put his twisted folded-up hand in yours as you said goodbye, you never knew whether you would be seeing him again. Each year when Miles and Laney and I left the cottage, we would walk seventy-five yards or so — nearly to the practice green — before we exchanged a word. My God, we felt good at that moment! We were so proud of Bob Jones! There was no need to feel sorry for a man like that. If *he* could rise above his misfortune, *you* could jolly well rise above his misfortune. I think that everyone who called on him responded this way.

Jones did not like his friends to talk about his illness, and they honored his wishes as best they could. However, in writing to him shortly after the 1968 Masters to ask a favor of him, I mentioned in closing how sorry I was that he had not been well enough to go out on the course in his golf cart and watch some of the play, as he usually did, and to attend the presentation ceremony, at which he customarily presided. In his reply, which I received the following week, he wrote, after dealing with the main subject:

> Really, I am not as far down the well physically as I appeared to be in Augusta. I picked up an intestinal virus a week or ten days before the Masters and could not shake the thing, even with a course of antibiotics. Even with that, I could perhaps have done a bit more than I did. Had I known in time that the scorecard episode was going to be present, I most certainly would have appeared at the presentation, both on television and on the putting green. This happened to be the one time that I felt I should have lent the weight of whatever authority I possess to these occasions.

From that paragraph, one would have assumed that, the virus past, Jones was now back in the pink of condition.

A few days later, I received another letter from Jones. The scorecard episode he had referred to in the first note was, of course, the one involving Roberto de Vicenzo and Bob Goalby in the Masters that year. Goalby and de Vicenzo had apparently finished the tournament in a tie with totals of 277. However, de Vicenzo's playing partner, Tommy Aaron, had written down a 4, and not the 3 that de Vicenzo had made, as his score on the seventeenth; de Vicenzo had signed the card; and, under Rule 38, Paragraph 3, de Vicenzo had to be charged with the 4. This gave him a total of 278, and Goalby was declared the winner. In my account of the tournament, I had attacked Rule 38 as a bad rule. Jones had this to say:

> I find myself differing with you in your stand on the propriety of Rule 38 under modern conditions. You make the point that in an event like the Masters, with hundreds of spectators at each hole and millions more watching on television, everybody knows the score.
>
> You may recall that on two occasions in Open Championship play, I ordered a stroke added to my score. In both instances, there were several hundred spectators around the green and, in each case, I had a scorer or marker, in addition to my playing companion. Both these men on both occasions were standing within fifteen feet of me. Yet each time I had to call the marker's attention to the extra stroke; and on one occasion this gentleman went so far as to appeal to the committee after the round, affirming that my ball had not moved. There is scarcely any way the spectators around the green and no way the viewers on television could know that de Vicenzo had not inadvertently moved his ball and reported the fact to Aaron between the seventeenth green and the eighteenth tee. . . .
>
> Believe me, I was thinking not only of de Vicenzo but of Goalby as well. Whereas de Vicenzo was the player penalized, both men were deprived of the opportunity to win the tournament in outright competition. This was as bad for one as for the other.
>
> The whole situation was tragic beyond expression. I like to think, though, that it served one useful purpose in emphasizing the respect which golfers must have for the rule book.

I find it pleasant to quote from these letters, because they so vividly evoke Jones's personality and his manner of expressing himself. He must have been one of the great letter writers of our time. Whenever one wrote to him — and my guess is that literally hundreds of people, from Sarazen, his exact contemporary, to youngsters just starting competitive golf, did so quite regularly — he answered very promptly and with obvious thought and care. It is an understatement to say that the arrival of a letter on the distinctive heavy bond stationery he used, with its familiar Poplar Street letterhead, could make your day.

While I gather from medical authorities that it would be wrong to credit Jones with living on for years after the average person would have picked up his ball and torn up his scorecard — how long anyone lives is not necessarily dictated by his will to live, they say — Jones deserves incalculable credit for *how* he lived out his life. Where he got the courage and energy to do all that he did there is no knowing. However, I think that Hogan put his finger on at least a part of the answer when he said, shortly after Jones's death, "The man was sick so long, and fought it so successfully, that I think we have finally discovered the secret of Jones's success. It was the strength of his mind."

About three days before Jones's death, when he knew he was dying, he said to the members of his family, "If this is all there is to it, it sure is peaceful." That is good to know. We were lucky we had Jones so long, for he had a rare gift for passing ideas and ideals on to other people. I think he probably enriched more lives than anyone else I have known. He enriched mine beyond measure.

(1972)

The Miller's Tale

One of the most striking aspects of early American golf is the number of surprisingly good courses that were built in the first dozen years of this century by men who had a clear idea of what the top British courses were like. Charles Blair Macdonald knew the Old Course at St. Andrews like the back of his hand, for he had attended St. Andrews University. It took him four years — 1907 through 1911 — to build the National Golf Links, near Southampton, the first outstanding American course. In 1910 Hugh Wilson, a young graduate of Princeton, was sent to Britain by the Merion Cricket Club, near Philadelphia, to study the famed courses. Wilson returned with a marvellous concept of what makes a golf hole fascinating and testing, and this was the basis of Merion's wonderful East Course. On the other hand, there was Oakmont, outside Pittsburgh, which was laid out in 1903 by H. C. Fownes and was later lengthened and strengthened by his son William. A punishing course, Oakmont kept the big boys in check the first four times the U.S. Open was held there, but in the 1973 Open heavy rains greatly altered the challenge of the course, and Johnny Miller took full advantage of this.

EVERY TIME THE UNITED STATES OPEN IS HELD AT THE OAKMONT Country Club, as it was a few weeks ago, when Johnny Miller carried the day in such spectacular fashion, it becomes a shade clearer that this wonderful old layout on the edge of Pittsburgh is without doubt both the most historic and the most epitomical of all the courses over which the national championship has been played since its inauguration, in 1895. The Open has now been staged at Oakmont five times: in 1927, 1935, 1953, 1962, and 1973 — once each decade, with the exception of the nineteen-forties, when the Second World War threw everything out of kilter. Only one other club, the Baltusrol Golf Club, in Springfield, New Jersey, has been host to that many Opens, but Baltusrol has held its five on three distinctly different courses. Not only has Oakmont used the same course all the way but it is unlikely that any other championship course in our country has been altered as little as Oakmont. For example, only two of its greens have ever been moved. In 1947, when the Pennsylvania Turnpike was cut through the course, the green on the short eighth hole had to be shoved about twenty feet to the left; twenty years before that, for no special reason, a similarly minimal re-siting of the green on the short sixteenth had occurred.

But, more to the point, Oakmont stands as the avatar of the ultra-stringent qualities that the United States Golf Association has always set such store by in choosing and preparing the venue of the national championship. To begin with, it is a long course. (As far back as the 1927 Open, it measured over 6,900 yards — an almost unreasonable length in those days.) Its fairways are kept so narrow for everyday play that this year the U.S.G.A., which always makes it a point to bring the rough in drastically on its Open courses, so that the fairways seldom exceed thirty-five yards in width, had to ask Oakmont to widen two of its fairways. On top of this, Oakmont boasts the fastest greens in America, which also happen to be among the truest. For several Opens, they have been cut to two-thirty-seconds of an inch — three times as short as is standard for the Open. Put it all together and you can understand why Walter Hagen spoke of Oakmont as "the ideal championship spot," and why Tommy Armour called it "the final degree in the college of golf."

As the old saying has it, behind every great golf course is a great man. The man behind Oakmont was Henry C. Fownes — pronounced "phones" — a pioneer Pittsburgh steel magnate, who in 1899, when he was already in his forties, decided to take up golf, a game that his fellow steel-maker Andrew Carnegie once described as "an indispensable adjunct of high civilization." Fownes, a short, compact man, first played his golf on the six holes of the Pittsburgh Field Club, but he switched the next year to the nine-hole Highland Country Club. In a short time, he became a surprisingly able player, particularly skillful around and on the greens. In 1901, he qualified for the United States Amateur and won his first match. He qualified for the Amateur in 1902 and again in 1903, when he won his first three matches. In 1907, when he was in his fifties, he qualified for the Amateur for the last time. There is no record that Fownes travelled to Britain around the turn of the century to play and study the classic courses of Scotland and England, but he obviously read a good deal about them in books and magazines. In 1903, when he made up his mind that the time had come for him to organize a syndicate and build a modern eighteen-hole course, there was no question whatever as to what his goal was: if Pittsburgh's distance from the ocean denied him the opportunity to build an honest-to-goodness British linksland course, he would jolly well build the next best thing possible — a real British moorland course. Assisted by his son, William C., Jr., who had been named for his uncle but was oddly given the "Junior" anyway, Fownes reversed the usual process. He first laid out on paper eighteen sturdy holes and then set out to find a suitable tract of land to build them on. He had been looking for a while when a friend of his, George S. Macrum, who lived in the village of Oakmont, some twelve miles northwest of downtown Pittsburgh, called his attention to a two-hundred-and-twenty-one-acre sweep of gently rolling farmland in that area. After inspecting it and consulting with the members of his syndicate, Fownes purchased the property. At seven o'clock on the morning of September 15, 1903, under the personal direction of the Fowneses, *père et fils*, a work force of a hundred and fifty men, along with twenty-five teams of mules, began construction of the course. Six weeks later, before wintry weather set in, the first twelve holes were completed — the tees and greens built, the drainage ditches dug, and the fairways and greens seeded, the latter with a mixture of South German bent. The next spring, the remaining six holes were finished, and that autumn Oakmont was opened for play. It was not a course to regale the eye. Fownes had had his crew chop down just about every tree in sight except for a few around the gabled clubhouse, and this, coupled with the flattish terrain over which the holes were routed, did indeed give Oakmont the not easily achieved British bleakness that Fownes was after. It was a terribly long course from the start — 6,600 yards from the back of the tees — and saturated with bunkers. Fownes left no doubt about his philosophy of golf. When a man did not hit an almost perfect shot, he was supposed to pay a stiff penalty for his error. From the outset, American golfers agreed on two things about Oakmont: if it was the most punishing course in the country, it was also the best conditioned. Under the Fownes family, it was treated like a living thing. As early as 1906, the club sank ten thousand dollars a year into it. As maintenance costs rose, so did the money set aside for its maintenance. During the Depression years, the Fowneses personally picked up all the bills.

The first national championship held at Oakmont was the 1919 Amateur — Davy Herron, an Oakmont member, defeated seventeen-year-old Bobby Jones in the final — but it was the 1927 U.S. Open that made the golf world really conscious of the course. H. C. Fownes, the club's first president, still held that office, as he would until his death, late in 1935, but he was getting along in years, and W. C. was now running things. Although he was neither as imperious nor as stubborn as his father, W. C. was far from reticent when it came to expressing himself on golfing matters, and with some reason. He was a talented enough player to win the Amateur in 1910, and he qualified for that championship twenty-five times in twenty-seven attempts — a terrific record. He made it a point to know the game from all sides, and after a long administrative career with the U.S.G.A. he served as its president in 1926 and 1927. Where Oakmont was concerned, as the perennial chairman of the green committee he meant to keep it a sanctuary of par in a world gone mad with birdies and eagles, 67s and 65s. Toward this end, beginning in 1920, the bunkers at Oakmont were furrowed — that is, Emil Loeffler, the greenkeeper, combed them with a heavily weighted metal rake whose triangular teeth were two inches long and set two inches apart. Oakmont's bunkers in those days were filled with a coarse brownish sand that came from the Allegheny River, and it had enough body to hold the creases. Exploding a ball from a furrowed greenside bunker wasn't too much of a problem — the golfer simply blasted out the ridge of sand behind the ball along with the ball — but if he caught a furrowed fairway bunker off the tee he could not hope to advance the ball farther than forty yards. A good many golfers felt that this was plain unfair, but the Fowneses had a ready rationalization. The fairways on many of the best British courses, they pointed out, were punctuated by deep, sharp-walled bunkers that restricted the length of the recovery shot. Since bunkers of comparable depth could not be installed at Oakmont — the soil was extremely clayey, and this would have presented a serious drainage problem — the only way to make the shallow bunkers a menace was to furrow them. What with its fearsome bunkers and its glassy greens (which were massaged by a fifteen-hundred-pound roller that required eight men to handle it), not to mention its sheer length (6,965 yards), it was not at all surprising that nobody in the field broke 300 at Oakmont — par 72 — in the 1927 Open. Armour tied for first with Harry Cooper at 301, thirteen over par, and then beat him in the playoff with a 76. Jones, incidentally, never broke 76 on his four rounds.

For the 1935 Open, the U.S.G.A. insisted that the furrowing of the bunkers be considerably modified, but, apart from that concession, Oakmont played at least as hard as it had in 1927. In the interim between the two championships, a good many of the holes had been remodelled, and in the process the course had been extended to 6,981 yards. There were thirty more bunkers than there had been for the 1927 Open, bringing the total to well over two hundred. (The largest was the Sahara, on the short eighth — a monster seventy-five yards long, into which eleven railroad carloads of sand had been dumped.) There were also twenty-one traversing ditches to worry about. Nevertheless, the Fowneses remained eternally fretful that some golfer would come along one day and reduce to a shambles the course they wanted to be accepted as the best test in the world. Gene Sarazen loves to recall a fascinating incident that took place about a month before the 1935 Open. One weekend when W. C. was out of town, a visiting power hitter carried a bunker on the seventh fairway — about two hundred and forty yards from the tee — that no one was supposed to carry. Loeffler, following instructions for such emergencies, immediately telephoned W. C. and reported what had taken place. W. C. did not terminate his weekend then and there and hop the next plane back, but the first thing he did when he returned on Monday was to go out to the seventh hole and, after appropriate study, order Loeffler to put in a small, flat bunker just beyond the one that had been carried. Measure for measure. In the 1935 Open, only one man broke 300. This was Sam Parks, Jr., a young pro from the Pittsburgh area, who drove well, carefully thought out his approach shots to the extremely firm greens, putted steadily, and brought in a total of 299. No one in the entire field broke 70. On the last round, none of the twenty leaders broke 75. Really!

W. C. Fownes succeeded his father as president of Oakmont in 1935, and continued to head up the club's green committee — W. C.'s first love. In 1949, the year before his death, his duties were assumed by an eighteen-man board. In November of that year, this board declared that it was well aware it had "inherited what had become known as the finest golf course in America" and dedicated itself to perpetuating Oakmont's lofty traditions. Under the new leadership, a few bunkers were filled in and the speed of the greens was reduced a shade. As a result, the course that the field confronted in the 1953 Open was a somewhat more humane proposition. That was one of the two reasons Oakmont was at length tamed by Ben Hogan, whose winning total was 283, five strokes under par. The second reason was that Hogan seldom in his long career hit the ball with such supernal control throughout four rounds. In this general connection, a few weeks ago, before the recent Open, a visitor to Oakmont happened to ask Frank Ingersoll, a contemporary and close friend of W. C.'s, what would have been Fownes' reaction had he been around to watch Hogan dominate the course so thoroughly. Would he have saluted Hogan for the brilliance of his shotmaking or would he have been chagrined that par had finally been flaunted? "Bill Fownes was in the habit, as you may know, of going out onto the course at regular intervals and checking on how the different holes were playing," Ingersoll said, in a slow, thin voice. "He'd go out to some hole and sit there on his shooting stick for three or four days. If he saw that a lot of drives were ending up safely in a certain spot, he'd do something to tighten up the shot — put in a new trap or extend the rough or enlarge an old trap. No, I don't think he would have been delighted by Hogan's performance. No, I think he would have probably said to himself, 'It's your own fault, Fownes. If you had spent more time out on the course studying how the holes were playing, this never would have happened.' "

There was an unusual sense of excitement in the air at Oakmont on the eve of the 1973 Open. While returning to a storied championship course generally produces this feeling, a good deal of it was directly attributable, I believe, to the high drama that had marked the last previous Open at Oakmont, back in 1962, when Arnold Palmer and Jack Nicklaus, after tying at 283 (the same total as Hogan's nine years before), met in the playoff in their first head-to-head confrontation, with Nicklaus winning by three strokes. For this year's championship, the course measured twenty-seven yards longer than it had in 1962. Par was again 71, as it had been in 1962, by which time the first hole had been converted from a short par 5 into a long par 4. There were more bunkers to worry about — thirty-three more, bringing the total to a hundred and eighty-seven. No furrowing, though. That indulgence had ended around 1964, when the sand from the Allegheny had thinned to silt. Now the bunkers were filled with finely ground 5Q rock from Mapleton, Pennsylvania, and raked smooth. The evening before the start of the tournament, I made a call on Lou Scalzo, Oakmont's exceptionally able superintendent, who, after caddying for a few years at the club, joined the greenkeeping crew forty-three years ago. Scalzo said he was quite pleased with the condition of the course, considering how wet the spring had been. "That heavy thunderstorm yesterday didn't help," he went on. "We'd like our greens to be a little faster for putting and not quite so soft for holding the approach shots. With a good break in the weather, though, they should get faster and firmer pretty quickly."

Thursday, the day of the opening round, was a perfect day for golf, the air dry and not too hot. The course played very well. Only one man broke 70 — Gary Player, the neat, precise little South African, whose neat, precise 67 put him three strokes in the lead. Player's performance was somewhat unexpected, inasmuch as he had undergone a fairly serious bladder operation in February and had not joined the American golf tour until three weeks before. The most sensational shot of the day, though, was made by Nicklaus, the top favorite, who, it might be mentioned here and now, hit the ball erratically throughout the tournament and remained in contention only because of his great fighting powers. This shot came on the seventeenth, for years an ugly, mongrel par 4 of some 300 yards which climbed straight up the lumpy face of a hill to a green surrounded by bunkers, except for a narrow opening at the left. Ben Hogan drove and birdied it in 1953, and Palmer drove and eagled it in 1962 — this on the poorest of all the holes the Fowneses had designed. For the 1973 Open, it had been tastefully revised: a new and longer tee was built to the left of the old one, and an arcing fairway was swung out to the right. With the hole now measuring 322 yards, the green was out of range of the Goliaths from the new, angled tee unless a good breeze happened to be behind them. There was one that afternoon, and Nicklaus, fretful at being two over par, was in just the mood to go for broke. His drive landed in the rough about fourteen feet short of the green, hopped on on its first bounce, and rolled to within twelve feet of the pin. He made the eagle putt. That tee shot must have carried close to three hundred yards, uphill, but it wasn't its sheer power that was memorable. It was the beautiful timing with which the shot was struck and its consequent pinpoint accuracy.

That evening, with the greens having attained just about the right degree of speed and receptivity, in their opinion, P. J. Boatwright, the executive director of the U.S.G.A., and Harry Easterly, the chairman of the U.S.G.A.'s championship committee, met with Scalzo to determine what steps, if any, should be taken to keep the greens playing that way the next day. It was finally agreed to sprinkle them for five minutes, which was done, but somehow or other — partly because there was already so much water in the ground and partly because of unexplained reasons — on Friday the greens were as soft as pudding. The players were quick to perceive that they could bang their approaches right for the pins and that there was no need to be squeamishly fastidious when faced with, say, a five-foot sidehill putt — the kind that often at Oakmont leaves you with a six-footer coming back if you have been unlucky enough to catch the high corner of the cup, even with the most gentle, gossamer tap imaginable. The handwriting was on the wall early in the day when Gene Borek, a club pro from Long Island, who is an excellent golfer but who makes only occasional appearances on the tournament circuit, brought in a 65, to set a new competitive course record. All in all, no less than twenty-seven golfers broke or equalled par. Player, with a 70, for a halfway total of 137, was still out in front — by a stroke — but there was already a suspicion of strain in his play, and the chances of his holding on didn't look too sanguine when one studied the leader board and saw such names as Palmer and Nicklaus, Lee Trevino, Tom Weiskopf, Julius Boros, and Lanny Wadkins bunched behind him. Indeed, the only three "big names" not in the running were Billy Casper, Bruce Crampton, and Tony Jacklin.

Whatever chance Oakmont had to snap back and become its slick old intimidating self was gone for good when Saturday morning brought several hours of heavy rain. Indeed, at one point it looked as if the third round would have to be abandoned. The downpour stopped just in time, however, and play continued through a humid, steamy afternoon periodically interrupted by showers. Under these conditions, the main consideration of the players was to keep out of the thick, wet rough. If they did that, what with Oakmont playing so slow, there was no need to worry about such subtleties as driving down the side of the fairway that offered the best opening to the green or trying to place an approach shot, loaded with backspin, on the side of the pin that presented the least treacherous contours. When the third round was over, a good deal had happened, and yet, in a way, nothing had. At the start of the day, fourteen players had been clustered within six strokes of the leader, Player; at the end of the day, after some shuffling around, eight players were within five strokes of the four men who now shared the lead, at three under par — Palmer, Boros, John Schlee, and Jerry Heard. Heard, with a 66, had made up the most ground, and Player, with a 77, had lost the most. Ahead lay the possibility of one of the great last days in Open history, particularly since Palmer, the adored local hero — he comes from Latrobe, which is only thirty miles from Pittsburgh — stood on the verge of winning a major championship for the first time in nine long years. En route to a 68 on the third round, he had looked like the Palmer of old when he erupted with a burst of birdies on the ninth, tenth, and eleventh holes, and there was a youthful vigor to his manner, ascribable in some degree, perhaps, to the fact that he had been paired with Boros, who, at fifty-three, is ten years his senior. A two-time winner of our Open, in 1952 and 1963, Boros has put on quite a bit of weight and now pads down the fairways at a sort of ursine lope, but age has not affected the lovely tempo of his swing or his almost disdainful calmness under pressure. The most dramatic shots of the day, far and away, were the series of longish putts he holed down the stretch to save critical pars. As for the best lines of the day, I would say they were uttered by Schlee, a student of astrology, when he explained why he was playing so well: "My horoscope is just outstanding. Mars is in conjunction with my natal moon."

What had Johnny Miller been doing all this time? His first two rounds were a par 71 followed by a 69 that was nowhere near as solid as the score might indicate — he had holed putts from all over the greens. On the third round, he had apparently shot himself out of the tournament with a wild 76. Partnered with Miller Barber, he began his final round on a muggy, overcast Sunday six full shots behind the four co-leaders, and playing seven pairs in front of the final twosome. With such a large number of fine golfers jockeying for the lead, it was not surprising that the spectators paid scant attention to Miller as they buzzed frenetically around the front nine trying to see as much as they could of the play of the last five twosomes: Nicklaus and Gene Littler, Jim Colbert and Trevino, Bob Charles and Weiskopf, Palmer and Schlee, Boros and Heard. There was a lot to see. For example, on the second hole, a drive-and-pitch par 4, Nicklaus picked up his birdie 3. So did the next four men to play the hole — Colbert, Trevino, Charles, and Weiskopf. (Trevino's putt was the first one of any length he had made all week, and I remember wondering if that might set the tough little Texan off.) When Heard came along and birdied the second, he moved into the undisputed lead, at four under par. Fifteen minutes later, we had a new leader — Palmer; he had birdied the long fourth, after which Heard bogeyed it. Twenty minutes later, we had another new leader — Boros; after birdieing the fourth, he had birdied the sixth, which Palmer had just bogeyed. And so it went, Boros, Palmer, and Weiskopf eventually making the turn four under par, with Trevino, Schlee, and Heard a stroke off their pace.

I mention these figures because I think they help to explain to some extent why it caused so little stir when the news went up on the scoreboards, while the leaders were still moving over the front nine, that Miller was two under par for the tournament — and five under par for the round — after eleven holes. A tall (six-three), supple twenty-six-year-old Californian, Miller has a history of shooting red-hot rounds in the low 60s, but not when they really count. Conversely, he has also been known to falter at the critical stages of important events. The 1971 Masters is the first instance that comes to mind. On the last round, after he had overhauled and passed the leaders with a splurge of birdies, he threw it all away by missing his pars on two of the last three holes. A highly emotional young man, his tactics under pressure have frequently been questionable, and never more so than on the sixteenth (or seventieth) hole of that Masters — a 190-yard par 3 on which the pin was positioned that afternoon on a raised terrace at the back right-hand corner of the green, dangerously close to a bunker. Under the circumstances, the right shot for Miller was a safe iron to the middle of the green — to make sure of his par — but he went boldly for the pin, caught the rear bunker, failed to make his par, and opened the door for Charles Coody, the winner. On occasion, Miller's nerves have let him down. For example, this winter, through a strange lapse on the seventy-first hole at Bermuda Dunes, he lost a marvellous opportunity to tie Palmer in the Bob Hope Desert Classic. Just off the green with his iron on this par-3 hole, facing a run-of-the-mill little chip shot, he ran the ball a full twenty feet past the cup. (I can only guess that in his preoccupation with hitting a ringingly crisp chip he lost his concentration.) No one has ever disputed Miller's superior golfing talent, though. He first came to attention under rather remarkable circumstances in 1966, when the Open was scheduled to be played at the Olympic Country Club in San Francisco, which he belonged to. Determined to be part of the championship in some capacity, Miller, a handsome, blond young man, who was then nineteen and attending Brigham Young University, signed up for the caddie corps, but then he went out and qualified for a place in the Open starting field and ended up by finishing in a tie for eighth place. He turned professional in 1969. There are times when his long, lashing swing — the reverse of Heard's in its complicatedness — seems too ornate for consistent control, but on his day Miller can be absolutely dazzling. For one thing, no one in the game sticks his irons so close to the flag. Two of his six birdies on the first eleven holes of the last round, for example, were the result of phenomenal approaches: on the first, he put a 3-iron five feet from the pin, and on the second he put a 9-iron a foot from the pin. (His four other birdies came when he holed a twenty-five-foot putt on the third, exploded from a bunker to within six inches of the cup on the long fourth, reached the long ninth in two with a 2-iron, and holed from fourteen feet on the eleventh.) Still, at that point in the afternoon, few people at Oakmont viewed Miller as a prospective victor. I know I didn't. His sensational closing dash, like almost all sensational closing dashes, would, I felt, fall a stroke or two short. As need hardly be said, there is a world of difference between coming close and actually winning.

The player the majority of the gallery wanted to see win was, of course, Palmer. For a while, it seemed that he had been ordained by fate to do so. After scraping out his par on the tenth despite driving close to a tree in the rough and then slashing his recovery over the green into a bunker, he punched a lovely little pitch six feet from the pin on the eleventh, a short par 4. Now if he dropped the putt, that birdie would put him five under par for the tournament — out in front all by himself, as far as he knew at that moment, although, up ahead, Miller had by then gone five under par. Palmer struck the putt smoothly, but it veered off the line in the last few inches. The psychological moment had passed for him. His rooters seemed to sense it, and so did Palmer. In any event, a sudden decline in the calibre of his play ensued. He failed to make his pars on the next three holes. He was out of it.

At approximately the same time that Palmer's slide began, Miller was striding up the eighteenth, on his way to a par that would wrap up a thoroughly stunning day's work. It was hard to believe, but it was a fact: he now stood five under par for the tournament (and eight under for the day), and he had swept into the lead. Instead of wavering down the stretch, he had continued to play superlative golf, attacking all the way, but prudently, flying one full-blooded iron after another right for the top of the flagstick. On the long twelfth, after driving into the rough, he hit his third shot, a 4-iron, fifteen feet from the pin and sank the putt. He followed this with another birdie on the 185-yard thirteenth, where he hit a 4-iron to five feet. On the fourteenth, a solid par. On the fifteenth, a 453-yard par 4 commonly regarded as the most difficult hole on the course, he made still another birdie: a 280-yard drive, a 4-iron to ten feet, a perfect putt. On the short sixteenth, a good, sure par. On the seventeenth, after barely missing a birdie from ten feet, a tap-in for his par. On the par-4 eighteenth, 456 yards long, he finished in style: he was nicely on in two (with a 5-iron) and down in two. His figures were 32–31 — 63, for a four-round total of 279. Ahead of him, despite his euphoria, lay an uncomfortable hour of sweating out the players still on the course, but whereas they had made a profusion of birdies on the front nine, now that they needed them desperately there were few to be had. Schlee, in fact, was the only contender who mounted a real challenge, birdieing the sixteenth and coming very close on the last two holes to picking up the remaining birdie he had to get to tie Miller. In retrospect, several of his putts could have been more in conjunction with the cup, but the old zodiac had given it a damn good try.

Miller's 63 is the lowest round ever shot in our national championship. It is also the lowest final round ever shot by the winner of any major championship, eclipsing Palmer's final 65 in the 1960 Open, at Cherry Hills, near Denver, and Nicklaus's matching 65 in the 1967 Open at Baltusrol. It was an astounding effort in that Miller was on each green in the regulation stroke and that his card — shades of Jones at Sunningdale in 1926 — contained not a single 5. Incidentally, he had twenty-nine putts, including three on one green, the eighth. Impressive as are these statistics (and the sustained high level of the courageous shotmaking that underlay them), I would suggest that we are still too close to Miller's round to appreciate its full significance. Over the century and a quarter since the invention of the gutta-percha ball made golf a vital international game, there have been many stupefying feats of scoring — such as Young Tom Morris's 149 for thirty-six holes in the 1870 British Open — but I would guess that the thousands who saw Miller's 63 at Oakmont and the millions who followed it on television witnessed one of the genuinely epic rounds of all time.

For the past few days, I have been wondering what Henry C. Fownes and William C. Fownes, Jr., would have made of that 63. I am sure they would have pointed out that it was made over an Oakmont that played nothing like the way Oakmont usually plays. I have an idea they would have suggested politely but emphatically that Miller, for all the inspiration of his golf, could never have placed his approaches so close to the pins or holed so many sizable putts had the greens possessed their characteristic temper. I can hear H. C. saying, "With the greens that soft, it was more like darts than golf," and I can see W. C. nodding his head in vigorous agreement. In a way — and this, to be sure, detracts not in the least from Miller's achievement — many of us who were at Oakmont were saddened when the rains took almost all of the fire out of the course, for there are so few old-fashioned, cantankerous, proudly individual tests like Oakmont left in a world of golf architecture that is becoming ever more svelte and superficial. Consequently, we had been looking forward keenly to seeing how the outstanding contemporary players would fare in their confrontation with this outstanding classic course. Well, I guess we'll just have to wait until the nineteen-eighties and hope that when the Open next returns to Oakmont the special qualities of the course will not be diluted by the weather.

(1973)

Bernard Darwin

As befitted a grandson of Charles Darwin, Bernard Darwin (1876–1961)
set out to study law. Finding the life of a solicitor dull, he became a
barrister. However, that kind of work palled on him also, and in 1907 he
boldly did what he wanted to do: he wrote about golf for The Times *and*
for Country Life, *a weekly magazine. Considered by Sir John Squire to be*
one of the six best essayists since Lamb, he wrote on a wide spectrum of
topics, from Dickens to famous murders, but, thank goodness, golf was
his first love, and Darwin devoted more time to it than to any other
subject.

THERE IS LITTLE DISAGREEMENT THAT THE BEST GOLF WRITER OF
all time was an Englishman named Bernard Richard Meirion
Darwin. Beyond this, there is a large body of readers, made up not
only of golf addicts but of addicts of other sports, who believe that
Bernard Darwin may well be the finest talent who has ever written
about sports, not excluding such towering figures as William
Hazlitt, Leo Tolstoy, William Faulkner, Siegfried Sassoon, and
Ernest Hemingway, all of whom occasionally wandered into the
field, or such regular writers on sports as Pierce Egan, Robert
Surtees, Ring Lardner, Neville Cardus (who was equally impressive reporting on both cricket and music for the *Guardian*), A. J.
Liebling, and Joe Palmer — to name some of those who come
most quickly to mind. Although Darwin's books for the most part
were published only in England, for decades they have been the
keystone of American golf libraries and have been faithfully read
and reread. This year, in this country and throughout the golf
world in general, there will be even more interest than usual in
Darwin, since 1976 marks the centennial — or, as they say in Brit-

ain, the centenary (pronounced "centeen'ry") — of his birth. A host of tributes will be paid him, with one of the most significant being the publication of a book about Darwin (containing many selections from his work) by Peter Ryde, himself a writer of the first order, who succeeded Darwin as the golf correspondent of the *Times* of London in 1953 — eight years before Darwin's death, at the age of eighty-five. (The book, entitled *Mostly Golf*, is due out this autumn.) I myself am often reminded of Darwin — whom I was fortunate enough to know — but never more so than when I attend some significant golfing occasion, such as this year's Masters tournament. We will get to that later.

As a man of exceptional ability and enormous personal charm, Bernard Darwin would undoubtedly have made his way in the world whatever his background, but it would be wrong not to acknowledge that interest in him and his work was inevitably heightened by the fact that he was a grandson of Charles Darwin, the great naturalist, who propounded his theory of evolution in 1859. The Darwins were and are an exceptionally brainy family. Certainly the seven children of Charles Darwin were an uncommonly gifted lot. Of the five sons, three were knighted in recognition of contributions to science: George was a Cambridge professor of astronomy and experimental philosophy; Francis, Bernard's father, an M.D. who never practiced medicine, became a prominent botanist; and Horace was an outstanding civil engineer. As for the two other sons, William was a banker, and Leonard, a major in the Royal Engineers, found his real lifework in eugenics and economics after leaving the military. As it turned out, Bernard, as a very young boy, saw quite a bit of his illustrious grandfather. Bernard's mother died when he was born, and Francis Darwin moved, with his son, from a small house in Downe, Kent, to the large house, in that same lovely, tranquil village, where his mother and father lived. Charles Darwin died in 1882 (Bernard was six then), and although Charles' widow continued to use the house at Downe for a summer home, the family moved to Cambridge. Some forty-four years later, in 1926, Bernard returned to Downe — though not to the old ancestral home — with his wife and their three children, and he lived there until his wife's death, in 1954.

It would have been most unusual if a member of a family as distinguished as the Darwins had chosen to plunge directly into golf writing as a career. Bernard didn't. While he was growing up, he followed the accepted educational path trodden in those days by the sons of upper-level, well-to-do families: He spent two years at a local primary school (Perse) in Cambridge; at eleven he was shipped off to boarding school (Summer Fields, near Oxford), where he starred as a Latin student; and from there he moved on to "public" school (Eton) and thence to a university (Cambridge, where his college was Trinity). Darwin's years at public school were remarkably happy ones, and throughout his life he had a very warm spot in his heart for Eton. He liked Cambridge all right, but confessed many years later, "As an institution for beating Oxford it has my deepest, perennially boyish devotion, but as for my own time there I have always been conscious of something missing."

At Cambridge, Darwin started by reading for the Classical Tripos (examinations for an honors degree), but in his third term he switched to the Law Tripos. After graduation, he went down to London and set out to be a solicitor, joining two Cambridge friends in a firm in the Temple. He underwent some private coaching and later passed the Solicitor's Final with no trouble. He appears to have been a competent solicitor, but the work bored him, and he soon decided that he would perhaps find the career of a barrister more to his liking. After three years of attending the required dinners in chambers and passing the necessary examinations, he was called to the bar in 1903. A few of his cases interested him, but for the most part he felt a dismaying coolness toward a profession that many embrace with unmodified ardor. In 1907 — mind you, Darwin by then was thirty years old — the pivotal moment in his life occurred: The golf writer of the *Evening Standard*, who was moving over to the *Morning Post*, recommended Darwin as his successor to do the weekly golf column, "Tee Shots." Darwin jumped at the chance. There was nothing seriously wrong with law, he conceded, but he had long since discovered that his true passion was golf. Now his first taste of professional journalism confirmed his suspicion that he had been throwing his life away. In 1908 — by which time he was writing about golf for the *Times* and also for the weekly magazine *Country Life* — he sold his wig and, as he later said, "walked out of the Temple a free man."

*

For the *Times*, Darwin reported the important tournaments and also undertook a regular Saturday essay-type feature on some phase or other of the game. His Saturday columns attracted a good deal of attention from the start, as did his slightly longer and more ruminative articles for *Country Life*. Down through the years, batches of his *Country Life* pieces and his Saturday columns for the *Times* were collected at intervals in such popular books as *Out of the Rough*, *Rubs of the Green*, *Playing the Like*, and *Second Shots*. Besides his felicitous style, Darwin had another big thing going for him: he knew golf inside out. He had started playing it at the age of eight, at Felixstowe, a resort on the North Sea, in Suffolk, where his father took his summer holiday for a number of years. Later, Francis Darwin shifted from Felixstowe to Cromer, in Norfolk, and then to Eastbourne, in Sussex, on the Channel. He was the first of the Darwins to take up the new game — "new" in that in 1889 only fifty-seven golf clubs had been organized in England. Until the middle of the century, in fact, there had been practically no clubs south of the Scottish border. Francis Darwin had been converted to golf by his brother-in-law Arthur Ruck. Mrs. Ruck, Bernard's grandmother, was Welsh, and the Ruck family had come to live in the Welsh county of Merioneth, in the Aberdovey area. Arthur, with his brother Richard, had laid out the first rudimentary nine-hole course in Aberdovey. Richard Ruck was later responsible for founding the Aberdovey Golf Club and designing its eighteen-hole course. Bernard, throughout his life, regularly returned to play this Welsh course, which he loved for deep and multiple reasons, but one gathers that when he was a boy Felixstowe was his favorite, partly because he liked the quality of the links and partly because the well-known Scottish professional Willie Fernie, who had won the British Open in 1883, was the resident pro. The portrait of his boyhood hero, which Darwin dashed off in quick brushstrokes many decades later, is well worth quoting, for it is wonderfully typical of the verve that infuses his writing:

His shop was opposite the Martello tower and close to the second tee, the starting-point of my daily adventures, so I had plenty of chances of adoring him in his yachting cap with a shiny peak and his white apron, as he came outside to waggle a half-finished club. He had in my eyes rather a fierce, buccaneering air, and fear mingled with my worship. I did not dare to go into the shop, unless my father was with me. It was a paradise of glue and pitch, of files and a vise, and heads in the rough, with a smell that still comes gratefully back to me. "God bless me," as Mr. Borthrop Trumbull (in "Middlemarch") remarked of the ham, "what an aroma!"

Literary quotations of this type in Darwin are as abundant as parsley on a roast. By far the highest number of them come from Dickens, several of whose books Darwin apparently knew by heart almost from cover to cover.

Spurred by an intense and exuberant devotion to the game from boyhood on, Darwin developed into a very capable golfer, who could be accurately classified as standing just a cut below the players who win championships. Well over six feet, and bony in build — he filled out in his later years — he had an effective but hardly graceful swing. He had been brought up in the days of the gutta-percha ball, and his effortful method reflected this. It was initiated by a backswing in which, his body bristling with tension, he took the club back well beyond the ideal position, in which the shaft is parallel to the ground. Then, with something less than a relaxed, Sneadian lyricism, he uncorked his downswing and hurled the club vehemently at the ball. However, as I say, he was a very good golfer. At Cambridge, he was on the university team, and captained it in his last year. He was selected to play for England against Scotland in 1902, and was a member of the English team in seven of the traditional International Matches. He won the prized *Golf Illustrated* Gold Vase in 1919 and the President's Putter competition of the Oxford and Cambridge Golfing Society in 1924. His two greatest triumphs were scored in the British Amateur and the Walker Cup. In 1921, a group of eight Americans, including Bobby Jones, Chick Evans, and Francis Ouimet, entered the Amateur at Hoylake. The British, traditional leaders in golf, did not feel exactly comfortable about this invasion. As it happened, during the early rounds at Hoylake, the men whom the British were counting on most heavily were eliminated, and when the amateur field had been whittled down to the last sixteen survivors the worst seemed imminent. Darwin, who was still in the tournament, rose to the occasion. In the morning, when the round of sixteen was played, he defeated Paul Hunter, a sound golfer from Chicago, and in the quarter-finals, in the afternoon, he ousted the last American threat, Fred Wright. That evening, as Darwin was walking down a street in a nearby village, a man with a menacingly intense stare — Darwin couldn't place him — bore down on him and confronted him eye to eye. Then, in a ringing voice thick with emotion, he blurted, "Sir, I want to thank you for the way you have saved your country." Darwin's Walker Cup experience took place in 1922 and has the quality of one of those dreams of glory every boy nourishes. This, the first official meeting of the best British and Irish amateurs with the best American amateurs, was scheduled to be held at the National Golf Links, in Southampton, Long Island. The *Times* sent Darwin over to report on it. Just before the match, Robert Harris, the British captain, fell ill, and Darwin was drafted to take his place, both as the team captain and as a player. He did quite well. Although he and Cyril Tolley were handled roughly in their foursome against Ouimet and Jesse Guilford, Darwin won his singles from Bill Fownes, 3 and 1.

Certainly no one has ever tried harder than Darwin did to become a top-class golfer. The game meant the world to him. He threw every last grain of concentration and willpower into his tournament play, and, being a man with an extremely high-strung temperament and a very short fuse, he sometimes simply could not control his frustration when things went wrong. His eruptions were often so spectacular and, from a safe distance, so hilarious that even today, years after they took place, it remains a regular pastime of his old friends to sit around of an evening retailing Darwin stories. Darwin was well aware of his predilection on the golf course for suddenly losing control of himself when he had played a series of bad shots. He came to believe that such a drastic change in personality is common to most golfers, and he elaborated on this in a memorable essay called "Hydes and Jekylls." In the foreword to his Darwin anthology, Peter Ryde made this adroit comment: "He [Darwin] was too agitated a player even to become a good putter and this may have prevented him from ever reaching the top in the game. His opponent in that Worplesdon final remembers him muttering as he addressed the ball for a short chip from off the green made with an old cleek, 'Now then Darwin, come along Darwin, come along, keep it smooth,' and occasionally, 'Oh Darwin, you bloody fool.' The patter sounds like the remedy for some incipient twitch, especially as it was accompanied by a leapfrog movement of the clubhead behind and in front of the ball before the stroke was played. He had a peculiar horror, once he was in the lead, of the holes slipping away. Once, in writing about himself in the Worplesdon Foursomes, he described how, seized with the old terror of this happening, he went 'weakly and weakly' into bunkers in front of his nose."

Except when he was tempting the fates on the golf course, Darwin was an essentially warm and kind person and a most lovable one. He was revered by his friends, who called him Bernardo. Although a happy family man, he was also a member of that species of Englishman who relishes his hours at his club sharing his enthusiasms with his cronies. At the same time, any picture of Darwin would be incomplete if it didn't mention that during certain stretches when his "perennially boyish" side was in the ascendant — and no one recognized this more clearly than he did — he was sometimes unable to check a mood of arrant stubbornness or impatience or to resist getting off a stingingly witty phrase. At the Commonwealth Tournament, at St. Andrews, in 1955, for example, his aesthetic sense was appalled by a sweater with a repeating pattern of loud, clashing yellow, pink, black, green, and violet vertical stripes, which one of the Canadian players wore. Darwin kept himself well under control for a while, but finally went up to the Canadian and asked, "I say, are those your old school colors or your own unfortunate choice?"

Darwin was a man with lively, speculative dark eyes, who in his earlier years wore a rather dashing mustache. He wrote on a great many subjects besides golf. He produced several children's books, for instance, as well as two books on Dickens, a guide to the historic landmarks of London, an appreciation of the English public school, and biographies of W. G. Grace, the famous cricketer, and John Gully, a bare-knuckles boxing champion who later became a Member of Parliament. At seventy-eight, Darwin published his autobiography, *The World That Fred Made*. (Fred was the name of the family gardener, who in the eyes of Bernard Darwin's young grandson could do or make anything, and it was also the name of his own grandfather's groom, whom Bernard had felt the same way about when he was a boy.) During Darwin's forty-five-year association with the *Times*, he frequently contributed "fourth leaders" — light, humorous pieces that followed the various lead editorials. However, the literary form he seems to have found most to his taste was the personal essay, and some of his most enjoyable books are collections of pieces on golf and sports in general, mixed with thoughts on a gallimaufry of other interests. In the twenty-nine essays in *Every Idle Dream*, a typical collection,

Darwin elaborates on such varied subjects as his boyhood attachment for tin soldiers; the sporting prints on the walls of his study; his "fundamentalist's" faith in Sherlockiana; Rufus, the family dachshund; his affection for small railroad junctions situated thrillingly close to some favorite golf links; his admiration for the vitality that Walter Shirley brought to his book *Leading Cases in the Common Law*; the requisites for a successful picnic; the Christmas spirit; his fondness for the Cotswolds (where during the Second World War he and his family sought refuge from the aerial pounding the enemy gave their corner of Kent); the pleasures of a day spent in bed, provided one's ailment is merely a mild one; the magic that results when an author has the knack of selecting appropriate names for his characters; the "restful excitement" of watching a cricket match; and Tony Weller, of *Pickwick Papers*, whose shrewd worldliness he rated a cut above that of Weller's son Sam. What distinguishes these pieces from the rambles of most essayists is the way Darwin wanders back and forth between life and literature as if there were no boundary. His contemporaries were enchanted by this penchant of his, but, of course, most of their lives were lived at a time when the TV set had not yet superseded a good read as the choicest entertainment available at home.

While Darwin wrote well on all the subjects he tackled, most of his readers have always felt that he was at his best when writing about golf, and I agree. He certainly saw the game much more completely then anyone else who has written about it. Nothing that touched on it was too slight to have meaning for him and to evoke a substantial response. By way of illustration, the penultimate paragraph of the essay mentioned earlier about railroad junctions goes like this:

Lastly, I come to the best of all junctions. I have seen it looming in the distance all the time, and so, I fear, must anyone who has ever read any book of mine. I need scarcely say that it is Dovey Junction where there is, in a Stevensonian phrase, an infinite melancholy piping of porters: "Change for Aberdovey, Towyn, and Barmouth way." There is, I think, something about the Welsh voice, or intonation, which has a natural melancholy. When the little boys at Moat Lane Junction . . . used to cry . . . "Papers, chocolates, cigarettes," it was with an unutterable sadness. So at Aberdovey, when the caddie, perched on the sleepered crest of the Cader bunker, announces, "On the green," it is not in a tone of triumphant delight but rather of resignation to inevitable fate. It is only when the cry is, "In the bunker," that a measure of cheerfulness seems to break in. I write in the present tense, but alas! it should be in the past, for the more sophisticated caddies of today remain silent and only signal our fortune, good or bad, with the hand.

Like no other golf writer, Darwin had the ability to take the reader right out onto the course with him. You can practically feel the wind in your face and the crunch of the hard-packed turf under your spikes. There are countless passages that illustrate this gift of Darwin's, but I have always particularly admired his description of Walter Hagen's rush down the stretch at Hoylake in the 1924 British Open, when the championship had narrowed to a two-man fight between Hagen and Ernest Whitcombe, an English pro. Whitcombe had just finished with a 78 — a highly commendable effort, inasmuch as he had gone out in 43 — when Hagen came to the tenth green needing to hole a twenty-foot putt to save his par. It was a critical stroke, for Hagen had wobbled out in 41, and to beat Whitcombe's total he would have to play the last nine in 36 — a tall order at Hoylake. Hagen made the putt. Now to Darwin's narrative:

With that putt began as fine a stern chase as could be imagined. It divides itself in my mind into two distinct periods: the first a brave scramble, the second a triumphant march. He had made a mistake at the Dee and recovered from it; he made a mistake at the Alps, at the Hilbre, at the Rushes, yet his net loss from those four errors was just one shot, so indomitable were his recoveries. At the Rushes he seemed a beaten man when he pitched a feeble tee-shot slap into a bunker in front of the green. "That's done it," said a famous golfer standing near to me. "He can never do it now." But Hagen took a good long look, pitched beautifully out of the bunker and ran down a five-foot putt. And then suddenly it seemed certain that he would do it. There was no holding a man who could recover and keep on recovering like that. True, he still wanted four 4s and a 5 to win — perfect play and that over the severest finishing holes in all golf. Still, it was borne in on us that he would do it, and Hagen looked as if he thought so too. He cast away that recovering mood. He looked no longer grave but radiant, and he played faultlessly.

Bang, bang, went his long wooden club shots, as straight as arrows, to the Field, the Lake, and the Dun. Now he wanted two 4s to win, and who that saw it will forget that wholehearted long iron shot smashed right up to the Royal green, with the road on one side and the bunker creeping in on the other? That finally did it. Hagen played the home hole with the very palpable intention of making sure of his 5 and so at least tying with Whitcombe. His second was a bold one and over the green. What happened after that I could not see. I could only hear, "He's played a good run-up, but he isn't dead," and then, after an infinite wait, "He's holed it." If ever there were a case for our friends "the ranks of Tuscany" who could "scarce forbear to cheer," this was the one.

That spurt was one for all the golfing ages. Whitcombe's spurt was as fine a one, but there is this difference between the two, as there is so often between Hagen and the other man. Hagen just won and the other man just didn't.

Possibly because he had personally experienced the rigors of competitive golf, Darwin was peerless in sensing the moods of the players. Not surprisingly, he had an especial affection for and understanding of that exceptional young American Robert T. Jones, Jr. Here is Darwin beginning a retrospective account of Jones's victory in the British Open in 1927:

> When he came back next year to defend his title at St. Andrews, having in the meanwhile won the American Open at Scioto, he played unquestionably better; he enjoyed the greatest single triumph he ever had here, but there seems much less to say about it, for the reason that it was "his" championship, he was winning all the while. By this time St. Andrews had taken a thorough hold on him. He was amused by its problems; he knew whereabouts were its hidden bunkers and was not annoyed by them, as some people never cease to be, because they are hidden; he had devised some three different ways of playing the Long Hole In according to the wind; he had realized that for a player of his parts the Road Hole need hold no excessive terrors, unless he is overambitious. In short he had proved the truth of Mrs. Malaprop's saying that " 'Tis safest in matrimony to begin with a little aversion," for he was now thoroughly in love with the Old Course and played it as if he loved it.

There was no one like Darwin, either, when it came to painting vivid scenes of the big moments in the championships — scenes that stay forever crisp and clear in the reader's mind. Here is how he ended that account of Jones at St. Andrews in 1927:

> His second to the last hole was a little cautious and ended in the Valley of Sin. Thence he ran it up dead and as he scaled the bank the crowd stormed up after him and lined the edge of the green, barely restraining themselves. He holed his short one and the next instant there was no green visible, only a dark seething mass, in the

midst of which was Bobby hoisted on fervent shoulders and holding his putter, "Calamity Jane," at arm's length over his head lest
she be crushed to death.

What produced the singularly vibrant enthusiasm that underlies Darwin's writing? Having pondered the question for years, I
would think that, when all is said and done, the answer lies in the
excitable and responsive nature of his personality. He fell madly
in love with games as a boy — indeed, invented imaginary rugby,
cricket, and soccer leagues of his own — and he stayed in love
with them all his life. Golf he loved most of all. He was hopelessly
enchanted by every aspect of the game and the special milieu that
grew up around it. This shows in the golf anthology he put together and in everything he wrote about golf, whether it is his
coverage (both immediate and reflective) of tournaments; an instruction book on which he collaborated with George Duncan; his
full-length biography of James Braid, the great professional; or his
mammoth book on golf-course architecture. But perhaps it comes
through most clearly of all in his essays, and particularly his humorous essays — a form of golf writing that hardly existed before
Darwin and disappeared abruptly with his passing. A good example of this type of piece, in my opinion, is one he did about Leo
Diegel, an outstanding American pro of the era after the First
World War, who was best known for his eccentric method of
putting, in which his elbows were stretched out stiffly like the
wings of an airplane as he crouched low over his putter, his chin
almost resting on the top of the shaft. Darwin moves directly to
the heart of his subject:

> I diegel, thou diegelest, he or she diegels, we all diegel or are
> about to diegel; and I trust that no golfer needs telling that the verb
> which I am conjugating signifies to try to imitate the putting meth-
> ods of the hero, on the American side, of the [1929] Ryder Cup
> match.

Some nine hundred words later, having commented on Diegel's
putting technique from every possible point of view, Darwin
wraps the essay up:

> We all laugh at our friends and sometimes even pretend to laugh
> at ourselves for imitating the styles of the eminent. Yet there is this
> to be said, that if we are going to do it at all, the imitation of a
> putting style gives much the greater satisfaction. When we attempt
> a champion's driving swing, nobody by any chance recognizes our

rendering of it. No total stranger will ever come up to us and say, "I beg your pardon, my dear sir, but I cannot help noticing that you are copying the effortless grace and free pivot of Mr. John Ball. I hope you are making good progress." On the other hand, we have only to contort ourselves for a single minute in front of the clubhouse windows and a dozen kind friends will shout, "How is the diegeling getting on?" The ball may not go in the hole but recognition is something. It encourages us to go on and, by the way, there comes to me, as I write, a most encouraging sound. It is a pleasantly purring sound as of one mowing. The gardener has been told to mow a patch for me and afterwards to roll it. Then I really shall be able to get down to it.

One of the more fortunate turns of my life was that, as I mentioned earlier, I got to know Bernard Darwin — nothing like as well, for instance, as his contemporaries at Eton but fairly well for an American. My real luck was meeting him in my early twenties, when, as a student at Cambridge, I went down to Royal St. George's, in Sandwich, to watch the 1939 Oxford-Cambridge match. The fact that I was attending — and, naturally, rooting for — Cambridge did no harm, because Darwin, though he was then in his early sixties, still regarded the "university match" as a most important affair. At that time, he was just beginning to suffer from gout, which plagued him increasingly the rest of his life, and at Royal St. George's he was forced to take up a more or less stationary position at a good watching spot on the course. In the classic Greek tragedies, as you may remember, it was the practice to threaten with death a messenger who arrived bearing bad tidings and to reward one who brought good news. I mention this because at the 1939 university match, with Darwin's mobility impaired, I acted as a sort of scout for him, reporting periodically on the state of foursome matches (on the first day) and singles matches (on the second) that were being waged at distant corners of the course, and I profited immensely from the fact that most of the news I bore was good: Cambridge led from the start and won by a comfortable margin, and our relationship from the outset was a very happy one.

Because of the Second World War, I didn't see Darwin again until I went over to St. Andrews for the 1950 British Amateur. By this time, he was in his middle seventies. His gout had become much worse — the measures we have today for controlling the disease had not yet been discovered — and he was able to do only a minimum of walking. Still, he managed to function astonishingly well. The large windows in the Big Room of the clubhouse afforded him not only a view of the first hole but also of the seventeenth green and the eighteenth hole, and by fusing what he saw with a few reports from friends coming in off the course he kept better track of what was happening — especially during the match-crammed first three days of the championship — than anyone else I saw there. The extent of his knowledge was borne home to me on Tuesday, when, during a dull spot in the afternoon, he was kind enough to invite me to tea, although this involved for him the painful ascent of a long flight of stairs to the second floor. We were catching up on things in general when, after glancing at the eighteenth fairway, Darwin asked my opinion of an American player who happened to be coming up it. I knew nothing about him — he had done nothing in our tournaments at home — aside from his home club and home town, which were supplied in the pairings sheet. Darwin, however, was well acquainted with this player's record in his earlier appearances in the British Amateur, and even went on to mention some minor changes he had effected in his swing.

Year after year, Darwin saw to it that he was on hand for the big golf occasions. In 1953, when Ben Hogan made his historic conquest of the British Open, Hogan and Darwin, so utterly different and yet so much alike, got together for conversations that they both enjoyed. At the completion of the championship, which Hogan won with rounds of 73, 71, 70, and 68, Darwin wrote perhaps the most perceptive comment on Hogan's victory: "If he had needed a 64 on the last round, you were quite certain he could have played a 64. Hogan gave you the distinct impression he was capable of getting whatever score was needed to win." At the 1959 Walker Cup match, at Muirfield, Darwin got a look at Jack Nicklaus, who was then only nineteen, and he immediately grasped the young man's vast potential. He wrote that Nicklaus "gives the ball a blow like the kick of a mule." However, the late-period Darwinism I recall with most pleasure was a little aside he made one day during the 1955 British Amateur, at Lytham St. Annes, in which a young Floridian, Don Bisplinghoff, played very well for several rounds. "Bisplinghoff. Bisplinghoff. Bisplinghoff," Darwin muttered one morning, his forehead creased in concentration. "That name's like putting. Some days you have it, some days you don't."

My last meeting with Darwin took place in the summer of 1960 — the year before his death. He was living then with his daughter Ursula, a gifted potter, in her house in a village near Lewes, in southern Sussex. (There has long been a strong artistic strain in the Darwin family. For example, Bernard's son, the late Sir Robin, became Rector and Vice-Provost of the Royal College of Art. A cousin of Bernard's, Gwen Raverat, wrote and illustrated the very successful family memoir *Period Piece*.) A rather bulky man by this time, Darwin was confined to an overstuffed chair in the living room, and though it was either late June or early July, I seem to recall that a blanket was spread across his knees. Nevertheless, he looked very well for a man of eighty-three. His eyes had a nice twinkle to them, and his mind functioned with its characteristic fastidiousness and animation. I can remember only bits and pieces of my visit with him: Darwin's shrewd estimate of the talents of Jack Kramer, who was handling some of the telecasting from Wimbledon; his evaluation of the South Africa–England cricket matches that had lately been held at Lord's; his considerable interest in Arnold Palmer, who had just shot to the top by winning our Masters and Open and was about to make his début in the British Open. I also remember that I asked him which writers he admired the most. He was silent for a good twenty seconds. "Dickens. I've always loved Dickens," he said gravely. "But, everything considered, I think I would place Hazlitt at the top of my list. He had an unusual combination of intelligence, spirit, honesty, and originality, and how beautifully he brought them all together."

When one thinks of Darwin — and many of us find ourselves doing it frequently — one finds that he presents a definite puzzle. He seems to have lived at a much earlier time than he did — to have been, in essence, more of a nineteenth-century than a twentieth-century man. How far away his world sometimes seems: a world in which his tutor at Eton once competed against two other whizzes in a quoting match to see who knew *Pickwick Papers* best; in which there were gardeners who mowed a portion of your lawn as short as a golf green so that you could go out and practice your diegeling; in which a golf correspondent, such as Darwin, repaired to the clubhouse for a cup of tea and there knocked off his day's report in longhand and asked a member of the club's staff to carry it to the telegrapher in the local post office. Nor does Darwin make any bones about what he considered to be golf's golden age. It wasn't the age of Jones or of Hogan or of Palmer. It consisted, he wrote, "of the last few years of the gutty-ball era and perhaps, though golf would have been better if it had never been invented, of the first few of the rubber-cored era" — say, from 1896 to 1906, when the group of British golf champions called the Triumvirate (J. H. Taylor, Harry Vardon, and James Braid) was in its prime. And yet, when you look at Darwin from a different angle he seems to be thoroughly modern — as up-to-date as next week's tournament, the newest magic-metal long-distance shaft, or the latest rumor of an impending change in the rule about cleaning the golf ball on the green. The explanation is obvious. Nobody ever knew more about golf than Darwin or wrote about it so intuitively.

(1976)

Nicklaus and Watson
at Turnberry

In the opinion of most Scots and most golfers from other lands, the best course on the west coast of Scotland is not Troon (over which the British Open has periodically been played since 1923) but Turnberry, thirty miles or so to the south. It was finally added to the rota of the British Open in 1977, and though it was in far from its best condition, it produced what many people on both sides of the Atlantic consider the finest and most dramatic stretch of golf ever played in a major event. In the third round the two leaders, Jack Nicklaus and Tom Watson, pulled away from the rest of the field with a pair of sensational 65s. On the fourth round Nicklaus added a 66, but it wasn't good enough: Watson had a 65. Far ahead of the pack, the two leaders were engaged virtually in match play. Their duel was not decided until the last hole, which both of them birdied.

ONE OF THE MANY POINTS OF DIFFERENCE BETWEEN THE UNITED States Open and the British Open — perhaps the two most important golf competitions in the world — is that the British championship, since its inception, in 1860, has been played on only fourteen courses, while ours, which was started thirty-five years later, has been played on nearly fifty courses. There are a lot of reasons for this disparity, such as the size of the United States and that of Great Britain and Northern Ireland (with a combined area smaller than Oregon); the unwritten law that the British Open is played exclusively on seaside courses; and the preference of the Royal & Ancient Golf Club of St. Andrews, which conducts the British Open, for limiting the number of courses in the championship rotation (or "rota," as the British say), as opposed to the policy of the United States Golf Association, which conducts our Open, of holding our championship in all sections of the vast continental spread of our country. In respect to this last matter, most golfers regard Baltusrol, in Springfield, New Jersey, and Oakmont, outside Pittsburgh, as exemplifying the traditional U.S. Open venue, because these two clubs have put on the most Opens. However, when you come right down to it, each has held the championship only five times (Baltusrol in 1903, 1915, 1936, 1954, and 1967; Oakmont in 1927, 1935, 1953, 1962, and 1973), and in Baltusrol's case, it should be noted, three different courses have been used. On the other hand, St. Andrews has been host to the British Open twenty-one times, and Muirfield, some fifteen miles east of Edinburgh, a good solid eleven. I mention all this because 1977 was a rather unusual year in that neither championship was being played at a truly familiar course. Southern Hills, that splendid course in Tulsa, where our Open was won in mid-June by Hubert Green, was staging it for only the second time, and the British Open, which Tom Watson won in early July, was played for the first time ever on the Ailsa course, in Turnberry, about fifty miles south of Glasgow. The Turnberry Hotel, a long, low white stucco building with a pinky-brick-colored slate roof, is perched atop a fairly high ridge and overlooks its two courses: the Ailsa, the championship layout, and the Arran, a very good one.

The wonder, I suppose, is that it took the R. and A. so long to award the Open to Turnberry (which is how golfers refer to the championship links), because for twenty years and more the course has generally been acknowledged to be the best on the West Coast of Scotland. However, the R. and A., as Wordsworth said of the Thames, glideth at its own sweet will. In 1961, it gave Turnberry a tryout by holding the British Amateur Championship there, and two years later it used the course as the site of the Walker Cup Match. Turnberry acquitted itself favorably both times, and this undoubtedly had a good deal to do with its receiving the ultimate laurel, the Open. Tied in with this is a somewhat more complicated story. Whenever you hold a golf event of some importance in Scotland — as a rule, the Open is played alternately in England and in Scotland — you must take pains to see that neither the East Coast nor the West is slighted. As far as championship courses are concerned, the East Coast has always been well endowed. To begin with, there is St. Andrews itself, which sits on a small bay off the North Sea. Then, there is Muirfield, undoubtedly the finest classic course in Britain. Muirfield, situated on the south shore of the Firth of Forth, first held the Open in 1892, shortly after succeeding grim, obsolete Musselburgh, on the outskirts of Edinburgh, as the home of the world's oldest golf club — the Honourable Company of Edinburgh Golfers, established in 1744. Add to this duo chill Carnoustie, on the north shore of the Tay estuary, which was admitted to the rota in 1931, and you have three excellent championship courses. What about the West Coast? Well, the Open was a West Coast monopoly during its first eleven years. The club that initiated the championship was Prestwick, which occupies a rambunctious stretch of duneland on the east shore of the Firth of Clyde, and from 1860 through 1870 the Open was played there. In 1871, the Open was temporarily suspended, and when it was resumed, the following year, a new pattern was introduced: Prestwick held it in 1872, St. Andrews in 1873, and Musselburgh in 1874, and it continued to be rotated over those three courses until 1892, when the championship underwent a number of revolutionary changes. Among other things, it was extended from a thirty-six-hole competition to a seventy-two-hole competition, and several new courses, including some in England — Sandwich and Hoylake, in particular — became regular members of the cast. It wasn't until 1923, though, that a second course on Scotland's West Coast, Troon, just north of Prestwick — the two courses are actually contiguous — was chosen for the Open. Troon shortly became the only West Coast course on the rota, for after 1925 Prestwick was dropped. Its grounds were not commodious enough to accommodate the swelling galleries, provide adequate parking space, and meet the sundry other demands of a modern golf championship. Moreover, the course did not have the necessary length to test the top golfers in the world, and, ironically, the very features of Prestwick's terrain which had caused the most excitement in the early years of the Open had become sadly outdated. For example, on the short fifth hole and the two-shot seventeenth, the greens were completely hidden from view by huge sand hills. The sand hill on the fifth was proudly called the Himalayas, and the one on the seventeenth the Alps, since in that period a blind approach shot was esteemed as the last word in golf-course *haute couture*, and other clubs envied Prestwick's good fortune in having been so generously endowed by nature. Today, the crusty old course serves as a fascinating museum of what golf was like in the days of the gutta-percha ball.

When a golfer thinks of Turnberry, the first thing that comes to mind, I suppose, is the glorious vista from the hotel on the ridge: the two courses below are spread out over the tumbling duneland along the Firth of Clyde; the Mull of Kintyre and the jagged hills of the island of Arran rise in the distance across the firth; and to the south Ailsa Craig, a colossal granite rock shaped like the top half of a Rugby football, thrusts itself out of the water.

Some two and a half weeks after the U.S. Open, a good many members of that band of gypsies that plays or follows international golf was gathered at Turnberry, and on the evening of the first day of the British Open a number of them were looking down from the Turnberry Hotel at the Ailsa course, on which the last threesomes were finishing their rounds. There has been a golf course on this strip of billowing duneland since before the turn of the century, when the owner of the property, the Marquis of Ailsa, had a private course constructed. In about 1909, shortly after the Marquis sold the land to the Glasgow & South Western Railway, two substantial courses were laid out over it by Willie Fernie, the professional of the Old Troon Golf Club, up the coast. The courses were converted into a training station for the Royal Flying Corps during the First World War. They recovered slowly but encouragingly in the nineteen-twenties. Then, in the Second World War, the land was requisitioned as a base by the Royal Air Force Coastal Command, and the two courses all but disappeared from sight as hangars, eighteen-inch-thick runways, and the rest were installed. In the early nineteen-fifties, the courses made a miraculous recovery. Mackenzie Ross, the golf-course architect who had been called in, was not only able to remove just about all traces of the wartime airbase but had improved both the Ailsa and the Arran beyond all expectation. In the case of the Ailsa, he did this by making perceptive use of the heaving, eccentric terrain on many of the inland holes, the precipitous sand hills near the shore and the narrow valleys they enclosed, and the handsome stretches of land directly alongside the Firth of Clyde. In recent years, it has become standard practice to refer to the Ailsa course as the Scottish Pebble Beach, because seven holes in a row — the fourth through the tenth — follow the firth. In a way, this appellation is misleading, for the holes are not edged by steep cliffs, like the ones along Carmel Bay, nor are they elevated nearly as high above the water. There are two particular beauties — the fourth and the ninth. The fourth is a par 3 of 167 yards on which the tee and the hard-to-hit green are separated by a thick growth of beach grass. The old custom, more common in Britain than here, of giving golf holes names as well as numbers has all but disappeared, because only too often it fostered the same kind of cute, vapid clichés as the naming of beach houses. The fourth hole on the Ailsa, however, is an exception, it is called Woe-be-Tide, which is extremely appropriate when the tide is high and a stiff wind is coming off the water. On the ninth, a 455-yard par 4, possibly the best and fiercest hole on the course, the tee is straight out of a Gothic novel: It sits atop a small, high crag that sticks out into the firth. From the tee, the golfer must carry his drive about two hundred yards across an inlet to reach the nearest part of the curving fairway. How much of the inlet the tournament golfer chooses to bite off depends on the wind. On British seaside courses — and this applies to the holes that do not actually border on the sea as well as to the ones that do — the principal hazard is the heavy, moisture-laden wind. It follows that under ordinary conditions the key to playing the Ailsa well depends on correctly judging the effect that the wind will have on your shots, and making allowance for this. On the Ailsa, as on most seaside courses, the wind keeps shifting — blowing first out of one quarter and then out of another. For example, on the sixteenth, a 409-yard par 4, I have seen a golfer playing with a following wind get home easily in the morning with just a pitching wedge on his second shot, and then, in the afternoon, seen the same golfer playing into the wind fail to reach the green after a solid drive and a well-struck 3-wood. For the 1977 British Open, the Ailsa measured 6,875 yards — two yards longer than Southern Hills. Par, as at Southern Hills, was 70 — 35 out and 35 in.

Before proceeding any farther, I should explain that for the Open the Ailsa did not look or play the way it normally does. To begin with, there was no rough to speak of. The last three years, Britain has been hit with uncommonly hot and parching summers, and the condition of many of the golf courses — those at Turnberry among them — has suffered severely. This year, the Turnberry area, like most of Britain, was also plagued with a long, wet winter, which prevented the grass on the golf courses from getting a proper start. In addition, the Ailsa, which sorely needed both water and sunshine as the Open drew near, went through a damaging stretch of five rainless weeks just prior to the championship. As a result, the fairways were edged by the wispiest kind of rough — a thin, random collection of fescue, buttercups, plantain shoreweed, Yorkshire fog, dandelions, and assorted other weeds, grasses, and wild flowers. As if this weren't disheartening enough, the weather was wrong for the Open. On the first day, the nice, light morning breeze shut down at noon. In the afternoon, the temperature climbed to about eighty-five degrees and there was seldom a breath of breeze. British linksland courses are designed to be played in a wind, and, inevitably, the scores on the first round ran rather low. John Schroeder, of California, led with a 66. Seven other players were in the 60s, and there would have been more had the pins not been placed in dangerous spots on the hard, kittle greens. Johnny Miller, the defending champion, who had brought in a 69, predicted that if there were more of these windless days on the roughless course the scores might run in the low 60s. Before leaving Turnberry that evening for Ayr, where I was billeted, I took a last look at the Firth of Clyde, silver with mist. It had been covered with mist throughout the day, and, while you could see Ailsa Craig, which is not far offshore, the island of Arran and the Mull of Kintyre had not been visible at any time.

Ayr is some twenty miles to the north of Turnberry, and the drive up the back road, which I took that evening, was the ideal anodyne for the long day in the sun. The road winds through Scottish countryside at its tranquil best. You drive past soft-green sloping fields, some of them thick with Ayrshire cows, others punctuated with hayricks, which in this part of Scotland have a sort of ziggurat shape. Ash, oak, and pine trees separate the fields and line sections of the road. Now and then, for a change of pace, you pass a well-kept ruin or slow down through a village where the gardens of the squat stone houses are aflame with roses, which bloom so brilliantly in Scotland. When you cross the Doon River, you know you are bearing down on Ayr and the heart of Robert Burns country. On this drive, two thoughts filled my mind: first, how wonderful it is that so much of Scotland's countryside remains comparatively untouched, and, second, how disappointing it would be if we had a continuation of this Tulsa-like heat and still air, rather than typical British Open weather, which sends you striding out into a bracing breeze with a tweed cap on your head and a sweater under your tweed jacket, and carrying a raincoat just in case. Well, the way it turned out, we were in for three more hot, sticky, un-Caledonian days.

On Thursday, the day of the second round, Miller was one of the earliest finishers. He had taken a 74, and wore a mournful expression. "I have thrown away any chance I had of winning the British Open," he said. "You can't shoot a 74 and expect to be in contention. There are going to be a lot of very low scores today, the way the course is playing." Miller had hardly finished saying this when Mark Hayes, a young Oklahoman, brought in a 63 — a new record low round for the championship. It could easily have been a 62, for Hayes had missed his par on the eighteenth. Then the word circulated that Hubert Green was burning up the course — seven under par for the round with five holes to play. I was one of the detachment that raced out to pick up Green, and saw him bogey three of the last five holes. He had to be satisfied with a 66. Just when it seemed that we were watching the old Tucson Open, things began to settle down, for no apparent reason. In any event, among the players in the running, the lowest round completed late in the day was a 66, by Roger Maltbie, the promising young Californian. This gave him the lead, at 137 — a stroke ahead of Green, Nicklaus, Tom Watson, and Lee Trevino, in a tournament that from this point on was almost totally dominated by American golfers. In the end, eleven of the top twelve finishers were Americans.

Late that Thursday afternoon, I was on hand when Henry Cotton completed his second round. The winner of three British Opens (in 1934, 1937, and 1948), and undoubtedly the finest British golfer of modern times, Cotton is now seventy. The oldest of five former champions who received special invitations to play at Turnberry (he had played in his first Open exactly half a century before), Cotton had jumped at the chance. When he holed a short putt on the home green for an 82 — since he did not make the thirty-six-hole cut, this putt undoubtedly represented his final stroke in a British Open — a round of applause erupted from the spectators in the stands. He doffed his cap in appreciation. This gesture evoked another round of applause. Visibly affected, Cotton tipped his cap again, and then, straightening his Lanvin sports shirt, slowly headed for the clubhouse.

*

In the years ahead, all that will probably be remembered about the final thirty-six holes of the 1977 British Open is the fantastic duel between Nicklaus and Watson, who were paired on both the third and the fourth day and threw some altogether stupendous golf at each other as they fought it out — neither of them ever taking a backward step — right down to the seventy-second green. In the high excitement provoked by their shotmaking and their admirable combativeness, many experienced golf hands were, understandably, ready to proclaim this the greatest of all British Opens, and, for that matter, the greatest championship ever played anywhere. I don't know if I am prepared to go quite that far, but I do know that I cannot remember a head-to-head battle that can begin to compare with the one that Nicklaus and Watson waged two days running. On the third round, a 66 put Crenshaw only three strokes behind Nicklaus and Watson, and he managed to stay within possible striking distance of the two leaders on the fourth round until, after playing twenty-six consecutive holes without a bogey, he took a six, two over par, on the ninth. Then he collapsed, utterly. In retrospect, over the last two rounds the tournament was, in effect, a match between Watson and Nicklaus, although technically, of course, they were engaged in a stroke-play tournament. In the end, the man who finished in third place, Green, was a full ten strokes behind Nicklaus and eleven behind Watson.

When the Watson-Nicklaus duel began to assume epic dimensions, midway through the third round, it virtually erased interest in everything else that had occurred, or would occur, on the Ailsa course that day. Nevertheless, I should like to mention — much too briefly — a few noteworthy performances on that third day before returning to the leaders. I am thinking of the 67 by Peter Thomson, the Australian veteran who has won five British Opens, the first of them in 1954; also of the 67 by Arnold Palmer, in the course of which, exasperated after foozling several short putts, he decided on the seventh green to try putting cross-handed — the left hand lower on the shaft than the right — and came roaring down the last nine in thirty strokes, holing for one birdie from fifteen feet, for three birdies from thirty feet, and for still another birdie, on the home green, from thirty-five feet. It is years since Palmer, who in his prime sank more long putts than any champion in history, has had a day like this on the greens, and — not only because it is his manner to understate his feelings — I can't remember when I last saw him so honestly delighted with his golf. (On the final round, staying with the cross-handed grip and putting well, he had a 69 and finished in seventh place.) I feel compelled to add one more detail. On the third round, Green, only one stroke off the pace, gave us, on the very first hole, a short par 4, an all too painful reminder of his old penchant for wrecking his chances in a tournament by messing up one hole dreadfully. After pulling his approach into a bunker, he muffed his first explosion shot, hit his second over the green, played a mediocre chip and a poor putt, and wound up with a 7. He had a 74 that day, but maybe winning our Open is beginning to give Hubert Green something he never had before, for he came back on the last round to play a confident, steady 67.

Now to Watson and Nicklaus. No sooner had they teed off on Friday, the day of the third round, than the air began to bristle. Just about everyone in the immense gallery was thinking about their classic encounter on the final nine holes of this year's Masters, when Watson, playing right behind Nicklaus and completely aware of what he had to do to stay with this tremendous finisher, refused to be awed, and finally beat him by birdieing the seventy-first hole. Nicklaus, who is now thirty-seven, has been the best golfer in the world for the last twelve years, or possibly even longer, and he sees no reason to cede his throne to any young pup, since he believes that in many ways he is a better golfer today than he has ever been. Watson, who is ten years younger than Nicklaus, is patently an improved player this year. His left side controls his swing just the way it should, and his footwork is very good — not that these are the things you are most conscious of while watching him. What impresses you most is the quickness and decisiveness with which he plays his shots, the freedom of his hitting action, and the sharpness with which he strikes the ball. Much as Watson respects Nicklaus, you felt at Turnberry that he relished the challenge of facing him head-to-head. On both days, he played the better golf from tee to green, but Nicklaus came through with so many stunning recoveries and got down so many long and difficult putts in key situations that until the very end he was the man in command and Watson the hard-pressed pursuer.

Perhaps the most effective way to get across the furious attacks and counterattacks that made this protracted confrontation between Watson and Nicklaus so memorable is simply to set down, with a minimum of embellishment, what took place on the significant holes. On Friday, Nicklaus, off fast, birdied the first hole, a 355-yard par 4, when he played his sand-wedge approach three feet from the cup. Watson answered this with a birdie 3 on the third, a 462-yard par 4; his second shot, a 5-iron, left him only a six-foot putt. On Woe-be-Tide, the par-3 fourth hole, both men hit 6-irons, Watson stopping his shot two feet from the pin. Nicklaus, however, holed from twenty feet. Two birdies. On the sixth, a 222-yard par 3 across a deep swale, Nicklaus moved out in front by two strokes. He smashed a 2-iron to twelve feet and made the putt. Watson, who was bunkered off the tee, missed his try for a par from eight feet. On the seventh, a 528-yard par 5 that moves uphill most of the way, Watson reached the green in two. Nicklaus, who was starting to pull his tee shots, was never on the fairway on this hole but curled in another good-sized putt — this one from twelve feet — to match Watson's birdie. Scores at the turn: Nicklaus, 31; Watson, 33.

Starting home, Nicklaus continued to pour it on, birdieing the tenth, a 452-yard par 4, with a twenty-five-foot putt. Watson then holed from ten feet for *his* birdie. The fourteenth is a 440-yard par 4 to an elusive green. Here Nicklaus made his first real error of the day, misreading the three-footer he had for his par. Watson, who had looked as if he might fall a stroke farther behind when his approach bounded over the green, got down in two from the rough with a perfectly gauged chip and actually picked up a stroke. Only one behind now. He got that stroke back on the next hole, the 209-yard fifteenth, when he knocked in a twenty-footer for a birdie 2. On the seventeenth, an eminently birdieable 500-yard par 5, both made their 4s. Nicklaus let a big chance slip away here: his second, a great 2-iron, finished three feet from the pin, but he pushed his putt for an eagle a shade off line. Scores for the round: Nicklaus, 65 (31–34); Watson, 65 (33–32). Each had made six birdies and one bogey. Nicklaus was never behind on this round, but the two short putts he failed to make on the in-nine had cost him the lead.

On Saturday, Nicklaus was again off fast. He jumped into a two-stroke lead with a birdie on the second, a 428-yard par 4, by playing a remarkable 7-iron from an awkward sidehill stance in the rough (the ball was well above his feet) ten feet from the pin. Watson bogeyed the hole, pulling his approach to the left of the green and taking three to get down. Nicklaus increased his lead to three strokes with another 2 on Woe-be-Tide, holing this time from thirty feet. Watson then mounted a terrific rally. He cut away one stroke of Nicklaus's margin with a birdie 3 on the 411-yard fifth when he followed a lovely 5-iron with a sixteen-foot putt. He cut away another stroke on the long seventh when he reached the green in two, using a driver off the fairway, and two-putted for his birdie. On the eighth, a 427-yard par 4, Watson cut away the last stroke of Nicklaus's lead with yet another birdie: after a 5-iron approach to the heart of the green, he rapped in a twenty-footer. (I don't believe I have ever before seen two golfers hole so many long putts — and on fast, breaking, glossy greens. They were also doing such extraordinary things from tee to green that it was hard to believe what you were seeing.) Then, having come all the way back, Watson once again fell behind. On the ninth, the 455-yard par 4, where the tee is set on the isolated crag, he pushed his drive into the rough on the right, pulled a 1-iron across the fairway into the rough on the left, and needed three more shots to get down. Nicklaus saved his par when he eased a touchy downhill twelve-footer into the cup. Scores on the front nine: Nicklaus, 33; Watson, 34.

On the twelfth, a par 4 only 391 yards long, Nicklaus, after pitching with a wedge, rolled in still another long putt — a twenty-two-footer — for a 3. This birdie moved him out in front by two strokes, and many of us felt at that moment that we had perhaps watched the decisive blow of the struggle. After all, holes were running out fast now — only six were left — and how often does a golfer of Nicklaus's stature fail to hold on to a two-stroke lead as he drives down the stretch? Watson was not thinking in those terms. At this point, he rallied once again. He birdied the thirteenth, a shortish par 4, with a well-judged wedge shot twelve feet from the pin and a firm putt. Then he again birdied the fifteenth, the 209-yard par 3: using a putter from the left fringe of the green, he stroked a sixty-footer smack into the middle of the cup. Now Watson and Nicklaus were again tied. Everything to play for.

Two pars on the sixteenth. On the seventeenth, the 500-yard 5, Watson was down the fairway with his tee shot, a few yards shorter than Nicklaus, who was in the rough on the right. Considering the circumstances, Watson then played one of the finest shots of the day — a 3-iron that was dead on the pin all the way and finished twenty-five feet beyond it. Nicklaus went with a 4-iron. He hit it a trifle heavy, and the ball came down in the rough short of the green and to the right. Throughout these last two

rounds, Nicklaus, on his frequent visits to the rough, had improvised a succession of astonishing shots to scramble out his pars
and an occasional birdie, and here he punched a little running
chip that climbed up and over two ridges in the green and came to
rest three and a half feet past the cup. Watson was down in two
safe putts for his birdie 4. Nicklaus, who hadn't missed a putt all
day, missed his short one. The ball started left and stayed left and
didn't touch the cup. A 5, not a 4, and at the worst time possible.
Now, trailing Watson by a stroke, Nicklaus's only hope was to
birdie the eighteenth, a 431-yard par 4 on which the fairway bends
to the left. After Watson had played a prudent 1-iron down the
middle of the fairway, Nicklaus, going with his driver, belted a
long tee shot that kept sliding to the right — far to the right, and
deep into the rough. He was faced with an almost unplayable lie:
the ball had ended up two inches from the base of a gorse bush;
and, to complicate matters, a branch of the bush, some two feet
above the ground, was directly in the line of his backswing. He
would be hard put to it to manufacture any kind of useful shot.
Watson to play first, going with a 7-iron. He couldn't have hit it
much better: the ball sat down two feet from the pin. Nicklaus
now, playing an 8-iron. Still not giving up. With his great
strength, he drove his club through the impeding gorse branch,
managed to catch the ball squarely, and boosted it over the bunker
on the right and onto the green thirty-five feet from the cup. He
worked on the putt, studying the subtleties carefully, as if the
championship depended on it. Then he rammed it in for his 3.
Tremendous cheers. Watson chose not to give himself too much
time to think about the two-footer he now had to hole to win.
After checking the line, he stepped up to the ball and knocked it
in. Another salvo of cheers — for Watson, and also for both Watson and Nicklaus and the inspired golf they had played over the
last thirty-six holes of the Open. The scores for the concluding
round: Watson, 65 (34–31); Nicklaus, 66 (33–33). (Nicklaus, incidentally, had only one bogey over the last two rounds.) Their
scores for the tournament: Watson 68-70-65-65 — 268. Nicklaus,
68-70-65-66 — 269. Both shattered to smithereens the old record
total for the British Open of 276.

For some reason or other, Jack Nicklaus always moves one more
in defeat than in victory. I don't know exactly why this is, for he is
an excellent winner. Anyway, he is probably the best loser in the
game. He was direct and honest in his assessment of why Watson

had won: Tom, he said, had played better golf than he had on both rounds. He had no alibis. Nevertheless, for all his self-possession, it was observable that Nicklaus had been hit hard by losing a second major championship to Watson this year on the final holes after giving the pursuit of winning everything he had. That last phrase is important. No matter what the odds are, Nicklaus never stops fighting, and you never know when he will contrive some small miracle like that impossible 3 on the last hole. In a word, I should say that over the past dozen years, without any question, he had been far and away the best competitor in any sport in which it is one individual against other individuals, not team against team.

How was Watson able to play so superlatively, to keep coming back so valiantly time after time? Alfie Fyles, his gnarled little caddie from Southport, near Liverpool, who also caddied for Watson when he won the British Open at Carnoustie in 1975, put it this way: "His swing is better, more compact. His approach to the game has improved a great deal. He thinks better. He's a mature golfer now." What underlies the confidence that Watson exhibited throughout his extended duel with Nicklaus? For one thing, his triumph in the Masters undoubtedly convinced him that he had reached the point where he could stand up to a giant like Nicklaus. For another, he is able to get himself up very high when he faces Nicklaus, for he appreciates that this is essential. He also knows that he is a sound driver and a sound putter, and, though he doesn't make this kind of pronouncement, he believes he hits the ball as well as anyone. Despite a sensitive temperament and an active imagination, he is now able to relax under pressure. This, of course, helps him to execute his swing well, and when a golfer like Watson feels that he is swinging just the way he wants to, it affirms his feeling of confidence and imbues him with an extraordinary resilience.

The general feeling at Turnberry after the Open was that the R. and A. is almost certain to award the Ailsa course a regular place on its championship rota. After all, if the course produced such a thrilling Open when it was in relatively poor shape, it is only logical to think that it will provide a first-rate test when it is its real self — bearded with some good Scottish rough, and swept by good Scottish winds that will bring the bunkers into play and make ball control critical. (It is, I admit, something of a mystery how the almost defenseless course yielded so few low scores — other than those by Nicklaus and Watson — on the last two and a half days. Some players I talked with thought that the hard-surfaced, rolling greens had effected this, making it difficult to stop one's approaches close to the pins and also to putt consistently well. This suggests that the two leaders, locked deep in their duel, simply forced each other to rise above the conditions.) Everything being equal, the British Open should be back at Turnberry in about seven years. By that time, we should have a much better idea whether Tom Watson is just a very talented golfer or a great golfer. While he is different from Bobby Jones in many ways, there is in him more than a touch of Jones. In seven years, Jack Nicklaus will be forty-four, and yet I wouldn't be at all surprised if at that distant date this prodigious athlete still loomed as a serious contender for the championship.

(1977)

Mr. Crosby

Inasmuch as they usually work at night, many entertainers play a fair amount of golf during the day. Several have become accomplished golfers, but none more so than Bing Crosby. He won the championship of the Lakeside Golf Club, in Hollywood, five times. He qualified in the sectional round of the 1940 U.S. Amateur. In 1950 he entered the British Amateur, and a tremendous crowd turned out to see just how good their idol was. Well, he birdied from the first hole by sticking his approach shot a yard from the pin. He parred the second and then birdied the third with another fine pitch shot. After that, as I saw it, he decided that his unexpectedly huge gallery was not setting the proper atmosphere for the championship, and he managed to hit a sufficient number of loose shots to insure his defeat. He loved the game and the company of people who played it well.

LAST OCTOBER 14TH, MOMENTS AFTER FINISHING A WELL-played round at La Moraleja Golf Club, outside Madrid, Bing Crosby died of a heart attack. He was seventy-three. His death, which deeply affected his family and friends, not to mention the millions around the world who knew him through the motion pictures and recordings he had made over half a century, also greatly saddened the golfing community — for, of all contemporary public figures, he was the one most intimately identified with the game. I did not know Crosby well, but in January I was moved to make a sort of pilgrimage to the Monterey Peninsula, in California, to attend the annual Bing Crosby National Pro-Am, the tournament he founded back in 1937, which set the pattern for many tournaments that have been sponsored in recent years by other stars of the entertainment world. This year, everything at the Crosby, as it is generally called, was much as it has always been.

There was, as usual, some terrible weather: On the night before the opening round, an inch and a half of rain fell on the already sopping courses, and, with several of the greens and fairways under water, the start of play had to be postponed a day. Most of the familiar faces — the celebrities, businessmen, and other amateurs who regularly team up with the professional golfers — were on hand, full of the spirit and enthusiasm that the event seems to generate. And, finally, the tournament itself was packed with excellent golf and high drama. At the end of the seventy-two holes, two of the most talented and appealing members of the new young professional band, Tom Watson and Ben Crenshaw, were tied for first at eight strokes under par. This called for a sudden-death playoff, and on the second extra hole Watson won out. It goes without saying that Bing was missed at every moment, and all the more because this was one of the best Crosbys ever. The tournament has apparently grown deep roots, and there seems to be no reason it should not go on and on.

There is no question that the prominent entertainers who over the last ten or fifteen years have become sponsors of tournaments on the rich P.G.A. tour are, with few exceptions, genuinely devoted to golf, but it is also unarguable that being connected with a nationally televised sports event watched by millions is a sizable promotional asset. Crosby's involvement came about quite differently. He was an outright pioneer. In 1937, when he inaugurated his tournament, at the Rancho Santa Fe course, near San Diego, the pro golf tour was comparatively small potatoes, but Bing Crosby was already firmly established as a national institution. What led him to set up his Pro-Am was his intense love of golf and the pleasure he derived from being in the company of crack professionals. For the first tournament, he invited sixty-eight pros (among them Henry Picard, Dutch Harrison, Sam Snead, Denny Shute, Olin Dutra, and Paul Runyan) and sixty-eight amateurs (among them such Hollywood figures as Richard Arlen, Guy Kibbee, Fred Astaire, Zeppo Marx, William Frawley, and Gregory La Cava). Scheduled as a two-day, thirty-six-hole event with a purse of three thousand dollars — which Crosby put up — it was washed out the first day by heavy rain. On the second day, Snead, who was just coming into his own, shot a 68; this won him the professional competition and first-prize money in the Pro-Am, making for a combined haul of $762.30, which wasn't bad in those days, when first-prize money in the United States Open was only a thousand dollars. The important thing was that everyone loved the informal atmosphere of the affair, during which the entire field gathered in the evening at Bing's nearby home, where a battery of cooks grilled steaks, and where the host led off the entertainment with a few songs. The Crosby became a regular fixture on the tour until, after 1942, like many other tournaments, it was discontinued for the duration of the war. During those first six Pro-Ams, Crosby, simply by the obvious pleasure he took in the company of the touring pros, helped to give them a position of much greater social respectability than they had previously held. It brought to mind how, just after the First World War, when golf pros were still regarded as hired help and were not allowed in clubhouses here, Walter Hagen had led the way in changing that situation. Before and after playing an exhibition or a tournament round, he would walk blandly into the clubhouse through the front door to dramatize his point that if a professional was good enough to associate with club members on the golf course he was good enough to associate with them off it as well.

One reason Crosby was so fond of golf was that he had discovered it at the age of twelve, when he started to caddie at the old Riverside Golf Club in Spokane, where he grew up. From then on, he was fascinated by the game. He played it periodically during his years at Gonzaga University, in that city, and much more often when he became a band vocalist, ending up with Paul Whiteman's orchestra as the lead singer of the Rhythm Boys — a marvelous group, which was as far ahead of its time as the band's cornettist Bix Beiderbecke. After the Whiteman band completed the motion picture *The King of Jazz*, in 1930, Crosby decided to go out on his own, and settled in Los Angeles. In no time, he had his own coast-to-coast radio program and was making two or three movies a year. During this period, he developed his fine golf game. He joined the Lakeside Golf Club, to which many people in the film industry belonged, and, despite the rigors of his schedule, managed to play nine or eighteen holes several times a week. A well-coordinated man with a natural sense of timing, he got his handicap down to 2 and carried off the club championship five times. In 1940, he won a spot in the sectional qualifying round for the United States Amateur Championship, but failed to make the match-play rounds in the subsequent thirty-six hole qualifying test held at Winged Foot, in Westchester, the scene of the championship. During the war, he played many exhibitions — as did his

friend Bob Hope, himself a more than creditable golfer — to promote the sale of war bonds.

Golf is a game that demands constant application, and during this
stretch of his career hardly a day went by when Crosby didn't
have a club in his hands. For example, he used to keep a shag bag
of balls at the Paramount lot and, between scenes, practice chipping with a 7-iron on a small strip of lawn. I first saw him in action
near the end of the war, when he was playing with some friends
at Cypress Point, one of the courses on the Monterey Peninsula.
Two things about that afternoon remain clear in my mind. First, I
had long wondered whether Crosby was really as good a golfer as
he was cracked up to be, and discovered that he was; he had a
very legato, nicely grooved swing, and, while he wasn't particularly long, he hit crisp, straight shots down the fairway or toward
the flag with the assurance of a man who knew exactly what he
was doing. Second, I recall the astonishing way his voice travelled. You would be walking down an adjacent fairway, anywhere
from a hundred to two hundred yards from his foursome, and,
while you couldn't hear the three other players in his group talking at all or you caught what they said merely as an unintelligible
mumble, Crosby's voice had such timbre that every word he
spoke in an ordinary conversational tone carried like the peal of a
bell, and he invariably sounded as if he were no more than forty
feet away. I was told this past January by a friend of his that his
hearing was equally exceptional, and that in a crowded room
where the average man could not make any sense out of the
babble Crosby could hear practically every word uttered and dis-
tinguish who was saying it.

At the end of the war, when golf and other sports started up
again, Crosby made a brilliant move that transformed his tournament into a far more significant fixture. In 1947, he transferred it
from Rancho Santa Fe to the Monterey Peninsula, the spectacular
tract of forest and seashore about a hundred miles south of San
Francisco. And he extended the tournament to fifty-four holes,
with the first eighteen played at Cypress Point, the second at the
Monterey Peninsula Country Club, and the third at Pebble Beach.
While the Country Club's layout is nothing special, the layouts of
Cypress Point and Pebble Beach are indeed. Cypress Point, which
measures less than 6,500 yards from the championship tees, was
designed in 1928 by Alister MacKenzie — the Scottish architect

who later collaborated with Bobby Jones on the Augusta National — and is loaded with original and charming golf holes. It is usually ranked by knowledgeable players with Hugh Wilson's Merion, outside Philadelphia, and Donald Ross's Seminole, north of Palm Beach, as in a class apart from the country's other medium-length courses. As for Pebble Beach, which was completed in 1919, it may well be the best golf course in the world. It was laid out by Jack Neville, an outstanding California amateur golfer, who had never built a course before and did very little golf-course architecture afterward. Nonetheless, at Pebble Beach, where he was given a breathtaking piece of terrain, including high, rocky headlands that plunge straight down into Carmel Bay, Neville came through with an absolutely inspired piece of work, taking full advantage of the natural assets. At present 6,815 yards long from the back tees, Pebble Beach has been lengthened very little and altered only in minor ways over the past sixty years. There are eight seaside holes, all of them magnificent challenges, and the inland holes possess subtle qualities that give the course the proper balance.

The move to the Monterey Peninsula, with its superior courses, gave a whole new dimension to the Crosby. It immediately gained a further distinction, and with time it grew more and more important. In 1958, the year it became one of the first tour tournaments to be nationally televised, its format was changed again: It became a seventy-two-hole tournament, and on Sunday the pros who had made the cut and the fifty low pro-am teams all played the fourth round at Pebble Beach. (By this time, the starting field had been enlarged to a hundred and twenty professionals and a hundred and twenty amateurs, and the purse, which had been raised to ten thousand dollars in 1947, was up to fifty thousand. It is now two hundred and twenty-five thousand.) In 1967, there was another notable change: Spyglass Hill, a rugged layout designed by Robert Trent Jones and completed the previous year, replaced the Monterey Peninsula Country Club as the third course used in the tournament. Down through the years, the galleries, lured partly by the famous professionals but perhaps primarily by the chance to watch celebrities like Jack Lemmon and Robert Goulet execute their patented finesse shots, continued to increase. So did the size of the television audience. This was due in good measure to the fact that beginning in 1958, after he had stopped playing in the tournament, Crosby served as the principal commentator.

In 1971, thanks unquestionably to its being broadcast directly after the Super Bowl and on the same network, the final round of the Crosby reached what is still a record audience for a golf telecast: It was watched in more than eleven and a half million homes.

Several times, as the tournament's popularity kept increasing, pressure was put on Crosby to change it from a pro-am to a straight seventy-two-hole stroke-play event for the touring pros. A tough man to budge once he had made up his mind, he would not hear of it. "Bing felt that amateurs are the backbone of the game," Bob Roos, of the San Francisco merchandising family, said not long ago. "He liked to have friends from all phases of business and all kinds of professions, and he wanted his tournament to be an amalgam of top businessmen — particularly those who had contributed something to the game — along with championship-calibre golfers and a diversity of lively, interesting, socially compatible people." In recent years, several thousand players have applied annually for the hundred and sixty-eight invitations now extended to amateurs. From the start, Crosby personally selected those whom the invitations should go to — a task he found increasingly painful, since it meant turning down more and more friends. All in all, though, he loved the tournament. He was proud of the way it had taken hold, and liked to recall how in 1947 it had required a staff of only five, while thirty years later the general chairman, Dan Searle, needed six hundred volunteers to get the show done right. Crosby also took satisfaction in another aspect of its growth: The tournament, which made only nine thousand dollars in 1947, from the sale of tickets and programs, has now raised a total of approximately four million dollars for charity. Most of this has gone to youth centers and to needy students, through scholarship funds that have been made available to over ninety colleges and universities, in forty states. In this year's tournament program, alongside a picture of Crosby in a double-page spread — he is seen carrying four irons and a wood over his shoulder — the following statement by Bing appears: "If I were asked what single thing has given me the most gratification in my long and sometimes pedestrian career, I think I would have to say it is this tournament."

Because of their marathon hoked-up feud and the many movies they made together, Bing Crosby and Bob Hope were linked in the public mind as the closest of friends. They were decidedly good friends, but, like most stars of their magnitude, each really went his own way. They were men of extremely different natures. Hope is essentially what he appears to be — a happy, pleasant extrovert who can be funny without a script, loves to be funny, and, as a friend of his once put it, looks forward eagerly to breaking up the next washroom attendant with a few well-tested one-liners. Crosby was far more complicated. He was fundamentally a rather private person, and liked to spend quite a bit of time by himself, reading (something he did extensively), looking into his various interests, or simply thinking. This led some people to refer to him as a loner — a tag he resented, and with good reason, for, while there was a streak of shyness in him, he was at times the soul of gregariousness. As long as a person was bright or amusing or congenial, it mattered little to Crosby how wealthy or socially prominent he might be, and his friends included studio technicians, musicians, chauffeurs, horse trainers, and proprietors of bowling alleys. He had few truly intimate friends. One person he saw a good deal of was Basil Grillo, who over the last thirty years has served as the operating head of Bing Crosby Enterprises. Most people agree that probably the three men who knew him best were George Coleman, a wealthy oilman; Vic Bergeron, who started the Trader Vic restaurants; and Phil Harris, the orchestra leader, whom he met back in 1925. Besides being comfortable companions, these men were in a position to lead flexible existences — to get packed and go fishing, golfing, or whatever at short notice. This was something that Crosby appreciated. When there was work to be done, he was the complete professional — always prepared, always punctual — but during his free time he liked to do what he wanted to do when he wanted to do it. If a friend phoned Crosby at seven in the morning and suggested something that appealed to him, he was one of those men who would be ready to be picked up in fifteen minutes.

Unlike most people of his degree of celebrity, Crosby travelled without an entourage. When the spirit moved him, he liked to mingle with everyday people; he enjoyed them, and the rapport he could establish with them was heartening to him. Once, when he was in New York and wanted to go to the races at Aqueduct, instead of hiring a limousine or a taxi he took the subway. Another time, in the early nineteen-fifties, when he was in Paris and was wandering by himself along the Champs-Élysées on a balmy night, he sat down on a bench near the Rond-Point to enjoy the world, fell asleep, and was roused the next morning by a puzzled *agent de police*. There was nothing singular about his working out with the Pittsburgh Pirates, a baseball team in which he had a financial interest — many owners derive pleasure from that — but it surprised me to learn that in the days when he had a ranch, in Elko, Nevada, he would get on a horse at seven in the morning and ride all day. The intense workout recharged him. If Crosby could be remote on occasion, he could also be extraordinarily thoughtful. One year when he went on safari in Africa with Virgil Sherrill, a New York businessman who had been a Crosby tournament regular for many years, and six other people, he busied himself in the evenings working out lyrics about the various members of the party and putting each set of lines to some familiar tune. On his return to the States, he hired a studio and a small band, and then sent each of his companions a copy of the recording he put together.

Most of Crosby's friends agree that when he moved from the Los Angeles area to the residential community of Hillsborough, south of San Francisco, in 1963, a few years after his second marriage, to Kathryn Grant, the new locale suited him admirably. The move took him out of the old hubbub, except when he wanted a taste of it, and he was able to lead a quiet, orderly family life, as was his wish. A man who basically thrived on routine, he rose quite early in the morning, breakfasted, read the paper, answered his mail, and then called in his butler, Fisher — whom he had found in England — to discuss the schedule for the day. He played his golf at the nearby Burlingame Country Club, where he was treated, as he wanted to be, as just another member. A lot of his rounds were with his sons by his second marriage, Harry and Nathaniel, two pleasantly intelligent young men. Three years ago, when Harry was sixteen, Nathaniel thirteen, and Bing seventy, each played to a 9 handicap. Harry has since spent less time on golf and more on music. A good classical guitarist, he is now studying at the London Academy of Music and Dramatic Art. Nathaniel, who is tall and slim, decided at the age of eleven that he would like to become a golf professional, and now, at sixteen, that is still his goal. He has an unmistakable talent for the game, and plays to a 1 handicap. This year, he took his father's place as the sponsor of the Crosby, and though the pressure on him was unrelenting, performed equably and well. It is pleasant to know that the family wishes to continue the tournament.

As was generally appreciated, Crosby had an extremely good

mind. He was fascinated by language and enjoyed concocting phrases that were out of the ordinary and had a little flick to them. He had a startlingly good memory. One friend has estimated that he knew twenty thousand or so people by name. Throughout his life, of course, he devoted a large portion of his time to sports — more, perhaps, than any other celebrity of our era. They were a source of both stimulation and relaxation. He did not sing very often just for the pleasure of singing, but when he was out on a golf course with old friends he would break into song, hardly aware that he was doing so, and, even more frequently, he would whistle his way down the fairways. He appeared to be just as honestly nonchalant as this when he played in the 1950 British Amateur Championship, on the Old Course at St. Andrews. The news that he would be appearing in the championship sent a wave of excitement through Scotland, a land in which he was a great favorite, and the morning that he teed off on his opening round, against J. K. Wilson, a carpenter from St. Andrews, dozens of buses and numberless private cars converged on that speck of eastern Fife, and approximately twenty thousand fans were soon packed along the borders of the course. Crosby did not let them down: He birdied two of the first three holes. I saw only the first birdie, and it was a beauty. The opening hole at St. Andrews is a drive-and-pitch par 4 only 374 yards long, but it is a ticklish proposition, because the green is set smack on the far side of the Swilken Burn, which twists across the fairway. After a good drive down the right side of the fairway, Crosby took what looked like a 7-iron and hit a very sweet pitch, which cleared the burn by a couple of yards and finished three feet from the pin. He eventually lost the match, 3 and 2, but I have an idea that he did not want to create such a crowd scene again — he hadn't expected anything like it — and intentionally let a few holes slip away as the round wore on.

I think I will always remember how well Crosby played the first hole of that championship — particularly that classic approach shot. It was a remarkable exhibition under the cirumstances, but this was a rather remarkable man — a very nice man who gravitated to high standards and who kept on growing all his life.

(1978)

Player's Incredible Last Nine
in the Masters

*By the time he was thirty-seven, Gary Player had won the national open of
his home country, South Africa, no fewer than nine times. In addition, he
had won our Open once, our P.G.A. twice, and the Masters twice. He
had carried off the British Open in 1959, 1968, and 1974; the Piccadilly
World Match Play Championship five times; the Egyptian Match Play
Championship; the Japan Air Lines Open; the Australian Open six times
and the Australian P.G.A. twice; the Brazilian Open twice; and had
teamed with Harold Henning to win the World Cup in 1965. He was one
golfer who could carry his best game a little further than his local airport.
In 1978, still as fit as ever but now in his forties, Player surprised the golf
world by capturing his third Masters when his chances seemed hopeless.*

EVER SINCE GENE SARAZEN HOLED OUT A 4-WOOD SHOT FOR HIS
double-eagle 2 on the fifteenth hole in the last round of the second
Masters tournament, in 1935, and went on to tie Craig Wood for
first and to defeat him in a playoff, the Masters has been known
for the high number of dramatic finishes it has provided. At the
same time, a certain law of averages has obtained, and golf fans
have learned that, after they have been treated to an especially
thrilling Masters, more likely than not a few years will follow in
which the tournament will probably be relatively placid, like the
P.G.A. Championship or a George Eliot novel. For example, after
the 1975 Masters, which was perhaps the most exciting three-man
battle in the history of the game — as you may remember, on the
last day Jack Nicklaus holed a twisting, uphill birdie putt of some
forty feet on the sixteenth green to edge out Johnny Miller and

Tom Weiskopf by a stroke in a four-hour struggle crammed with the most dazzling kind of golf, which was not concluded until the last green, where Miller and Weiskopf barely missed birdie putts — no one was really surprised when the 1976 Masters proved to be one of the most soporific tournaments ever: Ray Floyd took the lead on the opening day and was never seriously challenged thereafter. In 1977, however, most Augusta regulars, conditioned by the percentages, were unprepared for that year's Masters' tremendously stirring stretch duel, in which Tom Watson, playing half a hole behind Nicklaus and watching all the marvellous strokes that Nicklaus summoned, managed to stand up to the man who is the most awesome competitor in golf (and possibly in all of sport) and, finally, carry the day by sinking a curling birdie putt on the seventeenth green. And certainly none of us expected yet another historic tournament this April, but for the third time in four years we had an extraordinary Masters — one that will be discussed and dissected as long as the game is played.

The 1978 Masters had a different pattern from any of its predecessors. Four men, each with a chance to win, were bunched during the final hour and a half. I am not sure, but I don't think that there has ever been a four-horse race quite like it anytime, anywhere. During most of the afternoon, the interest centered on whether or not Hubert Green, the current United States Open champion, could hold off the challenges of Watson and Rod Funseth, both of whom had started the round three strokes behind him. Very little attention was paid to Gary Player, of South Africa — the ultimate winner — since he had started the final round seven shots off the pace. Slowly, quietly, almost indiscernibly, Player, the fourth horse, crept into contention. He was out in 34, two under par. This put him five under par for the tournament, and his name then went up on the leader boards, but he was still so far back that no one thought that even Player, a nerveless man who thrives on pressure and the big occasion, could mount a serious challenge on the last nine. Well, he did. In an incredible display of solid shotmaking and some fantastic clutch putting, he proceeded to birdie the tenth, the twelfth, the thirteenth, the fifteenth, the sixteenth, and the eighteenth holes while parring the other three. This gave him a 64, eight under par, for the round, and a seventy-two-hole total of 277, eleven under par. When he posted that score, there was no assurance that it would hold up and gain him a third Masters title, since Watson, Green, and Funseth were still out on the course with a chance to beat his total or tie it and send the tournament into a sudden-death playoff. While it would be completely wrong to say that Player did not *win* the forty-second Masters — I don't remember any previous golfer's playing the last nine holes of a major tournament in thirty strokes, as he did — Watson, Green, and Funseth also had, in effect, to lose it. For the most part, the decisive shots were played on the last hole, before an enormous horseshoe-shaped gallery that watched the drama in hushed silence. This, it should be noted, was one of the best-run Masters tournaments ever.

Of the men with a chance to tie or defeat Player, Watson, a twenty-eight-year-old Stanford graduate who is probably the most literate golfer on the pro tour, was the first to come to the eighteenth, a 420-yard par 4 on which the fairway swings to the right and runs steadily uphill to a two-level green that slopes from back to front and is protected by two bunkers — a shallow one on the right, and a deep one before the green. On the final round of the Masters, it is customary to place the pin on the lower level of the green on the left-hand side, bringing the front bunker very much into play. The pin was set in that position in this Masters. To tie Player, Watson needed only to par the eighteenth. He made his crucial error off the tee. Playing a 4-wood in order to be sure to end up short of the bunkers that patrol the left side of the fairway, he hit a bad tee shot, hooking the ball into the trees on the left, well short of the bunkers. From that difficult spot he had the option, as he later explained, of either fading his approach into the green from left to right or hooking it in from right to left. He decided on the former, and took a 4-iron. The fade, however, did not come off, and the ball plummeted down among the spectators massed to the left of the green. With his ball lying thirty-five feet from the edge of the green at the bottom of a sharp bank, and with only about fifteen feet of green to work with, Watson elected to play his third stroke with his putter. He hit a very good shot, which trickled some eight feet past the cup. He figured that his sidehill putt would break about an inch and a half from right to left. It did break, but not that much, slipping by just above the cup. What a hard way to lose after all the fine shots he had played throughout the tournament, and all the courage he had shown!

Then Green and Funseth, who were the final twosome, came to the eighteenth. Funseth needed a birdie to tie Player. A soft-spoken man of bulky build who, at forty-five, is one of the oldest touring pros, Funseth had been in the lead or near the lead from the start of the tournament, but, curiously, had remained a passive shadow during the four days, partly because his manner is inexplicably self-deprecatory for a golfer of his ability, and partly because he has seldom been a factor in any of the big championships. He flew his approach over the top of the flag. It sat down about twenty feet past the cup, leaving him with a slippery downhill putt. Now Hubert Green. After missing his par on the sixteenth, where he took three putts from fifteen feet, he now needed a birdie to tie Player. Following a good drive, he had only an 8-iron left. In this crisis, he played a superlative approach. On the pin all the way, it spun itself out two and a half feet to the left of the cup. Funseth read his twenty-foot birdie putt to break a shade from right to left, he later said. He played it precisely as he intended to. The ball moved slightly to the left, but as it neared the cup it seemed to veer a touch to the right, and finished on the right lip. Hard luck indeed. Funseth had played a splendid tournament from the first hole on. Green is an excellent putter, and I think that nearly everyone expected him to make his two-and-a-half-footer, although on that tricky green a putt of any length is not an easy one. He missed it. He pushed it to the right, and it slid by the cup without touching the rim. That putt brought back memories of the British Open at St. Andrews in 1970, when Doug Sanders, having only to hole a three-footer from behind the cup on the home green to win the championship, pushed it to the right of the cup; in the playoff the next day he lost by a stroke to Nicklaus. There was an added similarity between the putts that Green and Sanders missed: Each man had allowed his concentration to be broken before making the stroke. In Sanders' case, after lining up his putt he bent down from his position of address to pick up a piece of glinting brown grass, which he thought was a pebble. He did not step away and line up the putt again. As for Green, just when he was comfortably positioned over his putt he was distracted by the voice of a radio announcer. He walked away and then got set again for the putt, but he seemed to take insufficient time with it. In any event, as he was the first to admit, he played a poor stroke, lifting the putter up abruptly on the backswing and then opening the blade a trifle as he tapped through the ball. After Green missed this critical putt, it was almost as if reality were suspended for a moment, like motion-picture film jamming in the projector. Everyone at the eighteenth had been thinking only of hurrying to the first hole for the playoff. It seemed like ages before Green walked over and made the tap-in that didn't count. While he did this, the gallery remained transfixed. Then it slowly dawned on the vast assembly that what they had seen had actually occurred: The tournament was over, and Gary Player had won it. The victory brought to nine the total of major championships that Player has won: three British Opens (1959, 1968, and 1974); two P.G.A.s (1962 and 1972); one U.S. Open (1965); and three Masters tournaments (1961, 1974, and 1978). That equals the number of major championships won by Ben Hogan. Only three men have won more: Jack Nicklaus, with sixteen; Bobby Jones, with thirteen; and Walter Hagen, with eleven. At forty-two, Player is the oldest golfer to win the Masters.

I very much doubt if anyone with a chance to win has ever played the last nine holes of a major championship as supernally well as Player did the last nine of the 1978 Masters. An abbreviated review of that stretch run seems to be in order. On the tenth, a 485-yard par 4, he put a 5-iron twenty-five feet to the right of the pin and holed the birdie putt. On the eleventh, a 445-yard par 4, he pushed his 4-iron approach sixteen feet or so to the right of the green, then improvised a little wedge pitch that slowed down as it neared the cup, hit the rim, and twisted out. On the 155-yard twelfth, over Rae's Creek, he hit a high 7-iron fifteen feet to the left of the pin and holed that birdie putt. On the par-5 thirteenth, he was a scant twelve feet from the pin after a big drive and a gorgeous 4-iron; his putt for the eagle grazed the right edge of the cup. On the fourteenth, 420 yards long, his approach, an 8-iron, ended up only six feet from the pin, but he missed his try for the birdie. On the par-5 fifteenth, he was on in two, and two-putted from fifty feet for his birdie. On the sixteenth, 190 yards long, he played a 5-iron to within fifteen feet of the hole and made the slippery birdie putt. On the 400-yard seventeenth, he was on in two with an 8-iron, twenty feet from the pin, but did not make his birdie putt. Then, on the home hole — and he knew full well he needed still another birdie to have a real chance — he used a 3-wood off the tee and followed it with an excellent 6-iron approach fifteen feet from the pin. He read the all-important putt correctly and stroked it smoothly into the cup for the birdie that in the end spelled the difference. You simply cannot play nine holes any better than that.

In most record books, Player is listed as standing five feet eight, but he may be nearer to five-seven. He does not, however, give the impression of being a small man. He has a splendid physique, which he has built up and maintained by constant attention to diet and exercise. He weighed a hundred and fifty pounds when he turned professional, in 1952, and he still does. In 1957, when I first saw him play, I was terribly disappointed. He had an ugly swing, for he was intent on hitting the golf ball as far as the big men did, and in his pursuit of length he set up in an overly wide stance, wrapped the club around his neck going back, and practically jumped at the ball at impact. Besides this, he had a defective grip, and on many rounds he was all over the course. Nevertheless, he contrived to bring in some surprisingly good scores, for he used the wedge well and putted like an angel. (In those days, he employed a locked-wrist method of putting, with the movement of his shoulders controlling his stroke.) He was also aided incalculably by his persistence: Success at school sports had convinced him that he had athletic coördination, and he was determined to be a golf champion. When I saw him in action the next year, 1958, I barely recognized his swing. I don't know how he managed the change so quickly, but he had transformed it completely. He now had a good-looking orthodox American-type swing, and he hit the ball nicely and far. Over the last decades, he has had his hot streaks and his slumps, but he has never stopped working on the technical nuances of hitting the golf ball as well as he can. Since he understands clearly what the proper movements should be in the vital part of the swing — when the golfer moves into the ball and hits through it — he has been able to remedy bad habits (all golfers fall into them periodically) and come back ready for the next big event. Today, when practicing, he works mainly on tempo. Unquestionably, he has long been and still is the best bunker player in the world. In temperament, he is somewhat like Arnold Palmer, in that he can concentrate during the heat of tournament play on at least three different levels simultaneously. There is also a helpful theatrical streak in his personality, which enables him to respond well to the strident galleries, the spur of competition, and the dramatic moment.

Player lives with his wife, Vivienne, and their six children in a suburb of Johannesburg called Honeydew, where he raises race horses. He has won the South African Open eleven times. There has never been a golfer who has performed outside his own country as well as Player. This is an index of his remarkable talent, for the game is played under subtly different conditions in every land, and so requires the ability to adjust and readjust. Player has won more than a hundred tournaments around the globe. He has won the Piccadilly World Match Play Championship, at Wentworth, outside London, five times. Teamed with Harold Henning, he won the World Cup for South Africa at the Club de Campo, in Madrid, in 1965; that year, too, he won the trophy for the lowest individual total score, and he won it again last year, at the Wack Wack course, in Manila. He has taken the Brazilian Open twice. He has won in Egypt and in Japan, and he has carried off the Australian P.G.A. Championship twice and the Australian Open no fewer than seven times. He looks much younger than he is, possibly because he has never been out of top condition. "I believe that if a man takes care of himself, then, all things being equal, he should be as competent a golfer at fifty as he was at thirty," he said at the conclusion of the Masters. There is no telling, of course, whether Player at fifty will be a threat in the major championships of 1986, but, you know, he might.

(1978)

Back to Cherry Hills

In 1978 the U.S. Open was held at Cherry Hills, on the edge of Denver, for the first time since 1960. In preparing the article about the Open, it seemed a good idea to devote part of it to the 1960 Open, for it was his stirring, come-from-behind victory at Cherry Hills that really projected Arnold Palmer to stardom. The tone of this excerpt is nostalgic, and it flashbacks all the way to Francis Ouimet's epochal victory in the 1913 Open.

ON A GRAY SATURDAY IN MID-SEPTEMBER OF 1913, WHEN A CON-tinuous drizzle fell on the already rain-soaked course of The Country Club, in Brookline, Massachusetts, what was perhaps the most momentous round in the history of American golf took place: in a three-man playoff for the United States Open championship, Harry Vardon and Ted Ray, the celebrated English professionals who had come to this country for an exhibition tour, were defeated by Francis Ouimet, a twenty-year-old amateur who had grown up across the street from The Country Club and had caddied there for several years. Outside the Boston area, few people had ever heard of Ouimet, and even those who had were stunned to learn that this young fellow, the son of a gardener, had defeated the famous Englishmen and, furthermore, had come within a stroke of tying their best ball. The significant thing was that the news of his victory was read not only by the small number of well-to-do Americans who then played golf but also by millions of other Americans, of all strata, who weren't the least bit interested in golf. They read about Ouimet's victory because newspaper editors throughout the country thought that the story deserved to be run on the front page and put it there. The repercussions were enormous. A young man like Ouimet was someone whom the average American could empathize with, and thousands upon thousands proceeded to look into golf, many took it up avidly, and a large percentage of them converted their friends to their new passion. In 1913, fewer than three hundred and fifty thousand Americans played golf. Ten years later, two million did.

Ouimet's epic triumph, besides igniting the biggest boom a new game had ever enjoyed in this country, set the people who followed sports to following tournament golf. It made them particularly conscious of the United States Open, our national championship, which had been inaugurated in 1895, thirty-five years after the first British Open was played. The Open remains our most important tournament, and it is generally regarded as the most important tournament in the world — an eminence it gained toward the end of the nineteen-twenties, when it became apparent that Bobby Jones, Walter Hagen, Gene Sarazen, and the other top American golfers were clearly superior to the best players produced in Britain, the land that, ever since golf was invented, in Scotland in around the twelfth century, had been unrivalled in all aspects of the game.

While it is unarguable that no other tournament can compare with the Masters in the abundance of stirring finishes it has been blessed with, our Open has certainly not lacked for drama, despite the fact that prior to 1965 it was customary for the last two rounds of the championship to be played on the same day. (This meant that the men who were in the lead or close to it after the third, or morning, round were not necessarily grouped together in the last pairs to go out, after lunch, in the fourth round; they are so grouped now, of course, in the final round of a four-day, seventy-two-hole tournament, the standard format for a dozen years.) In any event, ever since the landmark championship of 1913 a third of our Opens have resulted in playoffs, and a good many others have come down to the last green before the outcome was decided. Fred Corcoran, the veteran golf entrepreneur who died last year, was fond of pointing out that no one had ever won the Open by sinking a long putt on the last green, but that is the only form of excitement the Open has failed to provide. For example, Tommy Armour in 1927, and Bobby Jones in 1929 — to name two memorable golfers and Opens — had to hole a sizable putt on the seventy-second green to tie the leader and force a playoff (which both won, by the way). Down through the years, the championship has treated us to an endless variety of glittering stretch drives that have changed what had appeared to be an inevitable outcome. There was Billy Casper's great rush in 1966 at the Olympic Club, in San Francisco, in which he caught Arnold Palmer by making up seven shots on the last nine holes. The next day, Casper went on to win the playoff after again trailing Palmer at the end of the first nine, though this time by only two strokes. More recently, on the gnarled old course of the Oakmont Country Club, near Pittsburgh, Johnny Miller, who few savants felt had a chance to win when he started the fourth round six strokes behind the leaders, turned the 1973 championship inside out and won it with a closing 63 — a score that seems a form of sacrilege at Oakmont, even taking into consideration that a heavy rain had made it possible for the players to shoot right for the flagstick. The course has long been notorious for its frighteningly hard-surfaced greens, which, when dry and cut short, are as slippery as glass to putt on.

The Open has also produced some unforgettable instances of sustained heroics, such as Ken Venturi's performance at the Congressional Country Club, outside Washington, in winning the championship in 1964 — the last Open in which the field played two rounds on the final day. That day turned out to be a scorcher, the temperature climbing high into the nineties. At the end of the morning round, on which Venturi had shot a 66 — four under par — despite missing tap-in putts on the seventeenth and eighteenth greens, he was only two strokes off the pace, but he had been close to collapse from the heat on the last four holes, and it was questionable whether he would be able to play the fourth round. A doctor examined him. He was allowed to continue, but the doctor walked the final eighteen holes with him, just to make sure. Venturi, who had played a succession of well-thought-out and sharply struck shots in the morning, continued his beautiful golf in the afternoon, matching par for the round and winning by the comfortable margin of four strokes. Many Open aficionados consider Venturi's Open the most thrilling since Ouimet's, and I must say that I thoroughly agree with them.

What, you ask, has brought on this nostalgic walk down the old Open fairways? Very simply, the fact that the venue of the 1978 championship, which Andy North won last month, was the Cherry Hills Country Club, on the outskirts of Denver. Cherry Hills has now been the scene of three Opens. The first of these, in

1938, was the first Open held in the Western part of the country. Ralph Guldahl ran away from the field that year, finishing six strokes ahead of the second man, Dick Metz. I missed that Open, but I was on hand in 1960, the second time Cherry Hills put on the championship — surely one of the great Opens of all time. Denver was a much smaller city then than it is now. Today, it has a National Football League team called the Broncos, which went to the last Super Bowl, and an excellent National Basketball Association team called the Nuggets, which went to the semifinals of the championship playoffs this year, and if Bowie Kuhn and Charlie Finley ever finish their squabbling, it may get a major-league baseball team, the financially beleaguered Oakland A's. But in 1960 one thought of Denver principally as the Mile High City — an old Western town slowly growing up, a town that was the home of the Brown Palace, and that offered a visitor intoxicatingly clean air, bright sunshine, and a view of the easternmost range of the Rockies. (In mid-June, Open time, the tallest peaks are still covered with snow.) In short, it retained the ambience of an earlier and vastly appealing America. Fresh in my memory are the young boys operating their lemonade stands beneath the cottonwoods and Chinese elms bordering the perimeter of the golf course. A large drink cost a dime, a small one a nickel. *O tempora! O mores! O denarii!*

Few clubs were as well organized to put on the U.S. Open as Cherry Hills was in 1960. There was, however, one unfortunate difficulty: the course was not long enough to be a bona-fide championship test. Designed by Bill Flynn, the able golf-course architect from Philadelphia, it measured 7,004 yards, but in the thin air a mile above sea level the flight of a golf ball was increased seven per cent. For example, on the seventeenth hole, a 548-yard par 5 on which the green was on an island in a large pond, Jack Nicklaus — he was still in college — flabbergasted everyone by reaching the green in a practice round with a drive and a 7-iron. It was the first nine, though, that caused most of the concern. At 3,316 yards, it was much shorter than the second nine and no match for the power-hitting pros. After walloping a big drive on most of the par-4 holes on this nine, they had just a short pitch left to the green. As it turned out, the vulnerability of this first nine accounted for the *Sturm und Drang* that took place on the final afternoon.

Up to that final round, Mike Souchak, a burly young man who

had played end for Duke, had dominated the championship. On the opening day, he moved into the lead with a 68, three under par. He had used only twenty-six putts, which was remarkable, inasmuch as the greens were so dried out by the sun and afternoon winds that they had to be watered at night. On the second day, Souchak added a 67, and his 135 broke the record low total for the first thirty-six holes of the Open by three strokes. After the morning round on Saturday, the third and last day, Souchak was still out in front, but his lead was down to two strokes. It had been four strokes on the tee of the eighteenth, or fifty-fourth, hole, an exacting 468-yard par 4 on which a golfer had to hit a long drive over the lake to reach the left side of the heaving fairway. Souchak, intent on hitting a safe tee shot, shoved it much farther to the right than he had meant to, and the ball bounced out of bounds — a two-stroke penalty.

A two-stroke lead is not a four-stroke lead. Souchak's costly error had brought the field back to him and revived many hopes. One of the men whose eyes took on a new gleam was Palmer. At this stage of his career, Arnie was regarded as a fine golfer, but the admiration he inspired was much more restrained than it would later become. While he had already won three major championships — the 1954 United States Amateur and the 1958 and 1960 Masters — and was enjoying a big season, no one as yet spoke about his charisma or imitated the way he hiked up his trousers or used his method of putting from an exaggerated knock-kneed stance, but golf fans knew how strong he was and loved his aggressive tactics. In any event, at Cherry Hills he had played so-so rounds of 72, 71, and 72, which placed him seven strokes behind Souchak with eighteen holes to go, and so his name never came up at midday on Saturday when one discussed the probable challengers. Shortly before he was due on the first tee at one-forty-five to begin his final round, Palmer said to Bob Drum, an old friend of his, "I may shoot a 65 out there. What'll that do?" Drum replied, "That'll do nothing. You're too many shots back."

The first hole at Cherry Hills in 1960 was 346 yards long — a straightaway hole with an elevated tee. To make certain that no one drove the green, a stretch of the fairway just before the green had been allowed to grow up into tangled rough. On his final round, Palmer threw every last ounce of power into his opening tee shot and hit a huge drive that hopped out of this barrier of rough and onto the green, twenty feet from the pin. He missed his putt for his eagle, but his birdie did wonders for him. During his top years, Palmer's state of mind under tournament stress was different from that of most great golf champions: he really did depend to quite a large extent on the emotional lift he gained from pulling off a daring shot or holing a monstrous putt in a critical situation. Then, feeling that the ball was running for him, his confidence grew and grew, and frequently there was no stopping him. In that fourth round at Cherry Hills, buoyed up by his opening birdie, he smashed another long drive down the second, a 410-yard par 4, but he misgauged his pitch, and the ball finished on the fringe of the green, thirty-five feet from the pin. He ran his chip into the cup for a second birdie. On the third hole, a 348-yard par 4 that bent to the left, he hit another big drive and put his approach, a wedge flip, a foot from the stick. Three under par for the round so far. On the fourth, 426 yards long, he needed only a wedge for his second. He played a rather ordinary shot, but rapped in a putt of eighteen feet for his fourth consecutive birdie.

If there was any one hole on the front nine you would have picked Palmer to birdie, it was the fifth — the only par 5 on that side. It was moderately long — 538 yards — but in the thin mountain air a top professional could get home with two solid shots. Palmer hurried his timing on his drive a fraction, however, and when his ball ended up in a poor lie in the matted rough on the left, he had to be satisfied with a par. The sixth hole was a somewhat tricky par 3 of 174 yards. The green sloped down from back to front, and most players tended to be cautious with their putts. Palmer's 7-iron shot left him with a sidehill putt of twenty-five feet. He hit it with evident assurance and holed it. (In recent years, when Palmer's putting has been the least dependable part of his game, some sports followers have tended to forget that during his best years he possibly made more important long putts than any other tournament golfer in history over a similar span of time.) He had five birdies in six holes now. He picked up another on the seventh, a 411-yard par 4, where he stopped a soft wedge six feet from the pin.

As Palmer stood on the tee of the eighth hole, he was surrounded by an exuberant, swelling gallery for the first time; it had taken a little while for the news of his dash to get around. He deliberated longer than usual before deciding on the club he wanted to use on that hole, a 233-yard par 3, on which the pin was set on the left side of the green, tight behind an intimidating front bunker. Perhaps the wise decision would have been to play conservatively, for the center of the green, but now, attacking with every shot, Palmer went straight for the pin with a 2-iron. He had the ball dead on line, and as he squinted at it in the distance, you could sense that he had hit precisely the shot he meant to, and that he felt it might end up close to the hole. No, the ball caught the far edge of the front bunker; he had underestimated the distance by about three feet. He played a first-rate sand shot a yard from the cup but then failed to sink the putt. Back to five under par for the round. He made the turn in 30 after parring the ninth.

At that point, it was far from a foregone conclusion that Palmer would go on to win. He had an excellent chance, of course, but muffing that short putt on the eighth had changed things. Generally, if a golfer stumbles into a bogey after a hot streak like Palmer's — birdie, birdie, birdie, birdie, par, birdie, birdie — it is not easy for him to regain his momentum, or the conviction that destiny is watching over him and has programmed a historic winning round stroke by stroke. There was another highly relevant matter to consider, too: Palmer's brilliant burst hadn't exactly scattered the field. An hour after he had started his round, no fewer than eleven other players had a reasonable crack at winning the championship. Souchak was still out in front, but Julius Boros, Dow Finsterwald, and Jack Nicklaus were only one stroke behind him, Ben Hogan was only two behind, and Jack Fleck and Jerry Barber (along with Palmer) were only three behind. Don Cherry, an amateur, still had a chance. There was no reliable news about Dutch Harrison, who had gone out early and was somewhere on the second nine, but he was rumored to have a terrific round going. Moreover, it was too early to write off two players who were among the last starters that afternoon — Billy Casper and Ted Kroll. As it turned out, Kroll began his round with a stream of figures almost as incredible as Palmer's: he birdied five, parred one, and bogeyed one of the first seven holes. Fleck had got off just as fast, with five birdies and one bogey on the first six holes.

Halfway through that final afternoon at Cherry Hills, more players were validly in the running than in any other U.S. Open I can think of. (It was impossible to know how all the contenders stood at any given moment, because there were only a few small scoreboards out on the course, and they were operated in such a haphazard manner that several of the men clustered near the lead were not even listed on some boards, and the data on those who were were often late in being posted and frequently varied from board to board. This was the only serious flaw at Cherry Hills in the staging of the Open — one of the most complex events in all of sport.) The only previous U.S. Open that could be compared with this one for sheer congestion was the 1925 Open, at the Worcester Country Club, in Massachusetts, when seven players came to the seventy-second tee with a chance to win or to tie for first. The finishing hole at Worcester, a typical Donald Ross product, was a 335-yard par 4 to a two-level plateau green guarded by an array of bunkers but in the main by a deep, gleaming pit cut directly in front of and below the green. The first of the seven contenders to tackle it was Leo Diegel, one of the most talented golfers of all time and, because of his high-strung temperament, one of the unluckiest. He needed a 4 for a total of 292. He took an 8. He was followed by Johnny Farrell. Farrell's approach ended up a fair distance from the pin, set on the lower level of the green, not far from the commanding front bunker. He two-putted for his 4. This gave Farrell a total of 292 and made him what most sportscasters now call "the leader in the clubhouse." In the good old days of 1925, he was probably referred to more sensibly as the golfer who had so far brought in the lowest seventy-two-hole score. Gene Sarazen came next. He got his par 4, but he had needed a 3 for 292. Then came Bobby Jones. A 4 would give him a total of 291 and the lead. He was on nicely in two and down nicely in two for his par. Shortly afterward, Willie Macfarlane came to the eighteenth. A tall, slim, scholarly-looking Scot from Aberdeen, Macfarlane could tie Jones if he finished with a par. Macfarlane's approach ended on the upper level of the green, but, fortunately for him, his playing partner, Francis Gallett, was a few inches outside him. Macfarlane, with the advantage of being able to watch Gallett putt first, gained a good idea of the speed and break of the green. Gallett had gone yards by, but Macfarlane lagged his approach putt a foot short of the hole and made his par to go into a tie with Jones. Two contenders later came to the eighteenth, each with a chance to join Jones and Macfarlane at the top if he could come up with a birdie 3. The first was Francis Ouimet. He had to be satisfied with a 4. (To protect himself from the wicked sun, Ouimet wore an Indian topee, and, as further protection, had placed a large leaf of lettuce inside it on top of his head — all this on the advice of a friend who had spent a few weeks east of Suez.) The second was Walter Hagen. A great short-iron player, Hagen tried to feather a delicate pitch inches over the front bunker to give himself a reasonable crack at the birdie he had to get. His pitch, which looked as if it might be just what he wanted, caught the high face of the bunker. In their playoff the next day, Jones and Macfarlane were tied after eighteen holes, so another round was ordained for the afternoon. Trailing by four strokes after nine holes, Macfarlane won by coming home in 33. He had two 2s on the two par 3s, and that did it.

Back to Cherry Hills and the 1960 Open. As was perhaps inevitable with so many players bunched so tightly, when things started to pop it was impossible to keep up with them. At four o'clock, Souchak and two challengers were tied for the lead at five under par for the tournament. Only minutes later, after Souchak had bogeyed the ninth, he lost his share of the lead and was never again in the battle. At about ten minutes after four, Nicklaus, all of twenty years old, was out in front by himself, five under par for the tournament, after going out in 32 and then starting back with three well-played pars. Ten minutes later, after taking three putts from ten feet on the thirteenth, Nicklaus had fallen back to four under and into a triple tie with Boros, playing a hole behind him, and Palmer, two holes behind him. On the fourteenth green, with a difficult hogback to cross, Nicklaus again three-putted, surrendering the lead to Boros and Palmer, and slipping back into a tie for second with his playing partner, Hogan, a slightly older man, two months short of turning forty-eight. There is little question that one of the elements that made the 1960 Open a championship to savor was that Hogan, the finest golfer of his time, and Palmer and Nicklaus, the finest of theirs, all had something to say about the winning and losing of it. They are to be cherished, these occasions when circumstance contrives for the graying heroes of a departing era to be locked in combat with the bright-faced young men who are moving up to take their places. The 1920 Open, at Inverness, in Toledo, had been one of those rare championships. Jones and Sarazen, both eighteen, and Diegel, a little older, had made their débuts in the big event that year, and Vardon, who was fifty — an old fifty — had come over from England for a final shot at our Open, which he had won way back in 1900. Had a severe storm off Lake Erie not swept over the course when Vardon was playing the last seven holes, he might well have won at Inverness, but the storm was too much for him, and he finished in a tie for second, a stroke behind his countryman Ray. Ray was forty-three, incidentally — the oldest player ever to win our Open.

Throughout the long, enervating double round on Saturday at Cherry Hills in 1960, Hogan, enveloped in his customary cocoon of concentration, had produced immaculate golf. When, only one stoke off the lead, he walked onto the tee of the fifteenth (or sixty-ninth) hole, a 196-yard par 3, he had hit the green on each of the thirty-two holes he had played that day in the regulation stroke. On the fifteenth, he made it thirty-three straight holes, whistling a 3-iron twenty feet past the pin. Had he been able to make just a few of the many holeable putts that his fastidious iron play had set up, he would have been out in front by several shots, but his putting stroke was no longer what it once was, and he had got down only one putt of any length all day. Here on the fifteenth, his lips set in that familiar half smile, he rolled in his twenty-footer for a 2. Now, if one could trust the information arriving via the grapevine, Hogan was tied for the lead. On the sixteenth, a medium-length par 4, he had a twelve-foot putt for his birdie but missed it. Still, he was in splendid shape as he came walking down the seventeenth, the 548-yard par 5 with the green on a small island that is separated from the fairway by about twenty feet of water. Two of the three contenders playing behind him had fallen off the pace: Boros had dropped a couple of strokes by finding bunkers on two holes, and Fleck had dropped a couple because of some errors in the green area. The only player holding up was Palmer; thus far on the in-nine he had collected one more birdie and, for the rest, a string of pars. However, it should be repeated that out on the course at this point in the late afternoon reliable information on the standing of the leaders was not readily available.

On the seventeenth, a light breeze was blowing against the golfers, and both Hogan and Nicklaus laid up short of the water with their second shots. Hogan's ball finished on the left side of the fairway, about fifty-five yards from the pin, which was positioned in the front right-hand corner of the green, some fifteen feet from the bank at the edge of the water. According to the reports that reached Hogan and Nicklaus via the walkie-talkie operator accompanying their group, several players behind them were still in the hunt. Since he felt that one of them would almost certainly birdie the seventeenth, Hogan, who never gambled in a tight situation, decided that this time he had to. The picture is as clear in my mind as if it were yesterday — Hogan getting the feel of his wedge in his hands as he studied the strip of water dividing the fairway and the green, only too well aware that in order to stop the ball close to the pin he would have to try to carry the water hazard by just two or three feet, since the surface of that corner of the green was extremely hard and a player could not count on getting any backspin on his pitch regardless of the precision with which he made contact with the ball. Hogan laid back the face of his wedge and, cutting crisply under the ball, sent up a soft, spinning pitch that had perfect line and looked to have perfect length. It was a foot too short. There was a gasp from the gallery as the ball slapped against the bank before the green and slid back into the water. Hogan subsequently exploded it out of the hazard and two-putted for a 6. Nicklaus, who had played superlatively well and who ultimately finished second, remembers glancing over at Hogan after he had failed by inches to bring off that crucial pitch and being struck by the instant change in Hogan's demeanor: he looked utterly drained. Hogan finished with a 7 on the home hole, hooking his first drive into the lake and finally taking three to get down from the edge of the green. In retrospect, this proved to be Hogan's last serious challenge to win the Open for a fifth time.

Palmer, as you will remember, was playing about two holes behind Hogan and Nicklaus. When he arrived at the seventeenth, he knew exactly what had happened and what he had to do: pars on the last two holes would win for him. On the seventeenth, he laid up short of the water with his second and made sure of his par 5. On the eighteenth, that tough par 4, he pulled his 4-iron approach slightly, a yard or two off the green, but then played a pretty running chip about four feet below the cup. He knocked the putt into the center of the hole and in almost the same motion, unleashing all his feeling, scaled his visor jubilantly across the green. His score for the round — 30 out and 35 back, for a total of 65 — was the lowest that had ever been shot by an Open winner on the last round. It gave him a total of 280, two strokes lower than Nicklaus's.

(1978)

Long Thoughts about Inverness
and Vardon

Inverness, one of Donald Ross's best-known courses, has been the venue of the U.S. Open in 1920, 1931, 1957, and 1979. The 1979 championship, which was won by Hale Irwin, did not quite come to life, but the first three were exciting, each in a different way. This is the part of the article that deals with them, and especially with Harry Vardon, the first really modern golfer and a thoroughly fine man. Vardon, who had won the first of his six British Opens way back in 1896, seemed to have the 1920 U.S. Open well under control with only nine holes to play, but a storm blew up off Lake Erie, and it proved to be too much for the old boy.

THE MOST PROLIFIC GOLF-COURSE ARCHITECT OF ALL TIME WAS Donald Ross, a pleasant, methodical Scot from Dornoch, in Sutherland, who became the professional at Pinehurst, North Carolina, in 1900, shortly after his arrival in this country, and remained there until his death, at seventy-five, in 1948. Ross, who quickly demonstrated his gift for building good golf holes when he remodelled Pinehurst's original eighteen-hole layout, later constructed three more courses there, making Pinehurst, shortly after the First World War, the first resort in America to offer its clientele seventy-two holes of golf. Because they enjoyed and admired Ross's work, a good many of the people who annually vacationed at Pinehurst approached him to do courses in their home towns, and he is credited with having built no fewer than six hundred in all parts of the country. This is a flabbergasting number, and one must assume that it includes not only the courses he himself worked on during his summers away from Pinehurst and those he looked in on from time to time to check on how his construction superintendents were faring but also those he merely laid out on paper. Apparently, it was not uncommon for Pinehurst regulars to bring with them topographical maps of property back home on which they and their friends intended to build a course, and for Ross to take these maps home with him in the evening and rough out nine or eighteen good, sound holes — a few of which inevitably possessed such Ross specialties as crown greens (formed by levelling the top of a hill) and small, slightly raised greens that were hard to hit because of the adroit positioning of the bunkers and hollows that set them off.

In 1918, the Inverness Club in Toledo, Ohio, which had been making do with nine holes since its formation, in 1903, felt that the time was ripe to build a modern eighteen-hole course. They got in touch with Ross, whose name had become an assurance of superior design. Giving the job his personal attention, he revamped the old nine and created a second nine. When the Ohio State Open was held over the new Inverness in the autumn of 1919, both the players and the spectators were enthusiastic about the course, and, as a result, the United States Golf Association selected it as the venue of the 1920 United States Open Championship. From the old golf hands who attended this Open, I gather that while Inverness proved to be a fairly testing layout, spread over nice rolling terrain, it struck no one as a truly great course. For one thing, its routing was uninspired: No fewer than eight holes (the second, the eleventh, the twelfth, the fourteenth, the fifteenth, the sixteenth, the seventeenth, and the sixth) ran more or less parallel to each other. Certainly it was not at all in the same class as the two courses that are today considered Ross's masterpieces — Seminole, in North Palm Beach, which was completed in 1929, and his wonderful wholesale revision of Pinehurst No. 2, done in the mid-thirties, when advances in agronomy made it possible to replace the old flat sand greens with subtly contoured grass greens. In any event, what made a newly golf-conscious America very much aware of Inverness was not the attributes of Ross's course but, rather, the exciting dénouement of the 1920 Open. It was won by Ted Ray, a burly Englishman with a soupstrainer mustache who always wore a felt or straw hat on the course and played with a pipe in his mouth. Harry Vardon, Leo Diegel, Jack Burke, Sr., and Jock Hutchison finished a shot behind him. Ray was then forty-three, and he remains the oldest golfer ever to win our national championship.

Since 1920, Inverness has held the Open three more times — in 1931, in 1957, and this past June, when Hale Irwin carried the day — and each time an interesting Open took place. Before dealing with the recent championship, it would be worthwhile, I think, to touch on the high points of the earlier ones. Their scenarios differed considerably in some ways, but in other ways they were oddly similar — such as in the crucial role that the eighteenth hole, a par 4 that is only a drive and short pitch, nearly always played in the winning and the losing of the championship. In the 1957 Open, it looked as if Jimmy Demaret, who was then forty-seven, had at last won his first Open when, on the climactic double round on Saturday, he posted a par 70 and then a 72, for a total of 283. (He finished with a great burst: birdie, par, birdie, par.) Half an hour later, though, Dick Mayer holed a sliding nine-foot putt to birdie the eighteenth and nip him by a stroke. Half an hour after that, Cary Middlecoff, having taken several prolonged azimuth readings on the nine-footer he had to sink to birdie the last hole and tie with Mayer, finally got hunched over his ball and stroked it dead into the center of the cup. An exceedingly highstrung athlete, Middlecoff had expended all his energy on Saturday's double round (he had put together a pair of superb 68s), and he had nothing left the next day in the playoff, which Mayer won by seven shots.

The 1931 Open was also decided by a playoff — the longest playoff ever in a major championship. George Von Elm, who had turned professional the previous year, after a distinguished career as an amateur, made a playoff necessary when he holed for a birdie from twelve feet on the seventy-second green to match Billy Burke's four-round total of 292. The next day, Von Elm, a rather dashing type, and Burke, a steady, placid one, met in a thirty-six-hole playoff. Burke had a 73 in the morning and a 76 in the afternoon. Von Elm had a 75 in the morning, and on his second round he again cooly holed a birdie putt of twelve feet on the last green, for a 74 and a matching total of 149. So the two weary golfers set out once more the next morning on yet another double round to see who would be king. Von Elm had a 76 and a 73, Burke a 77 and a beautifully played afternoon round of 71. On the second nine that afternoon, he had eight straight 4s and could have easily made it nine straight, since he was on in two, thirty feet from the cup, on the home green. However, knowing that all he had to do to win was to get down in three putts, he made sure he did: He lagged his approach putt four feet from the hole, cozied the ball to the rim of the cup, and then tapped it in.

For all this, neither the 1957 nor the 1931 Open was as stirring or as significant as the 1920 Open. That was in many respects a watershed Open. To start with, it marked a changing of the guard; it was the last big championship in which Vardon and Ray, who had come to the fore in Britain in the distant days of the gutta-percha ball, played a prominent part, and it was the first appearance in our Open of a clutch of young men, among them Bobby Jones, Gene Sarazen, Johnny Farrell, Tommy Armour, and Diegel, who went on to become outstanding golfers. It was also the first national championship, here or in Britain, in which the entire clubhouse was opened to the professional entrants. The men running Inverness simply made up their minds that it no longer made sense, if it ever had, to regard professional golfers as low-class workingmen who were the social inferiors of the club members and the amateur contestants. Inverness treated the professionals as its guests, and once it had shown the way, the long-standing barriers against the professionals began to disintegrate rapidly. With Walter Hagen, as usual, acting as their leader, the professionals did not fail to let Inverness know how deeply they appreciated "the Toledo spirit." They took up a collection at the close of the tournament and presented the club with a handsome cathedral-chime clock about eight feet high — a clock that still stands in the clubhouse foyer. On a brass plaque attached to the clock at that time is a short verse (no one has any idea who wrote it) that is quite moving:

> God measures men by what they are
> Not what in wealth possess.
> This vibrant message chimes afar
> The voice of Inverness.

Primarily, though, the 1920 Open was the story of Harry Vardon. People are forever debating about who is the greatest golfer who has ever lived. Today, the consensus would probably favor Jack Nicklaus. His credentials *are* awesome. He has won seventeen major championships — four more than the next man, Jones

— and has done it over a period of twenty years: from 1959, when he won his first United States Amateur Championship, through 1978, when he won his third British Open. Longevity, no doubt about it, is a significant consideration in any evaluation of the relative merits of athletic heroes. However, in my opinion the best and fairest way to describe his position in the game's long history is to say that there has never been a better golfer than Nicklaus, just as there has never been a better golfer than Ben Hogan or a better golfer than Bobby Jones. As has been said so often that it is beginning to acquire a patina of triteness, all that one can ask of an athlete is that he be the finest performer in his field in his own age. Jones, Hogan, and Nicklaus have all been that. It is only natural that today's sports fans should be less well informed about the deeds of earlier champions than about the contemporary paragons, but sports experts are another matter, and most of today's experts know far too little about the exploits of Jones and Hogan. As for Vardon, his name hardly rings a bell at all, and yet, on the basis of his record, his marvellous technique, and his overall contribution to golf, he deserves a place on the same level as Nicklaus, Hogan, and Jones.

There has surely never been a better golfer than Harry Vardon. A native of the island of Jersey, he won his first British Open in 1896, at the age of twenty-six. In that era, when the British Open was *the* championship, he won it a record six times, his last victory coming in 1914. In 1900, when he made the first of his three visits to this country, he won our Open, at the Chicago Golf Club, and sold golf everywhere he went by the grace of his style and the astonishing accuracy of his shots. No one had had any idea that a player could control the golf ball in the masterly fashion that Vardon did. A medium-sized man with a strong, athletic frame and extraordinarily large hands, he was undoubtedly the most brilliant fairway-wood player ever; it was nothing unusual for him to rip a full brassie shot right at the flagstick and have the ball flutter down like a leaf ten or fifteen feet from his target. On Vardon's second American tour, in 1913, on which he teamed up with Ray, a fellow-native of Jersey, the two invaders, as fate would have it, tied for first with Francis Ouimet, a twenty-year-old amateur, at The Country Club, in Brookline, Massachusetts, and were subsequently defeated by Ouimet in the playoff — possibly the most momentous round of golf of all time. When the war was over, Vardon and Ray returned to this country for another tour. Vardon was then fifty years old, which in terms of athletic vigor would be roughly the equivalent of being sixty years old nowadays. He had stayed at the top of his profession for a quarter of a century, and that is a rare achievement in sports. At Inverness, he qualified handily. At the end of the first thirty-six holes of the championship, which was played in mid-August, he was in an excellent position: rounds of 74 and 73, for a halfway total of 147, placed him two shots behind the pacemaker, Hutchison, one shot behind Diegel, and in a tie with Hagen and Ray. (The weather was broiling hot in Toledo that week, but Vardon and Ray were used to playing in loose-fitting jackets, and they did so on this occasion. They also wore shirts and ties — as did the whole field.) Despite Vardon's precise golf on the opening day, no one expected too much from the old boy from there on, because the final thirty-six holes were set to be played the following day, and this would work to the advantage of the young and hardy. Thereupon Vardon, in top form, stepped out in front of the pack with a splendid 71 on the morning of the third round. At two o'clock, when he started his afternoon round, he carried most of the spectators with him; they realized that even Vardon couldn't go on forever, and they wanted to cheer him home in what well might be his last crack at winning another big championship.

On the first nine, continuing to split the fairways and hit the greens, Vardon was out in 36. He added a par and then a birdie, and, with only seven holes to go, had a margin over the closest man of a full five strokes. He seemed to have the championship wrapped up. When he was standing on the tee of the twelfth hole, then a 522-yard par 5, the skies suddenly grew dark and a wind of almost gale force swept off Lake Erie and across Inverness. Playing into the fierce wind, Vardon required four shots to reach the twelfth green, and lost a stroke to par there. He lost another stroke to par on the short thirteenth, when he jabbed a two-foot putt wide of the cup. (Near the end of his career, Vardon's play from tee to green was as impressive as ever, but he could be skittish on the greens when he was faced with short putts. As he prepared to tap the ball, a small muscle in his right forearm would sometimes jump visibly, and when it didn't his anxiety that it might ruined his ease and concentration.) By the time Vardon moved to the fourteenth, the extra effort of coping with the wind was beginning to wear him down, and missing that short putt completed his undoing. He took three putts on the fourteenth, three on the fifteenth, and three more on the sixteenth, losing a stroke to par on each of them. He lost two more strokes to par on the seventeenth, a 430-yard par 4. He was plain unlucky here: his second shot just caught the far edge of the brook guarding the green. On the eighteenth, he made his par 4, but apparently he did not have any chance for a birdie, since no account of his round which I have seen mentions how far from the pin he put his pitch or describes his putt. It was all quite tragic, Vardon's collapse. After starting with a double bogey on the first hole on his morning round, he had played the next twenty-eight holes in four under par — a terrific pace in the circumstances — only to go seven over par on the last seven holes of the championship. He had taken forty-two strokes on the second nine in the afternoon. His 78 on the last round gave him a four-round total of 296 and tied him with Burke, an earlier finisher. Now the question was whether Ray, Hutchison, or Diegel, still out on the course, would be able to beat that figure. (Hagen had fallen away.) Ray finished soon after Vardon did. He brought in a rather loose 75, but it was good enough: 74–73–73–75 — 295. He had played erratic stuff on the last nine, bogeying the eleventh, twelfth, fifteenth, and seventeenth, but when he was confronted with the opportunity to win the Open he seized it, and that always takes some doing. Both Hutchison and Diegel eventually had to settle for 296. Hutchison's bid was over when his three-foot putt for a par on the fifteenth rimmed out of the cup. Diegel was in trouble after a double bogey on the fourteenth, but he pulled himself together and barely missed from eight feet on the seventeenth for the birdie he needed, and on the home green he failed to get down a longer but makable birdie putt. Had Diegel managed to win at Inverness, he might have gone on to win our Open several times, but, as it was, he never quite made it, and his two victories at match play in our P.G.A. Championship stand as the high point of his career.

The evening after the storm off Lake Erie prevented Vardon from achieving what had looked to be the perfect storybook climax to his long and illustrious career, he was his usual stoic self as he met with the press and went over his final round. "Even as tired as I was, I can't see yet how I broke so badly," he said. "Why, I am sure I could go out now and do better by kicking the ball around with my boot." It was easy to become fond of Vardon, for modesty and gentleness were deeply ingrained in his nature. His colleagues esteemed him highly, and the esteem was reciprocated. He thought the world of J. H. Taylor and James Braid, his chief rivals (each of them won the British Open five times), who, along with Vardon, formed what was called the Triumvirate, and his regard for them is not difficult to understand. Both were of humble background — Taylor started out as a mason's laborer, Braid as an apprentice joiner — and they typified the old yeoman virtues of strong fibre and generosity of spirit. In Vardon's mind, golf was an ennobling game, and he believed that Braid's and Taylor's closeness to it had a lot to do with their exemplary character. When one considers Vardon's own mild, pleasant manner, with its undertone of shyness, it is odd, and amusing, that the two best-known anecdotes about him present him as a very abrupt person. The first is set in 1900, the year of his first American tour. In one of his appearances in Chicago, his foursome included a left-handed player who on that particular afternoon could do no wrong. After the round, probing for praise, he asked Vardon who was the best left-hander he had ever played with. Vardon took a moment to clear his throat and then said, "Never saw one who was worth a damn." The second anecdote involves Bobby Jones. Some astute member of the championship committee for the 1920 Open thought that it might be an interesting idea to pair Vardon in the qualifying round with Jones, who was then only eighteen but already had the look of a champion. On the seventh, a drive-and-pitch par 4, Vardon hit his second, a little run-up shot, fairly close to the stick. Jones decided he would play a steep niblick pitch, which he intended to strike so crisply that the backspin on the ball would cause it to brake itself quickly on the green and draw back dramatically toward the pin. He looked up on the shot, however, and skulled the ball yards over the green. He did well to make a 5. Still smarting with embarrassment as the two men walked off the green, Jones turned and asked, "Mr. Vardon, did you ever see a worse shot than that?" "No," Vardon said.

Vardon was born in Grouville, on the eastern end of Jersey, which is an island about the size of Nantucket, and which, like the other Channel Islands, belongs to Great Britain, although it lies much closer to France — only fifteen miles or so off the Cotentin Peninsula. Harry was one of eight children of a gardener, and the fourth of six sons. What proved to be the pivotal event of his youth took place in 1877, when he was seven. That summer, some English visitors received permission from the constable of the par-ish of Grouville to lay out a golf course on part of the common land. This became the Royal Jersey Golf Club, and, like most of the local boys, Harry caddied at the club and picked up the game. A surprisingly large number of those Jersey caddies — among them the Gaudins, the Boomers, the Renoufs, the Becks, and, of course, Ted Ray — became very successful professionals. As a boy, Vardon developed into a proficient golfer in no time. This was more or less expected of him, because he was an exceptional all-around athlete — a fast sprinter and a standout at both cricket and soccer. His boyhood ambition was "to excel at cricket," but any idea he might have had about possibly becoming a professional cricketer was hardly more than a daydream, and when his schooling was completed he was apprenticed to a gardener. Had it not been for his brother Tom, who was a couple of years younger but far more enterprising and confident, Harry might never have left Jersey. Hoping to make a career in golf, Tom went to England and got a job as an assistant professional. He proved to be not only an able player but a talented instructor. When he had things under control, he lined up a job for Harry as the professional at Studley Royal, a nine-hole course in the North of England. Harry moved on from Studley Royal to Bury and then, in 1896, to Ganton, an inland course in Yorkshire with some of the characteristics of a seaside links. He was affiliated with Ganton until 1903, when he left to become the professional at the South Herts Golf Club, in Totteridge, north of London, and there he stayed until his death, in 1937. During his first season at Ganton, Vardon came into his own, winning the British Open, at Muirfield, by defeating Taylor in a playoff. He won the championship again in 1898, at Prestwick, and in 1899, at Sandwich. He had by then established himself as the premier golfer in the world, and what a delight it is to picture him during these years returning to Ganton after some signal triumph in a tournament or a challenge match and playing center forward on the town soccer team, which he had organized. Later, when he had slowed down a little, he shifted to goaltender. Tom Vardon, incidentally, never won the British Open but came close three times, finishing second, in a tie for third, and fourth. When he was in his late thirties, he emigrated to this country and became the popular and much-admired professional at Onwentsia, one of the oldest and best clubs in the Chicago area.

If Harry Vardon remains very much alive for a number of people both here and in Britain who are deep into golf, it is not so much because of the many championships he won as because he revolutionized the golf swing. In fact, he might be regarded as the first modern golfer. It is true that before he appeared on the scene several of the top British players had cultivated individual methods of hitting the ball. Taylor, for instance, had a wide, somewhat flatfooted stance and spanked his shots forcefully with his powerful arms. As a general rule, though, the leading players felt that the golf swing called for unconcealed muscular effort, like tossing the caber. They believed that the fundamentals of the swing included a long, low take-away followed by a strenuous lifting of the elbows and winding of the shoulders as the backswing progressed. Then came an emphatic forward lurch on the downswing, so that the weight and strength of the body could be poured into the shot at impact, after which the player followed through with whatever vigor he had not expended. Just why Vardon, isolated in Grouville, happened on a totally different and much more advanced technique is as much a mystery as how it was that Addison and Steele hit upon and developed the personal essay, Chopin utilized the full melodic range of the piano, or Manet and the other early Impressionists evolved a new approach to the depiction of light. A genius, it appears, can pop up anywhere, and there is no accounting for his special gift. In any event, Vardon had some very definite ideas about the difficult game of golf, in which a stationary ball is hit from a stationary stance. To begin with, he believed that the two keys to a good swing were a steady head position and a sound grip. Because he had large palms and long fingers, the grip that he found gave him the most control was one in which the little finger of the right hand overlapped the index finger of the left hand. Speaking of this grip, he once said, "It did not come naturally to me, but it was well worth the trouble of acquiring. It seems to create just the right fusion between the hands, and voluntarily induces each to do its proper work." He was convinced that there was no master hand in the golf swing — that the two hands contributed equally. Other golfers had happened on the overlapping grip before Vardon did — J. E. Laidlay, a Scot who won the British Amateur in 1889 and 1891, was perhaps the first player of prominence to use it — but the grip has always been referred to as the Vardon grip since the last years of the nineteenth century, when he popularized it by making the British Open practically his private property. The swing he gradually evolved included many other departures from orthodoxy. Instead of employing a closed stance, he opened the toe of his right foot slightly and the toe of his left foot to about a thirty-degree angle (anticipating Hogan in the latter respect, though Hogan's left foot was a little less open — to about twenty-two degrees). He took the club back from the ball in a much more upright and less flat arc than any golfer before him. This was a critical innovation. Besides facilitating a correct hip turn and a full shoulder turn on his backswing, it enabled him to execute his downswing and his release through the ball with an unimpeded flow and rhythm that, in the opinion of the best authorities, only two other golfers, Bobby Jones and Sam Snead, have matched. Vardon's upright arc also made it much simpler for him to pick a ball cleanly from almost any type of lie, even with a club like a brassie, which has a face with comparatively little loft, and to sweep it away in a high trajectory. With his irons, he did not take a large or a deep divot but merely brushed across the turf. He differed from the great stylists who came after him in that his left arm was not straight but bent slightly at the elbow when he took the club back, but, interestingly, at the start of the downswing he straightened the arm. He was, by the way, the first golfer who hit the ball so that in its flight it moved from left to right in a controlled fade, and since a left-to-right shot tends to come down much more softly than a shot that moves from right to left, this, combined with the precision with which he struck the ball, put him in a class by himself when it came to playing full fairway shots and having the ball drop softly on the green and expire almost instantly. Many golfers have tried to copy Vardon's fade, but none of them have made the hitting action seem as natural as he did. He was an incredibly straight player; he once strung together seven consecutive tournament rounds without ever hitting the ball into the rough or into a hazard. The refined tempo and the synchronization of his movements disguised his power, but Vardon hit the ball a long, long way.

In a word, Vardon, as noted earlier, was a genius. It was fortunate that he was, for in 1903, not long after he won his fourth British Open, he came down with tuberculosis, and during the next half-dozen years he had to take things rather easy. An illness of this seriousness would have ended the career of most athletes. Vardon, in truth, was never quite the same again, but he managed to play in the British Open each year, and often managed to finish in the top five. The simplicity and correctness of his grooved swing permitted him to do this, although the game of golf underwent a substantial change during this period when the rubber-cored ball — the modern ball — replaced the old solid gutta-percha ball that Vardon had grown up with and greatly preferred. In 1911, in much better health than he had been for some time, he amazed the golf world by emerging from the shadows and winning his fifth British Open, at forty-one. In 1914, he won the championship for the sixth and last time. He was not yet ready to pack it in, however. At the conclusion of the First World War, he felt strong enough to undertake his third American tour — the one that took him to Inverness. As I write, I am studying a splendid action photograph that shows Vardon following through on a drive off the fourteenth tee during the championship. In certain respects, the picture looks as if it were taken when it was — sixty years ago. Vardon is wearing knickers, a straw hat, and a two-buttoned, ventless jacket, which the force of his swing has sent billowing out at the bottom. The hat is probably an authentic panama, the jacket most likely pongee. On the other hand, as Vardon nears the finish of his swing, with the heel of his right foot high off the ground, he is as beautifully on balance as Hogan was in his prime. His hitting action on that drive was obviously as free as Tom Watson's is today. In short, he looks absolutely contemporary.

(1979)

Trevino

There has never been a golfer quite like Lee Trevino: the harshness of his early years; the lateness of his arrival on the national golf scene; the sharpness and consistency of his unorthodox method of striking the ball; and the charm he exudes on the days he entertains his galleries with his stock of one-liners and his witty spontaneous humor. When Trevino arrived, he arrived in force. He won the U.S. Open in 1968 and 1971, the British Open in 1971 and 1972, and the P.G.A. Championship in 1974. After that he continued to play well in spurts, but recurrent back trouble and the loss of his putting touch made it quite clear that his days of winning championships were over. Thereupon, in the summer of 1984 at the age of forty-four, this confounding character played four brilliantly controlled rounds at Shoal Creek and won the P.G.A. Championship ten years after his first victory in that event.

ON THE EVE OF THE RECENT UNITED STATES OPEN, WHICH WAS played last month at the Baltusrol Golf Club, in Springfield, New Jersey, and was eventually carried off with a flourish by Jack Nicklaus, there was, along with the usual resounding prognostications by the savants in seersucker, a good deal of conversation about the five earlier Opens held at Baltusrol — in particular, the last one, in 1967. This was understandable, for the 1967 Open was a sort of watershed championship. Among other things, it marked the final appearance in our Open of Ben Hogan. Nearly fifty-five years old at that time, Hogan fell well off the pace with a 76 on the third round, and ultimately finished seventeen shots behind the winner. Thirty-one years before, Hogan had appeared in the national championship at Baltusrol; he did not score low enough to make the thirty-six-hole cut, and no one at that time had the faintest intimation that the intense young Texan would go on to become one of the greatest golfers of all time.

The 1967 Open also marked the last head-to-head duel in a major championship between the arch-rivals of that period, Arnold Palmer and Nicklaus. In the 1962 Open, at Oakmont, outside Pittsburgh, Nicklaus, who had only just turned professional, was the victor in their first confrontation, winning a playoff for the title by standing up sturdily to one of Palmer's celebrated charges. At Baltusrol in 1967, it worked out that Nicklaus and Palmer were paired on both the third and fourth rounds. Neither was at his best on the third round; instead of playing the course, each seemed preoccupied with what the other was doing, as if it were match play. Nicklaus had a 72 (two over par), Palmer had a 73, and both stood at 210 at the end of the round. On the final day, the other contenders faded rapidly, and it became evident almost from the start that Palmer and Nicklaus were battling it out for the championship. Both played beautiful golf from tee to green. It was the putting that made the difference. Palmer failed to get down a number of holeable putts and had to be satisfied with a 69; Nicklaus, who missed nothing on the greens and made a few long ones, had a 65. This gave him a total of 275 for his four rounds — a stroke lower than the Open record that had been set in 1948 at Riviera, in Los Angeles, by Hogan. Nicklaus was twenty-seven when he won at Baltusrol, and his victory was his ninth in a major championship. Today, at forty, he has won eighteen major championships — which, as hardly needs to be pointed out, is a record.

The 1967 Open served to spotlight one other remarkable golfer, Lee Trevino. At that time, he was completely unknown except in his native Dallas, where he had worked at a combination driving range and par-3 course, and in El Paso, where he was then the pro at the Horizon Hills Country Club. He was already twenty-seven, but for some reason he had played in only a handful of tournaments. In 1965, he had been the runner-up to Homero Blancas in the Mexican Open. In 1965 and 1966, he won the Texas Open. He also finished fifth in the Panama Open in 1966, and later that year he picked up six hundred dollars by tying for fifty-fourth in our national Open, at the Olympic Club, in San Francisco. That was it. At Baltusrol, he started with a 72 and added a 70. A 71 in the third round put him within reach of the leaders, and for the first time people began paying some attention to this stocky, black-haired, garrulous young man. He was the grandson of a Mexican grave-digger, we learned, and he had put in a four-year hitch in the Marines. On the day of the fourth round, a group of us made it a point to watch Trevino play a couple of holes. We caught up with him on the third, a par 4 that slopes downhill to a tricky green. He played it easily and well: a drive down the middle of the fairway, a pitch twenty feet from the flag, two putts. It was impossible, however, to see what Trevino looked like. A golf cap was pulled down low over his forehead, and most of the rest of his face was hidden by large scuba goggles. In the El Paso area, we were later told, quite a few golfers wore scuba goggles to keep windblown dirt out of their eyes, and he had got used to them. For another thing, he was not reacting to the strain of the Open the way one would expect a newcomer with sparse credentials to do. As he came bouncing down the hillside on the third, swinging his arms confidently and patently enjoying himself, he was talking a mile a minute to his playing partner, Dave Hill. While Trevino's control of the ball was impressive, his swing wasn't. It was exceedingly flat, and he moved into the ball with an ungraceful, down-low lunge. He had a 70 on that last round, and this put him in fifth place and brought him six thousand dollars in prize money. There have been many occasions when a golfer without a clipping to his name has turned in an eye-popping performance in a big championship and never been heard of again. I confess that I wouldn't have been surprised if this had happened with Trevino. However, that summer and fall, on the strength of his showing in the Open, he received special invitations from many of the sponsors of tournaments on the Professional Golfers Association tour, and he played so well in their events that he picked up over twenty thousand dollars in prize money. In those days, this was a pretty fair haul. Gene Littler, for example, earned less than forty thousand that year over the full tournament season.

The following year, Trevino showed us just how good he really was. During the first five and a half months — up to the week of the Open — he won more than fifty thousand dollars on the P.G.A. tour. Then he won the Open, and that changed everything. The 1968 Open was played at Oak Hill, an old Donald Ross layout in Rochester, New York, which had been remodelled and lengthened to 6,962 yards. In retrospect, only three players were actually involved in the winning and losing of that Open: Nicklaus, who was in a contending position all the way; Bert Yancey, a Floridian with a handsome, Jonesian swing; and Trevino. At the end of three rounds, Yancey led Trevino by a stroke, so they were paired on the last round. Trevino went out in front on the ninth, which Yancey bogeyed. Trevino then drew away, widening his lead by a stroke on each of the next four holes. Two of these strokes came on difficult birdie putts — a thirty-footer across the slippery eleventh, and a twenty-two-footer rapped firmly up a slight grade on the twelfth. The prospect of winning the Open has overwhelmed and destroyed many men, but it didn't seem to bother Trevino. On the long thirteenth, as he walked up the fairway with Joseph C. Dey, Jr., the executive director of the United States Golf Association, he reached out impulsively and slapped Dey on the back. "I'm just trying to build up as big a lead as I can, so I won't choke," he explained. He didn't choke, but he wobbled a little on the last two holes. On the seventeenth, after mis-hitting his second shot he scrambled out his par by holing from fourteen feet. On the eighteenth, a demanding par 4, he hooked his drive into trouble, and his recovery shot ended up in a tight lie in matted rough some ninety yards from the pin, just on the brink of a steep gully. There was no way that Trevino, still in front by four strokes, was going to lose the championship, but when I looked at his lie I didn't think he'd be able to play much of a shot. He took out his sand wedge, got comfortable over the ball in a twinkling, and punched a lovely high pitch three feet from the pin. He made the putt. Trevino's third shot was one of those helpful reminders a spectator receives from time to time when he watches the best golfers up close. From a distance, it all looks much easier than it is, and one is apt to forget how skillful these players are. If you or I had had to play Trevino's third shot, we would have been lucky to chop the ball halfway to the green, but he made contact with the ball so precisely and smoothly that it looked as if it had been sitting on a hairbrush. That final par enabled Trevino to become the first man ever to play all four rounds in the Open under par and all four rounds in the 60s: 69, 68, 69, 69. It also enabled him to tie Nicklaus's record Open total of 275.

From his breakthrough at Oak Hill right up to the present day, Trevino has stayed at the top of his highly competitive and wearing profession. Over those dozen years, of the four major championships — the Masters, the U.S. Open, the British Open, and the P.G.A. Championship — only Nicklaus has won more. Over that

span, only Nicklaus and Gary Player have produced such consistently excellent golf. Trevino has now earned over two million
dollars on the P.G.A. tour and added a drachma or two in tournaments outside this country. He has been admirably generous with
his money. After his victory in the Hawaiian Open in 1968, he
gave ten thousand dollars of his purse to the family of Ted Makalena, the Hawaiian professional, who had died in a surfing accident. He and Makalena had been close friends on the tour, and
Trevino, as a person who grew up in poverty — his grandfather's
four-room shack had no running water or electricity — knows
what money can mean to people. Frequently when he has won a
tournament, he has donated a portion of his winnings to charity.
For example, after taking the 1971 British Open, at Birkdale, he
saw to it that forty-eight hundred dollars of his purse went to a
local orphanage. "The world's a funny place," he once said.
"When you have no money, no one will do anything for you. If
you become successful and pile up enough money to buy anything you want, people deluge you with gifts you don't need and
try to do all kinds of things for you."

Trevino probably reached the apex of his career in the summer of
1971, when, within the space of twenty-three days, he won his
second U.S. Open, the Canadian Open, and the British Open. The
following year, although he won the British Open again and collected over two hundred thousand dollars in prize money during
that season, his life had become more complicated and less pleasurable. His affluence had arrived so quickly that he hadn't had
sufficient time to understand some aspects of his new position. He
was also physically run down. Lured on by the pots of money that
could be made on the tour, he had pushed himself too hard,
playing in some thirty tournaments a year. In the early nineteen-
seventies, the stress of chronic competition at length got to him,
and he began to suffer all kinds of strange maladies. During this
period, he played some stretches of marvellous golf — in 1974 he
won his fifth major title, the P.G.A. Championship — but there
were also weeks when he was so tired that he showed none of his
characteristic bonhomie. What is more, his golf became uneven,
and this bothered him terribly. Some weeks, he was convinced
that he was overgolfed and should be back home taking things
easy. Other weeks, he was equally certain that he was under-
golfed and the cure was to stay on the tour and fight out his

problems there. He persevered, and got through this difficult phase, only to run headlong into some troublesome physical setbacks. In 1975, when he was playing in the Western Open, at the Butler National Golf Club, near Chicago, he was struck by lightning. It was a freak accident. There had been no distant thunder or lightning. When the storm suddenly broke, it broke directly over the course. The force of the lightning lifted Trevino off his feet and knocked him out for an instant. Jerry Heard, who was Trevino's playing partner, and Bobby Nichols were also hit. The three were rushed to a hospital. Trevino was kept in the intensive-care unit for twenty-four hours. Three weeks later, he was able to rejoin the tour, but he was by no means a hundred per cent fit. His muscle tone had been damaged considerably. However, the most serious aftereffect of the electrical shock was intermittent back trouble. (Trevino holds with a theory that electrical shock can cause a drying out of the intervertebral discs. He points out that Nichols and Heard have also been afflicted with back trouble since that afternoon at Butler and that Heard's career as a professional golfer has been in danger.) In June, 1976, a year after being struck by lightning, he injured his back gravely when, working around his house, he attempted to move a heavy potted plant. That November, he was operated on for a herniated disc by Dr. Antonio Moure, a Spanish-born neurosurgeon on the staff of the Park Plaza Hospital in Houston. It was a most successful operation. Three months later, Trevino returned to the tour. He had to be careful and space his appearances, however, and he played in only twenty tournaments. that year. He won just once, but his victory came in a fairly big event, the Canadian Open. He has had to continue to be careful not to overdo things, but his last two seasons have been active and productive ones. In 1979, for instance, he captured his third Canadian Open. This year, he has already won the Tournament Players Championship, which ranks just below the majors, and (last week) the Memphis Classic, making this year the seventh in which he has earned over two hundred thousand dollars in tournament prize money. Only Nicklaus has won more prize money during his career.

Although in many ways Trevino's achievements are not sufficiently appreciated — many people tend to regard him primarily as a colorful showman, who communicates with his galleries as do few other sports figures — this June, at forty, thirteen years after he came out of nowhere and announced himself so memorably at

Baltusrol, he returned to that course as a man who has gained for himself a secure position in golf history. He is one of only four players who have won both the U.S. Open and the British Open at least twice. (The others are Walter Hagen, Bobby Jones, and Jack Nicklaus.) From 1968 on, he has never gone a season without winning at least one tournament. Trevino, who is extremely modest when he talks about his accomplishments, thinks that his best claim to fame is his consistency. He likes to point out that since 1968 he has averaged under seventy-one strokes a round in all but two seasons — 1975 and 1977. In 1970, 1971, 1972, and 1974, he won the Vardon Trophy, which annually goes to the touring professional with the lowest strokes-per-round average over a minimum of eighty rounds.

He continues to approach competitive golf with the enthusiasm of a young man. This, he feels, can be explained by the fact that he did not begin to play a steady run of tournaments until he was twenty-seven, whereas Nicklaus, for instance, who is exactly his age but has played in relatively few events in recent years, was a youthful prodigy, who won the Ohio Open at sixteen and was then already carrying a rather full tournament schedule. Trevino's favorite relaxation is fishing — bass fishing especially — but even when he leaves the tour for a change of pace, he plays golf. "Golf isn't just my business, it's my hobby," he said when he and I had a nice long talk recently. "My idea of a perfect vacation is to go to Mexico with some friends and play golf." In his undiminished, and apparently undiminishable, enchantment with golf, he is like Sam Snead, who for over fifty years has played a round of golf just about every day. He also reminds one of Ben Hogan, whose idea of bliss is to practice hitting balls daily, cerebrating unceasingly before, during, and after each shot.

Three facets of Trevino's career and personality seem to me unusually fascinating and well worth further examination: his background, his singular technique, and some of the key moments of his major victories. His life has a strong Dickensian quality, partly because of the hard times he endured as a boy and a young man, and partly because of the improbable turns of fate that marked his road to the top. He left school when he was fourteen and in the eighth grade, and found a job helping out at a driving range in Dallas that was owned and operated by a professional named Hardy Greenwood. Trevino had already been around golf for several years. While his grandfather's shack had many limitations, it also had a few advantages. There was a lake behind it, along with some big willow trees and a beautiful cottonwood that he remembers wistfully. More to the point, the shack was situated a hundred yards from the Glen Lakes Country Club. Trevino had started caddying at Glen Lakes when he was eight. He also started playing at that age, for he got to know the greenkeeper's son, and they would go out together and hack around the course during the hours when it was empty. It didn't take Trevino long to become a pretty fair little golfer and also to become thoroughly enamored of the game. That is why he gravitated to the driving range in 1954 when he left school and went looking for a job. The following winter, he helped Greenwood build a nine-hole par-3 course on twelve acres adjacent to the driving range. They did all the work themselves: they designed the holes, installed the pipes for the watering system, mixed the sand and loam and peat moss for the fairways and greens, seeded the course, and, when the grass came through, mowed it and spruced up the green areas. The longest hole at Hardy's pitch-and-putt course was 120 yards, and the shortest was 65 yards. The course was lit at night, and it was a highly profitable operation. Trevino was happy with this life for a while, but late in 1956 he grew restless and signed up for a four-year tour of duty in the Marine Corps. He spent a good deal of it on Okinawa and got in a lot of golf on a course called Awase Meadows. At this time, Trevino was, in his own estimation, "just a good 4-handicap golfer," although he turned in some low rounds in interservice matches. (One of the golfers he played against was Orville Moody, then in the Army and stationed in Japan, who subsequently won the 1969 U.S. Open.) "My main trouble in those days was that I was a right-to-left player," Trevino recalled during our talk. "On some rounds, I would hit the most awful-looking hooks you ever saw, and I paid the price for them. I had to do something about my method of hitting the ball, I realized, or I would never become a really sound golfer."

Upon getting out of the Marines, Trevino went back to Dallas and to his old job at the driving range and the par-3 course. One day shortly after his return, he was invited to play at Shady Oaks, in Fort Worth, Ben Hogan's home club. As usual, Hogan was hitting out practice balls. Trevino stopped and watched him from a distance. He was impressed by two things: every shot that Hogan hit was cut slightly — that is, it curved a shade from left to right — and on shot after shot the caddie never had to move; the ball hopped up into his hand on the first bounce, as if it were on a string. Hogan, like Trevino, had struggled for years with a hook when he was a young man, and he didn't become a champion until, completely altering his approach to the game, he started hitting the ball not from right to left but from left to right and patiently mastered a controlled fade that made him the most accurate golfer since Harry Vardon. Trevino, like all golfers, had heard about this, but it was watching Hogan in action that drove the point home. In a word, when a right-to-left player hits the ball badly and hooks it, the spin on it carries it sharply and fast to the left, and it frequently ends up in heavy rough or even out of bounds, but when a left-to-right player hits the ball badly, it spins in a comparatively soft and slow arc to the right, often stops in the fairway, and rarely causes him much grief.

Back at the driving range, Trevino got down to the job of learning to cut the ball. He took a very open stance, aiming well to the left of his target, and, after some experimentation, he developed an individual way of achieving the results he was after. He used an exceptionally strong grip on the club, and he took it back with the club face closed. Then, as he came into the ball, he tried to open the club face just before impact. He worked on developing a firm left side on the downswing, knowing that if he didn't he'd spray the ball all over the place. He also worked on keeping his body down low in the hitting area; the longer a player stays down at impact, the less he can pronate his arms and hands, and too much pronation causes hooking. As he hit through the ball, he extended his club as far forward as possible. This exaggerated extension was not at all a natural move for him. One gimmick he found invaluable in training himself to do this was to pretend that there were four balls lined up in a row and on his downswing try to hit through all four of them, and not just the first one.

It took Trevino about a year of daily practice before he felt confident that he could fade the ball more or less as he wanted to. He began to play very well, so he continued with the method he had devised. Off the tee, he would aim for the left-hand rough and slide his low, buzzing drives ten or fifteen yards to the right and comfortably onto the fairway. On his irons, if the pin was positioned on the left side of the green he aimed for the left edge and slid his approach into the pin. It should be noted that in the mid-nineteen-seventies, after his back trouble, he had to modify his technique slightly. He couldn't stay down as low in the hitting area and also had to come up a little more quickly, and this meant he couldn't keep the club face on the ball as long. In addition, the right hand got into the shot more. Consequently, after setting up in his open stance he did not try to cut across the ball from the outside in on the downswing to give the ball the outer spin that made it fade; instead, he swung straight through the ball almost on the direct line to the target. This is the technique he employs today. On his full shots with his woods and most of his irons, the ball falls in a shade from the left. On some of his short irons, he actually draws the ball a fraction from right to left. Unlike most athletes with an unorthodox style, who are interesting mainly because they nevertheless manage to get results, Trevino is an aesthetic delight. On his best days, there is no visible exertion at all as he moves into his shots; his magnificent hand action and timing quietly do the work. He strikes the ball much more purely than most of the paragons of copybook style, and it flies toward the flag with perfect rotation and on just the right parabola. The fact is that he is not only one of the finest strikers of the ball in modern times but one of the best shotmakers in history. Trevino is generally content to let his golf speak for him, but he likes to point out that he thinks his unorthodox method is more than just an effective means to an end. "Do we know what the correct golf swing really is?" he asked me during our session. "I may have the best swing, the right swing." He broke into his impish grin, but when he resumed speaking there was an unmistakable serious-ness beneath his bantering tone. "The only reason the old Scots a couple of hundred years ago swung the way they did was that they played in heavy wool coats that were a couple of sizes too small for them, and they couldn't get the upright swing. They had to swing flat. They used a tremendous amount of pronation. They had to swing opening and closing the club face because, with all the clothes they wore, they couldn't get any body movement."

Down through the years, the leading golfers, whatever their method of hitting the ball, have more often than not been able to play their best when it counted the most; otherwise, they would not have been the leading golfers. Most of the time when Trevino has been in the hunt in a major championship, he has shown a gift for playing spectacular shots at the critical moments. When he won our Open for the second time, at Merion in 1971, after an eighteen-hole playoff with Nicklaus, he made only one faulty shot on that exacting course in the playoff round: on the first hole, he pushed a 9-iron pitch into a bunker and took a bogey. On the remaining holes, he rattled off fourteen pars and three birdies. A cluster of three splendid putts decided this hard-fought playoff. On the twelfth green, one of the slickest at Merion, he curled in a sidehill birdie putt of twenty-five feet, which increased his lead to two strokes. Then he held Nicklaus off by holing from ten feet to save his par on the fourteenth and from twenty-five feet for his birdie on the fifteenth. The final scores were 68 and 71. The week after the championship, Trevino played in the Cleveland Open, and finished back in the pack. The week after that, he played in the Canadian Open, and won it in a playoff with Art Wall by sinking a fifteen-foot birdie putt on the first extra hole. He should have been exhausted by then, but somehow he wasn't. He hopped a plane for London, hurried out to Birkdale, on the Lancashire coast, north of Liverpool, for the British Open, and won that championship. This must have been a particularly sweet victory, because the year before he had thrown away a wonderful chance in the British Open at St. Andrews. With a round to go, he was out in front, two shots ahead of Nicklaus, Tony Jacklin, and Doug Sanders. The spit of duneland on which the Old Course at St. Andrews was built is so narrow that, except for four holes — the first, the ninth, the seventeenth, and the eighteenth — an outgoing hole and an incoming hole share an immense double green. The flags on the outgoing holes are white, and those on the incoming holes are red. On the final round, Trevino had a most untypical mental lapse on the par-4 second hole. He fired his approach not at the white flag but at the red flag, which marked the sixteenth hole, on the left side of the green. With his ball lying about a hundred and eighty feet from the white flag, marking the second hole, he had to work hard to get down in three putts. At that time, Trevino was perhaps the best putter in the world, save for Billy Casper, but on this round, upset by his mental error and further bothered by a whipping west wind, he three-putted three more greens on the first nine and was out of the tournament. (Nicklaus won it after a playoff with Sanders.) At the end of the first three rounds at Birkdale, Trevino was once again the leader. A stroke behind him were Jacklin and Lu Liang-huan, the soft-swinging, polite Taiwanese known to the golf world as Mr. Lu. On the final round, Trevino rushed to the turn in thirty-one strokes, using only twelve putts, but on the last nine the edge began to come off his game, and his pursuers were closing the gap. On the seventeenth, a 526-yard par 5, he nearly blew the Open. He aimed his tee shot for the left rough, counting on his well-schooled fade to swing the ball back onto the fairway. His tee shot was ripped low and hard, but for some reason his fade didn't take, and the ball thudded into a scrub-covered sand hill. On his second shot, he advanced the ball only a few yards, and on this third he knocked it across the fairway and into the rough on that side. He wound up with a seven on the hole, and suddenly his lead was down to a single stroke. He held his poise and played the eighteenth, a 513-yard par 5, coolly and well. In those days, when the small, lively British ball could still be used in the British Open, he had no trouble getting home on the last hole with a drive and a 6-iron. He played a daring approach, going straight for the pin, which was tucked behind the bunker that guards the entrance to the green on the left. The ball landed close to the pin, but on that resilient green it rolled some forty feet past. He made no mistake with his approach putt. The ball died two and a half feet to the left of the hole, and he tapped it in for the winning birdie.

When Trevino defended his British Open title the following July, at Muirfield, near Edinburgh, he stole the championship back after he had seemingly kicked it away. For the third year in a row, he led the field into the last round, a stroke in front of Jacklin, six strokes ahead of Nicklaus. He had moved into the lead with a 66 in the third round, which he finished with a run of five birdies, twice holing out from off the green. On the par-3 sixteenth, where he was bunkered on his tee shot, he had skulled his explosion shot, but the ball had struck the flagstick on a fast bounce and fallen straight down into the cup. Then on the eighteenth, a long par 4 on which his second shot ended up fifty feet from the flagstick in the stubbly rough to the left of the green and beyond it, he had chipped his third into the cup. There were fireworks all over the place on the last round. Briefly, Trevino and Jacklin, playing together in the last twosome, both eagled the ninth, but the leader by a stroke midway through the afternoon was Nicklaus, who, in one of his most amazing fourth-round rushes, birdied six of the first eleven holes. However, he missed a five-foot putt for his par on the sixteenth, and after that the winning and losing of the championship came down to Jacklin and Trevino. It was decided on the seventeenth hole, a par 5 to a small, saucerlike green hemmed in by rough. Trevino could not have played the hole worse. After hooking his drive into a bunker and hitting a weak recovery, he hooked a fairway wood into the rough and then scaled his fourth shot, a little pitch with his sand wedge, clear across the green and up into a bank of thatchy rough close behind the green, twenty feet or so from the pin. The tournament looked like Jacklin's — he lay four only three and a half feet from the cup after missing his putt for a birdie. "When I walked over to play my fifth, I was totally red hot with myself about that fourth shot," Trevino told me. "I'd tried to put some spin on the ball, but I never got my wedge under the ball correctly — I did what you call dropkicked it. As I say, I was so damned mad with myself when I went over to play my fifth that I didn't take any time at all with it. I just grabbed my 9-iron from the bag and hit the ball. The film shows I didn't even have my feet planted when I chipped it. The ball just happened to go into the cup." Jacklin then carefully lined up his short putt and missed it. Trevino was out in front again. On the eighteenth, he played an absolutely airtight par, and that did it.

Trevino's victory in the 1974 P.G.A. Championship, the other major title he has won, is a different kind of story. (That season, he captured only one other tour event, the New Orleans Open — a tournament that is worth mentioning because he didn't make a single bogey over the seventy-two holes.) In 1974, the P.G.A. was held at the Tanglewood Golf Club, in Clemmons, North Carolina. As is his practice at many of the big championships, Trevino rented a private house for the week. The one he rented in Clemmons belonged to a widow, a Mrs. Mayberry. One day, when he was looking around the house, he happened to come across a bag of golf clubs that had belonged to Mrs. Mayberry's husband. He pulled out the putter, took a couple of practice strokes, and said to himself, "Isn't this something! This is the putter I've been looking for." It was the model that Arnold Palmer had designed for the Wilson company back in the nineteen-fifties — a blade-type putter somewhat resembling the immensely popular Tommy Armour model, which featured a small flange. Trevino asked Mrs. Mayberry if he could buy the putter. She didn't want to sell it, but said he was free to use it, which he did. During the tournament, in which he putted very well, he again asked Mrs. Mayberry if she would sell him the putter. She again declined, but told him that if he won the tournament she would be delighted to give it to him as a present. He played the last two rounds in 68 and 69, and edged out Nicklaus by a stroke.

Trevino changes putters quite frequently. He always uses the same type of putter, however, and carries six or seven spares with him. What he does when he doesn't like the way he is stroking the ball is to switch to a spare whose head has a slightly different look to it or one whose shaft has a slightly different feel. The change usually proves to be beneficial. In any case, Trevino has a wonderfully simple and direct putting stroke. He takes the club back low to the ground and uses a short backswing. He keeps the blade low as he brings it forward. His left hand controls the stroke entirely.

Let us retrace our steps a bit. One of the most important stretches of Trevino's life is the period we know least about — the years between his return home from the service at the end of 1960 and his sudden explosion on the national golf scene in 1967. Soon after getting back to Dallas and reëstablishing his ties with Hardy Greenwood's driving range and par-3 course, he turned professional and joined the Professional Golfers Association. He quickly fell into a daily regimen. He would rise before daybreak and arrive at Tenison Park, a public golf course, at around five. Tenison Park received a lot of play, but at that early hour it was empty, and Trevino, if he wished, could whirl around the eighteen holes in no time at all. Other mornings, if he had a match lined up — and he often did, since Tenison Park was a harbor for hustlers — he would play a few holes before the match to get warmed up for his morning's work. He nearly always wore Bermuda shorts, and as often as not he played barefoot. When his practice round or his match was over, he would move to the practice tee and hit dozens and dozens of balls. After that, he would take a shower, put on his work clothes (slacks and a golf shirt), and drive to Hardy's. He began work there at two in the afternoon and closed the place down between eleven and midnight. He alternated between its two facilities: one day he would run the driving range and the next day the par-3. During slow afternoons, he hit out more balls. Trevino estimates that during those years he had a golf club in his hands an average of fifteen hours a day. It is unlikely that any other golfer in the country in the nineteen-sixties practiced as hard or as long. By 1965, when he won the state open championship, he was probably a good enough golfer to have made it on the P.G.A. tour, but personal problems prevented him from taking that step. In any event, he was very much at home at Tenison Park and was prospering to some degree from his matches there. He was also able to augment his salary from Hardy's by playing matches on the par-3 course. His chief difficulty was that he had become so expert at pitching and putting on that familiar terrain that it wasn't easy to get people to play him. Finally, after running out of even those customers who were willing to take him on provided he played right-handed with left-handed clubs, he hit upon a gimmick that, once he was firmly ensconced in the big time, received reams of publicity. His new specialty involved the use of a twenty-six-ounce Dr Pepper bottle — made of very heavy glass — which he wrapped with adhesive tape, so that it would not shatter when he hit a golf ball with it. Wearing a glove on his right hand, he held the bottle at the neck, tossed the ball in the air, and batted the ball with the big end of the bottle. He practiced with the bottle almost as much as he did with his regular clubs. After a while, he could flight the ball in the proper arc for a golf shot, and he could also hit it 120 yards — the length of the longest hole on the par-3 course. He putted billiards style, with the neck. Trevino's average score for nine holes with the bottle was 29 or 30 — two or three strokes above par. He was able to persuade his opponents to give him half a stroke a hole, which meant that if he tied them on a hole they lost it. The stakes generally were fifty cents or a dollar a hole. He accepted all challenges for over three years and never lost a match with the bottle.

In the winter of 1966, the course of Trevino's life changed abruptly. Shortly before, he had quit his job at the par-3 and the driving range, and for a while his only income came from his matches at Tenison Park. One night that January, he received a phone call from El Paso. A man he had never met was calling him. "He was connected with the Horizon Hills Country Club, and he wanted me to come out and play a golf match for him," Trevino explained to me. "You see, quite a few people were getting beat pretty badly at Horizon Hills in matches with a certain guy. One young fellow who had lost his shirt had been asked, 'Do you know someone who can play — someone nobody knows?' This kid told them, 'Yeah. I know a Mexican boy in Dallas who can really play, and no one's ever heard of him.' Well, this man at the other end of the phone said he'd send me a plane ticket and give me three hundred dollars if I'd come out to El Paso and play for him for two days. I told him I'd have to ask my wife about it. She was working then as a file clerk at Blue Cross-Blue Shield for fifty-five dollars a week, and that's what we were basically living on. We were having a hell of a time making ends meet. So I told Claudia — that's my wife — about the proposition this guy had offered. When she heard the numbers, she said, 'O.K. You can go.' I flew out to El Paso, went to Horizon Hills, and played two rounds — one each day — against a very good golfer, a well-known pro on the tour. I beat him soundly both rounds. About a month later, this man from El Paso phoned me again. There was an amateur who wanted to play me, he said. I said I was interested. 'You got a job yet?' he asked me. I told him no, and after a moment he said, 'Why don't you come out to El Paso to stay?' I had a 1958 Oldsmobile, and I rented a small U-Haul trailer and threw everything into it. When we arrived in El Paso, that's all we had, along with fifty dollars in cash."

Trevino easily defeated the amateur challenger. He then went to work for Horizon Hills as the club professional. He received only thirty dollars a week for his services as the pro, but he gave some lessons and had ample time to play matches with the members, so his take-home pay amounted to a respectable sum. By spring, he was well started on a new life. He qualified for the 1966 U.S. Open, held that year at the Olympic Club, in San Francisco, and he made the thirty-six-hole cut, but he finished with two unimpressive 78s, mainly because of his inability to cope with the bunkers. There hadn't been a single bunker at Tenison Park. The next year, he didn't feel much like trying to qualify for the Open, but his wife set aside the necessary twenty dollars and sent in his entry. He did very well in the local and sectional qualifying tests. Two of the key men in the operation of Horizon Hills, Jesse Whittenton (who had played cornerback for the Green Bay Packers) and his brother Don, lent him four hundred dollars to help him meet the cost of the long trip East. At Baltusrol, he had the good fortune early in the week to meet a club member — Chuck Smith, now deceased — who found him delightful company. At the close of each day's play, they spent part of the evening together, Smith working on his gin-and-tonics, Trevino on a succession of beers. There is no question in Trevino's mind that Smith's friendship had a good deal to do with his feeling almost as much at home at Baltusrol as he had at Tenison Park, and that that put him in the proper frame of mind to play his best golf. After his fifth-place finish in the Baltusrol Open, he was on his way.

Trevino continues to be a tremendous drawing card. The crisp, sophisticated golf he plays accounts in good measure for the large galleries he attracts, but his popularity derives to a good extent from his outgoing, jovial nature and his incessant, high-velocity badinage with his colleagues and the spectators. He is the first to admit that he loves being onstage, and he is onstage from the moment he arrives at the golf course in a courtesy car until some eight hours later, when, with his pre-round practicing, his round, and his post-round practicing behind him, he steps into a courtesy car and is driven back to wherever he is staying that week. He is fond of referring to himself as "a complete hermit," by which he means that at the end of a day's work he seldom attends the après-golf parties or frequents the local glamour spots. His energy is depleted by that time, and he prefers to relax in the company of a few old friends. (These include the Salinas brothers, Arnold and Albert, who manage Lee Trevino Enterprises, in Dallas, and who take turns travelling with him on the tournament circuit.) On the course, it is no easy thing for Trevino to put on a show for his thousands of admirers over a period of hours, and there are stretches when he has to fall back on shopworn, comparatively corny material or on one-liners he has been using for years. However, few people in sport can be as entertaining as Trevino when he is away from the golf course regaling a group of friends with a series of anecdotes and opinions, supplying, as he goes, an obbligato of contagious laughter. In other moods, when he is more serious and reflective, he can be equally spellbinding, for he knows a little about life. Not many people talk golf as well as he does, either. Here are a few typical examples of his conversation as he flows from one subject to another:

On putting: "I don't putt as well now as I used to, but when I first came on the tour I was an exceptionally good putter. You know what made me into a good putter then? It was those terrible greens at Tenison Park and the other public courses I played on.

The grass on those greens was always too high, and the surface was bumpy and worm-cast and inconsistent and ragged. When I came out on the tour and looked at the greens, my feeling was: How does anyone ever miss a putt on these things? What a change! It was like sleeping on dirt floors and all of a sudden they let you sleep on a spongy carpet. I got a tremendous amount of confidence in my putting practically overnight."

On the importance of application: "There's nothing better for you than hard work. If a guy has the fundamentals — a basically good swing — then all he has to do is work on his golf. Of course, some folks are blessed with more natural ability and pick the game up quicker than others, but even those fellows have to work. When I first came out on the tour, in 1967, there was one man in particular I looked up to. He never got credit for being the player he was. That was Billy Casper. He was then in his prime, and he was a wonderful golfer. At that time, he was winning the most tournaments. I watched Billy Casper and I studied him as he hit balls, and I evaluated myself with reference to him. I asked myself, 'I wonder how much better he is than I am.' I concluded that he was three times as good. You know what I said to myself then? I said, 'He may be three times as good, but I'll practice three times as hard, and I'll eventually catch up with him.' "

On Jack Nicklaus: "A lot of people ask me why I've played so well head to head with Nicklaus, why I'm one of the few players who aren't overawed by him. I should begin by saying that Jack and I are good friends. Each of us respects the other's game. I consider myself a very capable shotmaker, but I would never put myself in the same class with Jack Nicklaus as a golfer. During my time in tournament golf, there has been no one else in his class. There are several reasons, I think, why I've done well when we've met. First, he'd already scaled the heights. He had everything to lose and nothing to gain. I started with a big psychological advantage. I was the underdog. I've always had the underdog image. I enjoy that role. It's like bringing two football teams together. You can have, for instance, a Notre Dame playing a William and Mary. If William and Mary wants it bad enough, they'll give Notre Dame all it can handle."

On why he thinks he was able to become a champion: "I believe that in order to play good golf you have to be able to feel what you're doing with your hands. I just happen to be one of the guys who can feel the golf club throughout the swing — where it's at and the position of the club face. Most people get up there hypnotized by the ball, and they have no idea whether their swing is upright or flat, whether they're coming down inside, outside, open, closed, or whatever."

On having the right approach to getting things done: "The problem for the majority of people is that they set goals that are too high. They're never able to achieve them, and that becomes demoralizing. I've been lucky. I've set goals for myself that I've been able to reach, and I could go on from there."

On the changing face of Dallas: "Many of the landmarks in the part of Dallas where I grew up no longer exist. Hardy's pitch-and-putt course is now a shopping center. I hear that they'll be closing down the range this year and that some outfit is planning to build apartments on it. Two years ago, a real-estate-development company started building houses on the old Glen Lakes course, where I caddied and learned to play. Mary Kay Ash, the head of Mary Kay Cosmetics, bought the lot where my grandfather's shack used to stand. She built what looks to me like a half-million-dollar house on it. When I drive by it, I say to myself, 'You didn't have it so bad.' My grandfather died in 1969, by the way. He lived long enough to know I had won the Open championship and had found a place for myself in golf."

On his return to Baltusrol in June for the 1980 Open, Trevino, while not in top form, gave a good account of himself. As the Lower Course at Baltusrol (on which the Open was held in both 1954 and 1967) was set up for the championship, it measured a little over 7,000 yards and played to a par of 70. (The Upper Course was used for the Open once, back in 1936.) Trevino led off with a 68 and then had rounds of 72 and 69. Going into the final round at one under par for the tournament, he was only five strokes behind the leaders, Nicklaus and Isao Aoki, of Japan, and still had an outside chance to get into the fight, but he fell away on the last nine holes and finished with a 74, for a total of 283 and a tie for twelfth. Trevino would undoubtedly have acquitted himself better if he had putted as efficiently as he normally does, but from the start he did not like the feel of his putting stroke, and the greens of Baltusrol, with their hard-to-read shimmers and weaves, bothered him all the way.

*

All this reminds me of a recent chat with Lee Trevino. I inquired at one point if he thought that he was too old, at forty, to win another big championship.

"How did you feel when you were forty?" he asked.

"I didn't give any thought to age then," I answered.

"That's right," he said, nodding. "You don't. I really don't feel much different today from the way I felt when I was eighteen. All a guy needs to keep going in tournament golf is good health, the same ambition he had when he was younger, and maybe two or three putts that fall at the right time."

(1980)

Graham's Great Finish

One of the special qualities Ben Hogan possessed was that, once having decided what club to play on his approach, he seldom changed his mind and struck the shot with no tinge of unsureness. This is not an easy thing to do. It takes confidence in your swing and uncompromising determination. When David Graham won the 1981 U.S. Open at Merion, the execution of his shots on the last five holes — particularly his irons to the pins, which were set in ticklish positions — was so superb it brought Hogan to mind. I particularly admired his 7-iron to the fourteenth green on which the pin was positioned just beyond the trough that divides the green in two. Graham's approach shot just carried the trough, and it left him with a seven-foot birdie putt that he holed to go out in front.

EARLY SATURDAY MORNING, A THUNDERSTORM HIT THE PHILA-delphia area. It was just what wasn't wanted. The course was soaked again, and there was not much that Richie Valentine, Merion's renowned course superintendent, and his staff could do about it. On the third round, the greens were far too receptive. It was like throwing darts at a dart board. Two of the early starters, Tom Kite and Jim Simons, were around in 67, and two others, Raymond Floyd and Craig Stadler, had 68s. Shortly after this, Ben Crenshaw really took Merion apart with a 64, tying the course record, which had been set in 1950 by Lee Mackey, of Alabama, one of the better-known unknown Open heroes. Crenshaw, an exceptional young man in many ways, is a golf-history buff. When he was congratulated by friends after his record-equalling round, he gave them a wide smile and declared, "Today, I putted like Walter J. Travis" — a reference to an early American champion, whose victories in our Amateur in 1900, 1901, and 1903, and in the

British Amateur in 1904, were directly attributable to his wizardry on the greens. "The greens are like poundcake," Crenshaw went on to say. "I'm a little afraid for Merion's sake."

All things considered, Merion got through the third round fairly well. It gave up a swarm of birdies, but, as it generally does, it exacted a good many bogeys and double bogeys. There were only sixteen scores under 70, and, except for Crenshaw's 64, none under 67. Many of the leaders started off fast, but as the afternoon wore on the pressure of the Open began to tell on them. The first of the favorites to go was Watson. He had not taken advantage of the ideal scoring conditions, but he was purring along nicely — one under par for the day, two under for the tournament — when he came to the fifteenth, a 378-yard par 4 on which the fairway breaks acutely to the right just before it climbs a gradual slope to a dramatically bunkered green. The tee shot on the fifteenth is one of the most worrisome on the course: it is hard to decide how much of the dogleg you should bite off. On one hand, you must not be too ambitious or you won't carry the rough and reach the fairway. On the other, you must not be ultraconservative, for a drive hit far to the left runs the risk of bouncing across the fairway into the rough and, sometimes, through the rough and out of bounds. The fifteenth proved to be disastrous for Watson. Driving with a 3-wood, he was quick coming into the hitting area and snap-hooked the ball across the fairway and out of bounds for a two-stroke penalty. With his second ball, he was on the left side of the green in two, but since the pin was set on the right side forty uphill feet away, it took him three putts to get down. This added up to a 7 — a triple bogey. He fought back and birdied the sixteenth, but then he missed his pars on the last two holes, and for all intents and purposes another Open was over for Watson. With a round to go, he trailed the leader, George Burns, by a full nine strokes, and there was no way that he was going to be able to make up so huge a deficit.

Burns, on his third round, had played a 68 and had widened his lead over the closest contender — the Australian-born David Graham — to three strokes. Bill Rogers, a most agreeable young pro, from Texarkana, Texas, and a solid golfer, was a stroke behind Graham. The group of players clustered a stroke behind Rogers included Nicklaus, who, after a burst of simply elegant shotmaking midway through his round, had fallen away on the last five holes. Burns' golf had been impressive. He had taken three bogeys, but he had immediately followed each bogey with a birdie — a classic sign that a golfer is in a winning mood. Burns, a powerful hitter, is anything but a stylist. He lifts his club back outside the correct path, his right elbow flying high. At the top of his backswing, he gives his hands an extra twirl to load them up, and then hurls himself down and through the ball with a lunging movement in which he is perceptibly off balance. Nonetheless, he was keeping the ball pretty well in play from tee to green, and he holed a large number of putts. He is a very good putter.

On the final round, Burns did not play as well as he did on the first three, but he could easily have won the Open. Graham, with whom he was paired, was the only one of his challengers to make a rush at him. A thirty-five-year-old veteran of the tour, Graham had quickly moved to within a stroke of Burns with birdies on the first two holes. Burns entered the last nine holding a one-stroke lead on Graham, but lost it on the tenth, which he bogeyed after a poor tee shot. The two men were still tied as they entered the last five holes — a stretch that has long been considered one of the great finishes in golf, along with the last five holes at Hoylake, in England, and the last three holes at Carnoustie. Graham's shot-making on those five holes was so superb that I think it is worthwhile to examine his progress hole by hole.

The fourteenth, a 414-yard par 4, is one of the most difficult holes on the course. A first-class tee shot is needed to hit the bending, pinched-in fairway and then a first-class iron to hit and hold a mean, tightly bunkered green, partially hidden from view, which is separated into two distinct sections by a trough running diagonally from the front left to the back right. On the final day, the pin was in the toughest position possible — in the back left corner, just beyond and above the trough. Burns, over the green in two, saved his par with a ten-foot putt. Graham had a birdie 3. He used his driver off the tee and hit the middle of the narrow fairway. On his approach, he went for the pin with a 7-iron — a very bold shot, because of the smallness of the target area and the danger implicit in missing it. The ball carried the trough by a couple of yards, landed seven feet to the left of the pin, took a little hop, and sat down. Graham worked hard on the putt and holed it with a confident stroke. He may have won the championship then and there. At any rate, he was now in the lead for the first time. He widened his margin to two strokes on the fifteenth — the dogleg par 4 on which Watson had driven out of bounds on the third round. Graham hit the fairway off the tee with a 1-iron, then lofted an 8-iron that spun itself out eight feet from the pin, which was set on the right, high side of the green. After Burns had missed an only slightly longer birdie putt, Graham made his — a sidehiller that broke a foot from right to left. On to the sixteenth — the famous Quarry Hole, a 430-yard par 4. From the low fairway, the second shot must carry across an old, worked-out quarry filled with trees, scrub, and sand to reach a plateau green that slopes up from front to back. Here Graham played two more wonderful shots — a 3-wood down the center of the fairway, followed by a 5-iron to the flat crown of the green, the ball stopping some ten feet from the pin. He almost made that putt, too — the ball just slipped by the rim of the cup. Burns had taken a 5 there, so Graham's lead was now three strokes. Merion's seventeenth is a 224-yard par 3 on which the golfer plays from a high tee to an undulating green hemmed in by bunkers and rough. Graham hit a crisp 2-iron that landed near the center of the green and ended up on the collar of the green, at the back and to the right, about twenty feet from the pin. Burns was away, his ball lodged in the rough to the left of the green. From there, he pulled off a miraculous shot, chopping the ball softly onto the edge of the green and watching it trickle down the slope and into the cup for a birdie. Graham digested this calmly. He then stroked his approach putt two feet from the hole and made the short one. A lead of two strokes, one hole to play. Many old Merion hands are of the opinion that the eighteenth, a 458-yard par 4, may well be the hardest hole on the course. The drive is blind — over the end of the quarry to an elevated fairway hidden by bushes and trees. From the championship tee, it takes a carry of two hundred and ten yards to reach the fairway, which tilts to the left toward the rough and a long line of out-of-bounds stakes. More often than not, the second shot must be played from a downhill lie, and this makes it a bit more difficult to stop it on a green that is perched at the crest of a mild slope. Burns finished with a 5 when he missed a putt of tap-in length. This gave him a 73 and a four-round total of 276. Graham was down the left side of the fairway with his drive and on the green, eighteen feet from the pin, with his 4-iron approach. He almost holed his putt for a birdie; the ball lipped out of the cup.

He was down in 4 for his par, a 67 for his round, and a total of 273 — a stroke above the Open record, which Nicklaus set last year at Baltusrol.

On his last round, Graham missed only one fairway off the tee — the first. He hit every green in the regulation stroke except the seventh, eighth, and seventeenth, and on those holes his approach finished on the trimmed collar of the green. The only time he faltered all day was on the fifth green, which he three-putted from fifteen feet. However, Graham's golf on the taxing and precarious last five holes is what will be especially remembered in the years to come. It had been a long time since we last saw a golfer play such brilliant, forceful, technically pure shots on the final holes of the Open. Burns did not lose the championship. Graham had the courage to try to win it, and he did so by hitting the kind of iron shots that one associates with Hogan: they were struck decisively; they travelled in the right trajectory; they covered the flag; and they pulled up abruptly when they touched down on the green. It was a genuinely memorable performance.

Graham, the first Australian to win our Open, is a purposeful, realistic man, who appreciates the long distance he has come in golf and the good life that the game has given him and his family. He has had to work his way up the ladder. A native of Victoria, when he was fourteen he became the assistant to the pro at a club outside Melbourne, where he ran the shop and handled other unglamorous duties. He did this for four years, then switched to a club in Tasmania, then worked as a clubmaker in a factory in Sydney. What he wanted was to be a player, though, and he went out on the Australian circuit, which is a lot less golden than ours. His first tour victory, in the 1970 Tasmanian Open, was worth only eleven hundred dollars. That year, he made his mark in international golf, when he teamed with his friend Bruce Devlin to win the World Cup for Australia at the Jockey Club in Buenos Aires. He came to the United States shortly after that and has remained here. Today, he and his family live in Dallas. In 1972, he won his first American tournament, the Cleveland Open. He has made it a practice to play in events held all around the world, and his record includes victories in the 1976 World Match-Play Championship, at Wentworth, in England; the 1977 Australian Open; the 1977 South African P.G.A. Championship; and the 1979 New Zealand Open. In 1979, he won his first major tournament — our P.G.A. Championship, at Oakland Hills. After almost throwing it away with a double bogey on the last hole, which enabled Crenshaw to tie him and sent them into a sudden-death playoff, he stayed alive by holing from twelve feet to halve the first extra hole and by holing from ten feet to halve the second, and then played the winning stroke on the third, a seven-foot birdie putt. A man of medium size with the leathery look that many Australians have, Graham has a sound, orthodox swing. You would never guess this from his stance at address: there is hardly any flex to his knees, and his back is as stiff as a poker. However, when he starts his backswing — he takes the club back a shade more on the inside than most golfers do today — the various elements of his swing begin to fuse smoothly, and from then on he is a pleasure to watch. Golf fans have known for some time that Graham is a player of talent, but until those last five holes at Merion few of us realized what a sturdy competitor and accomplished shotmaker he can be under the spur of a big occasion.

(1981)

An Old Master
Sarazen

The lead-in to the annual article on the Masters in 1982 was a portrait of Gene Sarazen, who had turned eighty that winter. He did not play in the tournament that year, but he and Byron Nelson were the honorary starters. They teed off first and played the front nine. Sarazen has lost some clubhead speed, but he still executes his shots with the same punch swing that identified him when he became the first golfer to win the modern Grand Slam (the Masters, the U.S. Open, the British Open, and the P.G.A.). Gene still plays the game seriously — very seriously — and still smiles like the Cheshire Cat when he comes off the course after a solid round.

THIS YEAR, FOUR OF THE FINEST GOLFERS OF ALL TIME HAVE reached or will reach milestones in their long careers. On February 4th, Byron Nelson turned seventy. Sam Snead will be seventy on May 27th, Ben Hogan on August 13th. On February 27th, Gene Sarazen turned eighty. What are the criteria that determine whether a man deserves to be considered an authentically great golfer or just a golfer of unusual talent? Well, along with a technical virtuosity that makes for exceptional longevity, the great golfers have had the ability to produce their best shotmaking in the most important tournaments — particularly in the four major championships: the United States Open, the British Open, the Masters, and our Professional Golfers' Association championship. While Nelson won only five major titles — one U.S. Open, two Masters, and two P.G.A.s — it should be pointed out that he had the misfortune to reach his peak during the Second World War, when most of the big championships were suspended. No one, certainly, has ever played more consistently superb golf than Nelson did in 1945, when he won eighteen tournaments on the P.G.A. tour, including eleven in a row, and averaged 68.33 shots per round over a hundred and twenty tournament rounds. Snead won seven major championships: one British Open, three Masters, and three P.G.A.s. Although our Open eluded him, he came tragically close to victory four times. Snead, the possessor of what may be at one and the same time the most natural, the most correct, and the most beautiful golf swing in history, captured a record number of P.G.A.-tour tournaments: eighty-four. The last of these was the Quad Cities Open in 1979, in which he became the first man to shoot below his age in a tour tournament when, on the fourth day, he finished with a round of 66. Hogan was in his mid-thirties before he managed to win his first major championship, but he won nine in all: four U.S. Opens, one British Open (in one attempt), two Masters, and two P.G.A.s. In 1960, when he was almost forty-eight, he was in sight of winning a fifth U.S. Open: with two holes to go, he was tied for the lead, but on the seventy-first, gambling on making a birdie, he failed by inches to carry the water hazard before the green, and that was it. There has never been a better striker of the ball or a more accurate player. As Al Laney, of the old New York *Herald Tribune*, once put it, "Hogan's control of the ball was such that he seemed to allow it no option but to go where he wanted it to go."

Sarazen won seven major championships: two U.S. Opens, one British Open, one Masters, and three P.G.A.s. He was the first to carry off all four of the major championships in which professionals play. (Three other men have done this since — Hogan, Gary Player, and Jack Nicklaus, in that order.) Sarazen was an excitingly aggressive player who made things happen, and he was also one of those people to whom things happen. The most memorable instance of both was in the 1935 Masters, when, trailing Craig Wood by three strokes midway through the last nine, he made a double-eagle 2 on the par-5 fifteenth (or sixty-ninth) by holing his second shot, a full 4-wood. This enabled him to end the seventy-two holes tied for first, and he went on to take the playoff.

Where these four golfers rank in the hierarchy of the game's champions has to be a matter of personal opinion. Hogan, to be sure, belongs at the very top, sharing that eminence, as I see it, with Harry Vardon, the pioneer of the modern golf swing, who won six British Opens and one U.S. Open between 1896 and 1914; Bobby Jones, a career amateur, who won four U.S. Opens and three British Opens in addition to five U.S. Amateurs and one British Amateur between 1923 and 1930; and Jack Nicklaus, who, starting with his victory in the U.S. Amateur in 1959, has amassed the incredible total of nineteen major championships — four U.S. Opens, three British Opens, five Masters, five P.G.A.s, and two U.S. Amateurs. It is easy to see why many authorities consider Nicklaus to be the greatest golfer ever, but I prefer to rank him alongside Vardon, Jones, and Hogan, who were also peerless in their eras. Just below them, I would place Walter Hagen, all by himself. An astounding competitor, Hagen, between 1914 and 1929, was victorious in eleven major championships — two U.S. Opens, four British Opens, and five P.G.A.s, then a match-play tournament. Sarazen, I believe, belongs on the tier below Hagen, along with Snead, Nelson, and Player, the sturdy South African who has not only won nine major events (one U.S. Open, three British Opens, three Masters, and two P.G.A.s) but more than a hundred tournaments throughout the world. On the tier below these four players, I would place Arnold Palmer, the winner of eight major titles — one U.S. Open, two British Opens, four Masters, and one U.S. Amateur — and this would complete this highly subjective ranking of the top ten players of modern times.

It is pleasant to report that Nelson, Snead, and Hogan, as they move into their seventies, continue to be very much involved in golf. Nelson, who lives on his beef-cattle ranch in Roanoke, Texas, north of Fort Worth, works with Tom Watson, Ben Crenshaw, and other young players on their games. Each spring, he is the host of the Byron Nelson Classic, which takes place at the Preston Trail Golf Club, in Dallas. Snead still lives to play golf. Wherever he is, he generally arranges to get in a round every day, weather permitting, and the enjoyment he derives from hitting the ball well is no less intense than it was forty-five years ago, when he came out of the Allegheny Mountains to become an immediate sensation on the tour. He still hits the ball a long way. Hogan's schedule varies a bit, but he usually spends his mornings supervising the production of golf clubs and in related activities at the Ben Hogan Company, in Fort Worth, where he has long made his home. Most weekdays, he lunches at the Shady Oaks Country Club, and afterward, arrant perfectionist that he is, he passes up playing a round in favor of practicing on a deserted stretch of the club's third nine holes. His is a probing, scientific mind, and nothing delights him more than to experiment with this nuance or that nuance of his swing to see if some minuscule modification might possibly lead to a slight improvement in the contact he is making with the ball, in the flight of the ball, or in his consistency in producing the precise type of shot he is after. Most winters, he spends some time in Palm Beach, where he plays and practices at nearby Seminole, his favorite course.

Sarazen, at eighty, is the most amazing of all. Seventeen years ago, the land developer Frank E. Mackle, Jr., who was then turning his attention to Marco Island, off the west coast of Florida some fifteen miles south of Naples, signed Sarazen as director of golf for his Deltona Corporation. During his first twelve winters in that post, Sarazen watched over the golf at the Marco Island Country Club. For the last five years, he has been superintending the renovation of the Marco Shores Country Club, a newer course, situated on the mainland close by the island. Since 1969, when he sold his farm in Germantown, New York, the Squire, as Sarazen has been called since the mid-nineteen-thirties, on account of his predilection for country living and farming, has spent his summers in New London, New Hampshire, a spot that he and his wife, Mary, enjoy because their daughter Mary Ann and her family live there. These days, he plays only a few rounds of golf each week, but on the days he doesn't play he gets in a good session on the practice tee, whether he is in Florida or in New Hampshire.

Over the last half century, Sarazen has had the gift of eternal old age, mainly because he was so young when he broke through in our Open at the Skokie Country Club, near Chicago, exactly sixty years ago. In 1932, when he won the British Open and his second U.S. Open, he was only thirty, but he was looked upon as a gnarled veteran, because he had then been around for a full ten years and, alone among the players he had vied with in the nineteen-twenties — Hagen, Jones, Tommy Armour, Leo Diegel, Jock Hutchison, Macdonald Smith — remained a force in the championships. Golfers much younger than he retired from competition year after year, but Sarazen kept popping up in the big tournaments decade after decade. In 1940, when he was thirty-eight and well past his prime, he made his last bid for a major title by finishing in a tie for first with Lawson Little in our Open, at the Canterbury Golf Club, in Cleveland, but he lost the playoff by three shots, 70 to 73. Rain drenched the course the night before the playoff, and there was no way that Sarazen could keep pace off the tee with Little, a burly young man whose tee shots — almost all carry — ended up as much as thirty-five yards beyond Sarazen's. Little, in fact, played an excellent round in every respect.

As a former P.G.A. champion, Sarazen was exempt for many years from having to qualify for that tournament. In 1947, he astonished the golf world by defeating Snead, who was then at his peak, 2 and 1 in the second round of the P.G.A. The following year, he pushed Hogan to the thirty-sixth green when they met in the third round of the P.G.A. He continued to make sporadic visits to Britain to play in the British Open. In 1958, when it was held at Lytham St. Annes, in Lancashire, he made a wonderful showing. His total of 288 (73–73–70–72) was only ten strokes behind the winner's, and this put him in a tie for sixteenth with three other players, among them Bobby Locke, who had won his fourth British Open the year before. Sarazen, then fifty-six, was paired with Locke on the last thirty-six holes. In the ensuing years, he kept on going. In 1963, he became the first man over sixty — he was sixty-one — to make the thirty-six-hole cut in the Masters. Rounds of 74 and 73 gave him the same total at the halfway mark as Arnold Palmer, the defending champion, and they were paired on the third round. Sarazen appeared in the Masters through 1973. After that, although he was on hand at the Augusta National Golf Club each April, he limited himself to playing in the nine-hole competition staged on the club's par-3 course the afternoon before the start of the tournament. Last year, Hord Hardin, the chairman of the Masters, asked Sarazen and Nelson if they would become the tournament's regular Honorary Starters, and they were pleased to accept. In that capacity, they are annually the first twosome to tee off on the opening round. In 1981, they played nine holes and then called it a day — the Augusta National, with its heaving hills, is not an easy course to play from the back tees as one gets on in years.

Sarazen's last "real" appearance in a major championship came in the 1973 British Open, at Troon in western Scotland. Fifty years before, in 1923, when Sarazen was our reigning Open champion, Troon was the venue of the British Open, and he made the trip across to play in it. After some successful tune-up appearances before the Open, he suffered a considerable humiliation at Troon. On the second day of the thirty-six-hole qualifying round — he had had a satisfactory score the first day on one of the nearby municipal courses — Sarazen's group was assigned the earliest starting time on another municipal course that was situated close along the Clyde estuary. That morning, a furious storm off the ocean swept over a boundary seawall and washed up to the edge of the municipal course. The fishermen in the village were not permitted to go out in the storm, but the golfers had to battle the chilling rain and fierce winds. Sarazen was blown off balance time after time as he attempted to play his shots. On the second hole, where his drive was buried in the face of a bunker, he took a 9. He also had big scores on the next three holes. Then, when he was playing the fifth, the storm began to abate. Pulling himself together, he played quite well the rest of the way, but his total proved to be a stroke too high; most of the later starters that day, who had the advantage of favorable conditions, had brought in low scores.

In 1973, when the British Open was scheduled for Troon, the Championship Committee of the Royal and Ancient Golf Club of St. Andrews, which conducts the national championships, came up with the happy idea of issuing special no-need-to-qualify invitations to three veterans: Arthur Havers, the victor at Troon in 1923; Sarazen; and Fred Daly, a somewhat younger man, who had won the British Open in 1947. On returning to Troon after a fifty-year absence, Sarazen, at seventy-one, broke 80 on both rounds — not at all a bad performance, inasmuch as it rained both days and the wind blew hard at times. While he missed making the thirty-six-hole cut by several strokes, he had stolen the limelight on the first round with a typical flourish. On the celebrated 126-yard eighth hole, known as the Postage Stamp, because of the minute size of its plateau green, he ripped a 5-iron through the wind. The ball landed on the front of the green, hopped a couple of times, and rolled into the cup for a hole in one. The following day, he birdied the eighth by holing a recovery from a deep bunker for a deuce. This summer, the Open returns to Troon — a course that suits Sarazen's game, because it doesn't require long carries to reach the fairways. Furthermore, the hard surface of the fairways gives a golfer who hits the ball on a line, as Sarazen does, a good deal of roll on his tee shots. Sarazen hasn't yet made up his mind whether or not to go across for the championship. It will depend on how he is playing at the time.

*

This past February, I went down to Marco Island and spent a few days with Sarazen just before his eightieth birthday. I was struck, as I am each time I see him, by how little he has altered over the years. He was brimming with health. His olive skin had been bronzed by the sun, and his eyes twinkled with animation — especially when he talked. When he smiled, I was reminded, as I always am, of how Bernard Darwin, the English golf writer, liked to compare Sarazen's smile to the grin of the Cheshire cat. Sarazen is a stocky man, five feet five and a half inches tall, but he looks taller than that, because he is so sturdily built. One particularly notices his broad back and his muscular legs (his legs are usually visible, for knickers have long been his trademark), and the general feeling one gets is that here is a man as strong as an oak. He takes good care of himself, and always has. These days, he rises early in a suite in the Emerald Beach Apartments, facing the Gulf of Mexico, that he and Mrs. Sarazen have occupied since they first came to live on Marco Island. After breakfast, he drives to his office at the Marco Shores Country Club. Its walls are covered with a mélange of photographs: the young Sarazen is holding trophies or posing with celebrities from the entertainment, political, and business worlds; the middle-aged Sarazen is shown mainly in his role as host of "Shell's Wonderful World of Golf," a series of international golf matches that ran for seven winters and that Sarazen feels reestablished him with the sports public long after he had ceased winning tournaments; the elder Sarazen, the statesman, is grouped with old friends at the Legends of Golf tournament, an event played in Texas each spring, and with new friends at the Gene Sarazen Jun Classic, an event played in Japan each autumn. Most mornings, Sarazen spends a couple of hours in his office, taking care of business matters and answering his correspondence. His letters are not long, and on the average he writes eight or nine. On days when he hasn't set up a golf game, before proceeding to the practice tee he sometimes checks those areas of the Marco Shores course on which alterations are being made. By nature an exceedingly fast player — in 1947, he and George Fazio, the first twosome to go out on the last day of the Masters, whipped around the course in an hour and fifty-seven minutes, and Sarazen had a 70 — he gets right down to business when he practices. He always has in mind one of two things he wants to work on, and he sticks to those. He knows every inch of his swing, and he should — in fundamental respects it has changed very little over sixty years. In the nineteen-twenties, his arc was a bit flatter than it later became. These days, because his muscles are less flexible, his swing is somewhat shorter; at the top of the backswing his hands are only shoulder-high. The most distinctive feature of Sarazen's swing was always, and remains, the speed with which he moves into the ball and the conviction of his hand action at impact. He is, in a word, a puncher. An incident that took place in 1923 comes to mind. Shortly before undergoing the ignominy of failing to qualify for the British Open at Troon, he had the privilege of being paired with Harry Vardon in the first two rounds of the North of Britain championship — which, incidentally, he won. It was played at Lytham St. Annes, which has an unorthodox opening hole, a fairly long par 3. Sarazen began his round by punching a 1-iron through a heavy crosswind onto the green, close to the hole. As he and Vardon walked to the green, Vardon told him, "Your style, I gather, is to hit the ball sharp and low. You are very strong. If I were you, I would never allow for the wind. I would always play directly for the flag."

On the days when Sarazen practices in the morning, he customarily lunches at Marco Shores and then returns home; later in the afternoon, he walks three miles or so along the beach to strengthen his legs. On the days when he has arranged a round of golf, the schedule is slightly different. For example, one day during my visit, when he was to play in the afternoon at the Hole-in-the-Wall Golf Club, in Naples, he taped an interview with a local television sportscaster at Marco Shores and took care of some routine matters before he headed for Naples. I had never heard of Hole-in-the-Wall, and after seeing it I was surprised that I hadn't. The course, which was designed by Dick Wilson, one of the best golf-course architects we have ever had in this country, is a very good test. It is only a medium-length layout, measuring a shade over sixty-four hundred yards from the men's tees, but to score acceptably a golfer must keep the ball well under control. A number of holes are tightly bordered by thick growths of vines and trees in a cypress swamp from which the course was reclaimed, and most of the greens are bunkered rather severely. In addition, Hole-in-the-Wall has an appealing low-key atmosphere — the kind that one often finds at clubs where only golf is played and where, in the small, tasteful clubhouse, lunch but not dinner is available. Before we had lunch, Sarazen went out to the practice tee to warm up. He hit three or four shots with his 7-iron and then shifted to his 5-iron. All his shots were hit crisply and flew as straight as an arrow. "This year, I decided to make one main change," he said. "I don't know if you noticed it, but I'm not taking any turf at all. I'm taking the ball clean, just the way Macdonald Smith used to do. Mac Smith sure impressed me when I was breaking in." At this reference to one of the great technicians of the nineteen-twenties, he winked an eye and grinned broadly. There is a lot of the young boy in Sarazen. Resuming his warmup, he hit a few shots with his 3-iron, the longest iron he carries in his bag nowadays, and then explained, "I don't believe in hitting out too many balls before a round — just enough to get loose. I'll hit a couple of shots with my 5-wood — I use that club a lot now — and then a couple of 4-woods. That will be it. I don't take any turf with those fairway woods, either." He didn't. He continued to meet the ball squarely and whistle it down the center of the practice area. I hadn't seen him swing as smoothly and hit the ball as nicely in a long time — perhaps not since the mid-nineteen-sixties. "I think taking the ball clean is going to help me," he said as we walked to the clubhouse for lunch. "Among other things, it stops you from pounding down with your right shoulder as you come into the ball. At my age, I could hurt my shoulder if I did that. The only time I take some turf is when I'm playing pitches with my wedge."

After lunch, Sarazen's foursome moved swiftly onto the course. It was made up of Andy Beljan, the club professional, and two members, both able golfers, who I guessed were in their early sixties. Since the front nine holes were crowded, they decided to play the back nine first. Par on that nine, the longer nine, is 37. Sarazen has a 39, and his score could have been one or two shots lower. He took a 6 on a long par 5 when his fairway-wood shot kicked into trouble, and he bogeyed a par 4 when he was too firm with his approach. These were his only errors. He hadn't missed a fairway off the tee. He played even better on the front nine. Par for that nine is 35. Sarazen had a 36, which included a 6. It came on the seventh, a 569-yard par 5, where he was on the green with his third shot but took three putts. On the eighth, a 408-yard par 4, he missed his first fairway of the day when his drive ended in a trap to the left. Going with his 5-wood, he picked the ball perfectly off the sand. Rising higher and higher in an ideal trajectory, it carried all the way to the green, and there, after hanging in the air for a moment, it floated down as softly as a leaf.

When Sarazen was sixty-nine, he shot his age for the first time. Nowadays, he expects to score lower than his age every time he plays, unless he is up against a course as long and demanding as the Augusta National. Accordingly, although he was happy with his 75 on this round at Hole-in-the-Wall, it was not the score in itself that pleased him but the way he had played — especially the success he had had in sweeping the ball off the grass à la Macdonald Smith. As we were driving back to Marco Island, it occurred to me to ask him exactly where he tried to have his club head make contact with the ball. "Oh, about an eighth of an inch from the bottom of the ball," he replied matter-of-factly. I don't think he has any idea what fantastic hand-and-eye coördination that requires, even for a young man. I don't think he appreciates, either, what astonishing depth perception he has. He reads distance so well that he was hole-high or thereabouts on most of his approach shots that afternoon. He still goes about playing golf as if it were the most natural exercise in the world. After studying the shot he is about to play, he never takes a practice swing. Unlike most of the contemporary young stars, who make their preparation for each shot a protracted ritual, he positions his body as he rocks into his stance. A squint at the target, and he is ready to go. When I watch Sarazen, a remark comes to mind that circulated twenty-odd years ago about the baseball player Smoky Burgess, a natural hitter who was a catcher and pinch-hitter *extraordinaire* for the Cubs, the Phillies, the Reds, the Pirates, and the White Sox. It was said that if you woke Burgess in the middle of the night and told him to get up and pinch-hit, he would line the first pitch cleanly into center field for a single. The ease with which Sarazen plays golf is in large part responsible for his longevity as a golfer, but the zest he brings to the game is no less important. During his round at Hole-in-the-Wall, it was clear from the start that he meant to play well. As the round wore on, he worked harder and harder on his shots, concentrating as if a tournament were at stake. He is something — very probably the best eighty-year-old golfer ever.

Sarazen's life, and particularly the early years, has much of the quality of a novel by Dickens. He was born Eugenio Saraceni, in Harrison, New York, on February 27, 1902, the first son and second child of Federico and Adela Saraceni, who had come to this country from Italy. Mr. Saraceni was a bitterly unhappy man. As a boy of scholarly bent, he had been sent to a monastery in Rome to prepare for the priesthood, but the year before he was to be ordained both his parents died, and he did not have the funds to continue his studies. He became a carpenter. In this country, he never learned to speak fluent English, and this was a handicap both socially and in business. Every night after dinner, to escape from his frustrations, he would retire by himself to the cellar and read for hours. As a member of a family that always needed more money, Eugene, from the time he entered school, worked at odd jobs. He was a newsboy, sold the *Saturday Evening Post*, collected scrap to sell to junk dealers, and, in the summer, picked fruit. For a period, he was hired by the town of Harrison to light its old street lamps each evening. When he was eight, he began caddying at the Larchmont Country Club. Three years later, he switched to the Apawamis Club, in Rye — there were many more golfers there, and a caddie could do much better. In 1913, his first year at Apawamis, Francis Ouimet, who had been a caddie at The Country Club, outside Boston, won our Open and became the special hero of American caddies. On learning that Ouimet used the interlocking grip, Eugene changed to that grip. He has stayed with it ever since.

Except for his hours on the golf course, Eugene's boyhood had been a grim one, and it continued to be. In 1917, his father, who had contracted to build some houses, lost every penny in the deal. At his bidding, Eugene, then fifteen, left school to go to work. At about this time, the United States entered the First World War. Mr. Saraceni not only found work for himself but was also able to get a job for his son as a carpenter's helper at Fort Slocum, an Army installation on Long Island Sound, near New Rochelle. Fort Slocum was slated to become an induction center, and barracks had to be built in a hurry to house the thousands of recruits who would be passing through. Eugene next worked as a carpenter's helper at the Remington arms plant in Bridgeport, Connecticut, to which the family had moved in 1917. Eugene's job at Remington was to drill the holes in the wooden racks in which artillery shells were shipped. While he was working at Remington, he came down with pneumonia and was rushed to Bridgeport Hospital. He was close to death for three days but pulled through, only to come down with pleural empyema, a complication of pneumonia in which the pleural cavity accumulates fluid. A young surgeon operated on him successfully, using a method that is standard nowadays in such cases but was then new and risky. When his patient was ready to leave the hospital, the doctor instructed him to rest for six weeks and also advised him not to go back to the Remington plant but to find an outdoor job. It was spring, and that meant only one thing to Eugene: golf. He started to spend his days at Beardsley Park, a nine-hole public course in Bridgeport, practicing longer as his health gradually returned.

Eugene and his father had never got along, and now the rift between them widened. Mr. Saraceni regarded golf as a form of loafing, but his son was determined not to go back to carpentering, and to find his way in golf. That summer — the summer of 1918 — he invented his name. Playing together one day, he and Al Ciuci, the Beardsley Park professional, had both had holes in one on the first hole, and this earned them a small writeup in the local paper. The pleasure of this taste of publicity was marred when Eugene saw what his name looked like in print. Eugene Saraceni was a suitable name for a musician but was all wrong for a golfer. It didn't have the right look, the right ring, the right anything. He spent the next few nights trying out variations on Saraceni, arranging the letters differently and substituting other letters. One night, after writing down "S-a-r-a," he added "z-e-n": Sarazen. He liked it immediately. Gene Sarazen — now, that was what he was after. That was a very good name for an athlete. Then and there he became Gene Sarazen.

Slowly, things began to look up for Gene Sarazen. In the autumn of 1918, he was taken on by the professional at the Brooklawn Country Club, the best club in Bridgeport, to help out in the pro shop. He mopped the floor and did other menial tasks, but he also wound grips, refinished shafts, and, in time, learned the essentials of clubmaking. He was permitted to play some golf, occasionally, with the members, and his game improved considerably. In the winter of 1919, he went south to Florida, where, presenting himself as the assistant professional at Brooklawn, he kept himself afloat by winning most of the money matches he played. Ramsey Hunter, the professional at the Fort Wayne Country Club, in Indiana, liked the way he hit the ball, and hired him to be his assistant. The next winter, Sarazen went to Florida again, and, with the aid of two professionals from Pittsburgh, who spent their off-season there, he landed the post of professional at the

Titusville Country Club, a nine-hole course in the northwest corner of Pennsylvania. In the late winter of 1922, he won his first significant tournament, the Southern Open. It was held that year at the New Orleans Country Club, and Sarazen ran away with it, finishing eight strokes ahead of the runner-up, Diegel. He acquitted himself well in six other tournaments on the infant winter tour that then swung from Texas through Florida and up to North Carolina. Most important of all, his friend Emil Loeffler, the greenkeeper at the renowned Oakmont Country Club, on the outskirts of Pittsburgh, told him that he had been able to arrange for him to be the professional at the Highland Country Club in that city. That July, at twenty, Sarazen won the 1922 U.S. Open championship.

Looking back at this awesome achievement, one is struck by the intelligent and thorough way that Sarazen prepared for the Open. In those days, William Fownes, a member of the family that had created Oakmont, was the most influential man in Pittsburgh golf. The city and the outlying districts had produced several winners of our Amateur (Fownes himself was one), but no golfer from the area had ever won the Open, and to this end Fownes had Loeffler take Sarazen to the venue of the championship — the Skokie Country Club, near Chicago — a month before the Open. It was a highly rewarding expedition. Sarazen reached the conclusion from his familiarization rounds that Skokie was a perfect course for his game. The key to scoring, he felt, was keeping the ball out of the rough off the tee. Back in Pittsburgh, he practiced his driving diligently. He returned to Skokie a week before the Open. He had played in the championship in 1920 and 1921, and though he hadn't done badly, he had never actually been in contention. He had hurt his chances both years by putting considerably below his usual level. Consequently, during his tune-up week at Skokie he devoted a sizable portion of his time to practicing his putting on the greens he would be playing, memorizing the grain, the speed, and the contours of each one. In the evening after dinner, ignoring the practice green — it is rare when a practice green resembles the greens out on the course — he spent as much as an hour on a single green. Aware that in previous Opens he had got off on the wrong foot on many rounds because of shaky putting, he made a special point of getting to know the first four greens.

On his opening round at Skokie, Sarazen, putting well and playing well from the outset, brought in a 72, two strokes over par. A second round of 73 placed him only three strokes behind the leader at the halfway point — John Black, a veteran Scottish professional then attached to a club in California. On his morning round on the last day, Sarazen began to feel the pressure of the Open. He couldn't stroke his putts up to the cup however hard he tried. He persevered, and, thanks to three birdies on the last five holes, got out of the round with a 75 and was still in the battle, three shots behind Black and four behind the co-leaders, Bill Mehlhorn and Bobby Jones. Sarazen then went out and played a tremendous last round, the first of the many thrilling finishing rounds that he was able to summon in major championships during his long career. He started the round with a wobbly par and a bogey — Open jitters. He was too tight, too tentative. On the third, he forced himself to go boldly for the twenty-five-foot putt he needed for a birdie, and made it. He holed from fifteen feet for a birdie on the fourth. Those two putts set him off, and after that he played attacking golf. He made the turn in 33. He kept pushing himself hard, and came to the last hole needing a par 5 for a 69 and a four-round total of 289 — a stroke better than Mehlhorn's total, the lowest that had been posted. The eighteenth, 485 yards, was not a long par 5, but it had its hazards. Out-of-bounds markers marched along the left, and there was a pond on the right side of the fairway about three hundred and fifty yards out. The green was bunkered on the left and the right. That afternoon, the hole was playing long, for the wind was directly against the golfers on the second shot. Sarazen felt that under the circumstances it was probably wisest to make sure of his par, but his caddie, a young man named Dominico, was against this. He thought that Sarazen should not change his tactics, and should keep charging. He also reminded him that Jones and Black were playing behind him and there was no way of knowing the score he would have to shoot to beat them. Sarazen took his advice. He lashed a long, low drive two hundred and fifty yards down the fairway. From there, the only club he could reach the green with was his driver. He had a good lie, and he went with the driver. He hit a screamer that tore through the wind, on line all the way. The ball bounced onto the green and rolled dead sixteen feet from the pin. He was down in two putts for his birdie, a 68, and a total of 288. As it turned out, he would not have won without that final birdie. Jones, after failing to par the seventeenth, finished one stroke behind Sarazen, and so did Black, who also ran into trouble on the seventeenth.

Sarazen's dashing play at Skokie — he was the first to win the Open by breaking 70 on the final round — captured the imagination of sports fans. His victory also served to popularize golf, then still a rich man's game in this country, for he was the first golfer of Italian descent to win the national championship. Like Ouimet, he had risen from humble origins and the caddie ranks. That August, Sarazen added to his reputation by winning the P.G.A. championship, which was played at Oakmont. On his way to the title, he defeated Jock Hutchison in the quarter-finals, Bobby Cruickshank in the semis, and Emmett French in the final. The only American star he had not accounted for in head-to-head competition was Walter Hagen, who had chosen not to enter the P.G.A. championship that summer. A confrontation between the two was a natural, and it was arranged that they should meet in a 72-hole match in October for what was ballyhooed as the "World's Golf Championship." Hagen then held the British Open title and Sarazen the U.S. Open and P.G.A. titles, so the billing was far more justified than most promotions of this sort. After the first thirty-six holes, played at Oakmont, Hagen held a two-hole lead, but when the scene shifted to the Westchester-Biltmore Country Club, Sarazen surged to the front and ultimately closed out the match on the seventieth green, 3 and 2. I cannot think of another young golfer, completely unheralded at the start of the season, who enjoyed a string of triumphs comparable to Sarazen's in 1922.

The following year, it was a different story. To begin with, there was Sarazen's misadventure at Troon in the qualifying round of the British Open. In the U.S. Open, he did not make a strong defense of his title. The general feeling in golf circles was that he was a skyrocket that had lit up the sky brilliantly but had now fizzled out. He had been playing so poorly that in the autumn, when the P.G.A. championship was held, at the Pelham Country Club, if he had not been the defending champion he would probably not have entered the tournament. Golf is an enigma. At Pelham, Sarazen won the P.G.A. again. He came onto his game in the early rounds, then beat Jim Barnes in the quarter-final, Bobby Cruickshank in the semifinal, and Hagen, the great match player, in the final. That final was a remarkably dramatic duel, and, perhaps for that reason, it is one of the few matches of the nineteen-twenties that golf fans who were born decades later seem to know about. It built to a terrific climax. Hagen, two down with three holes to play, squared the match by winning the thirty-fourth and thirty-fifth. The thirty-sixth was halved, and so was the first extra hole. The second hole at Pelham was a short par 4 that bent sharply to the left after the drive. There were woods along the left, and the threat of out-of-bounds territory. Hagen, with the honor, put his drive down the middle of the fairway, setting himself up for a little pitch — a shot he played better than anyone else in the game. Sarazen, for some reason, decided to risk carrying the trees in the angle of the fairway. He hooked the shot badly, and it disappeared into the trees. It could have easily ricocheted out of bounds or ended up in an unplayable position. He was lucky. The ball was found in bounds near the edge of the woods, and, more than that, he had a feasible opening to the green. His lie was difficult, though: the ball lay deep in a clump of high, heavy rough. He managed to gouge it out with his niblick, and it kicked onto the green and stopped two feet from the cup. This unexpected turn of events shook the usually unshakable Hagen. He flubbed his pitch into the bunker before the green, and that was the match. When I was with Sarazen this winter, I asked him how it was that he was able to stand up to Hagen in match play when Hagen's cool, imperious manner intimidated just about everyone else. "I don't think I had enough sense to know what pressure was," Sarazen said. "I was young, and, like most kids, I had lots of confidence when I was hitting the ball well. I knew that Hagen could play magnificent recovery shots, and I knew how good he was on the greens, but I figured I was a better shotmaker than he was. I felt I could beat him by outplaying him from tee to green."

Sarazen's triumph in the 1923 P.G.A. was his last in a major championship for a long, long time — until 1932. During this extended drought, his record was still quite respectable. In our Open, for example, he tied for fifth in 1925, tied for third in 1926, was third in 1927, tied for sixth in 1928, tied for third in 1929, and tied for fourth in 1931. For the average tournament player, this would have been regarded as a string of worthy performances, but when Sarazen arrived he had looked to be the stuff of which champions are made, and his inability to continue to win his share of the prestige tournaments was a disappointment. He recognized as clearly as anyone that a true champion is at his best when he has to be, but year after year he threw away his opportunities by making ruinous errors. By 1931, he had gained sufficient maturity to analyze his weaknesses and set about rectifying them. His natural way of hitting the ball was to swing on an inside-out arc and draw the ball from right to left. When he went on an exhibition tour with Jock Hutchison in 1923, he had made the mistake of trying to copy Hutchison's outside-in fade, and he had become so confused after fiddling with countless adjustments and constant compensations over the years that he had no confidence, no feel, no sense of where the ball was going. One thing he knew: under pressure he was susceptible to hitting disastrous hooks, which were brought on because he had lost control of the club with his right hand at the top of the backswing, letting it slip from his fingers down toward the thumb. He corrected this in 1931 through painstaking practice and with the help of two pieces of equipment. The first was the Reminder Grip. Unlike other grips, the Reminder Grip is not round at the top. A slim section of its left side has been sliced away, leaving a flat surface. When a golfer places his left hand on a Reminder Grip, he tends to grip the club properly: the key to this is that the pad of the palm, below the little finger, fits snugly against the flat surface. A Canadian golfer had devised this grip and sent it to the Wilson Sporting Goods Company, but there were no plans to do anything with it until Sarazen, who was retained by Wilson as an adviser on equipment, spotted it on one of his visits to Wilson's and had the grip put on several sets of clubs he was having made up. It was of incalculable value to Sarazen. His improved left-hand grip made it possible for him to grip the shaft correctly and firmly with his right hand. Before that, his right hand had been too far under the shaft. From then on, the club remained glued to the fingers of his right hand at the top of the backswing and did not slip down. To fortify his grip further, he had a twenty-two-ounce practice club made up — it was about fifty per cent heavier than his driver — and dutifully swung it for long periods every day. He began to strike his shots much more solidly. The following year, 1932, he thought it was high time to do something about his bunker play, which had never been as reliable as he would have liked. In the town of New Port Richey, on the west coast of Florida, where he and his wife then spent their winters, there was a mechanic at a local garage who was particularly good at soldering. Sarazen bought up all the solder at the local hardware store, and, at his direction, the mechanic applied it to the soles of twelve niblicks that Sarazen had collected. Sarazen then took the clubs out to a bunker on an abandoned course nearby and, shaping the solder with rasps and files — and sometimes adding more solder back at the garage — kept experimenting until he arrived at what he was after: a club with a heavy, wide, flanged sole that, when it struck the sand behind the ball, exploded the ball out of good lies, bad lies, and buried lies with an efficiency far beyond that of the niblick, the club traditionally used in bunkers. The new club was the first sand wedge. It soon became a standard club in every golfer's bag. It was in Sarazen's bag in 1932 when he reclaimed his position at the forefront of golf by winning both the British Open and our Open in the same year — an exploit that only Jones had brought off before him.

For pure human interest, few stories in the history of the sport can compare with Sarazen's victory in the British Open. It is almost too good to be true. It pulls at your heartstrings like an old Hollywood melodrama, and the main character, aside from Sarazen, is straight out of Central Casting. This was Skip Daniels. A professional caddie all his life, Daniels was a thin man with soulful eyes and a solemn manner. He was then in his sixties, and his mustache was turning gray. He always wore the same outfit: a soiled cap, a rumpled dark-gray suit, a shirt with a worn celluloid collar, and an old tie. He spoke softly, in measured phrases, but he had enormous enthusiasm for his work and he knew how to inspire a golfer. Daniels caddied at only three courses in Kent: Royal St. George's Golf Club, in Sandwich; Prince's Golf Club, which abuts it; and Royal Cinque Ports Golf Club, close by in Deal. During the First World War, he had patrolled these three linksland courses against a possible invasion by the Germans, and he knew every inch of them. When Hagen won the 1922 British Open at Royal St. George's, Daniels had caddied for him, and when the Open returned to Royal St. George's in 1928, Hagen had arranged for Daniels to caddie for him again. That year, Hagen and Sarazen made the Atlantic crossing together. One night at dinner, after Sarazen had confided that his greatest ambition in golf was to win the British Open, Hagen made what was much more than a gracious gesture. Long convinced that a foreign golfer needed one of the top caddies in order to win the British Open, he offered to let Sarazen have Daniels in the upcoming championship. By that time, Daniels was in his sixties. He limped a bit, and his eyesight wasn't as good as it had been, but he was still an exceptional caddie. From the outset, he and Sarazen got along extremely well. On the first round, Sarazen had a splendid 72, one of the lowest scores. He was purring along nicely on the second day until he came to the fourteenth, a 508-yard par 5, which is called the Suez Canal, after the stream that runs across the fairway about seventy-five yards from the green. Here Sarazen hooked his drive into fairly tall rough. Angry with himself and intent on carrying the Suez Canal with his second shot, he shook off Daniels' advice to play short of the hazard with a mashie, the equivalent of the modern 5-iron. Instead, he reached into his bag and took out his spoon. He threw everything he had into the shot and succeeded in advancing it barely twenty yards, still in the rough. By then, Sarazen was out of control. Playing the spoon again, he managed this time to at least get the ball onto the fairway. The price of his impetuousness was a 7 on the hole. It cost him the championship. He finished two strokes behind the winner, Hagen — the two strokes he had thrown away on the fourteenth on the second round. When he said goodbye to Daniels, he admitted how stupid he had been not to listen to him on that critical hole. "We'll try it again, sir, won't we?" Daniels said. "Before I die, I'm going to win an Open championship for you."

The 1932 British Open was scheduled for Prince's. Sarazen had lined up Daniels to caddie for him. Before checking in at Prince's, however, Sarazen played a round with friends at the Stoke Poges course, outside London. His golf was just about flawless. At the conclusion of the round, the young man who had caddied for him suggested that he caddie for him in the Open. They couldn't miss, he said. He went on to say that Sarazen could never win with Daniels. Daniels, he had heard, had been ill, and his eyesight was gone. After thinking things over, Sarazen told the young caddie to meet him at Prince's. On his arrival at Prince's, Sarazen went through the terribly difficult business of telling Daniels (who indeed showed signs of the passing years) that he thought he was too old to caddie for him in the gruelling championship. On Sarazen's practice rounds, it soon became apparent that he and the young caddie from Stoke Poges were not getting along. The young caddie was much too bossy, and acted as if his mind never entertained error. Sarazen's shotmaking grew increasingly uncertain. His friends noticed this with dismay, and one of them, Lord Alastair Innes-Ker, took it upon himself to call on Sarazen and suggest that Daniels was still available, if he should wish to change caddies. The next morning — two days before the opening round — Sarazen and Daniels were reunited. Sarazen's game and his assurance picked up immediately. On their final practice round, Sarazen promised Daniels that there would be no Suez Canal fiasco this time — he would go along with Daniels' decisions on how to play each hole, each shot. When they reached the eighth hole on this round, Daniels emphasized that it could be the hole on which the championship would be won or lost. The principal problem the golfer faced on the eighth was a blind second shot over a bunkered ridge about thirty-five feet high that straddled the fairway eighty yards or so before the green. Most of the time, the second shot had to be played from a slightly downhill lie, but Daniels said he was confident that on a still day or with a following breeze Sarazen would have no trouble carrying the ridge. If the wind was against him, though, the intelligent play was to lay up short of the ridge. On the first round of the Open, Sarazen had an airtight 70, four strokes under par. He proceeded to run away with the tournament, adding rounds of 69, 70, and 74, and won by five strokes. In the process, he lowered the previous record total for the championship by two strokes. On the eighth, the hole he was most worried about, he had used a brassie for his second shot on the first two rounds, and, clearing the ridge with yards to spare, had made two pars. On the last two rounds, he had had a mild wind at his back, and Daniels had handed him his spoon both times. In the morning, he had been on the green with his second and holed for an eagle 3 from thirty feet. In the afternoon, he had played an even better second. It had stopped only eight feet from the pin, and again he had made the putt for an eagle. Sarazen had lived up to his promise: he had let Daniels select the club for each shot and had never questioned his judgment. Daniels, for his part, had been as good as his word: by keeping Sarazen on an even keel over the seventy-two holes — there wasn't a 6 on Sarazen's card — he had won the British Open for him. A few months later, Daniels died, after a short illness.

Sarazen returned home from Britain about a week before the U.S. Open got under way, at the Fresh Meadow Country Club, on Long Island. The course, which had been designed by A. W. Tillinghast, was very familiar to him; he had been the professional there from 1925 until 1931, when he moved to the Lakeville Country Club on Long Island. He appreciated only too keenly that, as on many other Tillinghast layouts, a golfer had to play his approach shots carefully, since the pear-shaped greens, narrow at the entrance and wide at the back, were flanked by severe bunkers. On his first and second rounds, Sarazen was overcareful. A 74 and a 76 put him five shots off the pace. On the third day — the day of the last two rounds — this same diffidence hampered his play until he holed a sizable putt for a birdie on the short ninth. From there on, he played forceful, assertive golf. Six pars and three birdies gave him a 32 on the second nine and a 70 for the round, and placed him only a stroke behind the leader, Phil Perkins. In the afternoon, he was able to maintain his momentum. He reached the turn in 32: par, bogey, birdie, birdie, par, birdie, par, par, birdie. Victory was now in sight, and his golf on the second nine was a shade more prudent. He was back in 34: par, par, par, par, par, birdie, par, par, par. His 66 gave him a total of 286 and a winning margin of three strokes. Never before in an important championship had a golfer put on such a sustained finishing drive: beginning with his birdie 2 on the ninth in the morning, Sarazen had played the last twenty-eight holes in a hundred strokes. Jones, who was then writing fairly regularly for the *American Golfer,* summed up Sarazen's performance with his usual discernment: "Sarazen has ever been the impatient, headlong player who went for everything in the hope of feeling the timely touch of inspiration. When the wand touches him, he is likely to win in a great finish as he did at Fresh Meadow and Skokie, or in a parade as he did at Prince's, but if it touch him not throughout the four rounds, the boldness of his play leaves no middle ground. When he is in the right mood, he is probably the greatest scorer in the game, possibly, that the game has ever seen."

For all his flair for competition, Sarazen let several big events that he looked like winning get away from him. Armour beat him one up on the thirty-sixth green in the final of the 1930 P.G.A. championship at Fresh Meadow. In 1933, at St. Andrews, Sarazen lost the British Open by a stroke when, playing the long fourteenth on the last round, he caught the face of Hell Bunker with his second shot, needed two shots to get out, and ended up with a triple-bogey 8. The following year, at the Merion Golf Club (then called the Merion Cricket Club), near Philadelphia, he lost our Open by one stroke in almost the same way: on the last round, he hooked his drive on the eleventh into Cobbs Creek and took a triple-bogey 7. The surest solace for defeats as searing as these is victory, and Sarazen, fortunately, continued to have his triumphs. He won his third P.G.A. championship in 1933, at the Blue Mound Country Club, in Milwaukee, even though he had been far off form during his practice rounds. He removed from his bag the clubs that were giving him trouble, and relied on the seven he was most comfortable with: his driver, 4-wood, jigger, 5-iron, 7-iron, sand wedge, and putter. He leaned most heavily on the 4-wood and the jigger. The jigger, which became obsolete with the coming of matched sets, was a shallow-faced club with a distinctively shaped blade that was about halfway between the 3-iron and the 4-iron in loft. Sarazen loved to play the jigger, because at address he could see the ball riding above the clubface, much as he did when he played the 4-wood, a small-headed spoon with a shallow face and a good deal of loft. With either of these clubs, he felt he could get the ball up in the air with no difficulty. His command of the 4-wood figured large in his last major victory, the 1935 Masters. On the final round of that tournament, as Sarazen was walking down the fairway after his drive on the fifteenth, a roar went up in the distance from the gallery crowded around the last green to watch Craig Wood, the leader, finish his round. Wood had holed for a birdie. To gain a tie with him now, Sarazen would have to birdie three of the last four holes. His drive on the fifteenth, a par 5 that measured 485 yards, was out about two hundred and fifty yards, not far from the point where the fairway begins to slope gently downhill to a small pond that lies just in front of a slightly elevated green. Sarazen had planned to use a 3-wood for his second shot to be sure of clearing the pond, but when he saw that his ball had ended up in a very close lie he decided to go with a 4-wood. His 4-wood had a hollow-backed sole, and he would be able to go down after the ball with it. He hit a fine-looking shot that carried the pond with yards to spare. The ball bounced a little to the left after landing on the front edge of the green, rolled straight for the pin thirty feet away, and disappeared into the cup. That changed everything. Sarazen then needed only pars on the last three holes to tie, and he got them. The one on the eighteenth, a par 4 that is all uphill after the drive, took some doing. Ordinarily, the approach shot required no more than a 5-iron or a 6-iron. However, a strong wind had suddenly sprung up, and on the eighteenth it was blowing against the golfer and a shade from left to right. Rather than play a long iron, Sarazen opted for his trusty 4-wood. He played for the left edge of the green and let the wind bring the ball onto the green. He was down in two putts, and had tied

Wood. There had never before been a shot in an important tournament as sensational as that double eagle, and one can understand how nearly everything else about that Masters has been forgotten — Sarazen's three closing pars, for one thing, and the playoff, for another. (A widespread misapprehension persists that Sarazen won the tournament outright with the double eagle.) The playoff was necessarily anticlimactic, but Sarazen feels that he produced some of the most consistent golf of his career in defeating Wood by five strokes over thirty-six holes on an unseasonably cold day. He was in the rough only four times. He was never in a bunker. And from the eleventh hole through the thirty-fourth he ran off twenty-four consecutive pars.

Sarazen's double eagle popularized the 4-wood, and in a short time it replaced the brassie — the 2-wood — as one of the three wooden clubs most golfers carried. No one played the 4-wood better than Sarazen. He could do anything with it — hit the ball high or low, draw it or fade it, float it or rip it, dig it out of the rough. In crucial situations, if he had a chance to use the 4-wood, he did. For instance, in the 1940 U.S. Open, at Canterbury, in which he tied Little, who was already in, it came down to Sarazen's second shot on the seventy-second hole, a 441-yard par 4. He was about two hundred yards from the pin, which was on the left side of the green rather close to a bunker. It didn't take him long to decide to go with his 4-wood in preference to a long iron. His first concern was to make sure of his par, so he played the percentage shot, starting the ball for the right fringe of the green and drawing it onto the green, thirty feet from the pin. One day during my visit with Sarazen this winter, I found myself thinking of the many consummate wood shots from the fairway he had hit under pressure in the championships, beginning with the full driver on the last hole at Skokie, and ending with the 4-wood on the last hole at Canterbury, eighteen years later. I concluded that he was probably the best fairway-wood player of all time. When I later told him this, he shook his head. "No, I think that Jones, with his brassie and spoon, was the greatest I've ever seen," he said, in his direct, emphatic way. "Jones was a wonderful driver, too, so I'd have to say he was the best wooden-club player ever. He won most of his tournaments on the long holes. And we can't overlook Hogan. He was a strong, accurate driver, and in his later years his 3- and 4-woods were deadly."

Realistic and resilient, Sarazen has always lived in the present, but in certain respects he is typical of his generation. He objects to the current passion for overwatered greens. While he admires a number of today's champions, he is of the opinion that a good many of the promising young golfers would play better shots if they had better hand action. This decline in hand action he attributes to the passing of the age of the caddie: "When kids started to caddie at ten or eleven, at every chance they got they'd pull a club out of the bag and swing it, and in time they developed beautiful hand action." He enjoys recalling the youngsters and the old-timers who caddied for him: Dominico, who urged him to go for a birdie on the last hole at Skokie; Daniels, who guided him so surely at Prince's; Stovepipe (he got his name because he always wore a tall, beat-up silk hat), who caddied for him in the Masters the year he made his double eagle; and many others. One of his favorite stories is about Bill Cushing, who used to caddie for him in the Florida tournaments in the nineteen-twenties. One winter, Sarazen had a good chance of winning the Miami Open if he could break par on the final round. That afternoon, his wife Mary came out to the course to watch him play the final holes, but by the time she arrived he had finished. In the hubbub around the clubhouse, she couldn't find her husband, but she found Bill Cushing, and asked him how things had gone. "We didn't quite make it, Mrs. Sarazen," he explained. "We gave it a shot, though, We birdied the thirteenth, and we got our birdie 2 on the fourteenth, but then on the fifteenth Mr. Sarazen went and took a 7."

The weather on Thursday, April 8th, the opening day of the 1982 Masters — which Craig Stadler won on the first hole of a playoff with Dan Pohl — was appreciably less balmy than it generally is in Augusta in early April. When Sarazen and Nelson walked onto the first tee a few minutes before nine-fifteen, their starting time, the temperature was a little below fifty degrees and there was the feeling of rain in the air. Sarazen was dressed in blue knickers and stockings and a blue sweater, Nelson in gray flannels and a lavender sweater. Both were in a perky mood as they chatted with each other and with old friends gathered around the first tee. Usually, only a couple of hundred spectators are on hand to watch the first twosome go off, but this year, in addition to a crowd at the first tee, spectators were lined along the fairway ropes all the way to the green, some four hundred yards away. At nine-fifteen, Hord Hardin introduced Nelson and Sarazen with a few graceful words and indicated to Sarazen that he should tee off first. "Age, or what?" Sarazen asked, with a wide smile. He hit a good drive down the left side of the fairway, and Nelson followed with a beauty right down the middle.

Sarazen and Nelson played nine holes, the last five in a light drizzle. About five hundred spectators accompanied them all the way, and on each hole at least a thousand more were spread along the perimeter of the tee, the fairway, and the green. Sarazen and Nelson had not expected anything like such a large and exuberant gallery, and they responded with some first-class shots and some cheerful banter. Nelson, for example, birdied the second by holing a thirty-foot putt. He misread the speed of the third green, however, and took three putts. "How are those greens, Byron?" a fan in the gallery at the tee of the par-3 fourth asked him. "Fastest I've ever seen the greens here," Nelson replied. "I had no idea they'd be this slick." On the fourth, which is 205 yards long, Nelson's tee shot finished short of the green and to the right, about eighty feet from the pin, whereupon he holed his wedge chip for another birdie. On the fifth tee, he caught the ball a little thin, and the result was a low, skimming drive that did not reach the brow of the rising fairway but slid slowly back down the slope toward the tee. Nelson shook his head as he watched the ball. "My, even the fairways are fast!" he exclaimed. Some of the fans watching Nelson and Sarazen were on the young side, but the bulk of the spectators, as one would expect, were people who were contemporaries of the two stars or had seen them in their prime and obviously cherished happy memories of them. Whenever either man played a fine shot, the faces of the gallery lit up, and there was applause and spontaneous shouts of "Perfect, Gene," or "Great hit, Byron." It is only on nostalgic occasions, such as old-timers' games in baseball and tennis tournaments restricted to players forty-five or over, that one runs into galleries of this type. Theirs is a special mood, engendered partly by the delight and pride they take in watching the heroes of their youth still performing so creditably, and partly by the pleasure of recalling that earlier time when the spirit of the game was predominant in golf, baseball, tennis, and most other sports. Today, there is so much money at stake in golf tournaments, for instance, that it overpowers all other considerations. It is the rare player now who seems to enjoy his sport and to regard it as something more than a means to an end. In any event, walking the front nine with Nelson and

Sarazen was a treat. Nelson, in excellent form, had a 40, four over par. Sarazen had a 45, which could have been several strokes lower if he had putted better, but he hit some elegant shots: on the short fourth, a full drive that split the narrow opening to the green; on the long eighth, a running chip that had just enough speed to make the crest of a sharp ridge and slip down close to the cup; and on the ninth, where he was bunkered before the green, that familiar Sarazen calling card, an explosion shot that spun dead two feet from the cup.

(1982)

Pebble Beach and the Open

Without a doubt the most thrilling U.S. Open in recent years was the one at Pebble Beach in 1982. Many people consider Pebble Beach the best course in the country, and there are those who rate it the best in the world. Halfway through the final round, all of the contenders had been dismissed except those two well-acquainted adversaries: Tom Watson, who had never won our Open, and Jack Nicklaus, who had won it four years, including 1972, the last time it was played at Pebble Beach. With four holes to go, Watson, playing just behind Nicklaus, led him by a stroke. He lost his lead when he bogeyed the sixteenth. On the par-3 seventeenth, Watson pulled a 2-iron into thick rough. It looked as if that error might cost him the championship but, as we know, it didn't. Bob Jones, who had some experience in these matters, came to believe that before the first shot has been struck in a tournament, fate has already decreed who will win it and who will not.

THERE ARE FEW EXPERIENCES IN SPORT THAT CAN COMPARE with the thrill that the average golfer or the skillful golfer receives when he plays a famous course for the first time. Golf courses vary immensely as to how hard or how easy they are to comprehend for the first-time visitor. For example, the Old Course at St. Andrews, a sea of erratically rolling duneland, is replete with holes that give a golfer little or no clue in determining the correct line from tee to green. On many holes, a drive that whistles down the center of the fairway may end up in a pot bunker that is hidden from view at the tee. For another thing, there is no sure way of reading the undulations on many of the vast greens. When you study your line to the cup, what looks to be a definite break to the right turns out to be a slight swerve to the left. The Old Course must be memorized. There is no other way to learn the position of the hazards and the speed and roll of the various areas of each green. Inasmuch as this requires months of practice and application, the sensible procedure for a visitor is to take a caddie. Even then, the course manages to muffle a good deal of its personality. On the outgoing nine, your caddie will point out the salient features to aim at and the right club to use, and you must trust him. The same is true on the incoming nine, on which, after playing the loop, the golfer heads home, the old town looming in the distance like a watercolor of some medieval city. Down this stretch, the target that the caddie gives him on his drive and some of his other shots is more often than not a church steeple or an ancient building made of stone of a distinctive color. I once played a round with Willie Turnesa, a golfer of international stature, during which his drive on the thirteenth finished at the base of a rise so abrupt that all he could see was the sky. His caddie was resourceful. "Hit the middle of that big cloud," he said, pointing, as he handed Turnesa a 5-iron. Turnesa hit the ball exactly where he was told to, and when he climbed the bank and peered at the green, a hundred and seventy yards away, his ball was sitting eight feet from the pin.

On the other hand, when a golfer plays an exceptionally frank, straightforward course — three excellent examples would be Muirfield, near Edinburgh; Portmarnock, outside Dublin; and Royal Melbourne, outside Melbourne — the individual holes clearly disclose the perils he faces and the precise route he should try to take from tee to green. Nevertheless, when one plays these three courses, it is still advisable to take a caddie, for they are linksland courses, and, what with the shifting winds off the ocean, distance is harder to gauge than it usually is on inland courses. (Linksland is the stretch of sandy soil deposited by the sea as it receded slowly over the centuries. The soil drains well and produces splendid turf for golf.) Most of the other genuinely great courses lie about midway between St. Andrews and the likes of Muirfield, Portmarnock, and Royal Melbourne in the clarity with which they present themselves. In any list of the top courses in this country, the following would surely by included: Seminole, in North Palm Beach; the Augusta National, in Augusta, Georgia; Merion, on the edge of Philadelphia; Pine Valley, which is also close to Philadelphia; the Lakeside course at Olympic, in San Francisco; and Pebble Beach and Cypress Point, both of which are on the Monterey Peninsula, roughly a hundred miles south of San Francisco. In their separate ways, the challenges that each of these courses offers are stated explicitly, but it never hurts to have put in some time becoming acquainted with the subtleties of the land. The key to the endless fascination of golf is that it is the only game played on natural terrain — or, at least, on land that, however unpromising it was originally, has been fashioned to resemble attractive and interesting natural terrain. The finer the course, the more enticing the shots it asks the golfer to play. Moreover, on a great course on which many championships have been held there is an invaluable bonus: history comes to life every step of the way, and a golf pilgrim is continually reminded of the feats of the celebrated players who trod the same holes long before him.

All of this is by way of leading up to the fact that if there is any one course that is generally regarded as being the most dramatic in the world, and quite possibly the best, it is Pebble Beach, where the United States Open Championship was played last month, and carried off by Tom Watson after a tremendous duel with Jack Nicklaus that was decided by one of the most breathtaking shots in Open history. The official designation of the course is the Pebble Beach Golf Links, and this is odd, since it is not a true linksland course. It is made up of eight holes perched atop craggy headlands that overlook Carmel Bay and of ten fairly difficult, if less spectacular, holes, which are commonly referred to as the "inland" holes, although most of them lie within a driver shot of the bay. The moving force behind the creation of Pebble Beach was Samuel Morse, a shrewd, farsighted entrepreneur, who had been the captain of the Yale football team in 1906. In 1914, when he was in the employ of the Pacific Improvement Company, a subsidiary of the Southern Pacific Railroad, Morse got to know and appreciate the unspoiled grandeur of the Monterey Peninsula, with its pine-covered hills and its rockbound coastline. His assignment at the time was to liquidate the company's holdings on the peninsula and on the land adjoining it. He decided instead to form a firm of his own, the Del Monte Properties Company, and bought a tract of seven thousand acres of this land, including seven miles of coastline, for one million three hundred thousand dollars. Among the assets Morse acquired was the Del Monte Hotel, an immense Victorian structure above Monterey Bay, which at one time possessed — far more than any other West

Coast spa — something of the cachet of Newport. Attached to the hotel was the pleasant if obsolescent Del Monte golf course. Morse had the astuteness to realize that the hotel had seen its best days, and that in order to attract the wellborn and well-to-do from San Francisco and elsewhere who might purchase property and build homes on the Monterey Peninsula a much more modern golf course was necessary — preferably one with such a superlative layout that its fame would quickly redound throughout the world.

To this end, Morse, instead of selling his prize property on the high cliffs above Carmel Bay for plush private estates, as most real-estate developers would have, reserved it for the golf course. In 1918, he made a startling decision. He did not approach either Charles Blair Macdonald or Donald Ross, the two outstanding golf-course architects in the country, or any other golf-course architect of reputation, to design his course. He entrusted this considerable responsibility to Jack Neville, a real-estate salesman who had worked for the Pacific Improvement Company and had continued with the Del Monte Properties Company. A tall, laconic man with a nice dry wit, Neville had won the California State Amateur Championship several times and was rated to be as good an amateur golfer as there was on the West Coast, but he had never built a golf course before. He set about his task with no fuss whatever. He walked the site daily, spending most of his hours mulling over how to use the extraordinary land above Carmel Bay to maximum advantage. After three weeks, he settled on the way that the holes he had in mind would be routed. He got it absolutely right. His inspired plan went like this: The first three holes would swing inland and then back toward the bay. Holes four, six, seven, eight, nine, and ten followed along the edge of the cliffs. The fifth, a par 3 framed by woods, did not. Holes eleven through sixteen were inland holes, but the seventeenth returned to the bay, and the entire left side of the eighteenth, a long par 5, was bordered by the rocks, sand, and water of the bay. The course was completed in 1919. The golfers who played it came away stunned by its scenic beauty and the cornucopia of astonishing golf shots it offered.

It is well worthwhile, I believe, to describe in some detail the eight holes along Carmel Bay which Neville visualized and executed so brilliantly. The first one that the golfer meets is the fourth, a par 4 that is 327 yards long. Despite its shortness, it is a worrisome hole. Along its right side, a cliff about twenty-five feet high drops down to a rocky beach. Since such features have a particularly powerful subconscious effect on people wearing spiked shoes, most golfers hook or pull their tee shot far to the left, into the rough or into a bunker. Even if his drive stays on the left side of the fairway, the golfer faces a touchy shot: he must feather a soft pitch just over a frontal bunker in order to stop it on the green, perhaps the smallest of the eighteen — and the greens at Pebble Beach are smaller than those at any other of the world's great courses.

The sixth, a par 5 that measures 516 yards, presents a similar problem. Off the tee, the golfer must avoid the right side of the fairway, for it is bordered by a cliff that ranges from thirty-five to sixty feet high. Most golfers, in their concern to avoid this hazard, again play their tee shot farther left than they had intended to, and many drives wind up in a long trap that hugs the left side of the fairway. This complicates matters. Approximately three hundred and fifty yards from the tee, the fairway climbs a sudden hill nearly fifty feet high, to a plateau, at the end of which the green is situated. On a windless day, a big hitter can reach the green in two, but for the average golfer, unless he finds the fairway off the tee, a 6 is a most acceptable score. The tee on the short seventh, a mere 110 yards, is set about five yards below the level of the sixth green but at the edge of a cliff almost seventy-five feet high. When the golfer is addressing the ball on the tee, he has no protection from the sometimes fierce winds as he attempts to hit and hold the tiny, heavily bunkered green, far below him. On stormy days, when the wind is buffeting the rocks just behind the green and sending spray high into the air, a 3-iron is not too much club for a professional. On quiet days, a pitching wedge will suffice.

After this, the course begins to get tough. In playing the eighth, where the tee is only a short distance from the seventh green, the golfer, who has now turned around to face inland, must produce a long, controlled drive to reach the high land at the top of the hill that he had approached from the opposite direction when he was playing the sixth. From the tee on this 433-yard par 4, he takes in the cliff rising sharply along the right side of the fairway. When he has climbed to the top of the incline — a good drive will finish there — what may very well be the most awesome sight in golf awaits him. Here the cliff plunges straight down a hundred and fifty feet or more into Carmel Bay. He sees this and also notices that up ahead the fairway jogs slightly to the left, but what transfixes his attention is the sight of the eighth green in the distance, across the waters of an inlet of the bay. The green is guarded by a cortege of five bunkers, but it actually doesn't need any of them, since it sits just beyond the continuing cliffline, approximately fifty feet high at this point. Depending on the weather, the tournament-calibre golfer, who will usually choose to lay up off the tee with a long iron or a 3-wood or 4-wood, is usually left with a carry of between a hundred and seventy and a hundred and ninety yards across the inlet on his second shot. The average golfer, of course, having hit a somewhat shorter or more errant drive, most times faces a longer carry on his second if he chooses to go for the green. To pull it off, he must summon nothing less than a career shot. He should give it a whirl nonetheless. After all, if he manages to get home in two he will have something to talk about for the rest of his life. On the other hand, if he is working on a tidy round and scoring well, prudence dictates that he take a long or middle iron for his second and play a conservative lay-up shot down the fairway as it begins to bend to the right and follow the curve of the inlet. He will then be in position to hit the green with a firm pitch on his third.

The eighth leaves a golfer emotionally exhausted, but he must pull himself together quickly in order to cope with the ninth and tenth, two extremely exacting par 4s — 467 and 424 yards long, respectively — that continue southeast along the bay, which is on the right. On these two holes, the cliffs have dwindled to thirty feet, but this is enough to deter the golfer from flirting with the right side of the fairway. In addition, on both holes the fairway slopes from left to right, and, with the greens set close to the cliffs, hitting them in the regulation number of strokes in a swirling wind is no easy matter. I would guess that the eighth, ninth, and tenth constitute the most difficult succession of three par 4s in golf.

Pebble Beach has a formidable finish. The seventeenth and eighteenth return to the bay, and they can be destructive. The green on the seventeenth, a par 3 that is 209 yards long from the back tee, is situated on a rocky point that juts into the bay. The eighteenth is regarded by many experts as the premier finishing hole in golf. It curves like a scimitar along the bay, which flanks the fairway on the left. Out-of-bounds stakes patrol the right side practically from tee to green. As if the hole weren't stiff enough with these constraints, there are other hazards, such as clumps of trees and bunkers, that come into play with a strategic niceness. Then, there is the wind. Some days, it blows in so ferociously off the water that experienced golfers feel that the safest course is to aim their shots out to sea and let the wind bring them back onto the fairway.

The only trouble with emphasizing the grandeur of the seaside holes at Pebble Beach is that this may promote the impression that the inland holes are rather ordinary. They are not. The opening three holes are a short par 4 followed by a flat par 5 and another short par 4. Though original and provocative, they present good opportunities for birdies. As a matter of fact, the trick to scoring well on Pebble Beach is to get through the first six holes a shot or two under par, for, regardless of his skill, the golfer is almost certain to give a few shots back to par over the last twelve holes. Granted, life becomes a little milder after you walk off the tenth green, but each hole on the inland stretch from the eleventh through the sixteenth requires fastidious shotmaking. On the par-4 eleventh, for example, the drive must be placed on the left side of the fairway in order for the golfer to command the opening to the green on his approach. On the twelfth, a fairly long par 3, the surface of the green is hard and unreceptive, and the only way to stop a long iron or wood there is to hit the kind of shot that reaches the apex of its parabola above the green and floats down softly. On the thirteenth, a 393-yard par 4, the wide right side of the fairway beckons, but the tee shot should be played close to the large bunker on the left side, for otherwise you cannot come into the canted green from the correct angle. The fourteenth, fifteenth, and sixteenth also require knowledge and control. The greens, slippery and fast, as are all the greens at Pebble Beach, are full of quirky slopes and breaks, and you must place your tee shot — and on the par-5 fourteenth your second shot as well — with a good deal of care in order to be able to stop your approach on the proper part of the green in relation to the pin, and so avoid finding yourself in a position where there is almost no escape from taking three putts. All in all, the inland holes, with their emphasis on finesse, complement the seaside holes perfectly.

Before Neville worked his wonders on the marvellous land that Morse had set aside, there had never been a golf course quite like Pebble Beach. On the West Links at North Berwick, one of the older Scottish courses, there are a few cliffside holes. The green on the first is on an abrupt plateau twenty-five feet or so above the southern bank of the Firth of Forth. The second and third holes hug the shore, but the land drops quickly down from the high tee on the second and is only five feet or so above the water. Then, there is the fourteenth, the elegant hole called Perfection — a drive and about a 6-iron — on which the green is near the edge of a cliff some fifteen feet above the firth. At the beginning of the second nine, when the course heads back to the clubhouse, four other holes are situated close to the firth, but substantial hillocks and sand hills block off the sight of the water, and the golfer is hardly aware of its proximity. The course at Dunbar, near North Berwick, and the one at Stonehaven, twenty miles south of Aberdeen, also have some enjoyable cliffside holes. At Ballybunion, the renowned Irish course that winds through towering sand hills above the Shannon estuary, there are cliffs of a more heroic size, but they come into play on just three holes, and then only tangentially. After the First World War, when golf underwent a tremendous boom, Charles Blair Macdonald created Mid Ocean, the first course built in Bermuda. Formally opened in 1921, Mid Ocean is an imaginative layout, but for most golfers it proved to be a disappointment. They had assumed that such a lavishly publicized course on such a storied island would surely feature several arresting holes adjacent to the Atlantic, including a few in which the handsome coral cliffs were involved. Not at all. For example, the first three holes occupy a strip of land fairly close to the Atlantic, but the water is largely hidden by stands of trees, and when it is visible it plays a strictly decorative role. The only time a golfer really experiences the sensation of being next to the water at Mid Ocean comes when he walks onto the tee of the eighteenth, a grand finishing hole, where, just behind the back markers, the land drops vertically fifty or sixty feet to the ocean.

After the Second World War, the Ailsa course at Turnberry, in Ayrshire, Scotland, which is laid out over a glorious expanse of duneland along the Clyde estuary, and which during the war had been converted into an airfield for the R.A.F. Coastal Command, was revived and revised most successfully by Mackenzie Ross. Seven holes in a row — the fourth through the tenth — move along the coast, but for the most part a continuing ridge of duneland shuts off the view of the sea. The best-known hole, the ninth, has a tee that is set on a high, isolated crag, and it demands a fairly long carry over water to reach the fairway, but there were many other opportunities at Turnberry to build tees and greens at the water's edge, which were not utilized. I don't know the reason for this, but my guess is that in Scotland — and throughout the British Isles — improving on nature to this extent has not been seriously considered, because of the expense involved and because to do so would be impractical: on stormy days, holes that had been constructed too close to the sea might be inundated and damaged.

One course on which the popularity of Pebble Beach must have had an effect is Cypress Point, its neighbor on the Monterey Peninsula, which was completed in 1928. Cypress Point has an almost incomparable variety of holes: ordinary seaside holes, duneland holes, typical inland holes, pine-lined holes that climb and descend rolling hills, and, for good measure, three cliffside holes — the fifteenth, sixteenth, and seventeenth — which make magnificent use of the course's chunk of jagged coastline. Alister MacKenzie, who designed Cypress Point, was such a talented golf-course architect that he must have sensed on his first exploratory stroll of his acreage the possibilities of that wild corner where the Pacific beats against the cliffs, but if somehow he did not, the existence of Pebble Beach just a few miles down the road would certainly have thrust it into his mind. While there are a number of other courses around the world that have one or two or three memorable holes poised on cliffs by the sea, the only course that truly merits comparison with Pebble Beach is Campo de Golf Cajuiles, designed in the early nineteen-seventies by Pete Dye, on the southeastern shore of the Dominican Republic. As at Pebble Beach, a total of eight holes are strung along the sea, some of them with greens or tees built only a few feet above the water, others marching along coral cliffs, which Dye's Dominican crews patiently hammered into a workable substratum for the tees, greens, and fairways. On seven of these eight holes, it is necessary for the crack golfer to attempt risky carries across water on his tee shot or approach shot in order to match par. Campo de Golf Cajuiles lacks the dimensions and the majesty of Pebble Beach, but it is a remarkable achievement — a striking Caribbean version of the original.

And what about Jack Neville? After the smashing success of Pebble Beach, one would think that the world would have beaten a path to his door. For various reasons, this did not happen. He collaborated with George Thomas III on Bel Air, a superior course in Los Angeles, and, at Morse's request, he laid out plans for a number of other courses, none of which were ever built. Much later on, he designed a second nine holes at Pacific Grove, a nearby municipal course, and assisted in the design of the Shore Course of the Monterey Peninsula Country Club. All this time, he adhered to his old routine, selling lots for Del Monte Properties and living simply, almost forgotten. He was rediscovered in 1972, when the U.S. Open was held at Pebble Beach for the first time. Nearly eighty-one years old then, he remained modestly in the background during the championship, but there was no question that the tardy recognition he received as the man behind the masterpiece meant a great deal to him. He died at eighty-six, in 1978, not long after a banquet in his honor was held on the peninsula.

Down through the years, Sam Morse ran his beloved Pebble Beach as a home course for the residents of his private duchy and as a resort course for visitors — primarily those who were vacationing at the Del Monte Lodge, a hotel overlooking the eighteenth green and Carmel Bay, which was built to replace the old Del Monte Hotel. Technically, Pebble Beach was (and still is) a public course — the only public course, incidentally, on which the U.S. Open has been played — but, being well off the beaten path, in its early years it was seldom uncomfortably crowded. With few exceptions, a golf course's status depends to a large extent on whether or not it has been the scene of important tournaments. For instance, whenever the Royal and Ancient Golf Club of St. Andrews, which conducts the national championships in Great Britain, adds a new course to the rota of courses over which the British Open is played, this is tantamount to conferring knighthood on that course. A similar prestige accrues to courses in this country that are selected by the United States Golf Association for the U.S. Open. From the day that Pebble Beach was unveiled, knowledgeable golf hands thought that it would be a perfect venue for our Open, but it was not chosen until 1972 because the course lacked one fundamental requirement: it was not situated near a major center of population, and the general feeling was that an Open held there would not attract enough fans and bring in enough money in gate receipts to balance the considerable expense of staging the championship. The first significant tournament held at Pebble Beach was the 1919 California State Amateur Championship, which, incidentally, was won by Jack Neville. The site added incalculably to the event, and the California Golf Association was able to arrange for the championship to be played there annually, as it continues to be. In 1929, the course played host to its first national championship, the United States Amateur. This was quite a coup, for until then no national championship had been held west of Minneapolis. In those days, the Amateur was looked upon as Bobby Jones' personal championship. He had reached the final the five previous years and had won it four times. The 1929 Amateur is probably best remembered for the fact that Jones was eliminated in the first round, after a rousing match with the then unknown Johnny Goodman, who beat him one up over eighteen holes. The 1929 Amateur served to make golfers throughout the country much more conscious of Pebble Beach. Photographs of many of its spectacular holes appeared in newspapers from coast to coast and in magazines with a national circulation.

Pebble Beach's fame continued to grow. The United States Women's Amateur Championship was played there twice — in 1940 and 1948. The U.S. Amateur returned there in 1947 and again in 1961, when the young Jack Nicklaus dominated the proceedings from start to finish. There is no question, though, that the event that made Americans, non-golfers as well as golfers, aware of Pebble Beach was the annual P.G.A. Tour tournament that Bing Crosby devised and ran. Its official designation is the National Pro-Am, but it is usually referred to simply as the Crosby. Inaugurated as a thirty-six-hole competition before the war at Rancho Santa Fe, near San Diego, it was shifted to the Monterey Peninsula by Crosby in 1947. That year, it was extended into a fifty-four-hole tournament, with the golfers playing one round at Cypress Point, one at the Monterey Peninsula Country Club, and one at Pebble Beach. The critical year was 1958. The Crosby was further extended into a seventy-two-hole tournament, with the final round, appropriately, taking place at Pebble Beach. That winter, the Crosby became one of the first tournaments on the P.G.A. Tour to be televised nationally. From the start, it drew huge audiences. The presence of some movie stars in the lists and Crosby's personal popularity had a great deal to do with this — he did much of the commentary, fully indulging his penchant for polysyllables — but the main reason, I would have to believe, was the effect on the viewers of Pebble Beach's overwhelming beauty.

Apart from its high television ratings, the Crosby attracted large galleries. This undoubtedly led the U.S.G.A. to review its earlier position that holding the Open at Pebble Beach was too much of a financial risk, but for several other reasons as well the organization was ready to accept the invitation that Sam Morse tendered in 1966 and to agree, after some discussion, to hold the Open at Pebble Beach in 1972. In 1968, Morse and his son-in-law, Richard Osborne, who was associated in business with him, called in Frank D. (Sandy) Tatum, Jr., a San Francisco lawyer, to be responsible for the part of the course preparation which was the obligation of the Del Monte Properties Company. Tatum was an ideal choice for this assignment. When he was in his teens, he had spent his summer vacations working as a laborer on construction crews in Los Angeles, his home town, to accumulate enough money to play in the California State Amateur. "I'd blow it all in one wonderful week at Pebble Beach," he once told me. "It was one of the most intelligent things I've every done." An able golfer, Tatum won the National Collegiate Championship in 1942, when he was at Stanford. At Oxford, which he attended as a Rhodes Scholar, he was a member of the university golf team. Few people of my acquaintance know as much about golf or are as exuberantly passionate about it. As a longtime admirer of Pebble Beach, he knew that no changes had been officially authorized since H. Chandler Egan was asked to strengthen the bunkering in the green area on some holes before the 1929 Amateur, but he also knew that bit by bit, from 1929 on, as has happened at many courses, the physiognomy of individual holes had been altered by greenkeepers and work crews, and, in the case of Pebble Beach, by understandably spotty maintenance during the Second World War. Tatum concluded that the soundest procedure was to get in touch with Jack Neville and to restore any features of the original layout that Neville thought were significant but that somehow or other had disappeared over the years. Neville suggested restoring the following: the bunker at the front left corner of the first green, which made the approach shot more exacting; the bunker in the drive zone to the left of the fourth fairway, which he felt would work best if it was elongated into an L shape and carried into the fairway, and, additionally, if a small pot bunker was placed in the angle of the L; and the bunkering on the left shoulder of the hill on the sixth, which influenced the playing of the second shot. Neville also recommended that the bunker on the edge of the right rough in the drive zone on the sixteenth be deepened, so that a golfer couldn't play a relatively routine recovery onto the green from it.

He also felt that this bunker would pack more trepidation if it edged toward the fairway. Later on, P. J. Boatwright, Jr., the executive director of the U.S.G.A., came out to supervise the Association's part in preparing the course for the championship — a job he has done for years with enormous skill. Along with putting into effect such standard procedures for the Open as narrowing the fairways and letting the rough grow tall and dense, Boatwright proposed changes on the ninth and tenth that Tatum and Neville heartily concurred in. Both holes, exceptional par 4s, were playing extremely short at that time. The burned-out rough on the high, or left, side of their fairways was playing as hard as stone, with the result that on a solidly hit tee shot the ball would get so much bounce and roll if it landed there that the golfer would have nothing more than a wee pitch for his approach. On the ninth, new bunkering was established in the drive zone where the rough met the high side of the fairway. On the tenth, a new championship tee was built, on the left side of the ninth green, to add some length to the hole, and on the left edge of the fairway, some two hundred and thirty-five yards out, a long, irregularly shaped bunker that could not be carried was added. The effect of the new bunkers on these two holes was to force golfers to play for the fairway to the right of the hazards, and this put increased pressure on them.

The 1972 Open turned out to be everything that one had hoped it would be. The course played hard but well on the first three days, under blue skies and a warm sun and with a refreshing breeze coming off the water. It played perceptibly harder on the fourth, and last, day, when the golfers had to deal with a gusty wind that stirred up whitecaps in the bay. The 1972 Open had been expected to provide one of the most rigorous championship tests in years, and it did. For instance, Jack Nicklaus, who either was tied for the lead or held the lead from the first round on, posted a winning total of 290, which was two strokes over par. Only half of the hundred and fifty-two starters broke 80 on each of the first two rounds. On the windy fourth day, no one broke 70, and only two players broke or equalled par, 72. On that final round, there were several memorable moments. The first came when Nicklaus was playing the tenth. He held a comfortable lead at this point, but his tee shot sailed out to the right, over the cliff, and down onto the beach. His third shot could well have done the same thing, but it stopped at the brink of the cliff. Nicklaus was extremely lucky to get out of the hole with only a double-bogey 6. Not long after this, he botched up the par-3 twelfth and was faced with sinking an eight-foot putt for a bogey 4. At that same moment, Arnold Palmer, who had played a good, stubborn Open, was on the fourteenth green lining up an eight-foot putt for a birdie. If Palmer made his putt and Nicklaus missed his, Palmer would move into the lead by a stroke. It went the other way: Palmer missed and Nicklaus holed. On the fifteenth, Nicklaus nailed down his victory with an authoritative birdie. He went on to birdie the par-3 seventeenth when his 1-iron shot hit the flagstick on its first bounce and stopped six inches away. This is the shot that most fans who saw that Open remember.

There was no question after the 1972 Open that the championship would be returning to Pebble Beach. Before it did so, this year, a number of changes in the ownership, condition, and atmosphere of the golf course took place. Following Sam Morse's death, in 1969, the Del Monte Properties Company was reorganized. Under the new management, the role of Pebble Beach was altered. It was regarded primarily as a source of income. The cost of a greens fee rose steeply, as did the cost of renting a golf cart. The golf course was also looked upon as a principal attraction for luring visitors to the Del Monte Lodge — which, inevitably, was renamed the Lodge at Pebble Beach — and for selling lots on the peninsula. In 1976, the Del Monte Properties Company became the Pebble Beach Corporation, and three years later it was sold to Twentieth Century–Fox. Along with Pebble Beach, the old Del Monte course and Spyglass Hill, a new Robert Trent Jones course, which was completed in the mid-nineteen-sixties, were included in the purchase. (Twentieth Century–Fox had an abundance of capital at its disposal at this time, chiefly because of the colossal profits racked up by *Star Wars*.) In 1978, no fewer than fifty-six thousand rounds of golf were played over Pebble Beach. This total was attained by starting the groups of players off the first tee at nine-minute intervals. The average round took six hours, and under the constant tramp, tramp, tramp and whack, whack, whack the course took quite a beating. The installation in 1977 of a web of garish asphalt cart paths hardly improved its appearance. In 1979, a more enlightened attitude toward the course was observable. That year, the interval between starting times was increased to twelve minutes — a change that reduced the number of rounds to forty-two thousand. Pebble Beach gradually began to look like its old self again. This was due in a large measure to the work of John Zoller, an accomplished golf-course superintendent, who was appointed director of golf operations in 1978. (Before coming to Pebble Beach, Zoller, who had studied turf management at Ohio State, had been the course superintendent at the Eugene Country Club, in Oregon, for eighteen years, and then the course superintendent, and later the general manager, at the Monterey Peninsula Country Club. In 1980, Zoller became the executive director of the Northern California Golf Association, and, shortly after this, Tim Berg, who was also trained at the Eugene Country Club, was hired to be both the course superintendent and the professional at Pebble Beach.) One other change was in the offing. In June, 1981, Marvin Davis, a Denver oil man, bought Twentieth Century–Fox. Davis then formed a partnership with the Aetna Life & Casualty Company, and at the present time they operate holdings on the Monterey Peninsula and at Aspen, Colorado — ski runs, a ski school, a ski shop, and several restaurants. This year, the division that runs Pebble Beach hiked the greens fee at the course, which in 1979 had been raised from fifty to sixty dollars, to seventy dollars.

Pebble Beach underwent only minuscule changes in the months before the 1982 Open. After a visit to the course before preparations for the championship began, Tatum, who had meanwhile served as president of the U.S.G.A. in 1978-79, had a pair of recommendations to make. He believed that the shallow splash bunker that had been constructed before the 1972 Open in the angle of the L-shaped bunker on the fourth hole should be replaced by a classical pot bunker, sharp-sided and deep, since Neville had had that type of bunker in mind. And he believed that Neville had meant the bunker in the drive zone on the right side of the sixteenth hole to be more daunting from the tee and more punishing to play from. These changes were made. Apart from this, the 1982 Open course was really the same course that was played ten years before. This is evidenced by their over-all lengths: 6,812 yards in 1972, 6,825 yards this year.

The 1982 Open turned out to be one of the great Opens of all time. Before play got under way, there was a good deal of speculation about the chances of Craig Stadler, Severiano Ballesteros, Ray Floyd, who was on a hot streak, young Bobby Clampett, Tom Kite, David Graham, the defending champion, and a number of other players in the starting field of a hundred and fifty-three, but the two men at the center of most discussions were Jack Nicklaus and Tom Watson. No other golfer has played Pebble Beach as well as Nicklaus. In addition to winning the 1972 Open there, he scored his second victory in the U.S. Amateur there, in 1961, when he was twenty-one, overwhelming his opponent in the semifinals 9 and 8 and his opponent in the final 8 and 6. Aside from this, he has won the Crosby three times — in 1967, 1972, and 1973. Nicklaus's successes at Pebble Beach have been due in a large measure to his being that rare golfer, a power hitter with an instinctive sense of shotmaking. When he has been a bit off his game, he has been able to convert mediocre rounds into acceptable ones, because, first, he is an exceptional putter, as we have begun to appreciate more and more in recent years, and, second, he can concentrate under the strain of the big test like few other athletes. This uncommon amalgam of abilities explains why Nicklaus has won many more major championships than any other golfer — nineteen in all: two U.S. Amateurs (1959, 1961); four U.S. Opens (1962, 1967, 1972, 1980); three British Opens (1966, 1970, 1978); five Masters (1963, 1965, 1966, 1972, 1975); and five P.G.A. championships (1963, 1971, 1973, 1975, 1980). A proud man who is rightfully aware of his prodigious record, Nicklaus wanted very much to win the 1982 Open, for several reasons. Now forty-two and showing signs of slowing down, he was eager to bring his total of major victories to an even twenty. Then, too, if he carried the day at Pebble Beach he would become the first player to win our Open five times. (Willie Anderson, Bobby Jones, and Ben Hogan have also been four-time winners.)

As for Watson, he is the finest hitter of the golf ball to come along since Nicklaus's heyday. Over the past seven years, he has won five major titles — the British Open in 1975, 1977, and 1980, the Masters in 1977 and 1981. Watson is subject to spells of wildness, especially off the tee, but when he is in top form he can be dazzling. For a man of only medium size — he is five feet nine and weighs a hundred and sixty pounds — he drives the ball an astonishing distance, frequently more than two hundred and eighty yards. Around the green, he can improvise all kinds of stunning shots — a talent he has had since he was a boy. He is probably the outstanding bunker-shot artist since Gary Player. An attacking putter, he tends to be overbold, leaving himself plenty of those grisly four- and five-footers after running his approach putt past the cup, but he has streaks when he holes long ones from all over the place. Watson wanted to take the 1982 Open as badly as Nicklaus. Now thirty-two, he had failed in eight previous attempts to win it, although he was in a position to do so at Winged Foot, in Westchester, in 1974; at Medinah, outside Chicago, in 1975; and at Baltusrol, in New Jersey, in 1980. He knows only too well that since the mid-nineteen-twenties our Open has been the game's most important championship, and that a golfer cannot expect to be ranked among the great players in history, whatever his other accomplishments, unless he has won at least one Open. Many of us had begun to wonder whether the Open would always elude Watson, and I can well imagine that these same thoughts have gone through Watson's mind every day the last five years. Like Nicklaus, he has a special fondness for Pebble Beach. During the years he was attending Stanford University, which is only seventy miles or so away, he would hurry down to the Monterey Peninsula whenever he had a free weekend, and revel in the challenge of the course. Like so many young golfers who hoped for a career in the game, during his college days Watson used to fantasize about winning the Open while he was out on the course playing a round — "Tom Watson is now tied for the lead. To win this championship, he will need at least one birdie on the remaining holes. He has his work cut out for him. . . . " Watson was particularly prone to these fantasies when playing Pebble Beach.

As it turned out, in its final stages the 1982 championship was fought between Nicklaus and Watson, and was resolved by one of the Open's most exciting climaxes. It deserves to be described in some detail, but a few aspects of the first three days of play should be mentioned in order to set the scene properly for the stirring dénouement.

On Thursday, the day of the opening round, a fairly strong west wind swept over Pebble Beach. In the morning, the skies were gray and the air was chilly, and waking up to greet the new day brought one all the delight of rising in Glasgow in December. All during the morning and the afternoon, clouds from the fog banks in the bay rolled across the course. Apart from the fact that after the opening day the wind was appreciably gentler, the weather remained much the same throughout the tournament. The skies were generally overcast, and only now and then could one see the sun breaking through in Carmel Valley, fifteen miles away. It is testimony to the beauty of Pebble Beach that under such bleak conditions the course looked as handsome as ever. It was in first-class shape for the championship, the greens swift and smooth, the fairways tightly knit and resilient. The rough was not as high as it usually is in the Open, but it was thick, wiry, and sufficiently punishing. In one respect, Pebble Beach had a different mien: the bunkers were heavily fringed with shaggy, tall grass, which waved in the wind and gave the course a sort of Scottish look.

The tournament had hardly started on Thursday morning when Danny Edwards, a seasoned touring pro from Oklahoma, ripped off an eagle and three birdies to go five under par on the first six holes. As noted earlier, the first six holes at Pebble Beach are eminently birdieable, but one seldom tears through them the way Edwards did. However, after he had gone to six under par with a birdie on the eleventh, he double-bogeyed the fourteenth, bogeyed the sixteenth, double-bogeyed the seventeenth, and eventually had to settle for a 71, one under par. The lowest score that day was 70. There were two of them, one by Bill Rogers, the 1981 British Open champion, and the other by the veteran Bruce Devlin, a transplanted Australian who now lives in Houston. No one had looked for Devlin to make this much of a splash. Now forty-four, he is best known in the golf world these days as a commentator on the tournaments that NBC televises. Not many people remember that in the nineteen-sixties and the early nineteen-seventies he was one of the top dozen players in the world. When I think back to the period between 1955 and 1975, only two golfers come to mind who had the stuff to win a major championship but somehow didn't. Devlin was one, and Mike Souchak the other.

In the second round, on Friday, Devlin, instead of quickly fading from contention, birdied three of the last four holes for a 69, a total of 139, and a two-stroke lead at the halfway mark. Another pleasant surprise was the performance of Nathaniel Crosby, the twenty-year-old son of Bing Crosby. Smitten by golf at an early age, Nathaniel — everyone refers to him by his first name — is a slim, nice-looking, intelligent, and intuitive young man who attends the University of Miami. Last September, he astounded everyone by winning the U.S. Amateur Championship. His swing was so unimpressive that most observers felt there had to be at least a thousand better amateur golfers in the country. In many of his matches in the championship, including the final, he fell behind his opponent and seemed certain to be beaten, but he has courage and abiding determination, and in one crisis after another he produced the crucial shot or holed the vital putt and survived. Since the Amateur, he had done nothing to speak of. However, as the Amateur champion he automatically qualified for the Open, and he was paired on the first two rounds with two other automatic qualifiers, David Graham and Bill Rogers. This was a most attractive threesome, and I walked the second round with them. On the opening day, Nathaniel had shot a 77, which was not a bad score, but in order to make the thirty-six-hole cut, which seemed likely to come at either 150 or 151, he was faced with the necessity of playing a much lower round. I must confess that I did not anticipate golf of the quality he showed us. His technique had improved considerably since last summer. The arc of his swing was wider, his tempo slower and more rhythmic, his extension through the ball more assured. Indeed, there was little to choose between the shots he played and those of Rogers and Graham. Through the first thirteen holes, he was two under par. If he could stay close to that pace, he would almost surely qualify to play the last two rounds of the championship.

The fourteenth hole at Pebble Beach is a 565-yard par 5 that breaks acutely to the right in the drive zone and swings up to a very firm green, whose high left side, protected in front by a deep bunker, sits about ten feet above the fairway. In tournaments, the pin is almost always positioned on the left side, and so it was that day. Nathaniel's tee shot just failed to carry the bunker in the angle of the fairway, and he proceeded to play the hole about as badly as it can be played. He caught the lip of the bunker with his second shot. His third, from the bunker, was well out, but he hit his approach shot thin and it finished short of the green on the right side of the fairway. His fifth shot, a pitch with his wedge, rolled over the back of the green into deep rough. He tried to dig the ball out with his wedge but barely advanced it. He was on in seven with a deft wedge flip two and a half feet from the cup, but he missed the putt, and that gave him a 9. Now, according to my computation out on the course, in order to have a chance of making the cut he could not afford to drop another stroke to par. What a superb job he did! Quietly regathering his poise and his purpose, he played the last four holes flawlessly. On the par-4 fifteenth, he was on the green in two, twenty-two feet from the pin, and rolled in the putt for a birdie. He was on in two on the sixteenth, a dogleg par 4, and got down in two putts from about twenty-four feet. He had a crack at a birdie on the hazardous seventeenth, the 209-yard par 3, when he put his tee shot twelve feet past the pin, but his putt slipped by the cup. On the eighteenth, the par 5 that edges along Carmel Bay, he hit the narrow fairway with his drive, as he had done on both the fifteenth and the sixteenth. Safely on the green in three, he stroked his approach putt inches short of the cup, and tapped in for his 5. That was a 73 and a thirty-six-hole total of 150. Bob Sommers, the editor of *Golf Journal*, who is often a walking companion of mine at tournaments, thereupon lifted his shooting stick and speared the air in exultation. "A 73 with a 9! I won't forget this soon. You know, Nathaniel played so well after that disaster on the fourteenth that he could have birdied three of those last four holes." Nathaniel's 150 enabled him to make the cut, which came at 151. Only one other amateur, Corey Pavin, made it — at 151.

Nathaniel Crosby completed the tournament with creditable rounds of 76 and 77, and his four-round total of 303, a stroke lower than Pavin's, earned him the low-amateur honors. There is no knowing whether he will go on to become a truly outstanding tournament golfer, but I venture to predict that whatever he chooses to do he will do well.

The way to play a seventy-two-hole stroke-play championship is not to try to win it on the first three rounds. The main thing is to be patient those first three days, passing up the flamboyant or outright dangerous shot even when you may feel in your bones that you can bring it off. Your aim should be to be in a position at the end of the third round where you can win the championship on the fourth round. At Pebble Beach, both Watson and Nicklaus, working hard and carefully, played themselves into excellent position after fifty-four holes. Indeed, Watson, with rounds of 72, 72, and 68, for a total of 212, was tied for the lead with Rogers. He had been very lucky to escape with a 72 on the second round, for he had hit a number of loose iron shots. His putter had bailed him out: he sank two twenty-footers, a twelve-footer, and an eight-footer, and missed no putt he should have made. On the third round, his iron play was much sharper, but, then, the course was considerably more docile that day. Rain had fallen during the night and early in the morning, and, with the greens soft and holding, the players could fire right at the pin. The greens also did not putt fast, even though they had been triple-cut in the morning by the mowing crew. To further encourage low scoring, there wasn't so much as a puff of breeze coming off the bay. Incidentally, the galleries were so hushed and stayed so respectfully still that whenever a golfer was playing a shot on the holes along the bay it was impossible not to notice the movement and calls of the birds. The peninsula is well known for its many feathered species, but the only ones that I, a 36-handicap ornithologist at best, could identify were the California gull, the common swallow, and, I think, the lark sparrow.

One man who failed to take advantage of the easy scoring conditions on the third day was Devlin; after a birdieless 75, he stood at 214, two strokes behind the leaders, along with Graham, Scott Simpson, and George Burns. Nicklaus (74–70–71) was a stroke farther back. On his third round, Nicklaus had also failed to seize the day, and he knew it. He had played steadily and well from tee to green but had missed many holeable putts. "I'm not disturbed at the way I'm rolling the ball with the putter," he said at the close of the round. "These greens are very difficult to read." He added, with a rueful smile, "I've only been playing them for twenty-one years, and one of these years I'll learn to putt them." Twenty-one years ago, when he was twenty-one, Nicklaus was a different kind of golfer from what he is today. A heavyset, muscular athlete, he hit the ball "with the kick of a mule," as Bernard Darwin put it, and he sent it incredible distances. One year in the nineteen-sixties, he reached the green on the 525-yard fifteenth hole at the Augusta National with a drive and an 8-iron. In 1966, when he captured his first British Open, at Muirfield, the pivotal hole was the 528-yard par-5 seventeenth, the seventy-first hole of the tournament. Playing the small British ball and helped by a slight wind at his back, he set up the winning birdie by getting home with a 3-iron and a 5-iron. Nicklaus lost some of his power in 1969, when he took off twenty pounds, and over the last decade he has placed increasing emphasis on control at the expense of distance. Today, the ball doesn't explode off his club the way it used to, but he still hits it a long way. One other thing: he is still the most fearsome fourth-round player in the game.

*

On Sunday, under glum skies, Nicklaus, paired with Calvin Peete, started his fourth round at 12:38 P.M. His No. 1 son, Jackie, who is a student at the University of North Carolina, and is many inches taller than his father, was caddying for him. Nicklaus got off slowly, bogeying the opening hole, where his approach shot spun back off the green, and then missing his birdie on the second, a par 5 that is reachable in two. He appeared to be completely unfazed by this disappointing start. When he is out on the golf course during a tournament, you can practically feel the fierceness and continuousness of his concentration, and yet at the same time, despite being surrounded by pulsing thousands, he seems to be not only oblivious of the pressure of the contest but more relaxed than you and I are when we get home after work and watch the news in the living room with a drink in hand. On the third, Nicklaus holed a good-sized putt across the green for a birdie 3. That set him off. He birdied the fourth when he dropped a twenty-three-footer. For the first time in the Open, he was making some putts. He birdied the par-3 fifth after he stuck a 6-iron two feet from the pin. Continuing to roll, he birdied the par-5 sixth by reaching the hilltop green with a drive and a 1-iron, and two-putted from thirty-five feet. He birdied the seventh, the precarious 110-yard par 3, playing a crisp pitching wedge eleven feet from the pin and making the putt. His surge was stopped when he bogeyed the eighth, the hole across the inlet of Carmel Bay — here his iron to the green found the rough on the right — but, thanks to that rush of five consecutive birdies, he finished the first nine four under par for the tournament. He was in the thick of it now, tied with Watson and a stroke behind Rogers, who was the leader at that moment.

In the old days, news travelled slowly on a golf course, and the reports over the grapevine were not always reliable. Today, what with a large, well-operated leader board at nearly every hole, the players know almost instantly what their rivals are up to. Watson, paired with Rogers, certainly did. By nature a much more high-strung person than Nicklaus, he had felt a little nervous when he awakened on Sunday morning. After breakfast, he played for a spell with his two-year-old daughter, Meg, whom he adores. He then dug into two Sunday papers, taking his time as he read about the federal-budget controversy and the earthquake in El Salvador. He felt somewhat less tight when he put the papers down. He and Rogers were off at 1:05 P.M., three twosomes and twenty-seven minutes after Nicklaus. Throughout the round, Watson was two holes or a hole and a half behind Nicklaus, depending on the length of the holes they were playing. They were seldom in sight of each other.

Watson, who had started the final round four under par, turned the front nine still four under par. A bogey on the third had offset a birdie on the second. On the short seventh, he had wasted a big chance, muffing a two-and-a-half-foot putt for a birdie. This error obviously did not affect him as much as it might have, for on the eighth he made a difficult seven-footer to save his par. At this point in the round, Rogers was going through a very shaky passage, missing his pars on the ninth and tenth and, later, on the twelfth, and therewith dropping out of the race. By that time, Devlin, too, was out of it, a stout-hearted challenge by Graham was over, and the championship had become a two-man battle — Watson against Nicklaus.

In retrospect, the tenth hole looms large in Watson's eventual victory. On that 424-yard par 4 that marks the end of the glittering cliffside sequence, he managed to avoid a 5 and, possibly, a 6 or 7. This significantly changed the shape that his duel with Nicklaus took. Off the tee, he hit the narrow, slanting tenth fairway — it was only twenty-seven yards wide for the Open — but he hung his approach shot, a 7-iron, out to the right, and it found the bunker below and to the right of the green. That green is tucked close to the edge of the cliff, and if the ball had drifted a shade more it could conceivably have toppled over the cliff and down onto the beach. (Incidentally, in the distance beyond the tenth green one takes in the crescent beach of the town of Carmel, its bright white sand washed by the breaking slate-colored waves. It is something to contemplate. It looks the way one imagines the shore at Bali Ha'i might, except that one sees few people swimming, because the water is intensely cold.) From that sunken bunker on the tenth, Watson exploded to the edge of the green, twenty-five feet from the cup. Then he made the putt for his 4. This not only kept him four under par but boosted him into the lead, a stroke ahead of Nicklaus, who, minutes before, had three-putted the eleventh green from twenty feet.

Which player should one watch, Nicklaus or Watson? When in doubt, it is usually wise to go with the leader. I walked to the drive zone on the eleventh. This 382-yard par 4 runs uphill from the tee, but Watson, pumped up by holing that big putt on the tenth, whaled his tee shot two hundred and seventy yards up the fairway, at least forty yards beyond Rogers' drive. He was on with a pitching wedge, twenty-two feet from the pin. As he walked with his quick strides to the green, he acknowledged the gallery's applause with his ingenuous smile. Like Nicklaus, Watson is determined to play golf his way, and his way is to approach it as a game and to show in a natural manner his appreciation of the support that the spectators give him. The keystone of Watson's personality is his invariable honesty. This somehow comes through in his facial expression, and may explain why some people get the feeling that there is a certain vulnerability about him. It should also be noted that there is a lot of iron in his soul, for otherwise he would never have been able to accomplish the things he has. After studying the line of his birdie putt on the eleventh — close to the cup, the sidehill putt would dart from left to right — he stepped up and knocked it in. Five under par for the tournament now, a two-stroke lead on Nicklaus. Not for long. On the par-3 twelfth, 204 yards long, he left his iron shot out to the right and was bunkered. He played what was for him only an ordinary sand shot, leaving the ball fifteen feet short of the cup. He made a rather weak try for the putt. Back to four under par and a lead of only a single stroke on Nicklaus. Matters stood the same way after he parred the thirteenth. His tee shot on this hole must have been close to three hundred yards. Under tournament tension, Watson sometimes sprays the ball into trouble, because his hitting action gets too quick, but on this last round, swinging well within himself, he was clouting his drives a mile and dead straight.

The fourteenth, the long par 5 that swings to the right, proved to be another critical hole. After a good drive, Watson chose to lay up with an iron about eighty yards short of the pin, figuring that he would be able to put more backspin on a relatively full wedge than on an abbreviated wedge flip, and so would be able to stop the ball close to the pin, which, once again, was situated on the high left side of the green. I could not see what kind of lie he had, but, in any event, his shot had very little spin on it and rolled thirty-five feet past the pin to the back edge of the green. I think it was then — as Watson was walking to his ball — that most of us in his gallery noticed on the leader board adjacent to the green that a red 4 had gone up for Nicklaus on the fifteenth. This meant that he had birdied that hole and now stood four under par — tied for the lead. (We learned later that Nicklaus had holed a fifteen-foot putt for that birdie. The old Golden Bear is really a tough customer down the stretch in a championship.) Watson took a shade more time than usual reading the line of his thirty-five-foot birdie putt on this sleek, ripple-filled green. He hit the ball with a good-looking stroke. Halfway to the hole, the ball seemed to pick up speed. It was still moving fast when it dived into the middle of the cup. A terrific putt — especially in those circumstances. Five under par now, Watson had regained his one-shot lead over Nicklaus. Only four holes to play.

Up-and-down rounds are nothing new to Watson, but what was called for at this stage of the Open was sure, prudent golf: do nothing fancy, keep the ball in play, concentrate on hitting the green in the regulation number of strokes, get down in two well-thought-out putts. On the par-4 fifteenth, Watson was letter-perfect: on in two, down in two from twenty feet. On the sixteenth, however, the 403-yard par 4, which slides downhill as it doglegs to the right and drops to a green shut in on both sides by trees and further protected by immense bunkers, Watson made an almost fatal mistake. Off the tee, he missed hitting the fairway for the first time during the round. He started the ball off to the right, and it stayed to the right, finally plummeting down into the recently remodelled bunker in the crook of the dogleg. This is one of the two bunkers that Sandy Tatum, remembering Jack Neville's suggestions before the 1972 Open, had asked to have fortified for the 1982 Open, so that it would more accurately fulfill Neville's wish that it be both more intimidating off the tee and more difficult to recover from. Now its front wall rose straight up three feet high, the upper two feet sodded like a Scottish bunker. Talk about irony! Watson has no more fervent admirer or devoted friend than Tatum. A contemporary of Watson's father at Stanford, Tatum has been close to Tom ever since he came West to attend Stanford. Looking gravely at this bunker after it had caught Watson's tee shot, Tatum turned to some friends in the gallery and said, "That's what this bunker was meant to do." On the third round, Watson's tee shot had ended up in the same bunker, but the ball had finished at the back edge, and he was able to fly his recovery shot onto the green. On this round, though, his ball lay only a foot and a half from the base of the perpendicular front wall. Attempting to go for the green was out of the question. After some thought, Watson concluded that the best he could do was to explode out sidewise onto the fairway, which he did. The ball trickled several yards down the hillside and came to rest on a fairly severe downslope. It is not easy to put backspin on a ball from a downhill lie, and, with the pin positioned only fifteen feet from the low front edge of the green, which slopes down from back to front, backspin was necessary in order to stop the ball near the pin. Watson's third, a wedge pitch of some eighty yards, landed near the pin, but the ball had no spin on it whatever, and it rolled another fifty-five feet on up the green. At about this time, I began to wonder whether Watson should have exploded backward out of the bunker onto a flat stretch of fairway from which he could have played an approach with backspin. However, this was strictly second-guessing. His lie in the bunker had been such that he probably didn't have room enough to swing the club back and play that kind of shot. Anyway, from the high back edge of the sixteenth green he would be fortunate if he could escape with a 5. He came through with a beautiful approach putt. He lagged the ball downhill over the skiddy surface with its subtle slide to the right, and it died barely fifteen inches from the cup. He tapped in for his 5. With two holes to go, he was again tied with Nicklaus at four under par. It could have been worse. If he had three-putted the fifteenth, he would have been trailing by a stroke. He walked to the seventeenth tee at about the same time that Nicklaus, to resounding applause, was walking off the eighteenth green and heading for the scorer's tent to check his card. Except for taking those three putts on the eleventh, Nicklaus had played an error-less second nine. From tee to green, he had thought his shots out painstakingly and had executed each shot the way he had meant to. If his putting had been up to his normal standard, he could easily have been a couple of strokes lower. He had made his birdie putt on the fifteenth, but then he had missed a shortish birdie putt on the fourteenth, and on each of the last three greens he had had a crack at a birdie from seventeen feet or less. In any event, he had given one more unforgettable demonstration of how a golfer should play the final round of a championship.

Watson won the Open on the seventeenth hole, just when it seemed that he might lose it there. On the final round, the back tee of this celebrated par 3 was used, so the hole played its full length — 209 yards — into a moderate wind. (On the eighteenth, the wind was blowing across the fairway, off the bay. If it had been behind Nicklaus on that hole, and if he had got off a long drive, he might have tried to reach the green in two.) The seventeenth is a tester. The green is unusually wide and unusually narrow from back to front. It sits just above a very large front bunker. Beyond the green is a string of small bunkers, along with other trouble: the rocks and water on the left. You really cannot play for the right side of the green, because you then have to deal with the dangerous ridge that divides the green into two sections. In tournaments, the pin is almost always set on the left side. It was on this day — ten feet from the left fringe, about halfway between the front edge and the back edge of the green. Watson first thought he would use a 3-iron but then changed his mind and played a 2-iron. He hooked it a shade — or, to use the current expression, he "came over" the ball, instead of hitting under and through it. The ball finished hole-high, twenty feet to the left of the pin and eight feet from the fringe of the green, in a growth of thick, resistant rough. He would also have to cope with a downhill lie. If you were standing out near the ropes on the right side of the hole, you could not see the ball. However, Watson later explained that though it was down low, it was lying on top of the grass. "I had a good lie," he said. "I could get the leading edge of my club under the ball." Opening the blade of his sand wedge and cutting under and slightly across the ball, he hit an exquisite shot. The ball came up softly, about two feet high, and landed just on the edge of the green. Curving a foot and a half from left to right with the contour of the green, it rolled straight for the pin, hit it dead center, and fell in. The moment the ball disappeared from sight, Watson threw his arms up and broke into a wild Indian dance. The spectators packed along the seventeenth, reacting almost as immediately to this sensational birdie, which put Watson in the lead by a precious stroke, began jumping for joy and shouting and howling.

Under the circumstances, Watson calmed himself down quickly. By the time he stuck his peg into the ground on the eighteenth tee, he looked composed and confident, ready to wrap things up. A par 5 on the 548-yard eighteenth would do it. He played the hole just the way he meant to: a 3-wood tee shot down the right side of the fairway; a 7-iron laid up in the center of the fairway a hundred and thirty yards from the green; a 9-iron that sat down pacifically twenty feet behind the pin. Watson studied the green with care. His putt was a touch downhill, and he wanted to be sure he had the speed right, so that he would leave himself the shortest of tap-ins. He had no intention of trying to hole the twenty-footer, but the ball slithered into the cup. He had won the Open. He had finally won the Open. The fact that his margin of victory was two strokes was irrelevant. He had won the championship by holing his sand-wedge shot on the seventeenth when it would have been an achievement to get down in two from the rough. (I think his ball would have rolled about seven feet past the cup if it hadn't hit the pin.) That little cut pitch out of the heavy grass may well be the greatest winning shot that has been played in the Open since 1923, when Bobby Jones, tied with Bobby Cruickshank as they came to the eighteenth in their playoff for the title at Inwood, on Long Island, summoned a perfect-plus 2-iron, from a poorish lie, that rose in a high parabola over the water hazard before the green, came down on the green, and stopped six feet from the hole. The scores of the leaders in the 1982 Open: Watson, 72-72-68-70 — 282; Nicklaus, 74-70-71-69 — 284. Two strokes farther back, at 286, were Rogers, Clampett, and Dan Pohl.

Nicklaus, after walking off the eighteenth green, watched Watson's tee shot on the seventeenth on the TV monitor in the scorer's tent. When he saw the ball hook into the thatchy rough, he felt that the percentages were heavily against Watson's getting down in two from there and saving his par. He turned his attention to checking his scorecard, thinking that now he would probably win the Open and that the worst that could happen was a playoff, if Watson somehow birdied the eighteenth. When Nicklaus next looked at the monitor, what he saw was Watson dancing across the green. His first reaction was that Watson's recovery had probably lipped out of the cup.

Twelve minutes or so later, when Watson walked off the eighteenth green, Nicklaus was waiting there to congratulate him. "You little son of a gun, you're something else," he said as they shook hands. "That was nice going. I'm really proud of you, and I'm pleased for you." The two men have enormous respect for each other. They also like each other. In the last Ryder Cup match, they were always together. Nevertheless, it took an extraordinary sportsman to do what Nicklaus did at the conclusion of a championship that, not many minutes before, he had thought he would win. There is no other loser in sports as gracious and warm as Jack Nicklaus has shown himself to be. This quality is due in part to training he received from an exceptional father and in part to

Nicklaus's own character and sense of sport. He and Watson had previously fought three memorable battles down the stretch in major championships. In the 1977 and 1981 Masters, Nicklaus, trailing at the start of the final round, had mounted valiant rallies only to see Watson fight back successfully. In the 1977 British Open, Watson and Nicklaus happened to be paired on the third round. They both shot 65s. As the two leaders, they were paired again on the fourth round. Nicklaus had a 66, Watson another 65, with Watson prevailing on the final green. I can still see Nicklaus's yellow-sweatered, bearlike arm wrapped over Watson's shoulder as they came off that last green after their two-day, head-to-head confrontation.

And I am all admiration for Watson, for having the heart and the skill to play as he did under the stress of that long last hour. Now that he has at length won the championship, I am told by the experts and roving soothsayers that we will see a more majestic Watson. That would be fine. Apart from his superior personal qualities, he is one of the purest shotmakers since Harry Vardon. At the moment, though, the 1982 Open still fills my mind. I can think of only one U.S. Open since the Second World War that can compare with it in dramatic impact — Ken Venturi's triumph eighteen years ago at Congressional, on the outskirts of Washington. The 1982 Open is something to treasure. With the lone exception of that 1977 British Open at Turnberry, when Nicklaus and Watson duelled face to face over thirty-six holes — a rare combination of circumstances — I don't see how a tournament can be any better than the one we were treated to at Pebble Beach. It was just about as good as golf can get.

(1982)

Nicklaus in Retrospect

At this writing, Jack Nicklaus has won nineteen major tournaments: two U.S. Amateurs, four U.S. Opens, five Masters, five P.G.A.s, and three British Opens. Naturally, he would like to make it an even twenty. He well might. He has pulled off harder things in an altogether amazing career that has spanned a quarter of a century.

THIS PAST WINTER, MY THOUGHTS, LIKE THOSE OF OTHERS IN the North, often raced ahead to the Masters, the annual early-April tournament in Augusta, Georgia, which has come to signal the arrival of spring for golfers everywhere. This year, I found myself thinking not only of balmy weather, azaleas and dogwood, and the rolling green fairways of the Augusta National golf course but also about the incredible career of Jack Nicklaus, who, twenty years ago this April, when he was twenty-three, won the first of his five Masters titles — the most that anyone has won. When golf authorities rank the great golfers of all time, a sizable percentage of them place Nicklaus on the top level, along with Harry Vardon, Bobby Jones, and Ben Hogan, who were as preeminent in their eras as Nicklaus has been over the last two decades. While I am inclined to go along with this point of view, I can readily understand why many people close to the game consider Nicklaus nothing less than the greatest golfer ever. To a large extent, a golfer's place in history has traditionally been determined by his achievements in the major championships. Played on long, rigorous courses that require expert shotmaking, these championships are the British Open (established in 1860); the British Amateur (1885); the United States Open and United States Amateur (1895); our Professional Golfers Association (1916); and the Masters

(1934). Professional golfers, of course, cannot play in amateur championships, and amateurs cannot play in the P.G.A. Before Nicklaus came along, the highest number of major championships any golfer had won was thirteen. This mark was set by Jones in the eight-year period between 1923 and 1930, and was thereafter believed to be out of reach. Nicklaus, who should be competing for several years to come, has already won nineteen. To my mind, the most effective way to convey what Nicklaus has done is simply to set down the dates of those nineteen victories, championship by championship. Before turning professional, in 1961, he won the U.S. Amateur twice, in 1959 and 1961. He has won the British Open three times, in 1966, 1970, and 1978; the U.S. Open four times, in 1962, 1967, 1972, and 1980; the P.G.A. five times, in 1963, 1971, 1973, 1975, and 1980; and the Masters five times, in 1963, 1965, 1966, 1972, and 1975. Moreover, Nicklaus has been close to victory in these events on many other occasions. He has finished second or in a tie for second three times in the P.G.A., four times in the Masters, four times in the U.S. Open, and no fewer than seven times in the British Open. It is hard to believe, but for fifteen straight years, from 1966 to 1980, he finished among the top six players in the British Open. Altogether, in a total of eighty-four major championships he played from 1962 through 1982 he failed to finish in the first ten only twenty-three times. And Nicklaus has been as all-conquering and consistent in tournaments other than the majors. A golfer who travels well, he has, for example, taken the Australian Open six times. He has won sixty-nine tournaments on the P.G.A. tour — a total approached by none of his contemporaries. He is the only golfer who has earned more than three million dollars in prize money, and this February, by finishing sixth in the Bing Crosby National Pro-Am, he passed the four-million-dollar mark — not that this concerns him much. One could go on and on, but I think that these statistics are sufficient to indicate the enormous scope of his oeuvre. One wonders if there has ever been an athlete who has accomplished more in any sport.

Golf may be the most difficult of all games to play well. For one thing, it is the only major outdoor game in which the player must generate his own power as he strikes a stationary ball from a stationary position. To do this and at the same time hit the ball accurately toward a target requires mastery of a very sophisticated technique. For another thing, since the game is played on natural terrain the player must continually adjust his hitting action to the lie of the ball, not to mention the wind and weather. All the great champions have necessarily been extremely sound shotmakers, but what really separates them from the talented golfers on the level just below them is their deep, unshakable belief in themselves. This engenders the determination and the self-possession that enable them, in this game where the slightest faulty movement can lead to a costly error, and even to disaster, to rise to the occasion and produce their finest golf at the most important moments. For all the gracefulness of his swing, Jones was a highstrung young man who felt the stress of tournament play so acutely that during one championship he lost eighteen pounds. He had the ability, however, to gather his concentration as he prepared to play each shot. Hogan, from the beginning to the end of a round, could insulate himself from the world and go about his golf with white-hot intensity. He was oblivious of everything else. Nicklaus's mind works unceasingly during a tournament round, but at the same time he appears to be cooler and calmer than any other golfer of the modern era. He seems to actually thrive on pressure. Out on the fairway, surrounded by thousands of exuberant fans, he wears the tournament golfer's invariable frown of concentration, but he seems completely relaxed — as much at home as if he were taking a solitary walk in the country over a pleasant stretch of land he has known all his life.

In a word, Nicklaus has the ideal temperament for a golfer, and, combined with his physical stamina and phenomenal will to win, it helps to explain the miracles he has performed at many critical moments. Let me briefly describe three that come to mind. In the playoff for the 1970 British Open at St. Andrews, he held a oneshot lead over Doug Sanders as they came to the eighteenth, a straightaway par 4 only 354 yards long. When there is a good following wind, as there was that afternoon, a big hitter like Nicklaus can drive the green. Sanders, with the honor, played a fine tee shot that ended up a few yards short of the green. Nicklaus then removed the sweater he was wearing — he did not mean this action to be as dramatic as it was — and swatted a huge drive dead on line for the pin. He had, in fact, hit the ball too well. It bounced onto the green and rolled over the back edge into some fairly high rough. Sanders had his birdie all the way, so it was up to Nicklaus to get down in two to win. From a difficult downhill lie in the rough, he played a delicate wedge chip that stopped eight feet from the hole. His putt looked as if it might be slipping a shade too much to the right, but it caught a corner of the cup and fell in. By and large, Nicklaus has been a very solid putter throughout his career — an invaluable asset.

In the 1972 U.S. Open, at Pebble Beach, Nicklaus, with two holes to go, apparently had the championship won, for he led the nearest man by three strokes. Still, anything can happen on the last two holes at Pebble Beach. The seventeenth, a par 3, 218 yards long, is tightly bordered on the left by Carmel Bay, and the green is severely bunkered. With the wind in his face, Nicklaus chose to play a 1-iron. He ripped a beautiful shot through the wind which almost went into the hole on the fly. The ball landed inches short of the cup, bounced up and struck the flagstick, and came to rest inches away. He tapped it in for his birdie, and that was that.

Three years later, in the Masters, Nicklaus was involved in a tremendous battle in the fourth, and last, round with Johnny Miller and Tom Weiskopf. Throughout the long afternoon, all three played some of the most spectacular golf shots imaginable, and the outcome was not decided until the final green, where both Miller and Weiskopf, who were the last twosome, missed makable birdie putts that would have tied them with Nicklaus. In retrospect, Nicklaus had played the winning shot on the sixteenth. When he came to that hole, a 190-yard par 3 over one of the largest and loveliest water hazards in golf, he trailed Weiskopf by a stroke. The pin was set that day, as it usually is on the fourth round of the Masters, in the hardest position — near the front of the narrow terrace at the back right-hand corner of the green. It takes a superlative shot, with true backspin on it, to hit and hold that terrace, because there is little margin for error: a large bunker sits in wait just beyond the green. Nicklaus, going with a 5-iron, played a so-so shot that ended up on the left side of the green well below the slope of the terrace and some forty feet from the pin. He took a long time studying his putt, to make certain he had read the line correctly. He then rapped the ball firmly up the slope and watched it break some eighteen inches to the left in a gradual curve and dive into the cup. That birdie put him in a tie for the lead with Weiskopf, and when Weiskopf three-putted the sixteenth for a bogey 4 Nicklaus was out in front to stay.

Nicklaus is unquestionably the best fourth-round golfer there has ever been. Even when he starts the last eighteen so many strokes off the pace that his chances seem hopeless, it is not his nature to think for a moment of conceding the tournament to anyone else. He is never more dangerous than at these times, and it takes a stout-hearted competitor, such as Lee Trevino or Tom Watson, to stand up to the threat that Nicklaus poses. For most golfers trying to protect a lead on the last day, there is nothing more rattling than to look up at one of the leaderboards positioned around the course and see that Nicklaus, who has slowly mounted one of his celebrated rushes, has picked up three birdies in a row and, now in full flight, is within striking distance of overtaking them.

Nicklaus's awesome career impresses on one how valuable it is in golf, or anything else, to start with the proper fundamentals. His father, Louis Charles Nicklaus, Jr., a warm, companionable man who was a successful pharmacist in Columbus, Ohio, made his home in the suburb of Upper Arlington, and was a member of the nearby Scioto Country Club, the scene of Jones' victory in the 1926 Open. His son began golf at ten. Jack played some with his father; he joined the Friday-morning class for junior members that Jack Grout, the Scioto professional, held in the summer; and every two or three weeks he took a private lesson from Grout. Grout, a gifted student of the golf swing, had spent three years as an assistant to Henry Picard, who was then one of the top players on the tour, and, through Picard, he had been exposed to new theories on golf technique that had been advanced in the nineteen-twenties and thirties by Alex Morrison, a controversial West Coast professional. In many respects, Morrison, who courted publicity, was well ahead of his time. So, in his own quiet way, was Grout. In 1950, when he started to work with Nicklaus, he had arrived at a very sound understanding of the golf swing — a plexus of Morrison's ideas, Picard's ideas, and his own. As he saw it, there were three main fundamentals. First, the head must be kept still throughout the swing. It is the balance center, and if a golfer allows it to move it throws everything else off: the movements of his body, his arc, his timing. Second, balance also depends on footwork. The basis of footwork is rolling the ankles correctly. On the backswing, the left ankle and heel roll in toward the right foot, and the right foot remains firmly planted. On the downswing, the left ankle and heel roll back to their original position, where they remain planted, and the right ankle and heel roll in toward the left foot. Golfers with analytical minds, such as Jones, realized early that good golf is played on the inside of the feet, but Morrison was far more explicit and emphatic about this point, and it may have been his most significant contribution to modern golf technique. Third, when a golfer is young and limber he should try to develop the widest possible arc by making a full shoulder turn and fully extending his arms on the backswing, downswing, and follow-through. That way, he will be able to utilize all his latent power. The boy who learns to hit the ball hard and far can work on improving his accuracy when he is older. Nicklaus learned very quickly from Grout. The two not only communicated well but liked and respected each other, and they became fast friends.

Like Jones, who was only nine when he won his club's junior championship and only fourteen when he first played in the U.S. Amateur (and won his first two matches), Nicklaus was a prodigy. At twelve, after shooting eight straight rounds of 80, he broke the barrier with a 74. At thirteen, he broke 70 at Scioto for the first time. To do this, he had to eagle the eighteenth, a good par 5, which he did by reaching the green with a drive and a 2-iron and holing a thirty-five-foot putt. That was also the year he made his début in the U.S. Junior Amateur championship. At fifteen, he qualified for the U.S. Amateur. He played well in his first-round match but lost on the last hole to Bob Gardner, a golfer of Walker Cup calibre. At sixteen, he won the Ohio State Open from a field of experienced professionals after taking the lead on the third round with a 64. At seventeen, he qualified for the 1957 U.S. Open, which was held at Inverness, in Toledo. He played two loose 80s and failed to make the thirty-six-hole cut by ten strokes. In the summer of 1958, he strengthened his chances of making the Walker Cup team the next year by winning the Trans-Mississippi Amateur, a top tournament, and finishing twelfth in his first P.G.A. tour event — the Rubber City Open, in Akron, in which he was paired with such stars as Julius Boros, Tommy Bolt, and Art Wall. Many boy wonders in sports fade away when they are still young men. Sometimes they lose the precocious skill that had set them apart. Sometimes they lose their enthusiasm — they have had enough of the spotlight and wish to lead an altogether different kind of life. When Nicklaus, at nineteen, was named to the American Walker Cup team for the 1959 match in this biennial series against a team representing Great Britain and Ireland, it was as clear as could be that here was one young man who, given his background in golf and his ardent and justified ambition, would almost surely mature into a much more proficient player and possibly go on to become an authentic champion. In that Walker Cup match, which was played at Muirfield, outside Edinburgh, he adjusted splendidly to the demands of linksland golf and won both his singles and his foursomes. That summer, he captured his first national championship, the U.S. Amateur, at the east course of the Broadmoor Golf Club, in Colorado Springs. In the final — a classic final — he defeated the defending champion, Charlie Coe, on the last hole of their thirty-six-hole match by sinking an eight-foot birdie putt that broke just a hair to the right. He was on his way.

During his middle and late teens, Nicklaus remained as close as ever to Grout, and at this time Grout worked especially hard with him on two phases of shotmaking that were to become outstanding characteristics of Nicklaus's style of play: hitting the ball in a high parabola, and hitting it so that it moved in its flight from left to right. Thoroughly aware of Nicklaus's vast potential, Grout was looking ahead, as he had been from the start, to the years when his protégé might be competing against the finest players in the world. He thought it important that Nicklaus learn to hit the ball high, because this would be to his advantage when he was faced with playing long irons to resilient greens on which the pin was placed in a tight position that offered little margin for error. A ball that flies in a high parabola comes down softly and at a more nearly vertical angle than a long iron rifled on a low line, and so has a much better chance to hold the green and not run over it into heavy rough or a bunker. The value of fading the ball from left to right is that it is much safer than drawing the ball from right to left. When a golfer's timing is off — something that can frequently happen under tournament stress — a draw can easily turn into a hook, and there is nothing more costly to a golfer than a quick hook that darts into high, thick rough, or even out-of-bounds. Compared with the heavy sidespin that a hook carries, the side-spin on a badly hit left-to-right shot — a fade that turns into a slice — is relatively mild. The ball neither breaks as sharply in the air nor runs as fast when it lands. The very best golfers are able to play the ball either from right to left or from left to right, depending on the shot that is called for by the design of the hole and the way the wind is blowing at that moment. However, over the long haul, as Grout emphasized to Nicklaus, the man who fades the ball is bound to have better control than the man who draws it.

Grout is the only teacher Nicklaus has had. Since boyhood, Nicklaus has understood the workings of his swing extremely well, and as a rule he has been able to take care of small adjustments himself. He is one of the few golfers who can often do this even during a vital tournament round. There have been times, though, when he has accepted knowledgeable friends' suggestions, and these have proved helpful in correcting some faulty movement of a minor nature which he had been unable to pinpoint himself. This has been true especially in regard to his putting — a part of the game in which a player can easily lose his stroke without knowing just what has gone wrong. Then, too, early in 1980, recognizing that his execution of touch shots to the green and in the green area had never been up to the level of the rest of his shotmaking, Nicklaus went as far as to arrange for some instruction in pitching and chipping from Phil Rodgers, a master of the delicately cut lob and the rest of the short game. The last three winters, he has taken refresher courses with Rodgers. But down through the years, whenever something basic about the way he was hitting the ball was bothering him, or if he simply wanted to have his setup at the ball or his swing checked out, he has always gone to Jack Grout. When they are on the practice tee together, it generally takes Grout no time at all to spot the minutest departure from Nicklaus's customary swing pattern, suggest a remedy, and begin to work on it with Nicklaus. Grout remained at Scioto until 1961, when he became the professional at La Gorce Country Club, in Miami Beach. He stayed at La Gorce the year round for fifteen years, and during this period he and Nicklaus held most of their sessions there. Since 1965, Nicklaus has made his home in North Palm Beach, so getting down to La Gorce was an easy matter. In 1975, Nicklaus asked Grout to become the professional at the Muirfield Village Golf Club, in Dublin, Ohio, outside Columbus. Muirfield Village is a real-estate development in which Nicklaus has an interest; he was a co-designer of its golf course, the venue each May of the Memorial Tournament. Grout has been at Muirfield Village since 1975, except in the wintertime, when the course is closed. In 1976 and 1977, he spent the winter teaching at Cheeca Lodge, a resort in Islamorada, in the Florida Keys, that has a nine-hole course designed by Nicklaus. The last six winters, Grout, who is now seventy-three, has been teaching at Frenchman's Creek Golf Club, in the northern reaches of North Palm Beach. Frenchman's Creek is only a ten-minute drive from

Nicklaus's home, so during the winter Grout and Nicklaus, who have been devoted friends for over thirty years, get to see a lot of each other.

When old golf hands discuss when it was that it first occurred to them that Nicklaus might turn out to be not just a first-class golfer but a rare champion, more often than not they cite his performance in one or another of three events that took place early in his career: the 1960 World Amateur Team championship, at Merion, an exacting course near Philadelphia, in which his four-round total of 269 (66, 67, 68, 68) was thirteen strokes lower than the runner-up's; the 1960 U.S. Open, at Cherry Hills, outside Denver, in which he was second, only two strokes behind Arnold Palmer, then the premier golfer in the world; and the 1962 U.S. Open, at Oakmont, outside Pittsburgh, where he caught Palmer with an almost flawless last round of 69 and defeated him the next day in their playoff. While I concur that this cluster of events was significant, I would like to add some personal comments. At Merion, Nicklaus hit the ball so squarely and sweetly over the seventy-two holes that I thought he must be having one of those improbable streaks in which people play way over their heads — no one could be that good at twenty. I failed to appreciate the significance of Nicklaus's showing at Cherry Hills, because a large share of my attention was appropriated by Hogan's gallant bid for a fifth Open title and by Palmer's dashing last round of 65. And I must confess that Nicklaus's victory at Oakmont also surprised me. It was as if it had happened a bit ahead of schedule: I'd thought that it would take even a Nicklaus a year or two more to win the Open. I had underrated not only his skill but his fortitude.

Perhaps this is one of the reasons his victory in the 1963 Masters made such a profound impression on me: At Oakmont, he had patently arrived; after that every golf enthusiast, including laggards like me, realized that he could win whatever there was to be won. The other reason is that Nicklaus was tested in the 1963 Masters as he had never been before. With only seven holes to go on the final round, he was leading the tournament — a stroke ahead of Sam Snead, who was playing three holes in front of him, and two strokes ahead of Julius Boros, with whom he was paired. Then, as he was reading the line of his approach putt on the eleventh green, he looked up at the large leaderboard near the green and saw that Snead had birdied the fourteenth and was now tied with him. After getting his par on the eleventh, he shut out everything from his thoughts except the hazardous twelfth, a 155-yard par 3, where the narrow green is perched beyond the far bank of Rae's Creek. A steep slope of rough rises behind the green, and, for good measure, two bunkers are cut into this rough. A third bunker lies to the front right of the green just over the creek. That day, the pin was placed in the front part of the green — a relatively easy position. Boros, with the honor, played a handsome shot twelve feet past the pin. Nicklaus followed with a thinly hit 7-iron that barely carried the creek and landed in the front bunker. He was lucky to escape from the twelfth with only a bogey 4: his recovery from the bunker — the sand was soggy from the heavy rains the day before — had no backspin on it and ended up over the green in light rough; he misread the speed of the green on his third, which he putted, and ran it nine feet past the cup; after studying this nine-footer from all angles he read it to break about half an inch from right to left, and hit a perfect putt that veered left at the last moment and fell into the cup. Boros, meanwhile, had made his birdie. This moved him into a tie with Nicklaus. On the thirteenth tee, Nicklaus composed himself and got things in perspective. He decided that he would now think only about Snead, who was leading him by a stroke. Snead, he figured, would more than likely birdie the long fifteenth, which he was then playing. Nicklaus felt, however, that even if this happened the situation was far from hopeless, provided he could summon his best golf down the stretch. There are two par 5s on the last six holes of the Augusta National, the 485-yard thirteenth and the 520-yard fifteenth, and a long hitter like Nicklaus can usually reach the green on both with two well-played shots. If he could birdie them, he would be back in the hunt. Radiating cheer and assurance, he made his birdie 4 on the thirteenth, and was not at all fazed when he heard that Snead had indeed birdied the fifteenth. He parred the fourteenth. He had to settle for a par 5 on the fifteenth — he missed a four-footer for his birdie — but this wasn't very costly, because Snead had meanwhile bogeyed the sixteenth, the picturesque 190-yard par 3. At this moment in the long, exhausting afternoon, Nicklaus and Snead were again tied for the lead. On the sixteenth, as was to be expected, the pin was set on the terrace at the back right-hand corner of the green. Nicklaus went boldly for it and came through with a high, full-blooded 6-iron that dropped softly on the terrace and finished about fourteen feet from the hole. His putt was in from the moment he struck it. It proved to be the decisive shot, for Nicklaus protected his one-stroke lead with airtight pars on the last two holes. It was a tremendous triumph for him. The hardest way to win a tournament is to falter when you are in sight of victory, and still have the resolution to surge back and regain the lead. It doesn't happen very often.

At this point in his career, Nicklaus had established himself as a golfer who could play all the shots, but, understandably, it was his thunderous power off the tee that attracted the most attention. He was the Snead of his generation — the longest driver among the players who were regularly in contention in the big events. He lacked the ineffable rhythm and tempo that made Snead an aesthetic treat, but he was thrilling in his own way. Watching him unload on the ball and smash it three hundred yards down the fairway packed an excitement that never lessened, no matter how often an admirer had been in his gallery. Until 1969, when he went on a diet that radically altered his appearance, Nicklaus, who stands five feet eleven and three-quarters inches, weighed about two hundred and ten pounds. This young Percheron had especially heavy legs and thighs, which helped to explain his power, but the distance he hit the ball was not the result of brute force. Growing up under Grout's guidance, he understood from an early age the four main sources of power. He listed them like this in his book *The Greatest Game of All*, which was published in 1969: "1. a club of proper weight and balance; 2. a long, wide arc; 3. speed of movement from the right side to the left at the start of the downswing; 4. the speed with which the left hip, having stopped its move forward, spins to the rear in the hitting zone." As goes without saying, the body movements involved in a power swing are infinitely complicated, and few players succeed in mastering them. Nicklaus was able to because of his extraordinary talent and his willingness to put in the untold hours on the practice tee that finally make the synchronization of the multiple movements almost instinctive.

When Nicklaus's colossal power comes up in conversation, golf fans tend to recall different tournaments. Some go back as far as the 1960 World Amateur Team championship. (It was then that people started to speculate about Nicklaus's possibly being the longest driver in the game.) Others immediately think of the 1965 Masters — perhaps the most popular choice. That April, Nicklaus

flew the ball such great distances that he made the Augusta National, which measures 6,905 yards from the back tees, seem like
one of those little nine-hole courses that used to be operated at old
summer hotels in New England. He broke the previous Masters
record total of 274 by three strokes, with rounds of 67, 71, 64, and
69, and finished nine strokes ahead of his nearest competitor. On
his third round, in particular, he was driving the ball so far that on
the ten par-4 holes — only two are under four hundred yards
long — he had only a pitch left on his second shot: he used his 6-
iron once, his 7-iron once, his 8-iron three times, his pitching
wedge four times, and his sand wedge once. Jones, the founder of
the Masters, and its host, summed up Nicklaus's performance
perfectly when he said at the presentation ceremony, "Jack is
playing an entirely different game — a game I'm not even familiar
with." When I think of his power, as a veteran Nicklaus watcher, I
think of the shots he tore through a bitter wind off the North Sea
when, in a losing cause, he chased Gary Player down the final
holes at Carnoustie in the 1968 British Open.

Nicklaus's victory in the 1966 British Open, at Muirfield, also
comes vividly to mind. This takes a little explaining. That summer, Muirfield was modified a bit to keep the big hitters in check.
At about the 250-yard mark, the fairways, which were narrow to
begin with, were gradually pinched in so that at the 275-yard mark
they were scarcely twenty yards wide. Furthermore, the rough
bordering the fairways was allowed to grow almost two feet high.
Nicklaus made the adjustments called for. Over the seventy-two
holes of the championship, he used his driver only seventeen
times. He drove with his 3-wood ten times, and the rest of the way
he went with either his 1-iron or his 3-iron off the tee, depending
on how the wind was blowing. His decision to put accuracy ahead
of distance and his discipline in refusing to stray from this strategy
was the basis of his victory. At the same time, from the point of
view of power the most sensational single hole I have ever
watched Nicklaus play was the seventeenth hole of the 1966 British Open. The seventeenth at Muirfield is a 528-yard par 5 that
bends sharply to the left about two hundred and twenty yards
from the tee and then runs more or less straight to a smallish
green tucked in a hollow beyond a daunting mound. As Nicklaus
stood on the tee, he knew that he would have to birdie either the
seventeenth or the eighteenth to win. With the wind blowing
from right to left, he drove with a 3-iron, to make sure the ball

didn't carry too far and end up in the rough on the right-hand side of the twisting fairway. On his second shot, with the wind directly behind him, he selected a 5-iron. He played a superb shot. The ball landed on the small front apron about fifteen feet short of the green, as he had planned; it then hopped up and rolled to within eighteen feet of the pin. He was down in two for the crucial birdie. Even allowing for the helping wind and the lively British ball, imagine reaching a 528-yard hole with a 3-iron and a 5-iron!

While Nicklaus has a genius for hitting a golf ball, it should be brought out that he possesses uncommon physical coördination for sports in general. He got his size early: at thirteen, he stood five feet ten and weighed a hundred and sixty-five pounds. In junior high school in Upper Arlington, he was the quarterback, punter, and placekicker on the football team; the center on the basketball team; the catcher on the baseball team; and, surprisingly, a sprinter on the track team, who could run the hundred-yard dash in eleven seconds flat. He might well have had a career in baseball or football, but in high school he gave both of them up and concentrated on basketball, his favorite team sport. (Basketball hysteria has long been almost as rife in Ohio as in Indiana.) Switched to forward from center, he was a regular starter for Upper Arlington his last three years, and as a junior and senior he was named to the all-league team in the Central Buckeye League. In college — he went to Ohio State, his father's school — he limited himself strictly to golf. His range of sports interests is wide. He has been a devoted fisherman since boyhood. In conjunction with his golf travels, he has fished the world over. (For example, before playing in the 1978 Australian Open he fished for black marlin off the Great Barrier Reef, and last summer he stopped off in Iceland after the British Open to fish for salmon.) At his home in North Palm Beach, he has two grass tennis courts — a rarity in Florida. They are part of a grassed-over plot adjoining his house which serves Nicklaus, his wife, Barbara, and their five children as a playground. After the golf season ends, he plays a lot of tennis. The workout he gets from a couple of sets helps to keep him in shape, but, in addition, he is fascinated by the game, and he plays it well. (On most Saturday mornings in the autumn and early winter, Nicklaus and seven middle-aged friends, each wearing a special "Day Camp" T-shirt, assemble at his courts for doubles and singles.) At the side of the house, attached to the garage, are a basketball backboard and hoop. When the spirit moves him, Nicklaus still goes out and practices shooting by himself or with his kids. He also still enjoys throwing and kicking a football. He can be called, with no exaggeration, a brilliant passer and an astounding punter. (I have seen him boom kicks that were forty yards high and carried sixty yards.) During the last decade, he has developed one new sports passion — skiing. Since 1975, the Nicklaus family has spent nearly every Christmas holiday skiing at Vail, Colorado, or Park City, Utah. All seven Nicklauses are of one mind: skiing is the ideal family sport.

Nicklaus inherited both his love of sports and much of his athletic ability from his father. In high school, Charlie Nicklaus — he was always Charlie to his friends — starred in football, basketball, and baseball. He worked his way through college, and in his sophomore year he brought in some money by playing linebacker for the Portsmouth (Ohio) Spartans, one of the pioneer teams in the National Football League. The year he graduated from college, he won the Columbus Public Courts tennis championship. A low-handicap golfer, he had a long, smooth hitting action modelled on the swing of his idol, Bobby Jones. He and Jack, his only son, were close friends. (Jack has a younger sister, Marilyn.) They seldom stopped playing, watching, or talking sports. When Jack was six, his father started taking him to Ohio State football games. In fact, Jack didn't miss an Ohio State home game during the next fourteen years — not until Saturday, October 1, 1960, when he had to be at Merion to play on the American team in the World Amateur Team Championship. From the start of Jack's career, his father was always on hand at major events. His greatest joy was to watch his son play golf. Until his death, in 1970, he was a familiar figure at the championships, his name purposely removed from his tournament badge as he hurried along in Jack's gallery with his pals from Columbus. Of all the stage mothers and sports fathers I have met, I would put Charlie Nicklaus right up at the top. He was careful, for instance, to inculcate a deep sense of sportsmanship in his son. "My dad knew how to get his points across," Nicklaus recalled not long ago. "One day when I was eleven, I was playing with him at Scioto. We were on the fifteenth, and I had an 8-iron to the green. I put the shot in a bunker, and then I threw my club almost to the bunker. My father turned to me and said, very clearly, 'Young man, that will be the last club I'll every see you throw or hear of you throwing, or you're not going to be playing this game.' I've never thrown a club since." He was silent for a moment, started to laugh, and added, "I must admit that I've tossed a few over to the bag, but never with any kind of force behind them."

Jack Nicklaus and Barbara Bash were classmates at Ohio State — her father was a mathematics teacher at South High School in Columbus. They met the first week of their freshman year and began going steady that winter. They were married in July, 1960, the summer before their senior year. A tall, slim, fine-looking woman with an instinctive graciousness, Barbara Nicklaus is as exceptional in her way as Jack is in his. She is one of those people who, with no apparent effort, can keep a great many balls in the air at the same time. Over the last fifteen years or so, whenever the wives of young golfers have begun to attend tournaments, it has been standard practice for their husbands to tell them, "Just watch Barbara Nicklaus and you'll know exactly what to do." When Barbara is at a tournament, she walks the full eighteen holes each day in her husband's gallery. She knows golf, she knows Jack's game inside out, she knows the state of the tournament at every moment, and she knows which golfers are playing really well, and even why they are. She manages to keep her mind on all this while chatting with friends of the Nicklauses' who spend part of each round in Jack's Pack and meeting the stream of Nicklaus idolaters who come up to her and introduce themselves. She is at least as impressive at home. With her talent for organization, she knows what things have to be done that day, that week, and that month, and, with no bustle whatsoever, she is nearly always in the process of taking care of three or four matters exceedingly well.

I came to know Barbara Nicklaus in the late nineteen-sixties, not long after the family moved from Arlington Heights to Lost Tree Village, a North Palm Beach real-estate development built around a first-rate golf course that extends from the Atlantic, on the east, to Lake Worth, a segment of the Intracoastal Waterway, and Little Lake Worth, on the west. The Nicklauses first came to Lost Tree Village in the winter of 1965-66. They lived in a modest house that fronted on Little Lake Worth, and had Cary and Edith Middlecoff as their next-door neighbors. At this time, the Nicklauses had three children: Jack William II (Jackie), approaching five; Steven, three; and Nan, one. The family had originally planned only to winter in Florida. However, Jackie was scheduled to start kinder-

garten the next autumn, and as they came to realize the full impli-
cations of this they decided to live the year round in Lost Tree
Village. As Nicklaus puts it, "We wanted our kids to be able to
grow up right — in one place, with one set of friends, rather than
having to shift from one school to another each year." The thing I
probably remember most clearly from my look-ins on the Nicklauses in the late nineteen-sixties is how early in his children's
lives Jack introduced them to fishing. As soon as they were able to
stay in a boat, he would take them out with him when he fished in
Lake Worth or Little Lake Worth. In 1970, needing more space,
the Nicklauses moved to their present house — a spacious one-
story dwelling that looks out on the southern tip of Lake Worth.
When I saw them there this February, the two oldest children
were away at college. Jackie, who is twenty-one, is a junior at the
University of North Carolina at Chapel Hill. A tall (six feet four
and a half), serious young man with a nice independent quality,
he is a member of the college golf team. Last autumn, he won the
Campbell College Invitational tournament, in Buies Creek, North
Carolina, in which the members of twenty college teams from
Virginia and the Carolinas competed. He tied for first with rounds
of 74 and 67, and won the playoff with a birdie on the second extra
hole. Back in 1976, when Nicklaus's regular caddie in the British
Open became ill on the eve of the championship, Jackie, who had
come over with his parents, stepped in and caddied for his father.
He has since caddied for him in two U.S. Opens and in a number
of tour tournaments. Steve turned twenty this April. Rugged in
physique — he stands six two and a half and weighs a hundred
and ninety-five pounds — he is at Florida State University on a
football scholarship. A wide receiver, he is in his sophomore year.
Steve has never been interested enough in golf to work on his
game, but the four or five times a year he plays Lost Tree he
shoots around par. He occasionally caddies for his father on the
tour, and had the thrill of sharing in his victory last year in the
Colonial Invitation tournament, in Fort Worth. The middle child,
Nan, is eighteen and charming. Like her parents and all four of
her brothers, she is blond and blue-eyed. She is in her senior year
at the Benjamin School, a private junior high and high school in
North Palm Beach, and plays on the girls' socceer, volleyball, and
softball teams. Then comes Gary, an eighth grader at Benjamin.
Bright, disciplined, and determined, he is more like his father
than any of the other children are. A versatile athlete, he took to

golf when he was extremely young. When he was ten, it was his habit to go out by himself on the Lost Tree course, and he approached the game with the utmost gravity. He became very good very early. Last summer, when he was thirteen, the committee members at Lost Tree voted to lower his handicap to scratch. They were right to do so: Gary had scored a 66 from the back tees on the course. Michael, the baby of the family, is pushing ten. He is enjoying his childhood. He likes catching frogs, hitting a tennis ball, going to school, and playing video games on his own computer. Nicklaus is an especially good father. He expects his children to come up to certain standards of conduct, but he loves their company, and he is endlessly encouraging about their individual pursuits. I have never known a parent who derives more pleasure than he does from watching his children take part in sports. During the two seasons when both Jackie and Steve were on the Benjamin football and basketball teams, for example, Nicklaus missed only four games — this despite the commitments that so often take him away from home. After winning the U.S. Open at Pebble Beach in 1972, he did a characteristic thing: he spent the night flying back from San Francisco so that he could be on hand the next day when Steve and his teammates on the North Palm Beach Little League All-Star team played their big game against the Fort Pierce Little League All-Stars.

My visit to the Nicklauses this winter coincided with the first round of the Doral-Eastern Open, in Miami. Nicklaus shot a 70, two under par. Having been one of the early starters, he returned to North Palm Beach late in the afternoon in time to drive over to Frenchman's Creek Golf Club and watch the last few holes of the high-school varsity match in which Gary was playing. Gary won his individual nine-hole match with a 37, two over par. When father and son arrived home, they were talking golf. Nicklaus was explaining why he would like to see Gary take the club back a touch more on the outside: "It will put your arms and hands in a little better position at the top of the backswing." Barbara was in the kitchen talking with two old friends of the Nicklauses who were visiting from Columbus. Jack sat down with them and relaxed for a while, and then took me on a tour of the grounds. It had been ten years since my last visit, and some interesting changes had taken place. The swimming pool area at the back of the house now has an entirely different look. Ever since Nicklaus began to devote a large portion of his time to golf-course architecture in the early nineteen-seventies, he has been avidly studying horticulture, and he took charge of redesigning the informal gardens around the house — putting in small palm and citrus trees, tropical plants, and flowers that do well in a hot and humid climate. We turned left onto the grassed-over playground. One new addition immediately caught my eye. At the far corner, near the edge of the lake, a large satellite dish tilts slightly skyward. Nicklaus got it so that he could watch certain sports programs that the regular television networks don't carry. On my previous visit, there had been a putting green at the front end of the playground, but one that was so small it was hardly noticeable. It has been superseded by a sizable free-form green. The two tennis courts are at the opposite end of the playground. Originally, there was only one court, but the founding of the Day Camp made a second court mandatory. The grass on the putting green, a hybrid Bermuda grass called Tifdwarf, is cut very low, like the greens of a championship course on the eve of a tournament. The grass on the tennis courts, a hybrid Bermuda grass called Tifton 419, is kept at the height of grass on the tees of a championship course.

We swung left at the tennis courts, and Jack led the way past the garage (with its basketball hoop), down the driveway, and across a narrow road to two adjacent half-acre lots that constitute his nursery. He calls it "the yard." It abounds in trees, shrubs, and smaller plants, native and exotic. "It's quite a collection, really," he said as we walked past some lemon trees and lime trees. "Counting the different specimens we have around the house, I'd estimate that we've got thirty-four or thirty-five varieties of citrus trees here. Maybe nineteen varieties of mangoes. Eight avocados, I'd guess." He had paused briefly between these items, and now, as he continued to survey the yard, the cogitative pauses became a bit longer. "Five varieties of papayas. At least eight varieties of bananas. Seven or eight litchis — they're in the soapberry family. Six varieties of guavas. Eight or nine loquats. Maybe as many as twenty-five different kinds of palm trees. That's just the beginning. We've got lots of flowering trees — anything that will grow in this part of Florida." As we meandered through the yard, Nicklaus stopped periodically to identify and examine individual specimens, often rolling off their polysyllabic names as if he were Pliny the Elder.

On our walk, he told me that the yard had begun as a turf nursery a dozen or so years ago, when, after several years of serving as a consultant to golf-course architects and several more years co-designing courses, he decided to establish his own firm. He wanted to learn all he could about the new, refined strains of Bermuda grass, which is the most dependable grass for lawns, pastures, and golf courses in the southern part of the United States. Before he knew it, he was collecting plants and trees. Nicklaus has given more and more time in the past decade to building courses. He has found it stimulating and fulfilling. When he elects to retire from competitive golf, the bulk of his time and energy will undoubtedly go into golf-course architecture. He sees the yard as just the initial step in a long-range plan that will enable him in future years to set off and accent the playing areas of each of his courses with great colorful stands of plants and trees appropriate to its natural setting. The yard has also served another function, I learned as we completed our tour and headed back to the house. The man who heads the turf section of Nicklaus's golf-course-architecture enterprises is Ed Etchells, a superior golf-course superintendent, who first worked with Nicklaus at Muirfield Village. In this country, there are many young men who wish to become golf-course superintendents. Some of them are already employed at golf clubs; others are attending Mississippi State, Penn State, Michigan State, or other colleges that have agronomy programs. Etchells hears from a number of these young men or meets them on his travels. Over the last half-dozen years, he has had a program that calls for a promising young agronomist to join him as a trainee at the Nicklaus organization's headquarters in North Palm Beach, where Etchells has his office. These trainees study with Etchells for anything from three months to a year, depending on a number of circumstances, such as the need for an assistant at one of the courses that Nicklaus has designed and whose maintenance is supervised by Etchells. One of the duties of a trainee during his period in North Palm Beach is to take care of Nicklaus's own grounds — the putting green, the tennis courts, the gardens, and the yard. "It's been a very effective program," Nicklaus said. "When the fellows are here working with Ed, they get to feel at home with me, and they get to know the standard of maintenance we've set for our golf courses. Today, the head superintendents of seven of our courses are fellows who were trainees here. That's a big plus. When I drop in at one of those courses on an inspection trip, the superintendent will usually start by saying something like 'I think we've got the course the way you want it.' Almost always, it is. I can't describe the satisfaction you get when you see one of your courses looking and playing just as you meant it to. All too often, good golf courses aren't maintained properly, and, before anyone realizes it, they're no longer good courses."

The man I walked through the yard with this winter is essentially the same person I first met in 1959, at that year's Walker Cup match, but in several respects Nicklaus has undergone some noteworthy changes. He has expanded his vistas in many directions, developing a good mind, through exercise, into an excellent one. His memory can be astonishing. He has learned to understand other people better, and has become more generous of spirit. All in all, he has matured very well — particularly when one takes into account how long he has been in the spotlight and the disruptive effect that this kind of thing has had on many celebrities. My guess is that Nicklaus has always been a much more complicated man than most of us recognized. A profoundly private person of considerable sensitivity, he prefers to keep his problems to himself. He has had his share of them. To name only one, he could not have picked a worse time to burst onto the golf scene. The reigning hero in 1962, Nicklaus's first full year as a professional, was Arnold Palmer, the most popular golfer since Bobby Jones' heyday. A handsome, magnetic man who approached golf with a dramatic boldness, Palmer, who is ten years older than Nicklaus, had the gift of communicating his feelings to his galleries. He had another extraordinary gift: He was at his best when the going was hard, and would come charging down the stretch on the last round with a barrage of birdies that often carried him to victory. Small wonder that his galleries were so immense they became known as Arnie's Army. After winning his first major championship, the Masters, in 1958, Palmer won the Masters and the U.S. Open in 1960, the British Open in 1961, and the Masters and the British Open in 1962. In between these feats, he had torrid streaks on the tour, during which he performed his magic almost on a weekly basis, cheered on by his army and by the enraptured millions who watched him on television. Palmer continued to play fine golf for many seasons, but by 1965 it was clear, if it hadn't been before, that, remarkable as he was, he was not as good a golfer as Nicklaus. In the eyes of Palmer's fans, Nicklaus, the corpulent, expressionless kid who had supplanted their hero, was an unwelcome usurper. Nicklaus took all this in, stoically, and got through it. For several years, even when he stood alone at the top, he had a limited appeal for the average golf fan. Most of the regulars in his galleries were people who had been close to golf all their lives and could appreciate the beauty of his shotmaking. Then, slowly, starting in about 1970, the situation began to change. Nicklaus not only earned an ever-increasing esteem at home and throughout the world but also emerged as one of the most popular figures in modern sports. I can remember no occasion in golf quite like his victory in the U.S. Open at Baltusrol in 1980, eighteen years after he won his first Open. The upstart kid had become a venerated champion among champions. In Nicklaus's own opinion, he has never played a better nine holes than the second nine on the final round of that 1980 Open. The ecstatic, roaring thousands who greeted his sure progress down the last few holes seemed to me at the time to have something of the quality of the worshipful multitudes in Cecil B. De Mille's motion-picture extravaganzas about the heroes of the Bible and early Christian Rome. On reflection, the comparison is not inapt. If ever there was what has come to be known in sports jargon as a "living legend," it is Nicklaus. At Baltusrol that June afternoon, three generations of golf fans — most of them had often watched his exploits on television, but only on television — were ecstatic at being present to witness Nicklaus, in all his glory, once again outplaying and outscoring a strong field of challengers.

Since we live in the age of the "image" as well as the "living legend," it is perhaps not surprising that one factor in the new popularity Nicklaus gained was a drastic change in his appearance. In 1969, he let his blond hair, which he had worn rather short, grow longer, as other young men were doing. The reaction was very favorable, and this naturally pleased him. That autumn, when he and Barbara were flying home from London after the Ryder Cup match, the last event on his schedule that year, he began to think about his weight. He had always had a hearty appetite and had steadily become heavier. He now weighed two hundred and ten pounds or thereabouts. To his admirers, he was the Golden Bear, but to the claques of his rivals he was Fat Jack or Ohio Fats. He had let things go too far and too long, he told his wife on the plane, and he was determined to do something about it immediately. Once back home, he went on the Weight Watchers diet, and he stuck to it. The results were startling. In little over four weeks, he dropped twenty pounds, and in just the right places: He lost six inches around the hips and an inch and a half around the waist. The extra weight around his chin and neck also disappeared. The new Nicklaus was a younger-looking and much more attractive man. Realizing this, he watched his eating habits as vigilantly as a ballet star, and has continued to. The rise in Nicklaus's popularity rested on some things more meaningful than his new look, however. During his first years as a professional, when he sensed that the loyal followers of Palmer and other established stars begrudged him his sudden prominence, his reaction when he was playing tournaments had been to go into a sort of shell. In the nineteen-seventies, he began to relax more on the course and, at length, to be entirely himself. Watching him work on a round became an enchanting experience: one could follow his thinking practically step by step as he prepared to play each stroke, and this made the brilliant shots he brought off all the more spectacular. (Nicklaus believes that setting up correctly at the ball is ninety percent of golf.) As the years passed and the pressure of tournament golf became more and more intense, most of the new young stars flashed for only a brief period. Nicklaus continued to roll on and on, though. His longevity has been the product of his pertinacity no less than of his skill. He has been able to endure several long, discouraging slumps and play his way out of them. Four times, he has done this by winning a major championship — the 1967 U.S. Open, the 1970 British Open, the 1978 British Open, and the 1980 U.S. Open. There is nothing like carrying off one of the four majors to renew a golfer's confidence, and, apparently, there is nothing like confidence to restore the timing in a golfer's swing.

Few golfers know their swing as well as Nicklaus knows his. "In 1961 and 1962, I was very pleased with the way I hit the ball," he said the evening of my visit this winter, when he was reflecting on his play during different phases of his career. "I hit it long and straight those two years. In the middle sixties, I wasn't quite as good with the driver, but I was very sound with the irons. Then, toward the late sixties, my iron play went off. I played on power for several years. In the nineteen-seventies, I had some new problems. When I lost twenty pounds in 1969, I lost twenty yards. Being lighter was only incidental — I lost distance because my swing was starting to deteriorate. I got too upright. During the seventies, I wasn't a good striker of the ball at all. Oh, I won a lot of tournaments. In both 1972 and 1975, I won two major championships — my game happened to be at its best in those important weeks. Anyway, back in the middle sixties, at the top of my backswing my hands were well behind my head — deep, as we call it. That put me in position to hit the ball from the inside. My hip action was flat, and my head stayed level. In about 1970, I started to see my head bob a bit. I started to see my hips bobble. I was doing something on my backswing that pushed me up in the air, and at the top of the backswing my hands would be directly *over* my head instead of *behind* it. On my downswing, my left leg would sag. This would throw me outside the proper line, and I would wipe across the ball from right to left. That's why I lost so much distance. For years, I couldn't identify what caused that hip bobble. No one could — not even Grout. And I hadn't seen enough slow-motion movies of my swing in the sixties to know in what ways it had been different. In 1980, when Grout got me at the beginning of the season, he said, 'This year, we're going to go back to *deep*.' We worked on this hard. When I got to taking the club back deep again, I lost the bobble. You see, in order to get back into that position I was forced to move my hips in a different way — to make a flatter hip turn. Ever since I made that correction during those hours with Grout, I think I've struck the ball as well as I ever did. I made some other changes in my swing. I flattened my arc and levelled my shoulder turn. Now I come into the ball low and from the inside, and I hit the back of the ball more squarely than I ever did. When you do this, you can transfer all your power directly into your shot. I've got back the twenty yards I lost. Another thing — with this type of swing you get less spin on the ball. The ball has natural spin on it but not an exaggerated spin. That's an advantage. You can be more consistent. You can repeat the flight of your shots, as I did on the last nine at Baltusrol in the Open. I don't have much curve on the ball nowadays. I hit it more or less straight. Maybe it falls in a little from right to left. When you play from the inside with a complete release through the ball, you can hit it pretty straight. Of course, I practice now more than I used to. You have to when you get older. But I'm more excited about playing golf than I've been in a long time. I suppose the real reason for this is that I know I'm not going to play tournament golf that much longer. I don't want to go out of golf having let my game just dwindle away. I want to make sure that each year that I play I give it everything I've got. As long as I play tournaments, I'm going to work at it, I'm going to make it happen, and if I can't make it happen then I won't play."

This season, Nicklaus's plans call for him to play sixteen or seventeen tournaments. Between times, he will follow his usual procedure back at Lost Tree Village: he will relax with his family and friends, practice diligently, and keep abreast of what is going on at his business, the Golden Bear / Nicklaus organization. When the company was founded, in 1970, it occupied a two-room office on North Lake Boulevard in North Palm Beach. Aside from Nicklaus and a secretary, it had a staff of two, a bookkeeper and a treasurer, the latter being Tom Peterson, a banker from Fort Wayne. A sturdy, reliable man, Peterson is now the president and chief operating officer of Golden Bear / Nicklaus — a complex amalgam of many individual companies which has its headquarters in a two-story building on U.S. Route 1 in North Palm Beach and employs over a thousand people scattered across the country and overseas. The individual company in the group which is best known to the public is Golden Bear, Inc., which licenses the use of Nicklaus's name, nickname, and trademark to manufacturers and distributors of golf equipment, sports shirts, balzers, slacks, shoes, and other such items. Nicklaus has marketing contracts with a number of firms. He does television commercials for American Express, Pontiac, Magic Chef, and Uniden (Extend-a-Phone). His appeal is international. Golden Bear clothing, marketed by the Asahi Chemical Company, and Golden Bear jewelry, cosmetics, and soap, marketed by Taido, are the rage from Hokkaido to Kyushu, and their annual sales are estimated at over a hundred and fifty million dollars. Golden Bear / Nicklaus began to become big business in 1976, upon the arrival as chief executive officer of Charles E. (Chuck) Perry, a former president of Florida International University and later the publisher of *Family Weekly*. Under Perry's direction, the company expanded in three principal areas: real estate, insurance, and oil and gas development. Its ownership interests in these ventures has made it a multimillion-dollar conglomerate. Nicklaus, who is the chairman of Golden Bear / Nicklaus, has a good business mind. He takes a keen interest in the organization's diverse activities and is intimately involved in all significant decisions. Last year, his knowledge and enthusiasm were pivotal in the acquisition of the MacGregor Golf Company. From boyhood, he has always used MacGregor equipment.

Predictably, Nicklaus the businessman gives most of his time to the several individual companies under the Golden Bear / Nick-laus umbrella which design golf courses, supervise their construc-tion, and check on their maintenance for three years after they have been opened for play. Courses designed by Nicklaus are expensive, not only because of the power of his name but for another reason. Having often seen courses that were well laid out lapse into mediocrity because their upkeep was neglected, he pre-fers to make a deal with prospective clients that calls for personnel from two of his companies, Golforce and Golfturf, to undertake periodic inspection trips to recently completed courses over the first three years in order to make sure that proper maintenance procedures are established during that critical period. Nicklaus has now created twenty golf courses, and another twenty are in some stage of design or construction. These days, a golf-course architect seldom gets a crack at doing his stuff on choice natural golf terrain. Like other architects, Nicklaus frequently has to make a number of visits to a parcel of land that developers have ear-marked for a golf course before he can determine whether or not a course of merit can be built on it. For illustration, it took Nicklaus and Bob Cupp, his senior designer, six weeks and many trips to Shoal Creek, in the mountainous region of northern Alabama, before they were certain that there was room for eighteen holes in the narrow valleys. Then it took them four months to figure out a routing plan that satisfied them. Shoal Creek turned out to be a first-class course, and it has been chosen for the 1984 P.G.A. championship.

Nicklaus has a very definite approach to golf-course architec-ture. He abhors building holes that at first glance appear to be novel and intriguing but which have no genuine shot values. What he seeks during his first examinations of a new property are stretches of land whose contours lends themselves to sound, chal-lenging golf holes. In his mind, a well-designed hole will develop its own personality because of the way it plays and its geographic location. A good number of the courses he has worked on recently occupy unusually scenic sites. Castle Pines, south of Denver, is in the foothills of the Rockies. Bear Creek, twenty-five miles inland from San Clemente, is routed through a canyon in a valley just east of the coastal range. There were three hundred and fifty live-oak trees on this property, and Nicklaus routed his holes in such a way that only one tree had to be taken down. Desert Highlands, at Pinnacle Peak, in Scottsdale, is set in high desert country. The fairways, which are drained internally, are edged by decomposed granite that fills the same role rough and fairway bunkers usually do. Beyond this transition area is the real desert, abloom with four hundred varieties of plants and flowers. At the other end of the continent, at Hastings-on-Hudson, in Westchester, Nicklaus is beginning to renovate the course of the St. Andrews Golf Club, the oldest golf club in this country, established in 1888. Here the concept is to use modern techniques to produce eighteen holes with the aspect and the feel of the best courses designed here early in the century by Donald Ross and the other top architects of that day.

You can be sure that Nicklaus will be preparing conscientiously for the Masters, the U.S. Open, the British Open, and the P.G.A., for if he can win one of them his number of victories in the major championships will rise to a nice round figure: twenty. That is surely his goal.

When the day comes that designing courses replaces playing tournament golf as Nicklaus's chief occupation, he will be remembered for his sportsmanship as well as for his achievements. Considerate and gracious in victory, he stands alone in his time as a golfer who is able in defeat to go out toward his rivals with warmth and a genuine understanding of what winning means to them. Nicklaus's father instilled high precepts in him, but there is also something at the core of Nicklaus's character which underlies his attitude and conduct. He believes that there are definite ways a golfer must act in specific situations, and that if he fails to, the failure detracts immeasurably from the essence and worth of the game. There have been many examples of this in his career, but I will note just three. In the 1969 Ryder Cup match, at Birkdale, in England, the three-day competition came down to the last singles — Nicklaus vs. Tony Jacklin. All even as they played the eighteenth, a short par 5, Nicklaus lay 3 five feet from the cup, and Jacklin 3 two feet from the cup. Nicklaus's putt was a testing one. He took his time over it, and holed it. He then turned to Jacklin and told him his putt was good — he was conceding it. This halved singles made the final score of the team match 16–16. Some people thought that Nicklaus should have made Jacklin hole out, but Nicklaus felt that what he did was the right thing in those exceptional circumstances. In the 1977 British Open, at Turnberry, in Scotland, the championship turned out to be a two-man fight between Nicklaus and Watson, who, as it happened, were paired together on the last two rounds. Nothing in the history of golf quite matches their scoring and shotmaking over those thirty-six holes. Tied for the lead at the start of the third day, each was around in 65, six under par. On the fourth day, Nicklaus, despite a heroic birdie on the last hole, took 66 strokes — one stroke too many, for Watson had another 65. As they walked off the last green, Nicklaus flung his arm over Watson's shoulder and, smiling broadly, told him how wonderfully he had played. The two were involved in a similarly unforgettable moment at the close of the 1982 U.S. Open, at Pebble Beach. Playing three twosomes ahead of Watson, Nicklaus moved into contention on the last round with a string of five birdies on the front nine. Coming down the stretch, they were tied for the lead, but on the par-3 seventeenth Watson played what proved to be the winning shot: he holed a little wedge pitch from the greenside rough for a birdie. When Watson completed his round, there was Nicklaus, waiting off the eighteenth green to greet him heartily and congratulate him. Golf is one of the rare sports in which there has been no drop in the level of sportsmanship over the last decade, and I imagine that the example Nicklaus has set has had something to do with this happy state of affairs.

(1983)

The Masters'
Fiftieth Anniversary

In 1984 the Masters tournament became fifty years old — not that the Augusta National Golf Club, the home of the Masters, considered this reason for a formal celebration. How was it that an informal spring invitational tournament fostered by a private club had grown into one of the game's four major events during that period? It seemed to me a subject that warranted a detailed review. The result was a much longer article than I had intended to write.

IT IS GENERALLY AGREED THAT THERE ARE THREE KINDS OF GOLF: ordinary golf — the game the average golfer plays at his club; tournament golf; and major-tournament golf. The strain in tournament golf — be it an event for amateurs only, for professionals only, or for both — is much greater than it is in ordinary golf, where nothing much is at stake, but even a seasoned touring professional finds it infinitely harder to stand up to the pressure of major championships, because a victory in one of them can mean so much in money and prestige that it may well change a man's life. The British Amateur and United States Amateur championships still count for a lot, but they cannot today compare in stature with what are considered to be the game's four major tournaments. The oldest of these is the British Open, which was established in 1860. The field in the first British Open consisted of eight professionals from seven Scottish golf clubs, but the next year the men running the event made it clear that it was open to the crack amateurs of the day and, indeed, to all golfers in the world. This is why it came to be called the Open championship. The second-

oldest major tournament is the United States Open championship, which was started in 1895 by the newly organized United
States Golf Association. Our Open gained steadily in significance
as the game prospered in this country and as talented native players emerged to challenge the transplanted Scottish and English
professionals, but it was not regarded as a tournament on the
same level as the British Open until the nineteen-twenties. During
that decade, American-born golfers demonstrated — principally
through their astounding successes in the British Open — that
they were not only as good as the leading British players but
better. Walter Hagen, from Rochester, won the British Open four
times (in 1922, 1924, 1928, and 1929), and Bobby Jones, from Atlanta, won it three times (in 1926, 1927, and 1930). The United
States has continued to produce more first-class golfers than any
other country, and, as a result, since around 1930 the U.S. Open
has been considered — certainly by Americans — the most important tournament in golf. The third major tournament, the Professional Golfers' Association championship, was first played in
1916, the year the P.G.A. of America was founded. A match-play
event open only to professionals, it may have reached the peak of
its popularity in the nineteen-twenties, when the colorful Hagen
won it four years in a row and five times in all, and when Gene
Sarazen and Leo Diegel won it twice each. In 1958, the format of
the P.G.A. championship was changed from match play to stroke
play — a questionable move in the opinion of many golf enthusiasts. Over the last quarter of a century, Gary Player, of South
Africa, has won the P.G.A. championship twice, and David Graham, of Australia, has won it once, but the tournament has not
regularly attracted many of the outstanding foreign players, and it
does not compare in stature with our Open or the British Open,
or, for that matter, with the youngest of the four major events, the
Masters.

The Masters, which came into being in 1934, was then called the
Augusta National Invitation tournament. It was meant to be a
modest, informal get-together. Jones — who had retired from
competitive play following his Grand Slam, in 1930, of the British
Amateur, the British Open, the U.S. Open, and the U.S. Amateur,
in that order — invited his old friends in the game and its rising
stars to a tournament to be held in early spring at the Augusta
National Golf Club, in Augusta, Georgia, over the course that he

had designed with Alister MacKenzie, the well-known British golf-course architect. The players who received invitations had qualified for them through their achievements: they had won the U.S. Open, the British Open, the P.G.A., the U.S. Amateur, or the British Amateur. Filling out the field were the members of the current American Walker Cup and Ryder Cup teams. From the beginning, because the field at the Augusta National was composed of the game's most distinguished players, some members of the media took to referring to it as the Masters, but it was not until 1938 that Jones, who didn't want the tournament to lose the aura of the affable, relaxed reunion of friends which he had intended it to be — and which it was — yielded to the general pressure and, as the host of the tournament and the president of the Augusta National Golf Club, agreed that the annual tournament would thenceforth be known officially as the Masters. The recent Masters, won so impressively by Ben Crenshaw, was something special: it marked the fiftieth anniversary of the founding of the event.

How did the Masters — which is not a championship of a nation but simply a tournament run by a private club — manage to acquire such esteem that, before anyone had given real thought to its position in the realm of golf, it had come to be accepted as a major competition? Well, it was the result of the extraordinary concurrence of a number of factors. To start with, the tournament had both worth and glamour simply because it was played over the course that Jones had long dreamed of building — an altogether excellent course that turned out to be perhaps the most beautiful inland layout in the world, and one that introduced some revolutionary principles in golf-course design. The Masters also possessed a flavor distinctly different from that of all other golf tournaments. Leisurely in tempo, like a country fair, it was the first stroke-play tournament in which the field played only one round a day. (In the British and U.S. Opens, and in the lesser stroke-play events as well, it was traditional to play thirty-six holes on the last day.) Accordingly, the golfers had ample time to sit down together and catch up on things, either at the club or at the Bon Air Vanderbilt, the pleasant hotel at which just about all the players stayed in the years before the Second World War. A tournament is only as good as its field, and from the outset, because of its singular appeal, the Masters attracted the best players in the game. For another thing, the tournament was held at the perfect time of year — early spring. (The first Masters was played in late March, and then the tournament was moved up to April. Since 1940, it has usually been held during the first full week in April, when the azaleas, dogwood, redbud, and the other flowering trees and shrubs that make the Southern spring so glorious are busting out all over.) For American golf fans who had spent the long winter months in the cold Northern states, there was no cure like a week of balmy weather in Augusta. After the war, the Masters, as the first big tournament of the year, came to signify for golf fans around the globe the beginning of the new golf season. It also possessed two other incalculably valuable assets. In Clifford Roberts, a New York investment banker, it had possibly the most talented administrator that tournament golf has ever known. A man of perfectionistic zeal, Roberts came up with a series of innovations at the Masters which showed the game's other entrepreneurs how a modern golf tournament should be run. And, finally, there was Bobby Jones — or Bob, as he preferred to be called. The most idolized of all the athletic heroes of the nineteen-twenties — the Golden Age of American sport — Jones proved to be everything that his admirers thought he was, and a great deal more. Along with wide-ranging knowledge, true sensibility, and a charming sense of humor, he had an instinct for camaraderie that communicated itself instantly. Because he personified golf and sportsmanship at their best, his presence imbued the Masters with a spirit that few occasions in sports can come close to. The Masters did not set out to be a major tournament, but through the fusion of these disparate elements it became one. In golf today, the situation is just the reverse: unexceptional tournaments aspire by incessant self-promotion to elevate themselves onto the same plateau as the British Open, the U.S. Open, the P.G.A. championship, and the Masters, and to be acclaimed, as it were, genuine major events.

From the outset, the goal of the Masters was simply to put on the finest golf tournament possible. In the initial Masters, in 1934, Jones made his first appearance in a tournament since his retirement, and that assuredly served to thrust the Masters immediately into the spotlight. It didn't hurt the Masters, either, that in the 1935 tournament Gene Sarazen played what is without a doubt the most spectacular shot in golf history. On the last round, he was three strokes behind the apparent winner, Craig Wood, when he came to the par-5 fifteenth, then 485 yards long. He proceeded to hole his second shot, a 4-wood, for a double-eagle 2. This enabled him to tie Wood in the tournament and to go on to defeat him in their playoff. But what really made the Masters was the pleasure that the competing golfers derived from their week in Augusta — that and the exuberant endorsement of the tournament by the people who were lucky enough to attend it. My own case, I think, is typical. I saw my first Masters in 1947. By then, I had visited a number of famous courses, but none of them had quite the ambience of the Augusta National. It was the prettiest course I had ever seen. In those days, its Bermuda-grass fairways were overseeded with an Italian rye grass that gleamed a lovely shade of green in the sun. Most of the holes had a striking originality of design, and four or five of them possessed both a golf beauty and a scenic beauty that were inseparable. The galleries were still small. There couldn't have been more than two thousand people on the course on Thursday and Friday. On Sunday, five thousand at the most were on hand for the final round. It was a treat to be there. Inside the clubhouse, Mrs. Helen Harris and her staff provided a perfect blend of efficiency and hospitality. Out on the course, the players were courteous and approachable. The spectators knew their golf. The pimiento sandwiches at the refreshment stands were fresh and exotic. The clubhouse, an elegant ante-bellum manor house wrapped in wisteria, overlooked the course, and let you know you were in the Deep South as explicitly as did the mockingbirds' song and the abundant flora. (Each hole at the Augusta National is named after the tree, shrub, or plant that frames it from tee to green.) Everyone who attended the Masters before the Second World War or in the first few years afterward realized that its delightful intimacy was bound to vanish quickly. It did. The tournament was soon "discovered" during the postwar golf boom, and it wasn't too long before the number of spectators daily pouring onto the course mounted to ten thousand, to twenty thousand, to thirty thousand, and eventually to forty thousand and more. Considering the size of the galleries these days, the wonder is how smoothly the tournament continues to operate and how miraculously it has retained its ineffable charm.

When did the Masters become a major tournament? That is, of course, a matter of personal opinion. Some people I know feel that when the tournament started up again in 1946, after being closed down for three years during the war, it was tacitly regarded as a major event. My own feeling, which I share with many other old Masters hands, is that if there was any one year when the tournament arrived it was probably in 1954. That April, the two best golfers in the world, Ben Hogan and Sam Snead (each of whom had earlier won the Masters twice), held off a gallant bid by Billy Joe Patton, an amateur from North Carolina, and met in an eighteen-hole playoff that Snead won by a stroke.

When one looks back at the Masters from the vantage point of 1984, many phases of its development are amazing, but none more so than the dispatch with which the club and the course came into being. During his competitive career, Jones had often mentioned that one of the things he would like to do when his playing days were over was to design his "dream course." On September 27, 1930, he completed his Grand Slam by winning our Amateur at the Merion Cricket Club, outside Philadelphia. Shortly afterward, he announced his retirement from tournament golf. He was only twenty-eight, but he was wise enough to realize that anything he might accomplish in golf after that incredible sweep would be anticlimactic. He was instantly besieged with all sorts of business opportunities. A surprisingly large number of people remembered Jones' reference to building his dream course, and they lost no time in informing him that they had just the piece of land he was looking for. Since Jones was an Atlantan, the majority of the sites he was asked to consider were situated in the countryside on the outskirts of his home town. This was not what he had in mind. He was thinking about Augusta and wondering if there was some land there on which a really first-class course could be built. Whereas Atlanta is a thousand feet above sea level, Augusta lies in a valley that is only a little over an eighth that altitude. In the winter, it is considerably warmer than Atlanta, and in the eighteen-eighties it began to develop a reputation as a winter resort. It was particularly attractive to people who liked to play golf. There were three excellent golf courses — two at the Augusta Country Club, near the Bon Air Vanderbilt hotel, and the other at the Forest Hills Ricker hotel. Jones had loved to come over from Atlanta in the winter and play them. The course he intended to build would be one that would be used primarily for winter golf.

Through Jones' many friends, word of his interest in a possible site in Augusta reached the city's mayor, Thomas Barrett, Jr., who thought immediately of a three-hundred-and-sixty-five-acre property on the edge of Augusta. Originally an indigo plantation, it had been purchased in 1857 by Baron Louis Berckmans, a Belgian nobleman whose avocation was horticulture. The following year, the Baron and his son, Prosper, who was a professional horti- culturalist, had founded the Fruitland Nurseries there. They had imported many varieties of trees, shrubs, vines, and plants, and cultivated them with such success that Fruitland Nurseries be- came the first large commercial nursery in the South. After the death of Prosper Berckmans, in 1910, Fruitland Nurseries closed down and its trade name was sold, but in 1930 the property was still available for purchase. That autumn, after Mayor Barrett got in touch with him, Jones came to Augusta to look over the old Berckmans estate. Barrett drove Jones and some friends of his down the majestic entranceway to the old plantation manor house — a lane two hundred and fifty yards long, bordered by magnolia trees that arched overhead. He conducted the party to the back terrace of the manor house, which sits at the crest of a long, rolling hill. Jones slowly took in the spectacular view: the wide stretches of cleared land that tumbled gently down toward Rae's Creek, about a half mile away; the thick dark-green stands of longleaf pines, many of them rising a hundred feet on almost perfectly vertical trunks; the handsome clusters of shrubs and flowers that Berckmans and his son had cultivated, setting off the manor house and brightening the acres of cleared land. Jones smiled thoughtfully and then said, "Perfect. And to think that this ground has been lying here all these years waiting for someone to come along and lay out a golf course on it."

An option was taken on the property, and an organizing com- mittee of five, including Jones, was set up. Jones asked Clifford Roberts, who had an impressive background in finance, to serve as chairman of the committee. Jones and Roberts were well ac- quainted. A devoted golfer and a fairly good one, Roberts had regularly spent part of the winter season at the Augusta Country Club. Before the organizing committee went to work, Jones out- lined to Roberts the kind of club he thought the Augusta National should be. Inasmuch as he had friends in many states, he wanted the club to have a national membership. It would be called the Augusta National Golf Club, and it would be open from the first week in November to the end of April. It would be a men's club, and membership would be by invitation only. The operation of the club was to be as uncomplicated as possible: there would be no living quarters for the members at the club, and there would be facilities for no sport but golf.

Jones then turned his attention to building the course. An admirer of the work of Alister MacKenzie, who had designed Cypress Point, on the Monterey Peninsula, and many other superior courses, he was able to get MacKenzie to collaborate with him in laying out the holes at the Augusta National. Jones and MacKenzie started work in the spring of 1931. The course was ready for play in December, 1932, and was formally opened in January, 1933. It provoked immediate excitement, for it surpassed expectations in nearly every respect.

The unusually short time it took to build the Augusta National reflected the harmonious relationship between Jones and MacKenzie. They held similar views on the fundamental principles of course design. It was important, they thought, that a hole look natural — as if it had always been there. It was equally important that it be part of an over-all routing plan that offered a wide variety of holes in an interesting order. (What a triumph of routing the Augusta National is! No two consecutive holes run in the same direction. The sequence of the par-3, par-4, and par-5 holes is remarkable; there are no par 4s back to back until the ninth and the tenth. And there is not a single hole whose fairway is awkwardly tilted, as so many holes built on a hillside tend to be.) Jones and MacKenzie agreed on the value of creating holes that were scenically arresting as well as functionally sound. For example, they cut through large stands of trees to open up the stunning views on the second and tenth holes. They made imaginative use of Rae's Creek and the other small creeks on the property, turning them into ponds on some holes. (On five of the first seven holes on the second nine — the course's most precarious stretch — a water hazard either guards the direct approach to the green or is situated adjacent to the green.) Jones and MacKenzie were also of one mind about sand bunkers. They felt that there was an overabundance of them on most American courses. They objected particularly to our predilection for placing bunkers so close to the tee that they caught only the mis-hit drives of the high-handicap golfer, who had enough troubles to begin with. They laid out their par 4s and par 5s at the Augusta National so that there wasn't a single fairway bunker less than two hundred yards from the tee. Further aid and comfort were provided the high-handicap golfer by the paucity of rough and the breadth of the fairways — many of them sixty or seventy yards wide. The hills and slopes on the old Berckmans property were monumental in scale, and this suggested to Jones and MacKenzie that they should design greens that were much larger and more boldly contoured than the typical American green. Both men, as it happened, were fascinated by the huge double greens on the Old Course at St. Andrews, in Scotland, and this was a supporting reason for making the greens at the Augusta National such a challenge.

However, if there was any one overriding goal that Jones and MacKenzie were striving to achieve, it was to come up with a course that would be eminently playable from the regular tees for the medium- and high-handicap golfer while simultaneously presenting a stiff examination from the back tees for the low-handicap or scratch golfer. They were successful in bringing this off because they both staunchly believed that strategic design was much superior to penal design, which for years had dominated golf-course architecture in America. On a course of penal design, the golfer who hits a shot that strays the slightest bit from the narrow path from the tee to the green is punished for it drastically. His ball often ends up in high rough but even more often in a sand bunker. The Oakmont Country Club, near Pittsburgh, is probably the best-known penal-type course in this country. At the time the Augusta National was opened, Oakmont was sprinkled with well over two hundred bunkers. The Augusta National had only twenty-five. (Today, the number has risen to forty-four, but that is still an extremely small amount for a championship course.) Jones and MacKenzie were able to settle for so few bunkers because they were fortunate enough to be working with marvellous terrain and were intelligent enough to make the most of it. They had no idea that they were building a course on which a tournament would be held. They were simply out to build the best course possible on an exceptional piece of land.

In designing a golf course, the usual method is to first find natural sites for greens and tees. If it is possible, the architect prefers to work backward from a green site, deciding on the direction and swing of the fairway, the specific spot on the fairway that affords the ideal opening to the green on the approach shot, and, ultimately, the right site for the tee — a site that pulls everything together. As Jones and MacKenzie walked their acreage searching for golf holes, the first one they "discovered" was the thirteenth. It was there in its entirety — a 465-yard par 5 whose green could be reached in two if the golfer put together two excellent shots. Jones, it should be noted, was partial to short par 5s — par 4½ holes — because he felt that a long par 5, which required three shots to reach the green, was inclined to be dull. The basic principle of strategic design is to offer the golfer at least two routes to the green, and this the thirteenth does as dramatically as one could hope. The tee is elevated and gives the golfer a clear idea of his options on the hole. About two hundred and fifty yards from the tee, the fairway doglegs sharply to the left. At the bend, it slopes gradually up from left to right, like the banked corner of an indoor track. If the low-handicap golfer elects to gamble on taking the dangerous route down the left side of the fairway and succeeds in cutting the corner with a long, straight drive, he is in a position to reach the green in two, usually with a long iron or a fairway wood. Then if he hits the requisite second shot and gets down in two putts he has his birdie 4. On the other hand, the golfer who tries to cut the corner and hooks his ambitious drive pays a stiff price for his error. His shot will probably finish in the pine woods that border the left side of the hole, or in the narrow creek — an arm of Rae's Creek — that follows closely along the left edge of the fairway in the landing area of the drive. This creek later swings back across the fairway just before the green, and then bends so that it hugs the right side of the green. As is no doubt evident, unless a golfer needs to make up ground on his opponents there is ample reason for him to choose the right side of the fairway off the tee, the conservative route. If he hits a fairly long drive, though, he is faced with a difficult decision: should he go with a fairway wood on his second and try to carry the creek in front of the green, or should he lay up safely short of it? If he opts for the latter, he can be reasonably sure of his par 5, and there is always the chance that he can wedge his third shot close enough to the pin to get down in one putt for his birdie. All in all, as the thirteenth illustrates, a golf course of strategic design is not only fairer than one of penal design but much more stimulating. It rewards the aggressive golfer for his daring and his proficient execution of demanding shots. At the same time, it rewards clear thinking and prudence, for if a golfer tries to bite off more than he can chew he is punished for his poor judgment or his faulty execution of the shot. The Augusta National so entranced the erudite golfers who played the course themselves or watched the stars play it in the Masters that it is credited with changing the approach to golf-course architecture in this country almost single-handed. The penal course was out and the strategic course was in. One could often recognize the influence of the Augusta National in the designs of the multitude of new courses that were built after the war. For one thing, the extra-large green became practically standard. This was regrettable. The heroic-sized green is right only on a course of heroic proportions, like the Augusta National.

Alister MacKenzie unfortunately did not live to savor the praise lavished on the course when it was publicly unveiled, in 1934, at the first Masters; he had died in January. Jones was naturally pleased by the generous words that the players and the press had for the course. (He was less pleased with his golf in the tournament: he tied with Walter Hagen and Denny Shute for thirteenth.) In 1934, the par-72 layout measured about 6,700 yards, a little over 200 yards shorter than it does today. (The holes were remeasured by laser beam in 1980, from the ball-washers on the tees to the midpoint of the greens.) In Jones' mind, it is interesting to note, work on the course was by no means finished. He was aware that there were quite a few holes that needed strengthening, and he meant it when he told people who really knew golf that he would welcome any suggestions they might have for improving this or that hole. Perry Maxwell, a golf-course architect from Oklahoma who had been a protégé of MacKenzie's, was responsible for the first significant change. Originally, the green on the tenth, then a 420-yard par 4, was situated in a hollow at the bottom of a long and steep slope. The green area had presented drainage problems from the outset. It was Maxwell's idea to shift the green up onto higher land farther back and to the left, where it would be framed by a breathtaking backdrop of tall pines. Jones heartily approved of Maxwell's suggestion, which, carried out expertly by Maxwell himself, turned an indifferent hole into one of the most beautiful par 4s in the world.

Nearly every year, Jones made one or more minor changes in the course. The next major alteration came in 1947, when the sixteenth hole was completely revised. A par 3 about 145 yards long, the sixteenth was not one of the more memorable holes. A shallow stream curled close to the narrow green, which had a prominent mound in the center. The tee, when the course first opened, was located to the right of the fifteenth green; Jones later added an alternative tee, set to the left of that green. In 1947, he worked out an altogether different plan for the hole: a new tee would be built farther back on the left side of the fifteenth green; the stream would be dammed and a pond created between the new tee and a totally new green. Robert Trent Jones, already a well-established golf-course architect, executed Jones' plan very well. The ugly duckling turned into a swan — a 170-yard par 3 over a fairway of water to a somewhat kidney-shaped green that offered a wide variety of pin placements. The new sixteenth added palpably to the pressure the leaders felt when they came to the finishing holes at the end of a round. (Some Masters regulars regard the seventeenth, a 400-yard par 4 whose green cannot be seen from the area of the fairway where most drives end up, as the only ordinary hole down the stretch, and they wonder why no modifications of consequence have been made on it.)

In 1950, the Augusta National underwent its last major change. The eleventh was made into an incomparably better hole. The original eleventh was a drive-and-pitch par 4. Its tee was positioned above and to the right of the present tenth green, and the fairway swung from left to right and then downhill to a green of no particular distinction. Just who conceived the new eleventh is a controversial subject, but Clifford Roberts, who wrote a history of the Augusta National, stated there that it was he who suggested to Jones that a new tee should be built in the woods, far back and to the left of the tenth green. In any event, the new tee was set there, a chute was cut through the trees, and a new fairway was created which ran nearly straight until it veered a little to the right as it plunged down over large mounds to a new green. The redesigned eleventh measured 455 yards and was a terror. An extension of Rae's Creek, which was later dammed and turned into a small pond, menaced the left side and front of the green; a bank five or six feet high separated the water hazard from the putting surface. After studying the new eleventh, Ben Hogan made up his mind that it would be folly to go for the pin on his second shot — usually anything from a 2-iron to a 4-iron — considering the penalty he would incur if his ball struck the bank in front of the green and toppled down into the hazard. Hogan always aimed his second shot at the righthand fringe of the green, content to get down with a chip and a putt for his par. His decision on how he would play the eleventh prompted one of his most famous Hoganisms: "If you ever see me on the eleventh green in two, you'll know I missed my second shot."

Although from 1948 on Jones suffered from syringomyelia, a

crippling disease of the spinal cord, he continued to oversee the alterations made on the course, and through 1968 he always managed somehow or other to be on hand for the Masters. He died in December, 1971, at the age of sixty-nine. I often wonder how he felt as he watched the club's unpretentious invitation tourney blossom into an authentic major event. I also wonder what went through his mind as he directed, with his inveterate astuteness, the alterations that turned the very fine course he and MacKenzie had designed into both a more subtle and a more formidable one. Beginning in 1956, the Masters was televised annually, and by the time of Jones' death the Augusta National had become the best-known course in the world and a touchstone for a new generation of golf-course architects.

The Masters, it should be noted, would not have become the Masters without the unflagging ministrations of Clifford Roberts. Lean, dour, and gravel-throated, Roberts, an autocrat's autocrat, was the last person one would ever think of as an "idea man," but the Augusta National was inexpressibly dear to his heart, and he thought about the club morning, noon, and night. As chairman of the Masters, he thought no less incessantly about the tournament and how it could be made into a bigger and better event. Just as the Augusta National is unique in the continuing attention it gives to improving the playing qualities of its holes, so it stood alone for decades in trying to improve the lot of the spectator. From the start, the people who attended the Masters were not customers but "patrons." Roberts early saw to it that these patrons were provided with free parking on the club property — there was room for thousands of cars. (The main parking area was subsequently enlarged, and new parking areas were added; today there is space to accommodate over eight thousand cars.) Roberts was responsible for an endless series of innovations. For instance, the Masters' patrons were not asked to buy bulky programs; free pairing sheets were distributed each day. On the reverse side of each sheet was a map of the course, which also indicated where the various refreshment stands and rest rooms were situated. Another item available at no cost to the patrons was a small guide written by Jones in which he discussed the best vantage points for watching the play. Almost every year, new spectator mounds were built on a number of holes to afford more people a clearer view of the action. The new mounding was done with such care that it appeared to be natural terrain that one just hadn't noticed before.

Roberts had a lot of good ideas. The first time I attended the Masters, I was struck by how clean the grounds were throughout the day. This was no happy accident. Roberts had long before organized a uniformed trash squad that moved over the course picking up and bagging refuse. He appreciated that the Masters, as the only major tournament held on the same course each year, had certain advantages, and he meant to make the most of them. Underground telephone lines were laid to connect the scoreboards out on the course with Scoring Control, which is situated in the Tournament Headquarters building, close to the clubhouse. The phone lines allowed the scores of the players leading the tournament to be quickly posted, hole by hole, around the course. Roberts decided to call these scoreboards leader boards, and he had giant ones constructed which could be read from a good distance by spectators equipped with binoculars. His most important contribution in this area, however, was the simplified scoring system introduced at the Masters in 1960. Previously, in order to figure out how close to the leader a particular player was at any moment a spectator had to read the player's score for each hole, compute how he stood in reference to par, and then work out the number of strokes by which he trailed the leader. In the Masters' scoring system, each contending player's cumulative score in relation to par was posted hole by hole. A red number denoted how many strokes he was under par, a green number how many strokes he was over par, and a green zero that he was even par. It took hardly more than a glance for a spectator to know the state of the tournament. The Masters' system of scoring was soon adopted by tournaments everywhere.

In 1958, Roberts paused from his labors long enough to collaborate with George Cobb, a golf-course architect from South Carolina, in building a splendid nine-hole par-3 course to the east of the clubhouse, but his thoughts were never away from the big course for long. In 1962, the first observation stand for spectators was erected. Today, there are four observation stands, three of them on the second nine. Never lacking for energy, Roberts spent untold hours on such glamourless tasks as overseeing the installation of more efficient course drainage systems; improving the watering systems; working with turf experts on the seeding and overseeding of the fairways and greens, so that the Augusta National would continue to be the racy, fearsome test it was when the Masters was initiated; revamping the practice grounds and the spectator stands behind them; and superintending the telecast of the tournament, so that the action was interrupted far less frequently by commercials than was the case in other sports telecasts. He even selected the sponsors whose commercials would be run. In addition — often to the dismay of certain members of the club, who thought they should be consulted on these matters — Roberts called the shots on the expansion of the clubhouse. Before the Second World War, the old plantation manor house, with its two-story columns, nine-and-a-half-foot-wide porches on all four sides, and four-sided roof slanting up to a four-windowed cupola, was modernized into a cozy, functional clubhouse. One of the seven ground-floor rooms was made into a kitchen. After the war, an east wing was added. It contains a commodious dining room, called the Trophy Room, and living quarters owned by individual members — five suites on the ground floor, four single rooms on the second floor. A west wing was also constructed, which today houses a grillroom, a locker room, and guest rooms. Just beyond are the Tournament Headquarters, the pro shop, the press building, and the new media-interview building. It was decided in 1946 to grant permission to members to build individual cottages in the area southeast of the clubhouse. The cottages, following the old plantation custom, were referred to as cabins. The Jones cabin, the first to be built, faced the tenth tee. The Eisenhower cabin was at the east end of the vast practice green. Today, there are nine cabins, six of which are multilevel buildings.

Roberts, a one-man gang if there ever was one, ran the show at the Augusta National until he died, at eighty-three, in 1977, in his private suite in the clubhouse. William Lane, of Houston, then took over as Masters chairman for three years, and he was followed by the man who is currently the chairman of the club and the chairman of the Masters, Hord Hardin. A native of St. Louis, Hardin, now seventy-two, is a retired lawyer. As a young man, he was a capable golfer; he qualified seven times for the U.S. Amateur and once for the U.S. Open. He was president of the United States Golf Association in 1968-69 and chairman of the Masters Rules Committee from 1970 to 1980, when he took on his present duties. Hardin lives an enviable life. He and his wife winter in Naples, Florida, and summer in Harbor Springs, Michigan. He spends nearly three months of the year in Augusta, including the six weeks before the Masters. He plays golf about five days a week, and on the other days he hits out practice balls. He has shot a 69 from the members' tees at the Augusta National. A traditionalist who is pleasant in manner and diplomatic by instinct, Hardin is a good man for the job.

Early in its career, the Masters established a reputation for thrilling finishes. Horton Smith won the first Masters when he sank a twenty-foot birdie putt on the seventeenth — the seventy-first hole of the tournament. He won again in 1936, when he holed a fifty-foot chip shot on the sixty-eighth. In between Smith's two victories, Sarazen had lit up the skies with his double eagle. The other major events have had their share of sensational finishes, but the Masters has probably had a higher ratio of tournaments in which the outcome hung in the balance until it was decided fairly late in the fourth round by the kind of melodramatic dénouement that might have been co-scripted by Charles Dickens and Burt L. Standish. One possible explanation of this is the strategic verve of the last nine holes. If a contender hits a poor shot at the wrong time, his chances can be ruined then and there. Conversely, a number of these holes offer enticing birdie opportunities for the golfer who feels that fate has tapped him on the shoulder and nothing is beyond his doing.

Consider the roles that the twelfth and thirteenth holes played in the 1937 and 1939 Masters. In 1937, Ralph Guldahl, then just coming into his own, seemed to have the tournament locked up when he reached the twelfth, a 155-yard par 3, on which the thin, angled green is perched just beyond Rae's Creek. The pin that day was set at the back-right corner of the green — the toughest position. Instead of playing a conservative shot for the center of the green, Guldahl went for the flag. He may have cut across the ball a fraction, or the gusty wind may have caught it; in any event, the ball tailed off slightly to the right and dropped into the creek. Guldahl took a 5 on the hole, and this may have shaken him. On the thirteenth, the 465-yard par 5 that doglegs to the left, he played a mediocre second shot that wound up in the creek before the green, and took a bogey 6. About forty-five minutes later, Byron Nelson, a young man who had yet to make his reputation, came to the twelfth. He put his iron shot twenty-five feet from the pin and knocked in the putt for his birdie. On the thirteenth, he hit two big shots to the edge of the green and then holed his chip for an eagle. On those two holes, Nelson picked up no fewer than six shots on Guldahl. As he walked to the fourteenth tee, he was out in front in the tournament by two strokes, and he preserved his lead by playing the last five holes in par. Two years later, Guldahl was again in the thick of the fight at Augusta. He was a much more deeply respected golfer by then, having won the two previous U.S. Opens. On the last round, when he came to the thirteenth the grapevine had spread the news that Sam Snead had finished with a 68, to post a record low total of 280 for the Masters. Guldahl's drive on the thirteenth was not especially long, but he knew that any hope he had of catching Snead depended on his picking up a birdie. He decided without a moment's hesitation to go for the green on his second, although he had a sidehill lie and would have to carry the ball 230 yards to clear the creek. He went with a 3-wood and played an absolutely marvellous shot. It landed on the green, rolled straight for the flagstick, and finished six inches away. He tapped it in for his eagle 3. As it turned out, this courageous gamble won the tournament for Guldahl.

At about this time, it began to dawn on people who followed golf closely that most of the game's new stars were Texans. Guldahl was from Dallas. Nelson was from the Fort Worth area, and so was Ben Hogan, then emerging as a leading figure on the P.G.A. tour. Jimmy Demaret, from Houston, became more than just another promising player by winning the 1940 Masters. He finished four strokes ahead of the runner-up, Lloyd Mangrum, who was from Trenton, Texas. It was difficult to understand the sudden rise of Texas as a breeding ground of golf champions until the word got around that most of the impressive new pros from that state had grown up on courses with hard, resilient fairways, and that, as often as not, there were strong winds to be reckoned with. Consequently, these golfers had learned how to make contact with the ball on the downswing and to hit it in a low trajectory — "quail high," to use the local term. The playoff between Hogan and Nelson in 1942 — the year before the Second World War caused the suspension of the Masters — produced some of the finest golf that had been seen in the tournament. On the first five holes, Hogan jumped out in front by three strokes. He played the next eleven holes in one under par and lost five strokes to Nelson. Nelson ultimately won their duel by a stroke. Demaret won again in 1947 and once more in 1950, to become the first player to win the tournament three times. Demaret was an unusual man — kindhearted, companionable, and spontaneous whatever the circumstances. When he accepted the Masters trophy at the presentation ceremony in 1950, he told the crowd gathered around the practice green that he could best express his thoughts by singing a popular song. A former dance-band vocalist, he proceeded to render a properly professional chorus of "How Lucky You Are."

Demaret's third, and last, triumph in the Masters occurred during one of the most glittering periods in the tournament's history. In the stretch between 1949 and 1954, with the exception of 1950, Snead and Hogan, the two giants of the day, alternated in winning it. Snead's victories came in 1949, 1952, and 1954, Hogan's in 1951 and 1953. A good many of the game's cognoscenti were at a loss to know why it had taken Snead so long to win the Masters. The man and the course seemed made for each other — Snead, the powerful, picture-postcard swinger, and the beautiful rolling terrain of the Augusta National. A proficient all-around athlete, Snead had grown up in the resort town of Hot Springs, Virginia. He developed his classic golf swing without anyone's telling him what he had to do to improve his natural ability to hit a stationary ball from a stationary stance. He was exceptionally supple. For instance, when he was in his sixties he could still kick a seven-foot-high ceiling with no effort at all. This suppleness undoubtedly helped to explain the fluidity of his swing and its slow, rhythmic tempo. It was a thrill just to watch Snead hit the ball. Not only was his technique flawless but the ball really did seem to go practically out of sight as it whistled off the tee and climbed higher and higher until it peaked, say, 260 yards from the tee. Snead's weakness, as everyone knew, was his putting. He was a superior approach putter, but he had his troubles with the short ones, and this was often costly. Much later in his career, when his palmy days were over, Snead switched to a croquet type of putting stroke. He has putted so well since making the change that many people think he might have won many more championships if he had used this method during the years when he was at the top of his game.

When Snead finally broke through in the Masters, in 1949, he did it in style: he finished with a pair of 67s. He showed his fibre in winning his second Masters, in 1952. The leader at the halfway mark, he held on firmly the last two days, when heavy winds blew over the course, and won by four strokes. His victory over Hogan in their playoff for the 1954 Masters title was well earned. Both men played the first nine in 35, one under par. On the tenth, Snead went into the lead by holing a sixty-five-foot chip from the back fringe of the green for a birdie. He gave that stroke back by bogeying the twelfth after hitting his tee shot into a bunker behind the green. He moved out in front again with a birdie on the thirteenth, getting home with a drive and a 2-iron. He went ahead by two strokes when Hogan three-putted the sixteenth. On the eighteenth, Snead put his approach shot into the bunker to the right of the green, but he played a superb recovery five feet from the hole. Knowing he would win if he got down in two for a 5, he took no chances. He bunted his first putt inches from the cup, and then tapped the ball in.

In contrast with Snead, Hogan had to work hard and long to become a champion. People who went to high school with him thought that he had a limited talent for golf, and they didn't know what to make of it when he turned professional at nineteen, in 1931. The compact, functional, glistening swing that Hogan at length devised was the product of countless hours of cerebration, experiment, and practice. No one has ever devoted himself more assiduously to mastering a sport than Hogan did. What with his undeterrable concentration and his coolness under fire, it was small wonder that he was almost invincible during his best years. His first victory in the Masters, in 1951, is worth examining, because it brings out his aptitude for course management. The last of the leaders to go out in the final round, he played the front nine in 33, three under par. He learned at the turn that the other men in contention had not scored well and all he had to do to win was to play the second nine in even par, 36. That would beat the lowest total posted for the tournament, Robert (Skee) Riegel's 282. A good-sized gallery went out with Hogan on the last nine. A 36 didn't seem like too tall an order, but even a Hogan could run into trouble on those five hazardous water holes. Poker-faced and detached, as always, Hogan played two superb shots on the tenth, but he missed the short putt he had for his birdie. On the eleventh, he adhered to his practice of playing his approach shot away from the water hazard. The ball finished just to the right of the green, and he got down in a chip and a putt for his par. A routine par on the twelfth. On the thirteenth — one of two par 5s on the second nine, each of which can be reached with two big shots —

Hogan, after a solid drive, decided not to risk going for the green. He laid up short of the creek with a 6-iron, and then played a little wedge pitch about seven feet from the pin. He made the putt for his 4. On the fourteenth, a routine par. After a rather long drive on the fifteenth — the second par 5 — he chose to lay up short of the pond guarding the green. He played a nice wedge pitch, and was down in two putts for his par. A routine par on the sixteenth, and another on the seventeenth. On the eighteenth, the pin was set on the lower level of the terraced green, which slopes down-ward from back to front. From previous experience, Hogan was well aware that one should never be above the pin on that green. He deliberately played his approach a couple of yards short of the green. His crisp chip stopped four feet below the cup. He made the putt. He had a 35 on the nine, then, for a 68 and a total of 280, two shots below Riegel's. Many of the people in Hogan's gallery were a little disappointed with his golf on that last nine. They had been hoping for fireworks and had instead been treated to a ster-ling demonstration of how to stick with par by playing one well-executed shot after another. He made it all seem as easy as an-swering the phone.

When Hogan won his second Masters, in 1953, his control of the golf ball was even more astonishing than it had been two years before. In the course of his four rounds — 70, 69, 66, 69, for a record-setting total of 274 — he did not hit one really loose shot. His game was at its zenith that year. He went on to capture the U.S. Open and the British Open. No other golfer has won those three major events in the same year. He and Snead — both were born in 1912 — proved to be marvels of longevity. In the 1963 Masters, Snead, at fifty, finished only two strokes behind the winner, Jack Nicklaus. In the 1974 Masters, a month short of his sixty-second birthday, he finished only eight shots behind the winner, Gary Player, with rounds of 72, 72, 71, and 71. (I wonder if any other man that age has ever brought in a four-round total of 286 in a major tournament.) Snead continued to play in the Mas-ters until 1983, when, at seventy, he made his farewell appear-ance.

Hogan played in the Masters through 1967. On that last visit to Augusta, when he was fifty-four, he had a notable round on the third day. His play from tee to green was still sharp and consis-tent, but on the greens he now froze over the ball. It took him ten seconds or longer to take his putter back from the ball, and when he did the stroke was a terribly awkward one. It must have been a torment for him. (In his prime, Hogan did not hole many long putts, but he was a sound putter.) Anyhow, on that third round in 1967 he went out in even par. On the tenth, he planted his approach about five feet from the pin. He had a nasty downhill putt for his birdie but stroked the ball smoothly into the cup. This did something for him. He hit his tee shot so far on the eleventh that he broke his old rule and went for the green with his second. His 6-iron stopped a foot from the pin. On the twelfth, he holed from twelve feet for his third birdie in a row. He added another birdie on the thirteenth — on in two, and down in two. He saved his par on the fourteenth when he holed a touchy four-foot sidehiller. After a drive of only moderate length on the fifteenth, he tried to carry the pond in front of the green with a 4o-wood, and did. He got down in two putts for another birdie. Orthodox pars on the sixteenth and seventeenth. On the home hole, his 5-iron approach finished sixteen slippery feet past the pin, which was set on the lower terrace. He would have preferred to be below the pin, but he hit his try for his birdie with a confident stroke. The ball took the subtle break just right and fell into the middle of the cup. That gave him a 30 on the back side and a 66 for the round. The gallery packed around the green exploded with a tremendous salvo of appreciation, and Hogan, pleased by his performance, bobbed his head in response and smiled one of his rare broad smiles. The next day, after missing a couple of holeable putts early in the round, he was no longer in the race, and he eventually brought in a tired 77. Of course, it is his 30 on the second nine on the third round that lingers in one's memory.

One more thing about Hogan and the Masters: Since 1960, to entertain the patrons, it has been the practice for the field to compete in a tournament held on the nine-hole par-3 course on Wednesday, the day before the first round of the tournament. In previous years, a long-driving contest or a teaching clinic was generally held. However, in 1955, to mark the twentieth anniversary of Sarazen's double eagle, the field was asked to assemble on the fifteenth fairway, and each player was given two attempts to see how close he could come to getting the ball into the cup from about the same spot Sarazen had played from. Few of the pros expected Hogan to participate; he generally bypassed clinics and other such added attractions at tournaments. The two dozen or so golfers who preceded him in this contest had, with few exceptions, played rather ragged shots. Only a handful of shots had finished anyplace near the pin. When Hogan's name was called, a heavy silence fell. No one held him in more awe than his colleagues did. Hogan set himself up carefully before his first ball. He hit a nice low fade that landed on the front part of the green and finished about fifteen feet to the left of the flag. He then set himself up for his second shot, and hit an exact duplicate of the first. He shook his head a little and walked away.

The era of Arnold Palmer, the next distinct period in the history of the Masters, began in 1958, when he won the tournament for the first time. Palmer, who had turned professional at twenty-five, shortly after winning the 1954 U.S. Amateur championship, was certainly not an unknown quantity in 1958. In 1955, his first year on the P.G.A. tour, he had won the Canadian Open. The next year, he had won two tour events, and the year after that he had won four. In the 1958 Masters, Palmer shot a 68 on the third round to go into a tie for the lead with Snead. On the morning of the last round, I asked Bob Drum, a sportswriter for the Pittsburgh *Press*, if he thought Palmer had a chance to win the tournament. Palmer, the son of a club professional, comes from Latrobe, a town some thirty miles east of Pittsburgh, and Drum knew him and his golf game as well as anyone did. "I think Arnold can win today," Drum said. I asked him why he thought so. "Because all his life he's demonstrated an ability to win the tournaments he should win at that stage of his career," Drum replied. "As a young kid, he won the Western Pennsylvania Juniors three times. He had a good record in college golf at Wake Forest, and he won the Western Pennsylvania Amateur five years in a row. When it was time to see how he would stack up in national competition, he won the Amateur. He's had a pretty fair record on the pro tour. Yes, I think Arnold is about ready now to win something big, like the Masters." Drum hit it right on the nose. Palmer made a number of mistakes on his last round, a 73, but he won the tournament by a stroke. His eagle on the thirteenth may have been the difference. On his second shot — from a sidehill stance similar to Guldahl's in 1939 — he went down the shaft a little on his 3-wood. He met the ball squarely, and it rose in a low parabola. There was some draw on the shot, and it curved from right to left as it crossed the creek and landed comfortably on the green. The ball ended up hole-high, eighteen feet from the pin. His putt for the eagle was in all the way.

In 1959, Palmer won three tournaments on the tour and came close to winning the Masters again. Leading the field as he came to the short twelfth on the final round, he didn't allow enough for a deceptive wind puffing against him, and the ball splashed into Rae's Creek. He took a 6 on the hole, and the Masters suddenly became a free-for-all. (Art Wall won it.) It was a tough tournament to lose, but Palmer has a buoyant nature and snapped back quickly. He really arrived in 1960, when he won the Masters and seven other tournaments, many of them by pulling off miraculous shots down the stretch. His victory in the 1960 Masters was a perfect illustration of this. On the last round, with six holes to play, he was trailing Ken Venturi by a stroke. He missed the birdie he needed on both of the par 5s. On the par-4 seventeenth, however, he finally snagged it, holing for a 3 from twenty-seven feet. This put him in a position to win the tournament if he could birdie the eighteenth, a par 4, uphill all the way. He followed a well-placed drive with a great 6-iron. The ball landed hole-high two feet to the right of the pin, and the action on the ball set it twisting and twirling. It came to rest five feet to the left of the cup and a little below it. That 6-iron was one of the best shots ever played to the last green in a major tournament when the outcome was still to be decided. On his putt, Palmer aimed for the left corner of the cup. The ball broke to the right just a hair, and dived in. The gallery went wild. It was that year, at that Masters, that "Arnie's Army" was born. Thenceforth, wherever Palmer played, local regiments of his army sprang up to root their hero home.

What lay behind Palmer's enormous popularity? First, his galleries were attracted by the attacking style with which he played the game. He was not afraid to gamble, and three times out of four he pulled the shot off. He got into trouble quite often, because he was an arms-and-hands hitter who came through the ball with such velocity that he had to block out his shots a bit with his left arm to prevent his right hand from taking over and hooking the ball. Besides being an extremely strong and long hitter, he was a superlative putter. He holed many long, sinuous putts because he had complete confidence that if he missed them he would make the three-footer or four-footer coming back. Palmer brought Walter Hagen to mind in the way he could recover from seemingly impossible positions and, all in all, make a round of golf seem like an adventure. Like Hagen, he had the kind of personality that dramatized everything he did on the course. In other respects, though, he was the exact opposite of Hagen, the suave, pomaded, impeccably dressed internationalist. Palmer was a handsome, clean-cut, rugged, All-American type that people could easily identify with. He had a natural manner and an unusually mobile face, which expressed his thoughts and emotions vividly, and these traits enhanced the closeness the members of his army felt for him. People were charmed by his politeness and his patience. He was never too busy to autograph a book or a program. His coolness under pressure was the real thing. During a tournament round, he would walk over to a friend he had spotted in the gallery and begin a conversation. The friend would be as tight as a drum, fearful that he might be disturbing Palmer's concentration, but that was never the case. Palmer was the right man to be the dominant personality in golf at a time when it was enjoying a gigantic boom for several reasons — among them General Eisenhower's well-known fondness for the game, and the advent of color television and better coverage.

Between 1960 and 1964, Palmer won thirty-one tournaments, including three Masters, the U.S. Open (in 1960), and two British Opens (in 1961 and 1962). He did not win the Masters in 1961, although he was in an ideal position to do so. All he had to do was par the seventy-second hole to edge out Gary Player. He mis-hit his approach shot, though, and it hung out to the right and came down in the shallow bunker at the right of the green. Most people thought Palmer would still get his 4. He played a very bad sand shot, however. The ball carried too far, rolled over the green, and finished about twenty-five feet down the slope. When it took him three strokes to get down from there, he had presented the tournament to Player. Palmer did not let this bother him. He played first-rate golf that season, and the following spring he won his third Masters in typical Palmer fashion. On the fourth round, the chances of his winning looked bleak when he failed to birdie either the thirteenth or the fifteenth. The way things stood, he would have to pick up two birdies on the last three holes to tie for first place with Player, who was paired with him, and Dow Finsterwald, four groups ahead. On the short sixteenth, Palmer's 5-iron tee shot ended up in the fringe at the back-right corner of the green, about forty-five feet from the pin, which was positioned that day in the small tongue of the green that adjoins the pond on the left. Since the green slanted toward the pin, he played a soft pitching wedge. It looked as if he had hit the shot much too delicately, but the ball kept rolling and rolling, and on its last turn it fell into the cup. The shot itself and the ear-splitting roar his army sent up gave Palmer a discernible lift. He birdied the seventeenth, stopping an 8-iron pitch twelve feet from the pin and then holing the putt. Now that he had caught Player and Finsterwald, Palmer played the eighteenth conservatively, made sure of his par, and set up a three-man playoff. Finsterwald was never a factor in the playoff, but Player most certainly was. After the first nine holes, he held a three-stroke lead. Palmer then took off on one of his unstoppable charges. He birdied the tenth, the twelfth, the thirteenth, and the fourteenth. During that run, he made up seven strokes on Player and built up a four-stroke lead. That was it.

Two years later, in 1964, Palmer continued his mastery of the Masters in the even-numbered years, capturing the tournament for the fourth, and final, time. Many students of the game consider the golf that Palmer played in that tournament the best of his career, even a shade better than his performance at Troon, in Scotland, in the 1962 British Open, when he put together four almost impeccable rounds — 71, 69, 67, 69 — and won by six strokes. In the 1964 Masters, Palmer played rounds of 69, 68, 69, and 70, and again his margin of victory was six strokes. He showed us a different Palmer that April. When he needed distance, he still smashed the ball far down the broad fairways, but there was more restraint and more finesse to his shotmaking in general. On his approaches, in particular, he played well within himself. His irons did not come smoking into the greens full of fire, fury, and backspin. They dropped down as gently as snowflakes.

The next three years, Palmer was within striking distance of victory in each Masters, but he was destined not to win it again. His undoing — this was true not only at the Augusta National but wherever he played — was the loss of his putting stroke. He began to miss the three-footers and four-footers coming back. After that, as was inevitable, he could no longer go boldly for the long ones. Palmer is one celebrated champion who would rather play golf than do anything else, and everybody was delighted when he won the P.G.A. Seniors championship in 1980, the U.S. Seniors

championship in 1981, and a second P.G.A. Seniors this past winter. He has left quite a legacy. Wherever he plays, Arnie's Army,
its ranks only a little thinner, is still on hand, ready to swing into
action should the right moment arrive.

The age of Palmer interlocked with the next period of the Masters
— the years dominated by Jack Nicklaus. When Nicklaus teed up
at the Augusta National this past April, it marked his twenty-sixth
appearance in the Masters. Over that span, he has won the tournament a record five times — in 1963, 1965, 1966, 1972, and 1975.
Moreover, he has finished second or tied for second four times,
most recently in 1981. The Golden Bear has aged a little, but he is
still the worst man in golf to have chasing you if you are leading
the Masters on the final round. On the last eighteen holes, beginning in 1964, he has broken 70 ten times, closing with a 67, a 69, a
67, a 69, a 66, a 69, a 68, a 66, a 67, and a 69, in that order.

Each time that Nicklaus has won the Masters, the pattern of his
victory has been different. In 1963, he did it the hardest way
possible. It is exceedingly rare for the man who is the tournament
leader with nine holes to go, as Nicklaus was that year, to be able,
after being overtaken and passed, to come fighting back and win.
When Nicklaus stood on the thirteenth tee after bogeying the
twelfth, he had dropped one shot behind Sam Snead, who was
playing three holes in front of him. A moment later, Snead birdied
the fifteenth, boosting his lead to two shots. Nicklaus's composure in these circumstances was remarkable. He decided simply to
try to play the best golf he could — this might still see him
through. He reached the thirteenth in two, and birdied it. He did
not get his birdie on the fifteenth, but this wasn't fatal. Snead, he
learned, had bogeyed the sixteenth, so they were now tied for the
lead. That day, the flagstick on the sixteenth was positioned on
the narrow deck at the back-right corner of the green. Nicklaus
played a forceful, high 5-iron that sat down twelve feet from the
stick. He read his birdie putt to break a foot from right to left, and
it did. That was the winning shot.

In the 1965 Masters, after the first thirty-six holes Nicklaus was
in a three-way tie for the lead with Palmer and Player. He won the
tournament on the third round. Under ideal conditions — there
was only a slight breeze, and the fast greens still held well-struck
approach shots — Nicklaus posted a 64. This tied the record low
score for a Masters round, which Lloyd Mangrum had set a quar-

ter of a century earlier. It gave Nicklaus a five-stroke lead on the nearest man at the start of the final eighteen holes. Playing steady, judicious golf, he had a 69 — the lowest round of the day. This enabled him to set a new record total of 271 for the Masters. He also set a record winning margin of nine strokes — over Palmer and Player, who tied for second. Jones, in lauding Nicklaus for his four rounds of wonderful golf, said to the assembled spectators, "Jack is playing an entirely different game — a game I'm not even familiar with." What Jones was referring to was the colossal distance that Nicklaus was clouting the ball. On that round of 64, for example, he needed only a sand wedge for his second shot on the first hole, which measures 400 yards. In fact, on only five of the ten par 4s did he use more club than a sand wedge or a pitching wedge for his approach. He played a 6-iron on the 435-yard fifth, an 8-iron on the 485-yard tenth, another 8-iron on the 455-yard eleventh, a 7-iron on the 405-yard fourteenth, and an 8-iron on the 400-yard seventeenth. He birdied all four of the par 5s. He had to hole a long putt for his birdie on the 555-yard second, but he hit the green in two on the 535-yard eighth with a 3-iron, and got home with a 5-iron on both the 465-yard thirteenth and the 500-yard fifteenth. He birdied three of the four par 3s. It was an overwhelming performance because Nicklaus's accuracy was every bit as extraordinary as the power of his hitting.

The following April, Nicklaus became the first player to win two Masters championships back to back, when he defeated Tommy Jacobs and Gay Brewer in a three-way playoff. Nicklaus and Jacobs were very fortunate: Brewer had lost his chance for an outright victory when he missed a seven-footer on the seventy-second green. In the playoff, Brewer was not at his best, but Jacobs played a confident par round of 72. Nicklaus beat him by two strokes by holing three sizable putts: a twenty-foot downhiller to birdie the sixth, a twenty-five-footer to birdie the eleventh, and a fourteen-footer to match Jacobs' birdie on the fifteenth.

The dullest of Nicklaus's Masters victories was his fourth, which came in 1972. He led all the way. On his final round, he had a mediocre 74 — he made three bogeys on the second nine — but none of the contenders were able to take advantage of this lapse. He won by three strokes. On the other hand, Nicklaus's fifth victory in the Masters, in 1975, was assured only after what was perhaps the most stirring three-man battle in modern golf. As the last round got under way, Tom Weiskopf had taken over the lead with a 66 in the third round. He held a four-stroke margin over Johnny Miller, with whom he was paired in the final twosome. Miller, too, had caught fire in the third round, making six consecutive birdies on the front nine and finishing with a 65. Nicklaus, who started the last day only one stroke behind Weiskopf, was paired with Tom Watson, and they went off just before Weiskopf and Miller. Throughout the afternoon, Weiskopf, Miller, and Nicklaus played a succession of uncommonly brilliant shots. There was no sensing the probable outcome until the short sixteenth, where the pin was once again positioned in the back-right corner. Nicklaus, after a rather ordinary iron shot to the left-center of the green, knocked in a sweeping uphill putt of forty feet for a 2. It wasn't all over, though. Miller birdied the seventeenth, and both he and Weiskopf came to the home hole needing a birdie to tie Nicklaus. Both of them were on the green in two and had possible birdie putts — Weiskopf's was only seven feet away, past the cup. Miller made a good bid for his, and then Weiskopf hit a fine putt that hung on the right lip of the cup. It was a hard tournament to lose. Miller, by the way, had followed his 65 in the third round with a 66.

On the eve of the recent Masters, it was surprising how many people thought that Nicklaus, at the age of forty-four, had as good a chance of winning as Tom Watson and Severiano (Seve) Ballesteros, of Spain, his logical successors. Nicklaus's fans are an extremely loyal contingent. They were quick to point out how close he had come to winning the P.G.A. championship last summer and how well he has played this winter. (He was third in the Los Angeles Open, at Riviera, and second in the Doral-Eastern Open, in Miami.) They conceded that the eight years he had gone without a victory in the Masters was a long time, but they pointed out that he had been very much in contention in 1976, 1977, 1978, 1979, and 1981. Everyone in golf knows one thing for certain: Nicklaus would like to win one more major tournament and bring his total of major victories to twenty — a nice round number. This, of course, would make it infinitely easier for him to retire from tournament competition whenever he believes that he can no longer keep in step with the best young players.

As it turned out, Nicklaus, although discernibly not in top form, acquitted himself well in the Masters. Through skillful course management, he brought in rounds of 73, 73, 70, and 70, for a total of 286, two under par. He was never in the running, however, for from the outset the scoring in this Masters ran unusually low. For example, on Thursday evening, at the close of the first day's play, over half the field of eighty-eight golfers had shot rounds of 73 or lower. This came as a surprise to many of us, for the greens at the Augusta National were as glossy and fast as any I have ever seen in this country, except, perhaps, the greens at Pebble Beach on the fourth round of the 1972 U.S. Open. The players were frequently forced to putt defensively: if they were faced with, say, a twenty-foot sidehill putt, they cast aside any notion of trying to hole the ball, and concentrated on rolling it slowly just below the line of the break so that it would come to rest a couple of feet below the cup. (Even on a relative tap-in, it is much easier to hole an uphill putt than a downhill putt.) Though the greens putted very fast, an overabundance of rain had made them as soft as puddings, and they were more holding than they had ever been before in the Masters. Most greens, even those that are generally described as flat, tend to slope to some degree from back to front, and during this Masters — particularly on the first day but also throughout the tournament — the players had no trouble stopping their approach shots; in fact, the trouble was quite the reverse. The ball would make such an indentation in the green when it landed that it would often spin back ten or fifteen feet, and — when the terrain happened to encourage this — would keep rolling until it trickled off the green and was finally stopped by the higher grass of the fairway. Incidentally, the fairways at the Augusta National were just about perfect this year. There was more grass on them than I could ever recall, so that the ball sat up as if it were on a hairbrush, and this contributed to the exceptionally fine iron play throughout the tournament.

The leader after the first round was Ben Crenshaw, with a splendid 67, made up of thirteen pars and five birdies. Long recognized as one of the most gifted putters of our day — as well as one of its most wayward drivers — Crenshaw had played a most un-Crenshavian round: he had missed hitting only one green, the tenth, in the regulation number of strokes. He had driven the ball so straight and had hit his irons so accurately that he had set people to wondering if this could possibly be the year when Crenshaw would finally win a major tournament. When Crenshaw turned professional, in the autumn of 1973, prodigious things were expected of him. While at the University of Texas, he had won the national collegiate championship in 1971 and 1973, and in 1972 he had shared that title with his college teammate Tom Kite. He had made a lustrous début on the P.G.A. tour by winning the first event he entered, the 1973 San Antonio–Texas Open. In the years that followed, he established himself as one of the most genuinely admired young golf stars, but he never really fulfilled his promise. On several occasions, he had been in a position to win a major event, but, one way or another, it had always slipped out of his grasp. In the 1975 U.S. Open, at Medinah, west of Chicago, pars on the last two holes would have won the championship for him, but on the par-3 seventy-first he hit his 2-iron a shade too thin. The ball splashed into the water hazard before the green, and that was that. (Lou Graham defeated John Mahaffey in a playoff the next day.) In the 1976 Masters, he played four solid rounds, but his total of 279 was good enough only for a very remote second place, eight full strokes behind a fantastic performance by Raymond Floyd. Crenshaw is a regular commuter to the British Open. In 1979, when it was held at Royal Lytham and St. Annes, he was very much in the running on the last round until he took a disastrous double bogey on the seventy-first. (Ballesteros won.) Later that summer, he suffered his bitterest disappointment. After he and David Graham finished in a tie for the P.G.A. championship, at Oakland Hills, near Detroit, they went back onto the course to decide matters in a sudden-death playoff. On the first extra hole, Crenshaw seemed a certain winner, but Graham sank a twisting eighteen-foot putt to match Crenshaw's score. On the second extra hole, Graham had to make a ten-footer to stay alive, and did. Then, on the third extra hole, Graham won the championship with a brilliant birdie.

Crenshaw was able to put these dispiriting experiences behind him, and he continued to play good golf until 1982, when he apparently lost confidence in his swing. He was hitting the ball all over the place. His buddies on the tour (and off it) were only too eager to suggest remedies, with the result that total confusion set in. That summer, after missing the thirty-six-hole cut in the P.G.A. championship, Crenshaw left the tour and headed back to his home, in Austin, so down on himself that he didn't know whether he would be able to continue his career in professional golf.

For a person like Crenshaw, this was a much more grievous

prospect than for most professional golfers, because for him golf is much more than a way to earn fame and fortune. His father, a lawyer who was a scratch golfer at the Country Club of Austin, introduced him to the game when he was a young boy, and his progress was superintended by the club's greatly respected teaching professional, Harvey Penick. (Penick also brought along Tom Kite, the son of another member of the club.) Crenshaw early developed an intense enthusiasm for the other facets of golf besides the pleasure of playing it. He began to read every book he could find that touched on the game's fascinating past. Since he has never stopped reading and rereading the books he has assembled in his large golf library, I would say, without qualification, that he knows more about the history of golf than anybody else of my acquaintance. He is also an able writer, though up to now he has limited himself to prefaces for other writers' books, to instruction articles in golf magazines, and to essays for tournament programs. He is a keen, perceptive student of the golf swing. An active member of the Golf Collectors' Society and the United States Golf Association's Museum Committee, he is also, among other things, a connoisseur of golf art, and he recently put together a selection of his favorite golf paintings, which have been reproduced and put on sale under the aegis of the Nelson Rockefeller Collection. Crenshaw's passion for golf has caused him to go well out of his way to visit both famous and not so well-known courses that happen to be in the general vicinity of a course where he is playing a tournament. He is fascinated by golf-course architecture. In the summer of 1981, when he led a tour of golf aficionados to some of the historic championship courses of Scotland and England, he was not content to break for lunch after the group had played a round at Muirfield one morning. He suggested that they first go with him to North Berwick, an ancient course nearby, and there he walked the members of the tour out onto the links to study two of his favorite holes — the fourteenth (which is called Perfection) and the fifteenth (which is the original Redan). Then the party went to lunch. There is no doubt at all in Crenshaw's mind that when his playing days are over he will devote himself primarily to golf-course architecture. He will most likely be the type of golf-course architect who limits himself to working on only one or two courses at a time, so that he can personally supervise the many small but important touches that separate a fine golf hole from a trite one. Knowing all this about Crenshaw, one can easily understand the depth of his depression when he went home to Austin to think things out.

After a few weeks pondering his options, Crenshaw reached what turned out to be a remarkably sound decision. He chose to seek the assistance of his first teacher. Harvey Penick, then well into his seventies, had been made the professional emeritus at the Country Club of Austin, where he could usually be found most weekdays at the practice tee, giving lessons. He understood exactly how Crenshaw felt about the decline of his golf game, and made it clear that he would be very happy to help him all he could. He scrutinized Crenshaw's swing closely as he hit out dozens of balls on the practice range. At length, he gave Crenshaw this advice: "Every golfer must use the swing that is natural for him. There is nothing wrong essentially with your natural swing. It's a very good one." Penick told Crenshaw that he might benefit if he played the ball a little farther forward at address, but other than that he advocated no changes. He advised Crenshaw to work on getting himself set up properly at the ball. "After that, I'd work principally on my balance and my rhythm," Penick said. "You'll do much better depending on your own natural swing than trying to build a synthetic swing made up of all those 'do's and all those 'don't's." Crenshaw worked diligently on the practice tee for a good many weeks. Every now and then, he and Penick would talk over certain phases of the swing they felt needed to be further clarified. He was soon hitting the ball much better and more consistently, and with renewed confidence.

In 1983, Crenshaw returned to the tour and enjoyed a very successful season. This year, prior to the Masters, he had continued to play well, and now, after the first round at Augusta, here he was in the lead. Would he be able to play three more first-class rounds? This concerned him and also his many friends, who think of him not just as a young man with Hollywood good looks and a nice golf game but as a very substantial person who possesses a quality that is most unusual for a celebrity: when you are with him, it is *he* who goes out of his way for *you*. In the press-interview room after his 67, he said, "This is by far my best opening round in the Masters. I've had some terrible ones, as you know. It was an aggressive round, and it was a comfortable round. I didn't make many mistakes. I missed only one green. What helped, too, was that I missed only two fairways off the tee, the first and the seventeenth." Someone asked him if he was using a new driver. "That's right," Crenshaw said. "It's an old M85W MacGregor — about as old as I am. It has a stiffer shaft than my old driver, and it has two degrees more loft — about ten degrees. I'm straighter with it but about fifteen yards shorter." He paused a moment, and then said, "Like many of the players on the tour, I'm always shopping around for clubs. I found this driver in a barrelful of old used clubs and classic clubs in Houston. It cost me three hundred dollars and a box of balls. I would have bought that driver regardless of price." Crenshaw talked a little about how rare it was to have greens that were so soft and yet putted so fast. At the end of the interview, he narrowed his eyes and said, in a more serious tone, "I've got a very good start. However, that's just the beginning of my job. My job here is a four-day job. My job is to shoot four rounds as low as I possibly can. I've got a lot of work to do. Basically, it's a matter of concentration."

Friday, the day of the second round, was sunny and humid. A light wind wandered over the course, making the selection of the right club for the shot to the green a bit more difficult. The greens still putted frighteningly fast, but they were a touch slower than on Thursday. They were still very soft, and this was the chief reason that the scoring in general continued to be low. When a talented golfer knows that he can go boldly for the pin on his approach shot and the ball isn't going to take off like a rabbit and bounce into some punishing hazard, this knowledge helps him to relax and execute his shots with superior timing. At the end of the second round, Mark Lye was out in front with a two-round total of 135, nine strokes under par. He had added a well-played 66 to his opening 69. Who is Mark Lye? Until I saw his lanky figure moving down the fairways with the wide, clumping strides one usually associates with farm boys — and particularly those who grow up to be relief pitchers — all I knew about Lye was that one winter he had had a hot stretch on the Australian tournament circuit. I consulted my copy of the 1984 *P.G.A. Tour Book* and learned from Lye's bio that he is a thirty-one-year-old Californian who had indeed carried off the Australian Order of Merit in 1976 but had never won a tournament on our P.G.A. tour until last summer, when he led the field in the Bank of Boston Classic. As I watched him belt enormous tee shots and hit some approaches right at the flag, I realized very clearly that the reasons the 36-hole cut had come at 146, a rather low figure, included not only the favorable scoring conditions, the great distances the present lively golf ball can be hit by the pros, and the new sophistication in golf-club design and manufacture but also the fact that the quality of the swings and the overall technique of the young, somewhat unknown players on the tour these days is of a much higher standard than many of us have appreciated. I suppose we have been tardy in recognizing this because we don't pay much attention to a player until he has won a couple of tournaments and demonstrated past any doubt that he can really play.

Besides Lye's round, there were four other rounds on the second day that deserve brief comment. Ballesteros, with a 74 after an opening 73, missed the cut by a stroke. Nicklaus, far off his best game, just got under the wire by finishing his second round, a 73, with three consecutive birdies. On the short sixteenth, he almost holed his tee shot; it stopped three inches from the pin. On the seventeenth, he cut his approach with an 8-iron a foot from the pin. And on the eighteenth he holed a fifty-foot chip from the front fringe. Watson, after a 74 on the first round, got back into the tournament on Friday with a 67, which included seven birdies and two bogeys. On this round, Watson hit the ball with more sharpness than he had all winter. As for Crenshaw, his second round was a 72, even par. He was displeased with it, because he had diminished the value of the five birdies he made with an equal number of careless errors, such as taking three putts on the eighteenth. As I was leaving the course that evening, a rabid Crenshaw rooter I know made a remark that proved to be prophetic. "Ben always seems to have one poor round in just about every tournament he plays," he said. "If that 72 turns out to be his poor round here, he'll have an awfully good chance of winning this thing."

Last year, as you may remember, the Masters was plagued by the worst weather in its history. Heavy rains washed out one full day of play, and, despite a heroic effort to get the tournament back on schedule by playing two rounds in one day, in the end the final round took place not on Sunday, as it usually does, but on Monday. This year, on Saturday, the day of the third round, heavy rains, complete with thunder and lightning and periods of hail, twice halted the golf. The first suspension of play came at two-thirty and lasted about an hour. Play was then resumed, and it continued until five-thirty, when another storm, very much like the first, hit the Augusta area and forced the suspension of the round for the day. The last twosome to go off, Lye and Kite, had got as far as the twelfth green when Hord Hardin, the Masters chairman, who had been in constant communication with the local weather station, announced the cessation of play. Hardin later stated that at 8 A.M. on Sunday the golfers who had not been able to complete the third round would resume play at the point where they had had to stop. With the forecast for Sunday calling for pleasant, dry weather, the fourth round was scheduled to get under way at 10:54 A.M.

Despite the rain and the hour-long break in play, the standard of the golf on Saturday was extremely high. Larry Nelson, the 1983 U.S. Open champion, shot a 66, which gave him a total of 211 — five under par — after fifty-four holes. He was definitely in the tournament now, and so was young Fred Couples, who had won the Tournament Players championship, two weeks before. Couples got around in 67, and also moved to five under par. Lye, who had started the third round nine under par, was still nine under and still in the lead when play was stopped. He had just put his tee shot on the green on the twelfth, the dangerous 155-yard par 3 on which Rae's Creek skirts the right and front sides of the slightly elevated green. Kite had started the round six under, but he had picked up two shots on par and now stood eight under for the tournament. His last shot had been an iron that safely carried the creek but caught the bunker cut into the front bank of the green. Crenshaw stood seven under par, through thirteen holes. Watson, his playing partner, had not putted out on the thirteenth. On that hole, Watson had played a daring second from the pine-needle-strewn ground at the high right side, where the fairway adjoins a long line of pines. The ball cleared the creek by only a few feet and rolled about fifteen feet past the pin, which was set at the front of the green, on the right side. If Watson holed that putt for an eagle on Sunday morning, he would move to seven under par for the tournament; if he got down in two, he would be six under. Three other players were in a contending position: David Graham, the transplanted Australian who had won the 1981 U.S. Open, stood at six under after completing twelve holes; Nick Faldo, a tall young Englishman who now plays long stretches of our P.G.A. tour, was five under, through twelve holes; and Larry Mize, a twenty-five-year-old native of Augusta, was five under, through fourteen holes.

On that rainy Saturday, I spent most of my time following Crenshaw and Watson. Both were scoring fairly well. Through twelve holes, Watson had compensated for two bogeys with four birdies. Crenshaw had played impressively steady golf. On the first nine, he had backed up seven pars with two birdies — one on the long second and the other on the ninth, where he holed out from a greenside bunker. He started back with two pars, and then ran into his first bogey of the round when it took him three shots to get down from about ten feet over the back of the twelfth green. While he and Watson were on the thirteenth, lightning flashed, and it began to rain — lightly, at first. According to the U.S.G.A. rules of golf, at the first sight of lightning a golfer can stop play. In 1975, in the Western Open at the Butler National Golf Club, not far from Chicago, it was demonstrated beyond dispute that lightning is a serious danger on a golf course. During the second round of that tournament, Lee Trevino, Bobby Nichols, and Jerry Heard were felled by lightning. All three of them suffered severe back injuries. Trevino was later able to return to tournament golf after a successful back operation, but the careers of Nichols and Heard were virtually ended. A week earlier, in the U.S. Open at Medinah, Watson, who was due to start his round, had walked off the first tee when he saw a bolt of lightning strike not far away, and had headed for the locker room. Within a minute, lightning had struck very close to the course, and play was then officially suspended. The lightning on the third day of the Masters seemed more distant. Nevertheless, Watson, lying two on the thirteenth green about fifteen feet from the cup, followed his sensible custom and walked off the course. Play was suspended at about this time. Under the suspension-of-play rule, a golfer, if he so wishes, may exercise the option of completing the hole he is playing. Crenshaw did so. As he later explained, since he was on the green in two, some seventy feet past the pin, he did not want his first shot the next morning to be a very long putt on a green that was bound to be quite different in speed. He thought he would have a much better chance of getting down in two from seventy feet in the light rain, because he knew how the greens were playing that afternoon and, also, he had the feel of his putting stroke. He rolled his long approach putt close to the cup and made the short putt for a 4. I am sure that ending the unfinished round with a birdie on the thirteenth rather than with a bogey on the twelfth put Crenshaw in a more peaceful and happy frame of mind that night.

*

Sunday dawned clear and dry, and the Augusta National's course-maintenance crew had got the eighteen holes in A-1 shape by eight o'clock, when the third round was resumed. At the conclusion of that round, we had a new leader. Kite, after birdieing the fifteenth and eighteenth, had a 69 for the round. His three-round total of 207 — nine under par — put him a stroke in front of Lye, who had taken a 73, and two strokes in front of Crenshaw, Faldo, and Graham, each of whom had scored a 70 on the interrupted round. Watson was a stroke farther back, at 210, after a 69. (He had missed his try for an eagle on the thirteenth.) Nelson, Couples, and Rex Caldwell were five under par for the tournament. Shortly after eleven o'clock, when the fourth round began, the leaders, as is customary, were the last to go out. Nelson was paired with Couples, Graham with Watson, Crenshaw with Faldo, and Kite with Lye.

Crenshaw won the Masters by playing the best golf of any of the leaders — a 68 that was highlighted by his self-possession under the inevitable stress of a major tournament and was helped considerably by some remarkable putting, the part of the game he is noted for. He had a standard par on the first: on in two and down in two. He picked up a birdie on the long second when he stopped a little sand-wedge pitch a foot from the hole. Standard pars on the third, the short fourth, the fifth, and the short sixth. On the seventh, a 360-yard par 4 to a plateau green surrounded by bunkers, he got a good break: he cut his tee shot into the pines on the right, but his ball ended up in casual water, and he was permitted a free lift and drop. He then cut a pretty 7-iron pitch nine feet from the flag but missed the birdie putt. Now he entered what proved to be the crucial stretch of the last round for him. On the long, hilly eighth, he lobbed his third shot, a pitching wedge, nine feet from the pin and made the birdie putt. This put him in a tie for the lead with Kite, his friendly rival from Austin and the University of Texas. Crenshaw took the undisputed lead in the tournament on the ninth, a swaybacked 435-yard par 4. Here he put his approach, a 6-iron, ten feet from the cup and holed the birdie putt, which broke to the left. He coped well with the tenth, the beautiful par 4 whose green is set in a grove of tall pines. After splitting the fairway with his best drive of the day, he did not assess his distance to the pin correctly, and his 4-iron approach came down and stopped at the front of the green, about sixty feet from the hole. He rolled in that long, swinging putt for his third consecutive birdie. This gave him a two-shot lead over Kite, who was playing directly behind him, and over Nelson, two twosomes in front of him. Nelson, who had a hot round going, had just birdied the eleventh.

It is not an easy thing to be in the lead in an important tournament with eight holes to go — eight hazardous holes. Under the circumstances, Crenshaw's tactical decisions were exceptionally sound. On the par-4 eleventh, with its small pond guarding the left side and the front entrance of the cape-type green, Crenshaw chose not to go for the green on his second shot. Taking a page from Hogan's book, he played a 2-iron to the right of the green. With the pin set on the far left side, about ninety feet away, he had to be sure not to make too firm a chip, and he ended up by hitting a rather tentative one, which expired eighteen feet short of the hole. He was down in two putts, for his first bogey of the day. It must have made him feel a bit better to learn from the leader board that Nelson's rush had been stopped by a double-bogey 5 on the twelfth — his tee shot had fallen into Rae's Creek. At the same time, it must have been hard for Crenshaw to decide whether or not he should risk going for the pin on the twelfth. It was positioned, as it usually is on the last day of the Masters, at the back-right corner of a green that runs at a diagonal to the tee, rather like the hour hand of a watch at two o'clock. This, of course, is the most dangerous pin position on the hole. The player must hit a longer iron to clear the creek, and the ball must be hit sharply enough so that it will sit down quickly on a relatively small corner of the putting surface. I was still wondering whether Crenshaw would elect to go for the pin or play safely for the center of the green when he got set in his stance and, using a 6-iron, swung smoothly through the ball to a very high finish. The shot, on line all the way, carried the creek with yards to spare and stopped just about where it landed — twelve feet to the right of the flag. That brave shot may well have won the tournament for Crenshaw. He made the birdie putt, and now, with six holes to play, he led the closest contenders, Kite and Nelson, by three shots.

At that point in a tournament, the thing that the leader should do is to concentrate on playing one hole at a time. On the thirteenth, the famous par 5 that doglegs to the left in the landing area of the drive, Crenshaw hit a fine tee shot down the middle. He could have carried the creek in front of the green with a good 4-wood, but after thinking it over — and after noting that Kite had put his tee shot into the water on the twelfth — he chose to take the conservative route: he laid up short of the creek with a 5-iron, wedged his third twenty-five feet from the hole, and was down in two putts for his par. He didn't play the fourteenth well. His drive bounded into the left rough, and he yanked a 6-iron to the left edge of the slick, wide green, which is full of tricky breaks. He had a sixty-foot putt left and completely misread the speed of the green. His approach putt stopped twenty feet short of the hole. Then he made that twenty-footer for his par. On to the fifteenth, the 500-yard par 5, whose green is guarded in front by a small pond. Tactically, Crenshaw played it the same way he had the thirteenth. After a well-hit drive, he laid up short of the water hazard with a 6-iron and then lobbed a sand wedge fifteen feet from the flag. This time, though, he made the birdie putt. Now on to the last water hole, the 170-yard sixteenth. The pin was set near the front of the green. Crenshaw's main concern was to clear the large pond between the tee and the green. He hit a firm 5-iron thirty-five feet past the pin and onto the shelf at the back-right corner. He read the finicky downhill putt perfectly. He barely tapped the ball, and it kept on rolling and rolling, very slowly, until it eventually stopped close to the cup. He made the short putt for his 3. He later said that when he walked to the tee of the par-4 seventeenth he had the feeling that he should be able to win the tournament. After all, he now held a four-stroke lead on the nearest man, and he felt fairly sure that he could prevent himself from losing more than two strokes to par on the last two holes.

On the seventeenth, after a good drive, he hooked a 7-iron to the back fringe of the green, made a bad chip with a sand wedge which went twenty-five feet past the pin, and took two putts for a bogey 5. Simultaneously, Watson had holed a breaking downhill putt of about sixteen feet to birdie the eighteenth — a fitting climax to a well-played 69. This meant that Crenshaw, in order to win, could take no more than a 5 on the eighteenth, a 405-yard par 4 that runs uphill. He used a 3-wood off the tee — to make sure that his tee shot would not be long enough to reach the bunker on the left some 250 yards out — and faded the shot nicely into the center of the fairway. The pin was placed that day on the left side of the lower terrace. The huge gallery thickly lining the fairway and the green was still discussing how Crenshaw might choose to play his approach shot when, with little ado, he hit a soaring 5-

iron that landed in the middle of the lower terrace and finished about twenty feet beyond and to the right of the pin. Crenshaw walked up the fairway, his face aglow with a wide smile as he acknowledged the loud applause of the gallery. I wondered at the time if he really knew what was happening — that he was actually going to win the Masters, that this was reality, and not one of those dreams that all golfers of the top level have of walking up the eighteenth fairway at Augusta as thousands cheer. (Crenshaw later acknowledged that, for some reason, as he climbed the hill to the home green he thought about his high-school golf team.) However, when he studied his downhill, sidehill putt — it broke from right to left — it was obvious that he now knew precisely what remained to be done and was in full command of the situation. He hit exactly the right kind of putt. He purposely played it for the "amateur's side" of the cup — in this case, a shade to the left of the line — so that the ball would not pick up too much momentum but would end up just below the cup, leaving him a short uphill putt of two feet or so. He holed it smoothly. The man who everyone in golf had been hoping for years would win a major championship — his fellow-professionals, golf fans and golf organizations around the world, the golf press and the veteran golf telecasters, and, of course, golfers old and young — had finally pulled it off. How superbly he had played in achieving this: 67-72-70-68 — 277, on a very testing course! And how appropriate it was that a golfer in the mold of Jones should win the Masters on the fiftieth anniversary of its founding!

The victor in the Masters goes through two presentation ceremonies. The first one, presided over by the Masters chairman in a television studio in the basement of the Butler cabin, brings the telecast of the tournament to an intimate close. The second ceremony, at which the Masters chairman again presides, takes place on the spacious practice green, which is ringed by thousands of spectators. The low amateur is cited for his performance, and then comes the pièce de résistance: the presentation of the green Augusta National jacket to the winner, and his response. Then the winner is driven by golf cart to the media-interview building. In recent years, I have skipped the ceremony on the practice green, knowing that the press interview was on tap, but this year I attended it, for the sheer pleasure of seeing Crenshaw helped into his green jacket by Ballesteros, last year's winner. At many moments during the tournament, I had wondered whether Crenshaw would seize the opportunity before him and go on to win this Masters, or whether he was fated to be another Bonnie Prince Charlie, and never win a major title. No need to worry about that anymore. Crenshaw the historian had earned a permanent place in golf history.

Crenshaw's half-hour session with the press was warm and informal. At the same time, he had some interesting and thoughtful things to say. Here are a few of them:

"I must admit that as I came up the fairway on the eighteenth I had a feeling of relief more than anything else. I was relieved that I had not let my supporters down. I had put a lot of pressure on myself to win an important tournament. Today was my day. I was determined not to let shots slip away, and to hit the fairways and the greens. . . .

"The two people I have to thank most are my father and Harvey Penick, my teacher and a great gentleman. I must also mention Jack Burke. He gave me a pep talk today. 'Think fairways and greens,' he told me. 'Just put the ball on the fairways and greens.' He made me believe in that. During my round, I emphasized setting up well at the ball and then swinging with good timing. You can think of only one thing during your swing. Jones said that, you know. . . .

"Good night! Golf must be the hardest game in the world. I *know* it is. . . .

"That long putt for a birdie on the tenth helped me a lot. It must have been about sixty feet, and it broke left about eight feet. I should mention that my caddie, Carl Jackson, read that putt perfectly. Carl has caddied for me in the Masters eight years. My regular tour caddie doesn't read greens. These greens, I think, are the hardest greens to read in the world. . . .

"Until I bogeyed the eleventh, I had really played solid golf today. Darn, I was proud of that 6-iron I hit on the twelfth. I was determined to make that putt, because I'd just made a bogey. On the thirteenth, after my drive I had a 4-wood to the green. It was only two hundred and thirty yards away. Then I started studying the leader board, and when I saw the double bogeys some of the other guys were making on the water holes I thought of laying up and making sure of my par. . . .

"I began to think I had a good chance to win after that slippery downhill putt I hit on sixteen had just the right pace. I didn't play the seventeenth well, but I felt good on the eighteenth. I love this course that Bobby Jones designed, and I love this tournament that he and Mr. Roberts started. It should always be preserved. It stands for dignity."

At the end of the interview, we all went back to our places in the press room, and there we continued to express our delight in this happy occasion. Many discerning remarks were made, but I think that Renton Laidlaw, of the London *Standard*, expressed our sentiments best when he said, "This is a great victory for golf."

(1984)

St. Andrews and
the British Open

Whenever the British Open — the Open, as the British refer to it — is held in St. Andrews, it is an occasion. The town itself has such extraordinary charm that a visitor doesn't have to be a golfer to enjoy it. For the golfer, it is heaven. Golf has been played over its tumbling linksland since about the year 1100. The famous Old Course is now about a hundred and fifty years old, but when a breeze is stirring the gorse, it still presents the world's best golfers with a formidable challenge. Behind the first tee stands the august clubhouse of the Royal and Ancient Golf Club of St. Andrews, the governing body for all golf-playing countries in the world except the United States. Three other courses lie close to the Old Course, as do several public putting greens. In St. Andrews the spirit of golf fills the air as nowhere else. To be in the old gray town when a crackling good Open is being played — what more can one ask?

TO JUDGE FROM THE FREQUENCY WITH WHICH FRAMED PRINTS OF it appear on the walls of the offices and studies of devoted golfers throughout the world, the most popular piece of golf art ever created may well be the map of the Old Course at St. Andrews, in Scotland, which was "surveyed and depicted" in 1924 by Alister MacKenzie, the British golf-course architect. MacKenzie's map was produced and sold to the public by W. C. Henderson & Son, Ltd., the University Press, St. Andrews. The map is remarkable for its accuracy and detail. The undulations of the linksland are carefully noted, and so are the stretches of gorse — or whins, as the Scots call the prickly bush — that edge many of the fairways. The names of the most celebrated of the numerous sand bunkers that have so much to do with the strategy and character of the holes are printed legibly on the map. The bunkers are a vivid white, the fairways a pale green, and the greens a darker shade of green, while St. Andrews Bay is a soft ochre. The card of the course — the yardage of each of the eighteen holes — is set in a box at the top left corner. When MacKenzie drew his map, the Old Course was the most famous golf course in the world and had been for roughly a century. His map was so evocative of the singular test presented by the Old Course that golfers from all over who had played there and those who hoped to enjoy that experience in the future made sure to acquire it in order to be able to commune with it on a steady basis. As for MacKenzie, the year after he executed the map — a gesture expressing his immense admiration for the course — he left Britain, where he had designed such excellent courses as Alwoodly and Moortown, to pursue his career overseas, mainly in Australia and the United States. His major triumph in Australia was the West Course of the Royal Melbourne club. In this country, he laid out a dozen or so fine courses, including the two at the Ohio State University golf club; Crystal Downs, in Michigan; and dazzling Cypress Point, on the Monterey Peninsula, in California, which was completed in 1928. When Bobby Jones, having retired from competitive golf in 1930, following his Grand Slam of the British and United States Amateur and Open championships, turned his attention to building his dream course — the Augusta National, in Augusta, Georgia — he asked MacKenzie to serve as his co-designer. One reason Jones selected MacKenzie was that Cypress Point had made a deep impression on him, but, as a fervent admirer himself of the Old Course, he had been a fan of MacKenzie's from the day he first set eyes on the superb map of St. Andrews.

The town of St. Andrews (present population: just over eleven thousand) edges into the North Sea at the tip of the Fife Peninsula, between the Firth of Forth, to the south, and the Firth of Tay, to the north. The town itself sits on top of a rocky plateau that falls gently downhill to the Old Course, which occupies a sweep of linksland running north along the shallow curve of St. Andrews Bay to the mouth of the Eden River. As the crow flies, St. Andrews is only thirty miles from Edinburgh. Since 1964, when a bridge for motor traffic across the Firth of Forth was completed, the touring golfer on a tight schedule has been able to breakfast in Edinburgh, drive to St. Andrews for a round on the Old Course, get in a pleasant stroll around the town, and return to Edinburgh in plenty of time for dinner and some entertainment in the capital city. (Close by the motorway bridge stands the Michelangelesque railroad bridge that spans the firth. A mile long, its tracks a hundred and fifty-seven feet above the inlet, it was considered a marvel of engineering when it was finished, in 1890, seven years after work on it began. Whenever an old-movie buff takes in this gigantic, muscular structure, his thoughts invariably go back to *The 39 Steps*, Alfred Hitchcock's first great success, and to the theatrics aboard the train on which Robert Donat and Madeleine Carroll were crossing the firth.) For the golf enthusiast who is making his first visit to the Old Course and has a malleable schedule, perhaps the best time to arrive in St. Andrews is around six o'clock on a summer's evening, when the sun is streaming across the links and turning everything to gold. At this hour, there are many golfers still out on the course, and there will be until darkness falls. On such a long, lingering evening, the weather-beaten sandstone clubhouse of the Royal and Ancient Golf Club of St. Andrews looms sturdier and more regal than it does on any official R. & A. Christmas card. Beyond the clubhouse, nearer the bay, the vast eighteen-hole municipal putting green on the Bruce Embankment is filled to capacity with residents of the town, ranging from tots scarcely as tall as a putter to perky octogenarians. Everybody is totally absorbed in his match. The fee for a round is thirty British pence — about forty cents. A little north of the embankment is the three-acre green of the Ladies' Putting Club, a private club, established in 1867, which is now composed of a hundred and forty members and approximately thirty gentleman associate members. They all pay annual dues of five pounds. Because of its fanciful undulations, the green is referred to by the members as the Himalayas. In good weather, they are out in force, full of merriment.

For the visitor fortunate enough to hit St. Andrews on such an evening, this glistening, animated scene is almost too good to be true: the storied "cradle of golf" has turned out to be all that he hoped for and much more. Whenever the British Open is played at St. Andrews it is a special event, and unusually large galleries turn out. They did in 1873, 1876, 1879, 1882, 1885, 1888, 1891, 1895, 1900, 1905, 1910, 1921, 1927, 1933, 1939, 1946, 1955, 1957, 1960, 1964, 1970, and 1978, and again in July, when the championship was held on the Old Course for the twenty-third time. An average of more than thirty-six thousand spectators were on hand daily to watch an exciting tournament, which Severiano (Seve) Ballesteros, of Spain, won by summoning his best golf down the stretch and edging out Tom Watson, the defending champion, and Bernhard Langer, of West Germany, by two strokes.

How old is the Old Course? The late Sir Guy Campbell, a longtime St. Andrean who was a soldier by profession and a first-rate golf-course architect and golf historian as well, was of the opinion that a rude form of golf probably started being played at St. Andrews around the year 1100, and that by 1411, when the University of St. Andrews was founded, an elementary version of the Old Course was in existence. Along with other old Scottish towns on the North Sea, from Dornoch, in the north, to North Berwick, in the south, St. Andrews was a target of the well-known act of the Scottish Parliament promulgated in 1457, during the reign of King James II, which provided that "the Fute-ball and Golfe be utterly cryit doune, and nocht usit." England and Scotland were old ene-mies, and the Parliament did not want the country's young men to neglect their archery practice and fritter their hours away on pas-times that had no military worth. The first written evidence specifi-cally connecting St. Andrews with golf was a covenant issued in 1552 by the provost and bailies of the town permitting Archbishop Hamilton to raise rabbits on the north end of the links and grant-ing to the townspeople the right to use the links for drying their fishing nets, bleaching their linen, and pursuing such recreations as shooting, football, and golf. Nature was the architect of the Old Course. The linksland that the course was built on — indeed, the linksland that all the renowned Scottish, English, and Irish courses were built on — was a stretch of sand that had been washed up by the sea as it slowly receded over the centuries. Strong winds tossed the sand into gently rolling duneland, which was accented by fancifully shaped knolls interlaced with gullies, sharp declivities, hollows and whorls of all shapes, and small plateaus along with others of considerable extent. Birds pausing on the linksland fertilized the silt that streams deposited on their way to the sea. "Thus eventually," as Sir Guy Campbell wrote in a notable essay some thirty years ago, "the whole of these areas became grass-covered, from the coarse marram on the exposed dunes, ridges and hillocks, and the finer bents and fescues in the sheltered dunes, gullies and hollows, to the meadow grasses round and about the river estuaries and the mouths of the streams and burns. Out of the spreading and intermingling of all these grasses which followed was established the thick, close-growing, hard-wearing sward that is such a feature of true links turf wherever it is found."

Sir Guy goes on to describe in a brilliant passage how heather, whins, and other shrubs sprouted on the links and attracted animal life; how the rabbits, in particular, multiplied, and attracted foxes to their warrens; and how man, in turn, came down to the linksland to hunt the foxes, tramping the tall grass down into paths and wide, walkable "rides." Generations after this, when the Scots were looking for grounds on which to play the new game of golf — which may or may not have been suggested by the Dutch game called *kolven* — they wisely recognized that the linksland was the perfect place. In the beginning, golf was a point-to-point game: the golfers began at a starting point and tried to reach an established point a good distance away in the fewest number of strokes; then they played back to the starting point. They gradually learned how to control the ball in the wind, how to get increased roll on some shots by taking advantage of the downhill and sidehill slopes, and how to stay away from such calamitous hazards as burns, thickets, and sand bunkers. Many of the sand bunkers were dug by the sheep that huddled together behind high dunes to shelter themselves from the piercing winds off the sea. Other sand bunkers had a more banal genesis. On some holes, because of the undulation of the land, a high proportion of the golfers' tee shots ended up in natural gathering spots at the base of a slope or several slopes. As was inevitable with so many players hacking away in these spots on their second shots, the turf there became sparser and sparser. More often than not, these scrapes — as they came to be called — ended up as areas of exposed sand, indented by only a finger or two of thin turf. When the people charged with maintaining the links in good condition decided that reseeding such scrapes was not a sensible solution, they generally converted them into permanent hazards — clearly defined sand bunkers.

Golf in time developed from a point-to-point game into a game made up of a number of separate holes. At St. Andrews, this may have taken place as early as the fifteenth century. On the Old Course and the other early Scottish courses, the flatter areas of the tumbling land were used for the tees and greens. On whichever course the pioneering Scottish golfers learned the game, they soon came to understand that a basic reason they were so mad about golf was that a player had to think well in order to score well. The trick was to stay out of the hazards. The more talented the golfer, the more consistently he evaded them as he tacked his way — very much like a sailor — down the fairway from tee to green. These early golfers, both the silky swingers and the duffers, could not explain precisely why golf was so bewitching, but they sensed that it had something to do with the happy circumstance that it was played over natural terrain. Much later on — in the second half of the nineteenth century, when golf swept south of the Scottish border and, ultimately, all over the world — courses began to be constructed, not simply discovered. It became commonplace to move large quantities of earth in order to create tees, fairways, greens, and hazards that resembled those on the most respected Scottish courses. Underlying the charm of golf, whether one is tackling the Old Course at St. Andrews or some spanking-new American eighteen-hole layout, is the fundamental fact that the game is the only one played either on natural terrain or on ground molded at great expense into gently rolling land that resembles natural terrain. It is astounding how ideal the features of the linksland at St. Andrews happened to be for developing the skills and finesse that make golf such an alluring and addictive game.

The Old Course originally consisted of twenty-two holes. Like many of the first courses, it was routed so that the holes going out marched away from town in a relatively straight line and the holes coming in marched back in much the same pattern. One of the singularities of the Old Course was the narrowness of the fairways. In the beginning, they were only about forty yards wide. They were hemmed in on the west by the arable land along the Eden River, and on the east, shutting out the sight of the sea, there rose a succession of humpy sand hills crusted with bushes. Because of this extreme tightness, the outgoing holes, bordered on the right by the sand hills, were forced to share fairways and greens with the incoming holes. Another singularity of the Old Course was its shape: it looked like a serpent, or like a knobby walking stick with a curved handle. As the outgoing holes neared the mouth of the Eden, four holes performed a loop, twisting to the east and south and then swinging to the northwest. The loop completed, the holes headed back to town in staid single file. In 1764, ten years after "twenty-two noblemen and gentlemen" founded the Society of St. Andrews Golfers, the Old Course underwent a historic change. The first four holes were deemed too short and were replaced by two stronger holes, and the last four holes were similarly converted into two holes. St. Andrews became an eighteen-hole course. (The loop was composed of the eighth, ninth, tenth, and eleventh holes, and it still is.) In those faraway days, the number of holes on a golf course varied from course to course. The links of Leith, at the north edge of Edinburgh, had only five holes. Musselburgh, seven miles east of Edinburgh, had seven. Montrose, south of Aberdeen, had twenty-five. By the beginning of the nineteenth century, well before King William IV, in 1834, permitted the Society of St. Andrews Golfers to style itself the Royal and Ancient Golf Club and shortly afterward agreed to become its patron, St. Andrews had come to be looked upon by the other Scottish golf clubs as the game's rules-making and governing body, and its eminence was such that newly founded clubs almost automatically followed St. Andrews' example and built eighteen-hole courses.

Between 1840 and 1850, the Old Course started to take on the dimensions of the course we know today. The fairway land was widened to between ninety and a hundred yards. This allowed each hole to have a fairway of its own, so to speak: the golfers used the east side of the fairway going out, the west side coming in. Most of the greens were enlarged into mammoth double greens, almost the width of the fairways. On the first nine, the hole was cut on the east side of the green, and on the second nine another hole was cut on the west side of the green. Altogether, there are seven of these monstrous double greens at St. Andrews. Two holes on the first nine, the first and the ninth, have greens of their own, as do two holes on the second nine, the seventeenth and the eighteenth. The double greens are unique to the Old Course. The largest one, which serves the fifth and thirteenth holes, is about an acre in size. Bobby Jones once birdied the fifth by rolling in a hundred-and-twenty-foot putt, and it is possible to be confronted with putts more than twice that length. (On the greens, a golfer must also be prepared to cope with undulations so abrupt and severe that if, say, a member of his foursome were to lie down on the far side of an especially steep rise in the golfer's line to the cup at the moment when the golfer turned his head away to get his putter from his caddie, the golfer wouldn't be able to see the stretched-out body as he studied his line, addressed his ball, and stroked it.) By mid-century, the widened fairways and the double greens had become a necessity at St. Andrews. In 1848, the gutta-percha golf ball had begun to replace the old feathery — a ball made from a top-hatful of boiled feathers stuffed into a leather cover and pounded into shape. The gutty was cheaper than the feathery and lasted longer. It was also easier for the average golfer to hit, and when he hit it squarely it went farther. The advent of the gutty occasioned the first big boom in golf's popularity. Droves of new players took to the links, even in the old homes of golf like St. Andrews. On the wings of the gutta-percha ball, golf spread through England, most of Europe, the United States, and, of course, Canada and the other British Commonwealth nations, where failure of the local gentry to construct a sporty layout posthaste was equivalent to their giving up afternoon tea and virtually going native.

As golf took root around the globe, the R. & A., because of the continuing zeal of its members and the quality of the Old Course, came to be held in such awe and esteem that many of the new aficionados were shocked to learn that it was not the oldest golf club in the world. That distinction belonged to the Honourable Company of Edinburgh Golfers, which was founded at Leith in 1744, ten years before the Society of St. Andrews Golfers came into being. Furthermore, the Honourable Company was responsible for the first code of golf rules — thirteen rules, set down in 1744, which combined sense and clarity so effectively that the founders of St. Andrews adopted the code with only minimal changes. In 1854, its centennial year, the R. & A. nailed down once and for all its position as the game's legislative authority when it issued a recodification, consisting of twenty-two rules, and discovered that all the other golf clubs accepted it as instructions from Olympus. Today, only one national golf association does not recognize the R. & A. as the game's top governing body. That is the United States Golf Association. In December of 1894, six years after the first permanent golf club in this country came into existence — naturally, it called itself St. Andrew's — five of the leading American clubs, upset by the bickering about rules that had turned our attempts to hold a national amateur championship that summer and autumn into one long squabble, sent emissaries to a meeting in New York City, at which the U.S.G.A. was formed. Over the years, the U.S.G.A. and the R. & A. have differed on small points, but generally they have got along very well. In 1951, they reached an agreement on a unified set of rules.

The only thing that is different in the realms of the two organizations is the size of the ball. Our ball is 1.68 inches in diameter and weighs 1.68 ounces. The British ball also weighs 1.68 ounces, but it is only 1.62 inches in diameter. The smaller ball, being denser, bores through the wind more successfully. Most golfers believe that in almost all other respects the American ball plays better, though there are some who think that the ball that meets the O.D.S. (Overall Distance Standard), which the U.S.G.A. adopted in 1976, can be hit so far by the top-level tournament players that it renders many of our old championship courses obsolete and promotes a type of golf that is not the best expression of the game. Interestingly, the British Professional Golfers' Association decided in 1968 that thereafter the American ball was to be used in all its tournaments. Since 1974, the R. & A. has required the entrants in the British Open, which it conducts, to play the American ball. Being more difficult to control in the wind, the American ball tends to safeguard the traditional shotmaking values of St. Andrews, and also of Muirfield (which since 1891 has been the home of the Honourable Company), Royal St. George's (in Kent), and the half-dozen other classic linksland courses on which the British Open is played.

The emergence of the R. & A. as the capital of the golf world, along with the enthronement of the Old Course as the game's premier test, could not have come at a more opportune time for the town of St. Andrews. Its beginnings — probably as a fishing village — are lost in the haze of antiquity. We do know that it was founded in the seventh century as a Celtic ecclesiastical settlement. Later on, it went through periods of soaring glory and desperate conflict which today seem incredible for a town set off by itself, far from the heart of Scotland. The key to this turmoil was the wide circulation of the legend that St. Regulus had carried to the town the relics of St. Andrew, the patron saint of the Picts and later of the Scottish nation. In the Middle Ages, aside from being a port that conducted a thriving trade with the Low Countries, St. Andrews was the headquarters of the Roman Catholic Church in Scotland. On its cliffed headland stood a magnificent Norman–Early Gothic cathedral, the largest in the country. When the Reformation broke out in Scotland, St. Andrews was at the center of the controversy and violence, of which a chief protagonist was the fiery John Knox, a former student at the university who had returned to the town as a preacher. Calm and order were finally restored, but at the very end of the sixteenth century and during much of the seventeenth St. Andrews was ravaged by plagues that killed off most of its inhabitants and left it little more than a ghost town. Its population in 1793 was a mere 2,854. It slowly made its way back in the nineteenth century, as a seaside resort noted for its salubrious air. There was something about the town that appealed to intellectuals. It was a favorite place for masters of prominent English public schools and universities to take groups of students on "reads" during the summer vacation. Writers as different in personality as Thomas Carlyle, Anthony Trollope, and Charles Kingsley were regular visitors, as were Sir Edwin Landseer, Sir John Millais, and other painters of the top order. It would be wrong, however, to play down the salient part that the ever-increasing reputation of St. Andrews as the cradle of golf played in the recovery of the "auld grey toun."

In time, St. Andrews became the mecca of golf. During the summer months, thousands of pilgrims from all over the world made their way to it. They loved the town itself — a nice, cheerful conjoining of the past and the present. With its three very wide main streets — South, Market, and North — and the stepped roofs of many of its buildings, it looks more like a Flemish town than a Scottish one. The handsome buildings of the university add immeasurably to its charm, and so do the students in their bright-red gowns — particularly the pretty young women. In St. Andrews, everyone knows golf and talks it. Approximately seventy-five percent of the residents play it. Most of the townspeople of wealth and position, along with the lairds from the Fife countryside, are members of the R. & A. As a rule, the businessmen and professional men of the town belong to the New Club, established in 1902; it has a small clubhouse on The Links, a narrow road that runs along the right-hand side of the eighteenth fairway. A hundred yards or so up the road is the equally unpretentious clubhouse of the St. Andrews Club, which was established in 1843 and, down through the years, has been the club of the artisans and tradesmen. On days when the Old Course is jammed — each year, over forty thousand rounds are played on it, a third of them by visitors who are delighted to pay the twelve-pound greens fee — the residents of St. Andrews have three other eighteen-hole courses at their disposal. The New Course, which was laid out in 1895 on reclaimed duneland adjoining the Old Course on the east, has some stretches of arresting terrain and, all in all, provides a fairly good examination in golf. The Jubilee Course lies east of the New, on even more recently reclaimed duneland. Its first twelve holes were opened in 1897, the year of Queen Victoria's Diamond Jubilee. The Jubilee has been revised at least twice since, but it is best regarded as a sort of kindergarten retreat on which newcomers to golf can get the feel of the game before moving on to sterner challenges. And then there is the Eden Course, designed in 1912 by Harry Colt on the relatively flat land to the west of the Old Course. It is a most agreeable layout but, like the New, not a distinguished one. All these courses are open to the public. This was decided in 1894, when Parliament passed the St. Andrews Links Act. Under the terms of the act, the townspeople of St. Andrews were given "a servitude of golf" over the links, which became "a Public Park and Recreation Ground." The act entrusted the R. & A. with the responsibility of maintaining the Old Course and of building and maintaining the New Course. In return, the R. & A. was given exclusive use of the Old Course four weeks of the year. (It has been the custom of the R. & A. to set aside that time for its Spring Meeting, in May, and its Autumn Meeting, in September, when members of the club flock to St. Andrews from all over the United Kingdom — and often from overseas — to engage in a number of traditional competitions.) As costs continued to rise, maintaining the courses imposed a serious financial burden on the R. & A. In 1946, the Town Council was prevailed upon to offer some assistance, and it enacted a Provisional Order whereby the residents of St. Andrews, who up to that time had not paid a fee for using the courses, were thenceforth assessed a small amount each year for the privilege. Today, a Links Management Committee, made up of representatives of the Town Council and the R. & A., is responsible for the maintenance of the four courses.

However, what finally solved the recurring financial problems was the dramatic expansion of the British Open in the nineteen-sixties. After being relatively somnolent for years, the British Open — the oldest of the four major championships — began to regain its old stature and appeal when Arnold Palmer, the magnetic American star, made it a point to come over each summer — starting in 1960 — to play in it. By doing so, he impressed upon the other top American professionals the importance that being on hand regularly for the championship, and possibly winning it, could have for them. (Palmer won it in 1961 and 1962.) In 1967, the American Broadcasting Company, appreciating the allure of the revitalized British Open, bought the American television rights to the event. During the next decade, television rights to the Open were sold to companies in Japan, Australia, and a dozen other countries. The British Broadcasting Corporation, meanwhile, enlarged its coverage of the Open, and this was a signal factor in the championship's renaissance. In 1967, a total of fewer than thirty thousand spectators had turned out at the Royal Liverpool Golf Club, in Hoylake, to watch the practice rounds and the four rounds of the championship. By 1978, when St. Andrews was host to the Open for the twenty-second time, the total attendance for the practice rounds and during the championship had risen to over a hundred and twenty-five thousand devotees of golf.

A few more words about the R. & A., since it is perhaps the foremost international club in the realm of sports. It has had a long-standing policy of limiting its membership. At present, the club has eighteen hundred members. Seven hundred and fifty of them are Overseas Members. Two hundred and seventy-five of these are Americans. Two Americans have been elected captain — the club's highest office. The first, appropriately, was Francis Ouimet, America's first golfing hero, who as a twenty-year-old amateur up from the caddie ranks defeated Harry Vardon and Ted Ray, two illustrious British professionals, in a playoff for the 1913 U.S. Open. Ouimet was chosen to captain the R. & A. in 1951. In 1975, this honor was bestowed on Joseph C. Dey, Jr., who is the most outstanding golf administrator that this country has produced. From 1934 to 1969, Dey served as the executive director of the U.S.G.A., and, beginning in 1969, he put in five years as the first commissioner of the Tournament Players' Division of our Professional Golfers' Association.

The R. & A. is strictly a men's club, but this should hardly come as a shock. Indeed, women were not allowed into its hallowed halls of Canadian yellow pine until the 1955 Commonwealth Cup match, when a cocktail party for the players and their wives was given in what is known as the Big Room. This went over so well that another such mixed party was held in 1958, on the eve of the first World Amateur Team championship for the Eisenhower Trophy. Women, to be sure, can play the four courses — the British Ladies championship has been staged on the Old Course three times (in 1908, 1929, and 1965) — but the R. & A. remains the embodiment of the unindented male stronghold. The Big Room is its most celebrated room; a spacious rectangle sixty feet long, twenty-seven feet wide, and twenty-five feet high, it is lined on three sides by six-foot-high wooden lockers. On the fourth side, a tall, eight-pane bay window provides a wonderful view of the Old Course. (All the play on the first hole, a short par 4 on which the green sits just beyond the twisting Swilken Burn, is visible, and so is all the play on the eighteenth, a short but insidious par 4 on which the front-left section of the green is a large and deep hollow called, for good reason, the Valley of Sin. With the aid of binoculars the play on the green of the seventeenth, the notorious Road Hole, can also be followed.) Even on days when no competition is being held, the area around the bay window is the favorite haunt of the leather-armchair brigade — gruff, old regulars who make it their business to find out if Ladysmith has fallen and otherwise keep abreast of current events. On my first visit to the Big Room, shortly after the end of the war (the Second World War, not the Boer War), I quickly got the drift of things in the bay-window area, vacated the comfortable chair I had eased myself into, and focussed my attention on the handsome paintings that hang on the walls: in particular, I gave over most of my time to studying a portrait done in 1925 of the Duke of Windsor (then the Prince of Wales), looking smashing in a wide cap, a patterned tan sweater and plus fours, and a grouping of The Triumvirate — Harry Vardon, J. H. Taylor, and James Braid — whose noble characters as well as their feats on the links had so much to do with the rise of golf's popularity at the turn of the century. In recent years, the atmosphere of the Big Room — and of the R. & A. in general — has become more informal and cordial, and this trend is sure to be continued under the newly appointed Secretary, Michael Bonallack, who, among his other distinctions, is a five-time winner of the British Amateur.

Americans have long been enamored of St. Andrews, and their affection has been warmly returned, but in the entire annals of sport there have been few love affairs that can compare with the one between St. Andrews and Robert Tyre Jones, Jr. — the immortal Bobby. It was not love at first sight between Jones and the Old Course. In his first tussle with it, in the 1921 British Open, Jones — then nineteen — thought it was a rotten course. He was not the first or the last American to feel that way. To a golfer from a country where with few exceptions the finest courses are set inland, the fairways are lined with trees, the greens have a receptive give to them, and the bunkers and water hazards announce their presence in loud, clear voices, the Old Course doesn't even look like a golf course. A tawny sea of billows, it has only one tree on it — an apple tree to the right of the twelfth green. On some of its holes, the golfer, as he stands on the tee buffeted by the moisture-laden winds off the sea, cannot make out exactly where the fairway runs. Not infrequently, when he rips a drive that appears to have split the middle of the fairway he discovers that his ball has ended up in a fairway bunker hidden from view by the heaving land. He adjusts with comparative ease to the hard, close-cut turf of the fairways, but the resilience of the greens throws him off. His best approaches — the ones that land a dozen feet or less from the flagstick — take off like kangaroos. When his caddie tells him that on many holes he must land his approach short of the green and allow for the ball to bounce and roll up to the cup, his first reaction is that this type of pitch-and-run golf is as inferior to American target golf as British plumbing is to ours back home. On top of that, the chore of developing the proper touch on the very fast greens is made all the harder by the difficulty of reading the line to the hole. A putt that looks as if it would break a shade to the right sometimes breaks to the left. The visiting golfer has the option of either trying to memorize every green or taking a caddie. The second course of action is by far the wiser.

In the 1921 British Open, Jones scored reasonably well on his first two rounds. On the first nine holes of his third round, playing into the teeth of a strong wind, he made a series of costly mistakes and reached the turn in 46. An extremely high-strung young man, he was furious with himself. The best he could do on the easy tenth was a double-bogey 6. On the short eleventh, when he lay 5 on the green with a putt for a triple bogey, the indignity of it all was too much for him. He picked his ball up, which was tantamount to dropping out of the tournament. This incident, fortunately, had a beneficial effect on young Jones. He was so thoroughly ashamed of himself for quitting during the championship — in his mind, it went directly against the true spirit of sport — that he went on from there to set the highest possible standard of sportsmanship throughout his career.

Some St. Andreans had sensed in 1921 that Jones was an extraordinarily talented striker of the ball, but it wasn't until five years later that they began to realize just how exceptional he was. In the spring of 1926, the Walker Cup match was held at St. Andrews. Jones and a fellow-Georgian, Watts Gunn, won their foursome handily, and in the singles Jones overwhelmed Cyril Tolley, the formidable British amateur, 12 and 11. The townspeople took note of his new maturity. They loved his natural manner on the course, and the way he could gather his full concentration when he played a shot. They recognized that he now understood the subtle, variable demands of linksland golf and that he obviously enjoyed devising the exacting, ticklish shots that were required. They admired his swing, so full and yet so compact in the hitting area, and they were smitten by its beautiful, almost lazy tempo. They had been waiting for decades for their dream golfer, and now they were fairly certain that he had arrived. The following year, they were positive he had. The 1927 British Open was held at St. Andrews, and Jones, after starting with a 68, which tied the course record, stayed out in front with rounds of 72, 73, and 72, and finished a full six strokes ahead of the runner-up. The spectators, understanding the pressures that weigh on a tournament golfer, never disturbed Jones when he was working on a round, but on the last day of the 1927 Open they were thickly crammed around the home green, and when Jones' final putt went down they broke loose and mobbed their hero. As Bernard Darwin, the English golf writer, remembered the scene, "He holed his short one and the next instant there was no green visible, only a dark seething mass, in the midst of which was Bobby hoisted on fervent shoulders and holding his putter, 'Calamity Jane,' at arm's length over his head lest she be crushed to death."

Jones next returned to St. Andrews in 1930, shortly after captaining the American team in the Walker Cup match at Royal St. George's. That year, St. Andrews was host to the British Amateur, a championship that Jones had failed to win in two previous cracks at it. He looked to be in excellent form in winning his first three matches. In the fourth round, he met the defending champion, the redoubtable Tolley. Just about everyone in town streamed down to the links to watch this match. (Noting this, Gerald Fairlie, the British mystery writer, used that afternoon in one of his books as the time when a murder is committed in St. Andrews. Though stained with the blood of his crime, the murderer is able to make his way undetected down the empty streets of the town.) The Jones-Tolley match was one to remember. Both men were on their game. Neither was able to build up a lead of more than one hole. Coming to the seventeenth, they were even. There Jones was very lucky to halve Tolley's 4. His second, a slightly cut spoon that he hoped would sit down quickly at the back of the green, took a high, fast kick and might have bounded onto the nearby road if it had not been stopped by the spectators bunched behind the green. The eighteenth was halved in par. On to extra holes. The ending, which came on the nineteenth, was anticlimactic. Jones was on in two. Tolley, off to the right with his pitch, played a rather loose chip, and Jones' approach putt left Tolley with an uncircumventable stymie. In the fifth round, Jones defeated Harrison (Jimmy) Johnston 1 up, though he had been four holes down with five holes to play. Then he beat George Voigt 1 up after being two down with five holes to play. This put him into the final against the tall, accomplished Englishman Roger Wethered. After the morning round, Jones stood 4 up. He had only one 5 on his card: on the seventeenth, he had missed a two-foot putt. In the afternoon, continuing his sure, steady play, he closed Wethered out on the thirtieth green, 7 and 6. At the time, the general mood was one of immense gratification: after surviving so many close calls, Jones had finally won the British Amateur, the one major championship (among those in which he was eligible to play) that had eluded him. As the year spun on and Jones won the British Open and the U.S. Open, and, at length — four months after his victory at St. Andrews — concluded his epic Grand Slam by winning the U.S. Amateur, the significance of the wonders he had worked at St. Andrews became increasingly clear.

Jones' next visit to St. Andrews took place in 1936. He and his friend Grantland Rice, the syndicated sports columnist, made a brief visit on the way to the Olympic Games in Berlin. They had been stopping at Gleneagles, and Jones could not bear to be so close to the Old Course and not play it. Somehow, word of his plans leaked out. Stores closed down, and five thousand people were gathered at the course to welcome "our Bobby" when he teed off. At least a thousand more subsequently joined the gallery. Although Jones had been playing very little golf and had not been hitting the ball well, he responded to the occasion with some sensational shotmaking, reaching the turn in 32. On the back nine, he made a few errors en route to a round of 71, but he also brought off some thrilling shots that enchanted his gallery.

Jones did not return to St. Andrews again until 1958. The first World Amateur Team championship for the Eisenhower Trophy was scheduled for that October, and St. Andrews was the logical venue. Jones, a close friend of Eisenhower's, was asked to captain the American team. He agreed to do it, even though he had been suffering for some time from syringomyelia, a crippling disease of the spinal cord. Looking back at that vivid international competition, one remembers two things above all else: Australia's victory by two strokes over the American team in the playoff for the championship; and the evening at the university's Younger Hall when Jones was formally made a Freeman of the Burgh of St. Andrews. (The last American to have been so honored was Benjamin Franklin.) That night, some two thousand people — the bulk of them townspeople — jammed the hall literally to the rafters. The town clerk read the citation. The provost made a first-rate address about the warm and abiding friendship between Jones and the residents of the town. Jones then rose and moved to the lectern. It was his preference at functions of this kind not to deliver a prepared address but to talk spontaneously, expressing the thoughts and feelings that had struck him during the evening. This was one of the occasions when he forgot entirely about the notes he had in his jacket pocket. Speaking in his Georgia drawl, his tone both intimate and earnest, he told his audience how much it meant to him to be in St. Andrews once again, and remarked that "you people of St. Andrews have a sensitivity and an ability to extend cordiality in an ingenious way." He spoke of the Old Course and the patience and restraint it demands. He said, "The more you study it the more you love it, and the more you love it the more you study it." A bit later in his talk, which lasted about twelve minutes, he said, "I could take out of my life everything except my experiences at St. Andrews and I would still have had a rich and full life." He concluded by speaking of friendship. "When I say to a person, 'I am your friend,' I have said about the ultimate. When I say, 'You are my friend,' I am assuming too much, for it is a possibility that you do not want to accept my friendship. When I have said as much about you, and you have done so much for me, I think that when I say, 'You are my friends,' then, under these circumstances, I am at the same time affirming my affection and regard for you and expressing my complete faith in you and my trust in the sincerity of your friendship.

Therefore, when I say now to you, 'Greetings, my friends at St. Andrews,' I know I am not presuming, because of what has passed between us." At the end of his talk, Jones left the stage and got into the golf cart he used to help him get around. He guided it slowly down the center aisle of the hall. As he did, the whole auditorium suddenly erupted in the most stirring rendition imaginable of the old Scottish song "Will Ye No' Come Back Again?" It had all the strange, wild, emotional force of the skirl of a bagpipe. Hardly a word was said as the people filed from the hall, and for many minutes afterward it was impossible for anyone to speak.

Jones died in December, 1971. His admirers in Britain and America soon thereafter formed the Robert T. Jones, Jr., Memorial Trust, the Robert T. Jones, Jr., Memorial Scholarship Fund; and also the Robert T. Jones, Jr., Scholar Exchange Program Endowment Fund, whereby four students from the University of St. Andrews are selected annually to come to Atlanta for a year's study at Emory University (where Jones attended law school), and four students from Emory are selected to study at St. Andrews. If an applicant for one of the scholarships happens to be a golfer, fine. What the committees are looking for, however, are young men and women of scholarly bent and personal merit who would stand to widen their vistas incalculably during a year abroad.

It was not St. Andrews but Prestwick that founded the British Open. In 1860, eight professionals from seven Scottish clubs competed in the first Open, a thirty-six-hole event in which the field played three rounds over Prestwick's twelve-hole course. The Prestwick era of the Open ended in 1870, when Young Tom Morris — the nineteen-year-old son of Old Tom Morris, who had himself been the Open champion four times — won for the third straight year and so retired the Challenge Belt that Prestwick had put up. No Open was played the next year, but in 1872 a new arrangement was agreed on. Musselburgh and St. Andrews would join Prestwick in conducting the championship, which would be rotated over the three courses. This procedure continued until 1892, when the Open was extended to a seventy-two-hole event and some major changes in the championship rota were initiated. In that year, Musselburgh was dropped and Muirfield added; in 1894, Royal St. George's became the first English course to hold the championship. The next move of consequence came in 1919. Because of the reputation that the R. & A. had gained as British golf's governing body, it was asked by the other prominent clubs to assume responsibility for running both the British Open and the British Amateur. It was pleased to do so.

American golf fans first became conscious of the British Open in the nineteen-twenties. Out of a clear blue sky, a flock of upstart crows from our country went over for the championship and demonstrated that they could play the game better than the British could. Walter Hagen won the British Open four times, and Jones won it three times. In the mid-thirties, our interest in the British Open began to wane, and after the Second World War our top professionals seldom played in it. Sam Snead won it in 1946, at St. Andrews, but did not bother to defend his title the next year. Ben Hogan, in his first appearance in the championship, put on a magnificent display of shotmaking in winning it at Carnoustie in 1953, but he never played in it again. Palmer's enthusiasm for the British Open, and his two victories in it — at Royal Birkdale and Troon — turned everything around. American players began to go over in swarms, and to win it: Tony Lema in 1964, Jack Nicklaus in 1966, 1970, and 1978, Lee Trevino in 1971 and 1972, Tom Weiskopf in 1973, Johnny Miller in 1976, Bill Rogers in 1981, and Tom Watson in 1975, 1977, 1980, 1982, and 1983. American golfers have almost invariably been great favorites with the British galleries, because of their pleasant manner and their attacking style of play. A number of them have had their reservations about the merits of the Old Course, but the course has never lost its attraction or its importance for them. When Nicklaus won the championship there in 1970, after an exciting playoff with Doug Sanders, he was so stirred by having accomplished this on the historic course that although he had theretofore not been regarded as a particularly gifted speaker he found his voice for the first time in his career as he addressed the cheering crowds.

A large part of the appeal that the Old Course holds for a golfer, be he a Nicklaus or a nobody, is its age. When a golfer walks down its fairways and onto its greens, he is intensely aware that more than nine hundred years ago the town's pioneering golfers trod the same strip of land as they played their rough version of the game. He is also aware that the eighteen holes of the Old Course are basically the same ones that existed a hundred and fifty years ago, when Old Tom Morris was a young sprout. There have been some changes, inevitably. When the improvement of the golf ball and of golf clubs made it possible for the ball to be hit farther, new back tees were constructed, so that the strategy of the individual holes would not be impaired. Today, the course measures nearly 7,000 yards from the championship tees, and 6,550 yards from the regular tees. Other changes have taken place. The fairways are not as fast or the greens as kittle as they were fifty years ago. They haven't been since 1969, certainly, for that year a sprinkler system was installed — a dubious improvement in the opinion of many members. Some bunkers that underwent repairs have emerged with their playing qualities slightly altered. Other bunkers have just disappeared. It should be emphasized that at St. Andrews the way the bunkering ties in with the terrain is more responsible for the strategic concept of the holes than it is at any other course. Because the wind changes frequently, the golfer must be continuously alert. If the wind happens to be blowing into his face on a certain hole, he must not attempt to carry a bunker he can carry on a still day only with a big shot; he must be content to aim for the safe side of the fairway. When he notices on the tee of another hole that a breeze is kicking up behind him, he should feel encouraged to let out on his tee shot and try to fly it over a bunker that ordinarily menaces the direct line to the green. If he pulls this off, he not only will have a shorter approach to play but also may be rewarded for his daring with the perfect opening to the green. To play the Old Course well requires discretion. Even when there is no wind to worry about, it provides the average golfer with a nice exercise in maneuvering the ball, but for the likes of our modern power hitters the course is hardly a challenge on a calm day. The holes are simply too short, and the hazards rarely come into play. For example, on the first round of the 1970 British Open, when there wasn't any wind to speak of, no fewer than forty-three players broke par — 72 — and twenty-one equalled it.

Probably the best way to convey the unique personality of the Old Course is to describe briefly the incoming nine holes — much the superior nine, in the opinion of most authorities. On the outgoing nine, only the first, fourth, and fifth holes really seize the golfer's imagination. They have distinct personalities of their own. As for the six other outgoing holes, they are on the short side, and on four of them the tee shot is blind, or semi-blind, which may explain why most golfers do not score as low on the front nine as they expect to. In addition, there are numerous pot bunkers to gobble up errant shots, and along the right side there is the danger of thick patches of whins to be reckoned with. On the second nine, too, as a matter of fact, it is a good idea to keep the ball to the left whenever one feels a little uncertain about the shot he is playing.

The tenth hole happens to be an exception to this. A flattish, rather straight par 4, which measures 342 yards from the championship tee, it is bordered on the left by a bulge of heavy rough backed up by whins. When a power hitter has the wind at his back, he is tempted to see if he can carry the rough and reach the green, or at least leave himself with a short chip or pitch on his second. There is a lot of room out to the right, but the best target for the good club golfer is a well-defined fairway bunker, whose high front face, revetted with closely knit bricks of turf, lies about two hundred and seventy yards out, in line with the right edge of the double green. If the golfer hits a solid drive just to the left of this bunker, he is in great shape. The tenth is typical of many holes on the Old Course. It looks like a possible birdie hole, but a golfer must have some firsthand knowledge of it to be able to judge how much run to allow for on his pitch to the slightly elevated green, and most times it is only after he misses his putt that the break of the green clearly reveals itself.

The eleventh is a 172-yard par 3, whose fairway cuts across the seventh fairway. It is the last hole of the four-hole loop, and by far the most dangerous. The green slants from back to front at a very steep angle; if a modern golf-course architect were to design a green with the same degree of slope, his client would reject it. On days when the wind blows forcefully from the back of the green to the front, the astute player never soles his putter, for then, not having formally addressed the ball, he cannot be penalized a stroke if the wind happens to move it. (On windy days, some players also chase their approach shots up the green and hurriedly tap in their short putts, for there is always a chance that a gust will blow the ball back down the green.) Under ordinary conditions, however, a golfer's main concern on the eleventh is to avoid the two punitive bunkers guarding the entrance to the green — Strath Bunker, on the right, and Hill Bunker, on the left. It is the old story of Scylla and Charybdis. Hill, which is ten feet deep, does a good deal of business. In trying to stay away from Strath, golfers have a tendency to steer the ball too far to the left and into Hill. This is understandable, in a way: few bunkers are as mean as Strath. In the afternoon round of their singles in the 1938 Walker

Cup match, Charlie Stowe, of Britain, and his American opponent, Chuck Kocsis, both put their tee shots up against the base of
the steep, five-foot-high front wall of Strath, which noses well into
the putting surface. Kocsis, being away, played first. His explosion shot failed to clear the wall and toppled back into the sand.
Thereupon, Stowe, with little hesitation, played his second not
toward the pin but out the back of the bunker and onto the fairway. From there he got down with a fine chip and a putt, and his
bogey 4 won him the hole.

The twelfth is the first of the holes that thread their way, one
after another, back to town. If there is a north or northwest wind
at the back of a world-class golfer, it ruins this succession of holes.
He can then whale the ball such distances that the length of its
carry renders irrelevant the hazards that in a harrying wind make
these last seven holes one of the most fascinating stretches in golf.
The twelfth measures only 316 yards from the championship tee,
but there is more to this short par 4 than first meets the eye. For
instance, about two hundred yards out, smack in the middle of
the fairway, are four bunkers that are not visible from the tee,
because they lie beyond a sudden dip in the terrain. From experience, or from his caddie, a golfer learns that the proper line on
that particular day is either toward the heathery hillside on the left
or straight down the rough on the right. The twelfth has a thin,
tiered green; the low strip at the front rises quickly to the higher
tier. It takes an eye for distance and a sensitive touch to toss up a
pitch or a pitch-and-run shot that will finish within birdie range of
the flagstick. Nevertheless, the twelfth, being just over three hundred yards long, has yielded a few eagle 2s in its time. Joe Carr,
the long-hitting Irish star, made one in the final of the 1958 British
Amateur when he drove the green and holed a huge putt.

The thirteenth is 425 yards long, and a brute. I know of no other
par 4 that even vaguely resembles it. To the left of the narrow
fairway are three good-size bunkers. They are known as the Cof-
fins, doubtless because they catch a great many tee shots. This is
only the half of it. Just beyond the area where most tee shots
finish, the fairway abruptly sweeps up fifteen feet or so, shutting
out all view of the continuing fairway and the green. The caddie,
after cautioning his man to play to the left of his line to the pin,
climbs to the top of the fairway, gives him the line to the pin, and
then, after watching where the shot has finished, usually contorts
his face into an expression even glummer than the one he was

wearing. Blind holes are bad holes, but the thirteenth has a grandeur about it that makes it an exception. One other thing. There is
a small bunker twenty yards short of the green. It is called Lion's
Mouth, and it is voracious.

The Old Course has only two par 3s, the eighth and the eleventh, and only two par 5s, the fifth and the fourteenth. The fourteenth, 567 yards long, has no fewer than ten bunkers. It can turn
a promising round into a woeful one. "The drive on the fourteenth, especially from the championship tee, makes a fearsome
play on courage and technique," the British golf writer Pat Ward-
Thomas has stated. "The paramount thought is to avoid going out
of bounds over the low greystone wall which angles sharply into
the line, and separates the Old from the Eden course, but only a
slight pull can be trapped by the Beardies, a threatening cluster of
bunkers scarcely visible from the tee. For most golfers there is no
greater sense of relief on the Old Course than to see the drive
finishing safely on the lovely sweep of fairway known as the Elysian Fields." Even if a player has found the Elysian Fields with his
tee shot, plenty of work remains to be done. The temptation to try
to carry Hell Bunker, which lies straight ahead down the fairway,
is understandable, for if one brings it off with an aggressive fairway wood one is then less than a hundred yards short of the
green. It is wise, though, to pass up this gamble. To cite just one
example, Gene Sarazen, in the 1933 British Open, caught Hell
Bunker with his second, took two shots to get out, and ended with
an 8. It proved to be fatal to his chances: he lost the championship
by a stroke. The smart golfer will elect to play his second to the left
of Hell — down the fifth fairway, in fact. Not only is this a much
less precarious route but he is left with a much easier third shot.
The front part of the left side of the green — a green that is high at
the front and slopes down toward the back — presents only a few
minor ripples to contend with, whereas the front of the right side
rises like a breaking wave.

The fifteenth, a 413-yard par 4, is generally considered to be
something of a letup hole. The town of St. Andrews, which looms
in the distance as one plays the last seven holes, is now close
enough so that, depending on the wind, the caddie generally
gives his player some architectural feature as the line — a church
steeple, say, or a row of light-brown buildings, or the blocky red
facade of the old Grand Hotel, now a university dormitory. While
the fifteenth may be the least publicized hole in the finishing

stretch, it is anything but an automatic par. It contains many of the course's familiar appurtenances: a hidden bunker (Sutherland) in the landing area of the drive; a fairway full of bumps and hollows that frequently add the complication of an uphill, downhill, or sidehill lie to the approach shot; four pot bunkers at the far end of the fairway; and a green that has a good many delicate rolls.

The sixteenth is a marvellous hole. A 382-yard par 4, it is made by its feature hazard, the Principal's Nose — a good-sized mound that has a deep, pitlike bunker carved into its front side and two similar bunkers carved into its back side. It is situated in the fairway about two hundred yards from the tee and directly on the line from tee to green. The golfer who in an east wind aims for the twenty-yard-wide strip of fairway to the right of the Principal's Nose runs the risk of having his ball blown into the rough, or farther right and out of bounds. The golfer who in a crosswind aims eight or ten yards to the left of it often discovers that he has underestimated the force of the wind and that his drive has caught the hazard. This happened to James Braid in the 1905 British Open, to Jones in his match with Tolley in the 1930 British Amateur, and to Palmer in the qualifying round of the 1960 British Open. The best line to choose is far to the left of the Principal's Nose — there is plenty of room there — and to take your chances on playing the splendid iron shot needed to hit and hold the terraced green.

The seventeenth, the Road Hole, may well be the most admired and feared hole in the world. A 461-yard par 4 that doglegs to the right, it gets its name from the paved road that runs just behind and a few feet below the right edge of the diagonal green. Just beyond the road is a stone wall. The road plays as a hazard; you cannot ground your club on it. From the back tee, the golfer must decide whether he should play a careful drive down the left side of the fairway or an audacious drive over the angle of the dogleg. If the golfer fails to make the long carry, he is out of bounds. If he succeeds, he is in a position where he can reach the lean, diagonal, slightly elevated green with a long, or even a medium, iron. Some golfers consider that trying to land the second shot on the green is hardly worth the risk. An approach hit a shade to the right can end up on the road, and an approach hit a shade to the left will be funnelled most of the time into the Road Bunker, a fearsome hazard from which it takes a well-executed explosion shot to stop the ball on the green safely short of the road. Accord-

ingly, the old St. Andrews man usually plays his second intentionally short of the bank in front of the green, preferring to gamble on getting down from there in a little pitch and a putt.
Sometimes, of course, the circumstances are such that the golfer
must throw caution to the winds and go boldly for the seventeenth green on his second shot. This is what Dr. David Marsh did
in the 1971 Walker Cup match. Standing 1 up on Bill Hyndman
with two holes to go in the crucial singles of a very close team
match, Marsh played a perfect 3-iron to within fifteen feet of the
pin. He halved that hole and the eighteenth, and Britain had won
the Cup for the first time since 1938.

The Old Course has an ideal finishing hole. A straightaway par
4, it measures 354 yards. With a strong following breeze, a Nicklaus can drive the green, but for most golfers the hole generally
plays as a drive and a well-hit 6-iron or 7-iron. Since the out-of-
bounds line runs tight along the right side of the fairway from tee
to green, most golfers favor the left side of the fairway off the tee.
But then the Valley of Sin comes into play, and that large, deep
basin, which occupies the front-left section of the green, changes
the whole nature of the eighteenth. In tournament play, the pin is
almost always positioned behind it. The golfer approaching the
green from the left should always make sure to take enough club
on his second. He knows full well how rarely a player is able to get
down in fewer than three putts from the Valley of Sin. Nevertheless, an amazingly high percentage of golfers — perhaps because
of fear of going over the green, perhaps because of an illusion that
they are nearer the green than they actually are — put their approach shots into the Valley of Sin, and this has changed the
outcome of countless important matches and tournaments. The
green is very hard to read. It is common knowledge that it slopes
down ever so slightly from the back right-hand corner. Yes, but
just how much break does one allow for? In the 1970 British Open,
Doug Sanders had only to sink a three-and-a-half-footer — he
was just beyond the cup — to beat Nicklaus and carry off the
championship. His putt slipped by the right edge of the cup. The
next day, Nicklaus was faced with sinking an eight-footer from
about the same angle to win their playoff. As his ball neared the
hole, it started to veer to the right, but it caught a corner of the cup
and fell in.

For the 1984 Open, that stimulating second nine measured 3,432
yards, the first nine 3,501 yards, and the total yardage of the Old

Course 6,933 yards — a very respectable length. However, in calm weather the course, with its fast fairways, tends to play somewhat shorter than those figures suggest. This was a principal reason the thousands who gathered at St. Andrews for the 1984 Open were hoping not only for fair weather but also for a pleasant breeze, to make the course more interesting for the best players in the world.

St. Andrews is an enchanting town for a traveller to return to, I discovered again this summer. The townspeople are genuinely friendly, and their politeness bowls you over. The imminence of another British Open championship on the Old Course had put an almost tangible tingle in the air. After dinner on the evening of my arrival, it was impossible for me to restrain myself from walking over to the Old Course to see how it was looking. It was then almost half past nine, but in a latitude as northerly as St. Andrews' the light still holds in July at that late hour. I walked past the entrance of the R. & A. clubhouse and onto the course, with the eighteenth green on my left and the tee of the first hole on my right, just in front of the bay window of the Big Room. Two hundred and more St. Andreans were strolling here and there over the large grassed rectangle that serves as the fairway for both the first and the eighteenth holes. I found myself instinctively patting the grass of the eighteenth green to see if it felt as smooth and as tightly knit as the greens of the Old Course generally do. The grass felt fine, but it was a little higher than I had expected it to be. The greens evidently had not as yet been mowed to championship height. As I walked on in the gloaming toward the Swilcan Burn, I became increasingly conscious of how brightly green the eighteenth green, behind me, and the first green, across the Swilcan, were in comparison with the dun color of their joint fairway. The fairways had relatively little grass on them, and, though they are a pale brownish-green when in prime condition, they were browner and drier than I remembered ever having seen them before. On the first hole, which is 370 yards long, the green begins at the far side of the Swilcan, which is generally about a foot or so deep and is lined with walls of stone or wood on both sides. At the edge of the Swilcan, I picked up a ball-retriever that was lying there, and when I dipped the handle in the burn I found that the water was only half an inch deep. I headed back to my hotel a little concerned about the condition of the course. Clearly, this corner of Scotland had been undergoing a protracted drought. I was sure that everyone connected with the Open was praying for rain and more rain in the days remaining before the first round of the Open. I went to bed early that evening, not long after the distant lights of Carnoustie, across the Firth of Tay, had gone on.

The next day, around noon, I happened to run into Michael Bonallack, the Secretary of the R. & A., and I asked him if any chance of rain was mentioned in the weather forecast. "I hope not," he said, with his characteristic calmness. "We've been hand-watering the greens, as you can see. In this drought, that was necessary. We were fortunate to be able to do it. In many parts of Scotland, the drought, which began in April, has been so severe that water rationing has had to be invoked. But the last thing we want at St. Andrews is rain. The greens are a bit slower and not quite as firm as we would like them, and a heavy rain would only make them too slow and too spongy for the championship."

I had overlooked that critical point. Not being a long course, the Old Course depends on having greens that are extremely firm and fast, so that a golfer cannot shoot directly at the flags when he is playing his approach shots but must figure out where he should try to land the ball given the direction and force of the wind that day, the degree of firmness of the fairways and the greens, and the position of the flags. (The flags, by the way, are yellow going out and red coming in, with the exception of the flag on the home green, which is white.) As it turned out, that corner of Fife had a couple of light showers in the next two days, which didn't slow down the speed of the greens but greened up the fairways notice-ably.

At ten o'clock on the Tuesday morning before the first round, a significant ceremony took place in Younger Hall — the audito-rium where, twenty-six years before, Bobby Jones had been made a Freeman of the Burgh of St. Andrews. That morning, the Uni-versity of St. Andrews paid a splendid tribute to Jack Nicklaus, the finest golfer of the last twenty-odd years (and, incidentally, the winner of the last two Opens held in St. Andrews, in 1970 and 1978), by awarding him the honorary degree of Doctor of Laws. In delivering the laureation address, Stuart McDowall, senior lec-turer in economics and a former Master of the United College, said, "Jack Nicklaus's contribution to the game is monumental, and it is by no means confined to his achievements as a player. He has written authoritatively and perceptively about the game. He has designed or redesigned over forty golf courses in many parts of the world. Indeed, it may well be that he would prefer to be remembered as an outstanding golf architect rather than as the game's outstanding player." McDowall went on to mention some of Nicklaus's achievements in tournament golf, and added, "Equally important has been the manner in which he has achieved success. Obviously, he tries and loves to win. Much as he prizes his victories, though, he prizes his integrity more, and he sets a shining example by his conduct in a profession where the standard of behavior is already high."

Clad in a black university gown and a scarlet-and-white cowl, Nicklaus knelt before the vice-chancellor of the university, Dr. J. Steven Watson, who, speaking in Latin, awarded Nicklaus his degree. Nicklaus then rose and responded. "My participation in higher education came through one of America's largest universities, Ohio State," he said early in his address to the packed house. "I learned many things at Ohio State, the chief among them being the great importance of institutions such as yours, not only in educating young people but in helping them to achieve complete and fruitful lives as civilized members of society." He spoke of his first visit to Scotland, in 1959, as a member of our Walker Cup team, and of his many subsequent visits. "I love the style and atmosphere of Scottish golf and the great Scottish linksland courses. I am also in constant awe of the variety and beauty of the Scottish terrain. But what has always made me love Scotland the most is the people. Nowhere on earth have I been received more warmly, more affectionately, or with greater understanding than by the people of this country. I can assure you that the memories of my times here will never fade."

In the days before this Open, as before every Open championship in Britain, there was the deep pleasure of greeting old friends and enjoying their company. On Wednesday afternoon, I was one of six or seven people who had a nice informal tea with Henry Cotton, who exactly fifty years ago had stopped the run of ten straight victories in the British Open by golfers from the United States, and had gone on to win two more British Opens and to gain the distinction of being among the world's finest strikers of the golf ball. (Earlier this summer, during Wimbledon, Fred Perry, a three-time winner of that championship, also celebrated the fiftieth anniversary of *his* first victory; each was present when the other was fêted.) That evening, I also had the good fortune to run into two valued friends from Australia, Peter Thomson and Kel Nagle. Nagle won the British Open only once — in 1960 — but Thomson carried it off five times between 1954 and 1965. Thomson, who didn't fare nearly as well as most people expected in American tournaments during those years, was very amusing in recounting how in the last few years, which have seen the startling expansion of the veteran golfers' tournament circuit in our country, he has become much better known and has carried off far more prize money than he did when he was at his glittering peak.

And then there were the always happy hours visiting at 3 Pilmour Links, a block from the Old Course, with Laurie Auchterlonie and his wife, Bea, who for many people epitomize the spirit and the savor of St. Andrews. Laurie, who turned eighty this summer, is the honorary professional to the R. & A. As such, he tees the ball up for the incoming club captain when he drives himself into office, and he handles other such formal duties, but the main service he renders the club is to give the members a sense of the true worth of the game. He succeeded his father, Willie, in the post in 1964. Willie Auchterlonie won the British Open in 1893 — the last Scot who was still residing in Scotland at the time of his victory in the championship. Besides his skill as a player, Willie was famous worldwide for the superb handmade clubs he produced, along with his brother David, for their company, D. & W. Auchterlonie. Laurie, a very proficient player but a man for whom the life of a tournament golfer had little appeal, served a four-year apprenticeship under his father before being made a member of the firm. "I remember my father as a very kind man and a person of the highest principles," he said, in his soft Fife accent, during one of my visits. Breaking into a chuckle, he went on, "Oh, he could be stingy, though, with his compliments where clubmaking was concerned. I can remember that when I was a young lad I would show him certain hickory shafts and persimmon heads of which I was especially proud. The most I ever got from him was an offhand 'Tha's na bad' or 'It's sitting like a cocking hen' — a hen sitting on an egg." A huge man, with hands larger than Tommy Armour's, Laurie Auchterlonie became a celebrated clubmaker, and golfers from every green corner of the world beat a path to his shop — the old D. & W. Auchterlonie shop, which occupies the ground floor of the Auchterlonies' home. When, around 1930, the era of steel-shafted clubs arrived and wooden-shafted clubs were superseded, Laurie adjusted smoothly and put out handsome steel-shafted sets. He remained the Balenciaga or the Dior of the clubmaking profession. Many well-to-do golfers wanted clubs tailored to their individual specifications, and Laurie was about the only craftsman who could make clubs with the exquisite workmanship that gave such customers the feel and swingability they were after. I don't remember ever going to St. Andrews and not spending a lot of time in the Auchterlonie shop. Sometimes I would buy a lovely wooden-shafted putter, or a 7-iron shafted with a wood from the Caribbean called blue mahoo, or a new wedge that Laurie had fashioned, but my real reason was to chat with Laurie and the golf-obsessed people from here, there, and everywhere who had journeyed for thousands of miles to see him — say, a count from Denmark, the editor of an American golf weekly, the eloquent head of the French Golf Federation, a literate businessman from Johannesburg, a Canadian ice-hockey player, the retired editor of a Glasgow daily newspaper. What an unforced tang the conversations had at the Auchterlonies' this summer as they shifted, for instance, from the significance of the unusual movements of Jones' wrists at the top of his backswing to the way the old gutta-percha golf ball rested for a fraction of a second longer on the face of the club than the modern ball does, and on to how the building of the new back tees after the Second World War had given new life and pertinence to the Old Course's fabled hazards, to the restoration this year of the famous hickory- and persimmon-drying sheds in the angle of the fairway on the seventeenth, and then to the timeless book *F. G. Tait: A Record*, which John L. Low wrote early in the century about the appealing young Scot who won the British Amateur in 1896 and 1898, before going off to a war from which he did not return. Laurie Auchterlonie, a warm man who expresses his thoughts with an easy clarity and is also one of the best listeners in the world, has always been in a class by himself in enlarging his friends' knowledge and love of the game of golf.

Until noon on Thursday, the first day of the Open, the weather was almost too mild for golf. Then a pleasant breeze from the east — or, from time to time, from the east-southeast — started to blow across the links and made play on the incoming nine tougher. On the last seven holes, it slanted into the back of the left shoulder of a right-handed player and threatened to push him off balance. As it happened, a freshening breeze came up at about two o'clock on each afternoon of the tournament. However, all things considered — the greens were still holding the approach shots almost too well, and they tended to putt a little slower than is common in most British Opens — this was an ideal day for scoring. About a third of the field of a hundred and fifty-six either broke or matched par. Tied for the lead at 67 were Peter Jacobsen, the affable young Oregonian; Greg Norman, of Australia, who had been on a roll that saw him win the Kemper Open, lose to Fuzzy Zoeller in the playoff for the U.S. Open, beat Nicklaus by two strokes in the Canadian Open, and lose to Tom Watson in the sudden-death playoff in the Western Open; and Bill Longmuir, a sturdy Scot, whose tendency to hook the ball under pressure has prevented him from ever winning a big tournament. Alone at 68 was Ian Baker-Finch, an almost totally unknown Australian, who is the New Zealand Open champion, and who qualified for the British Open by finishing among the top six in the Australian Order of Merit. All the good P. G. Wodehouse fans, who appreciate the kind of double-barrelled name one would run into at the Drones Club, immediately announced that they would be supporting this Baker-Finch chap, and they were delighted to find that he was a tall (six-foot-three), good-looking fellow of twenty-three with a becoming naturalness and modesty. Behind him at 69 were Seve Ballesteros, Nick Faldo, and Tom Kite; Lee Trevino was at 70; Bernhard Langer and Tom Watson, a five-time winner of the British Open, were at 71. The only big name missing among the leaders was Jack Nicklaus. He had been under the weather all week with a mysterious virus and hadn't been able to prepare for the championship with his customary thoroughness. On his opening round, he bogeyed the first hole when he put his wedge pitch into the Swilcan. He birdied the third but three-putted the fourth, fifth, sixth, and seventh. After making the turn in a horrendous 41, he pulled himself together and played the second nine in 35, to post a 76. He looked very tired at the end of his round, but most people around golf are well aware of Nicklaus's incredible pertinacity. The consensus was that he would probably manage to play a fairly low round on Friday and that even though he now stood nine strokes behind the leaders he would somehow manage to make the thirty-six-hole cut. As for playing himself back into the tournament, that was another thing.

A record crowd of over thirty-four thousand spectators had turned out — five thousand more than had been on hand for the opening round in the 1983 Open, at Royal Birkdale. Keith Mackenzie, who preceded Michael Bonallack as the Secretary of the R. & A., had concentrated on reviving the stature and the revenue provided by the British Open. One of Mackenzie's key innovations was setting up grandstands around the various courses over which the Open was played, with the largest ones flanking the right and left sides of the eighteenth fairway and green. This year, Bonallack did a tremendous job of installing the grandstands at St. Andrews. (There is something about sitting in a grandstand which seems to encourage applauding, shouting, and other methods of letting a player know that you appreciated, say, the boldness of the iron shot he just played.) There were grandstands at all the double greens, and the finishing holes were very well handled. The seventeenth had a long, high grandstand along the right edge of the fairway and the beginning of the green area — the perfect spot for watching the action at the historic Road Hole, on which so many championships have been won and lost. Along the left side of the eighteenth fairway — which is also, of course, the right side of the first fairway — there was a long, major-league grandstand, which afforded an excellent view of all the shots on the dramatic finishing hole. There were two grandstands directly behind the eighteenth green which provided equally good vantage points. All told, the grandstands could accommodate seventeen thousand people. The news of such unprecedented spectator facilities on the Old Course spread rapidly through Scotland and was largely responsible for the record number of season tickets sold. However challenging its playing qualities, the Old Course had long been considered one of the worst in the world for watching the action in a championship. Because of the routing of the holes, it is just one long slog out and one long slog back, with most of the spectators heavily bunched in the ambulant galleries of the most popular golfers or of the golfers seriously in contention. This is a most frustating way of watching critical action. However, with seventeen thousand grandstand seats available, such a large percentage of the spectators was siphoned off that the golf fans trudging along on foot had a much easier time than heretofore of getting where they wanted to go and watching the shots they wanted to see played. Up to now, we haven't made much use of grandstands in our major tournaments (the Masters excepted) in this country, and perhaps we should do some thinking about it.

The weather on the day of the second round — and, for that

matter, throughout the tournament — was very much the same as it had been on the opening day. The early starters, who had been the last players to go out on the first round, benefitted from the windless conditions in the morning. Then, early in the afternoon, the east wind began to sweep across the course, blowing — sometimes vigorously — against the players on the last seven holes. Nick Faldo, one of the prime British hopefuls, seemed to be out of a recent slump and very much back in the groove when he followed his opening 69 with a 68, which put him close to the lead at the halfway point. Ballesteros, the moody and exceptionally talented Spaniard who won the British Open in 1979 and has twice won the Masters tournament, also appeared to be back in top form after a dull stretch in the months before the championship. The British golf fans look upon Ballesteros as one of their own boys, and they were pleased when he scored a 68 on his second round to stand at 137, tied with Faldo and Trevino, with two rounds to go. On this second day, Tom Watson played almost errorless golf until he reached the Road Hole, where, after driving into the rough on the left, he put his 3-iron recovery into Progressing Bunker, and ended up with a 6. Watson, who has won four of his five British Opens in Scotland but has never won one at St. Andrews, finished his round in 68 despite his aberrations on the seventeenth. He was in the thick of things at 139 with two rounds to go, and happy to be. Tom Kite and Peter Jacobsen, two solid golfers who have done well on the American tour but have somehow never won a major championship, were in a position to do so with halfway totals of 140. The time is long overdue for a number of proficient American golfers in their late twenties and early thirties, such as Kite and Jacobsen, to break through and push their way past the aging veterans in some of the major championships. One such player they would not have to worry about that week at St. Andrews was Nicklaus. He had just managed to make the thirty-six-hole cut by adding a 72 to his opening 76, but his shots lacked their customary resolution. One other thing: Greg Norman, who had been playing such consistently good golf for two months, dropped out of the running on the second round by taking six consecutive 5s on the second nine.

What really made the second round arresting was that Ian Baker-Finch continued to play excellent stuff. If any player in the field was the logical candidate to fall apart on the second round, it was Baker-Finch — or Hyphen, as his friends call him. Not only did he not crack but he brought in the lowest round of the day, an ultra-suède 66, to lead the field at the midway mark with a total of 134. Though most touring pros these days try to develop a compact swing without any unfunctional décor, the better to be able to repeat it time after time under tournament stress, Baker-Finch uses a long, full, Sneadian swing. He gets the ball out there a good distance. On the first nine holes of his second round, he picked up five birdies on his way to the turn, and then, taking his time and setting himself up unhurriedly before each shot, he came home in 34 (seven pars and two birdies). This supple, self-collected young man had pulled off some brilliant golf shots, let me tell you. In his press conference after the second round, Baker-Finch was peppered with questions, which he fielded ably. He gave considerable credit to his fellow-Australians, Peter Thomson and Kel Nagle, for helping him to understand and adjust to St. Andrews. "I think the secret of this course is to drive your tee shot into the correct position, so that you can put your ball onto the green in the correct position," he said, and he added, "Sometimes it's better to be fifty feet from the pin with an uphill putt than to have a much shorter putt downhill." He said that he started playing golf at ten and turned professional at eighteen. He comes from the state of Queensland, and also plays tennis and cricket. He confessed that he was astonished at what he had done so far in the British Open. "The next two days, I'm going to try to stay calm and relaxed," he said. "I won't think of winning until the last nine holes, or even the last four."

Baker-Finch, by the way, was one of the few leaders to make his par 4 on the seventeenth, where he got down· in two from the Road Bunker. Speaking of the seventeenth, that hole attracted extensive attention that Friday. Over the last two years, Frank Sheridan, the new owner of the Old Course Golf and Country Club, which overlooks the seventeenth fairway on the inland side, had redesigned the hotel, added some new facilities, and generally spruced things up. In the old days, the long hitter, to prevent himself from driving his tee shot across the fairway and into the rough on the left side, would try to fly his drive over the walled-off angle on the right of this left-to-right dogleg hole. Sheridan pondered what steps, if any, he should take in redoing the land in the angle of the dogleg, which belongs to the hotel. The first, and only previous, owner of the hotel had razed the buildings in the angle and covered the dangerous area with a free-style, rather

Tennysonian tent of white gauze and rope to prevent anyone from being struck by an errant tee shot. In the years before the hotel was built, the land inside the angle had been occupied by a garden tended by the stationmaster of the railway that ran between St. Andrews and Leuchars, six miles away; some piles of coal used by the railway; and the drying sheds where the Auchterlonies and D. Anderson, another local golf-club company, dried their hickory and persimmon planks. When I first played St. Andrews, in 1950, "D. Anderson" was painted on one of these sheds, and the correct line for a long hitter to take in cutting the corner was over the "d" in "Anderson." In any event, Sheridan elected this year to erect some shedlike buildings in the angle of the dogleg where the old sheds had stood. They are painted a muted dark green, and on the side facing the course the words "Old Course Golf & Country Club" are painted in soft lime. The correct line to take from the tee, I was told, is over the ampersand. Some people feel that the words on the new sheds carry too commercial a tone. Perhaps they do, but the sheds make getting a par 4 on the seventeenth a lot harder than it had been since the departure of the original sheds. This year, many of the players would step up on the tee and take their line over the ampersand, and then, at the last moment — only too aware that if their drive did not carry far enough it would end up out of bounds and they would be hit with a stroke-and-distance penalty — they would flinch a little, alter their swing, and pull-hook the ball over the left corner of the sheds. That kind of drive would bound across the fairway and into the left rough. From there, it took a brilliant recovery to get the ball onto the green, or even in a good position near the green from which the golfer could get down in a chip and a putt for a par 4. In short, the restored sheds make the Road Hole play the way the Road Hole used to. The poor drives induced by the terror of the sheds also brought those historic hazards, the Road Hole Bunker and the road behind the green, more frequently into play.

Much as I admired the smooth mechanics of Baker-Finch's swing and the courage he had displayed in refusing to be over-awed by the Old Course, I was fairly sure that sooner or later he would not be able to go on playing such amazing golf under the pressure of the Open. Here he was, this practically unknown young man of twenty-three, leading the championship by three strokes. Like everyone else, I hoped that when he folded it would happen almost invisibly. That was the least he deserved. Baker-

Finch, it became evident, had no such palliative thoughts on his mind when he teed off with Faldo at 3:20 on Saturday afternoon — ten minutes after Ballesteros and Trevino, twenty minutes after Lanny Wadkins and Bill Longmuir, thirty minutes after Bernhard Langer and Fred Couples, and forty minutes after Tom Watson and Jaime Gonzalez. On the first green, Baker-Finch rolled in a long putt for a birdie. That gave him quite a boost. He holed a twenty-five-footer to birdie the fourth. On the 564-yard fifth, playing downwind, he was on the green with two big blows and down in two putts for another birdie. Since he had parred the intervening holes, he was already three under par for the round. He made routine pars on the sixth and seventh. It was then that I took up a watching post near the tenth green, and saw the leading twosomes play the loop. It was easy to keep an eye on Baker-Finch's progress on the loop holes, since he was wearing a pink sweater, and nobody else was wearing a sweater with anything like that hue. He made his par 3 on the short eighth. On the tee of the 356-yard ninth, playing into the wind, he hurried his swing for the first time that day, and pulled his drive down the left rough and into a bunker called Mrs. Kruger. About fifty yards shorter, smack in the center of the fairway, is a double bunker called Kruger. Though no one I asked knew the story behind it, the existence of Kruger surely had something to do with the reason the bunker in the rough was named Mrs. Kruger. The latter effectively discourages the guileful golfer who is out to gain maximum distance off the tee by taking the line down the short, dry rough. Through my binoculars I saw a pink-sweatered golfer play a wedge shot from Mrs. Kruger, but I couldn't see the ninth green or the tenth tee from my position. Baker-Finch must have played a rather good sand shot, because several minutes later the leader board near the tenth green showed that he had parred the ninth. (There was a well-run leader board near each green on the course.) Baker-Finch's par on the ninth put him out in 33, three under par for the round and thirteen under for the tournament — not bad at all for a nobody who everyone had expected would disappear early in the Open. Some of the players close behind him were also scoring well. Langer had set up several birdies with some deft iron shots. Ballesteros, who is an actor through and through, had on his jut-jawed, Captain Ahab scowl of determination, and was hitting the ball sharply with the slightly shorter and more dependable swing he adopted a couple of years ago. On the greens, he had his touch and was coming close on every putt under twenty feet. But the man who really had things going was Watson. Consistently driving the ball into the bunker-free areas of the fairway with that disciplined repeating swing of his, he had finished the first nine in 32, and had picked up a shot on the leader. I decided, however, not to go in with Watson's twosome or with Ballesteros' but to wait for Baker-Finch and follow him on the in-nine. How often does an unknown golfer stay the pace in a major championship, as he was doing? The most recent case I could think of was Billy Joe Patton, who qualified for the 1954 Masters on the shoestring credential of being an alternate on the 1953 Walker Cup team, and then almost snatched the tournament away from Ben Hogan and Sam Snead. The short wait also offered an opportunity to add to my clothing, the better to suit the weather. On the walk out, I had been almost too warm wearing a Shetland sweater and a Harris-tweed jacket, but now I put on the raincoat I had been lugging along, and felt much more comfortable. Two holes later, I added a wool scarf. I believe that you can never trust the weather in Scotland, and I regularly carried an umbrella onto the links, drought or no drought.

The question still remained: How much longer could the unheralded Baker-Finch hold on? Hooking his tee shot into Mrs. Kruger showed that his timing might be beginning to unravel, but, with the wind behind him, he drove the green on the tenth, a poke of nearly 350 yards. He failed to take advantage of this: he left his slightly downhill approach putt ten feet short, and then missed from that distance. He took three putts again on the short eleventh, misplaying a sidehiller on that slanting green and missing the one coming back. On the 316-yard twelfth, though, he showed us something. His drive avoided all the fairway bunkers. Then, instead of playing a pitch-and-run shot at the pin, which was positioned on the back upper level, he punched a low pitch into the wind, and had the satisfaction of seeing it come down on the upper level and stop sixteen feet from the pin. He played an aggressive putt for the birdie and made it. Back to thirteen under par for the distance. You had to applaud the poise and courage of this young man. On the hard thirteenth, he made a copybook par, but he had a spot of trouble on the par-5 fourteenth, where the wind was blowing against him. He pulled his tee shot, and it finished in the second of the four bunkers known as the Beardies. On his recovery, he was able to advance the ball only a few yards, but he had the nerve to try to carry Hell Bunker on his third, and did it. He then played a pretty pitch dead on line for the pin on the left side of the green, but here he was unfortunate: the wind blew the ball back just far enough for it to catch a downslope, and he did well to two-putt from there for a 6. Back to twelve under par for the tournament. Regulation pars on the fifteenth and sixteenth. On the seventeenth, another spot of trouble. He drove into the rough on the left, and his second also finished in the rough. He tried to sneak a little run-up safely past the Road Bunker, but he was short with it and was semi-stymied by the left edge of the bunker. However, he played a dexterous chip to about seven feet and made the putt. He then finished a gutsy round by getting down in two putts from the Valley of Sin — a feat that few players pull off. The par on the eighteenth gave him a 71, which under the circumstances was not bad at all. His three-round total was 205, and this meant that on the fourth and final round he would be paired in the last twosome with Watson, who had the same total after a great 66. Except for misreading the length of his iron shot on the second hole, Watson had played an almost faultless round. He had hit a number of tasty little pinches next to the pin from some of those dusty Gobi Desert fairways. He had missed several holeable putts, as everyone had. The cups seemed to have no corners.

On Sunday, the day of the final round, the general feeling was that playing with a golfer as solid as Watson would not be to Baker-Finch's benefit. The only other players who seemed to be in the picture were Ballesteros and Langer; tied at 207, they were paired in the next-to-last twosome. I walked the first three holes with them. They were both hitting the ball well from tee to green, but on the third Langer missed a shortish putt for his par. Ballesteros seemed to be in an excellent frame of mind, relaxed but determined. All of Britain loves Ballesteros, because he has demonstrated that he is a winner — he can beat the Americans at home and abroad. They also think highly of Langer, a shy, straightforward West German, who is as good as anybody from tee to green but is a shaky putter. On some putts he uses the standard overlapping grip, on others he uses the reverse overlapping grip (the index finger of the left hand overlapping the little finger and the third finger of the right hand), and occasionally he holds the putter with his left hand lower on the shaft than his right.

On the fourth round, Baker-Finch finally went — and, when he went, he went quickly. His pitch on the first hole carried only a couple of feet beyond the Swilcan Burn, and the backspin on the shot drew the ball back into the hazard. He took a penalty stroke, played a chip from the back side of the hazard, and got down in 5, but this unlucky start patently bothered him. His confidence began to erode, he started to lose the rhythm of his swing — on his tee shots particularly — and he missed a couple of short putts. He amassed five bogeys on the first nine, and reached the turn in a wretched 41. His run of top-class golf was over, but what a run the young man had made! As happens so often in golf, and in many other pursuits, the gallery soon all but forgot old Hyphen and was absorbed in the duel between Ballesteros and Watson. By the sixth hole, Ballesteros had made up his deficit of two strokes, thanks to his own errorless golf and some unexpected mistakes by Watson, who had misjudged his pitches to the second and fourth greens and had three-putted the fifth. On the short eight, 178 yards long, Ballesteros moved a stroke in front by holing from six feet for a birdie. Then, on the tenth and eleventh, a sudden shift in the battle between them took place. After driving to the edge of the green on the 342-yard tenth — the wind was behind him — Ballesteros, who had been reading the greens expertly, left his approach putt twelve feet short and missed the second. He followed this by playing the eleventh, the 172-yard par 3 with the severely banked green, with an unsureness not at all typical of him. As was to be expected, the pin was placed about fifteen feet behind the high front wall of Strath Bunker. Ballesteros' tee shot, which he played with an 8-iron, had the right line — it was a couple of yards to the left of the pin — but he had hit the shot so badly that the ball plopped down a good twenty feet short of the green. His effort to play a touchy run-up shot through the heavy grass fringing the edge of the bunker did not come off. He needed two more strokes to hole out for his bogey 4. Watson, on the other hand, birdied the tenth. He drove the green, and ran his approach putt inches from the cup. He played the eleventh equally well, hitting what looked like a 7-iron about fifteen feet from the pin and getting down in two putts. Watson, who had trailed Ballesteros by a stroke after the ninth, now led him by a stroke after the eleventh. I stayed with Watson the rest of the way, for several reasons — the best one being that it is usually wisest to stay with the leader. I also felt that Watson would probably win. He was not hitting the ball with the assurance that he had on the third round, but I thought he would be able to make his slim lead stand up down the stretch.

Before the crucial action in this two-man fight took place on the seventeenth hole, there were several brave thrusts and parries, and at least one costly error on Watson's part. In the lead again as he stood on the tee of the twelfth, that short par 4, he hooked a drive that landed high on the heathery hill well to the left of the fairway and bounced into the congregation of whins there. Unable to play the ball, Watson had no alternative but to take a penalty stroke, and to lift the ball and drop it at the edge of the whins. He put his third shot, a wedge, about twenty feet past the pin, and was down in two putts for a bogey 5. Since Watson hadn't hit a hook all day, that big hook on the twelfth may have been the result of trying to hit the ball too hard in an effort to drive the green and consolidate his lead. He made up for the bogey to some degree by birdieing the 425-yard thirteenth. Here, after driving to the left of the Coffin Bunkers and onto the sixth fairway, he whistled a 3-iron over Lion's Mouth on the upthrust fairway, and the ball finished on the green fourteen feet beyond the pin. The putt was in all the way. Only seconds after the cheers from Watson's gallery for his birdie had subsided, however, a huge roar — the kind that usually follows the sinking of a long putt — went up from the gallery with Ballesteros and Langer, a hole ahead. As we suspected then and found to be the case later, Ballesteros had holed a twenty-foot birdie putt on the long fourteenth. He had negated Watson's birdie on the thirteenth and evened their duel again: both men were now eleven under par for the championship.

On the fourteenth, the 567-yard par 5, Watson avoided all the classic bunkers by playing three fine shots. On the green, he got settled comfortably over his fourteen-foot, slightly downhill putt, but he let it slip to the left. Down the stretch, Ballesteros, completely confident and concentrating keenly, parred the fifteenth and sixteenth. Watson subsequently parred them, too — he barely missed the Principal's Nose with his drive on the sixteenth — but his approach shots were not close to the pins. On the seventeenth, 461 yards long, Ballesteros' drive finished in the rough on the left side of the fairway. On his three previous rounds, he had not made his par 4 on that hole, and he sensed that a 4 on it this day might determine the outcome of the championship. The pin was positioned in the center of the green, about fifty feet from the front edge, which meets the fairway at the top of a long, sweeping, lateral mound. Ballesteros has magnificent hand action, and here he really hit through his second shot with a 6-iron. It climbed the mound and finished about thirty feet from the pin. He then played a fine putt that shivered to a halt on the lip of the cup. Highly emotional applause greeted the putt and the tap-in for the 4. Ballesteros nailed his drive a good way up the 354-yard eighteenth and put his wedge pitch about fifteen feet below the hole. Watson knew exactly what had taken place: to tie Ballesteros the first requisite was to get a 4 on the seventeenth. Off the tee, he set up on the ampersand painted on the sheds and blasted a long drive. It had a high parabola, and as it started to come down it faded several yards to the right. Watson, uncertain whether the ball had stayed in bounds, spread out his arms, palms up, waiting for some official down the fairway to give him the word. It was in bounds, he learned. More than that, it was on the right side of the fairway. He was in the perfect spot to play the hole the way the old Scots have always recommended. With the Road Bunker filled quite high with sand, making a good recovery shot from it was not too demanding. The one hazard a golfer had to avoid at all cost was the paved road at the back of the green. The best way to do this was to play about a 4-iron from Watson's lie. If the ball bounced up the mound and onto the green, fine. If it landed and stopped on the mound or below it, fine. He would probably get down nicely with a chip and a putt. But Watson read the situation and the shot differently. Out about a hundred and eighty-five yards from the green, he felt he needed a 2-iron or a 3-iron to land the ball well on the green, and he planned to play a right-to-left shot into the wind, which was blowing from the left and slightly against him. As he was finding his stance at the ball, a mighty shout went up from the eighteenth hole: Ballesteros had put his pitch to the eighteenth fifteen feet below the cup. Put off by the roar, Watson walked away from his shot and waited until the cheering had subsided before exchanging a few words with his caddie and then setting up at the ball with his 2-iron. He hit it badly. He had pushed the shot, and, as the ball drifted more and more to the right, one anticipated that it would probably land on or near the road, and that anything could happen. The ball bounced onto the road and into the stone wall behind it, but instead of ricocheting back toward the green, as it might have done, it settled in a little rut in the surface of the road only two feet from the wall. Getting down in two from there would take a miraculous shot. It wasn't in Watson's bag. He went down the shaft of his 7-iron and, with a necessarily restricted backswing, flicked the ball up the narrow bank of grass before the green and watched it roll some thirty feet past the pin. At about that moment, another loud, extended roar came from the eighteenth: Ballesteros had made his birdie putt, the ball tumbling into the cup on its last rotation. When I got my binoculars on him, Ballesteros was punching the air in ecstasy time and time again. Now Watson's chance of gaining a tie rested, no question about it, on his holing his putt for a 4. He made a good bid, but the ball was never in. Another salvo from the eighteenth: Langer had holed for a birdie. That was fine but irrelevant. As Watson stepped onto the eighteenth tee, he knew that his chances of tying Ballesteros boiled down to his making a 2. He hit a long drive, and, authentic sportsman that he is, he came up the eighteenth with a cheery smile on his face as the thousands around the home hole applauded him. By his own measurement, he was ninety-three yards from the flag. He went with a pitching wedge and hit the ball well past the flag. He walked to the green with that nice, natural smile of his, and got down in two putts. He waited until his playing partner, Baker-Finch, had putted out and he had shaken his hand, and then went over and warmly congratulated Ballesteros on his great finish and wonderful victory. It is not an easy thing at all to behave as graciously as Watson did after he had lost a championship he might well have won. I especially admire him for remaining himself in front of thousands of spectators, not to mention the millions watching on television. Most of the big names in sports these days make themselves into a character that they think will go over big, and proceed to act it out. With his high personal standards, Watson is one of the few who stay themselves. He is an unusual guy. For example, after driving off the fifteenth and heading down the fairway he felt he might have ignored the two R. & A. men who were with his twosome, the referee and the official observer, so he slowed down his walk and said to them cordially, "This has sure been some tournament!" In his press session after the championship, when he was asked if the first roar for Ballesteros on the eighteenth had bothered him as he prepared to hit his second shot on the seventeenth, he said,

"No. I was just trying to figure out with the caddie whether the 2-iron or the 3-iron was the right club."

A final word about Ian Baker-Finch. On the last day, after going out in 41, he added two more bogeys, along with a double bogey on the fourteenth, where he underwent the ignominy of having to take two shots to get his ball out of the fourth bunker of the Beardies. But, mind you, Baker-Finch finished his round 3,4,4,3 — birdie, par, par, birdie — for a 79 and a tie for ninth. Some knowledgeable professionals I talked with think that the young Australian has the built-in timing to control his long swing and become a most successful player. He is a likable young man, and as he drove his small car away from the R. & A. clubhouse an hour or so after the end of the championship the crowd that had gathered around the entranceway gave him a loud round of applause. I hope we get to see him often.

And what about Seve Ballesteros? His moods are as changeable as a matador's or a Trollope heroine's, but when he is on his game he is very, very good. He deserved to win this championship, because of the superlative fashion in which he played the fourteenth (birdie), the fifteenth (par), the sixteenth (par), the seventeenth (a par that had the weight of a birdie), and the eighteenth (birdie). He was both generous and apt when he said in his television interview only moments after the end of play, "I feel great to beat the best man in the world, and at the home of golf, St. Andrews." Later, in his press interview, he said, "This game is great and very strange" — a sentiment expressed for centuries but never put better. The most dramatic way to indicate how firmly in charge of his golf Ballesteros was on the fourth round is to set down his scorecard:

$$444\ 444\ 424-34$$
$$444\ 444\ 443-35 - 69.$$

I can't remember ever seeing a card quite like that.

It was appropriate that so exciting an Open broke all attendance records for the championship. During the four days when the field was warming up for the big event, more than forty thousand people paid to watch the practice rounds. As for the four rounds of the championship, 34,312 people paid their way in for Thursday's round; 38,484 for Friday's round; 38,136 for Saturday's round; 35,686 for Sunday's round. The total attendance over the eight days came to 187,736, eclipsing last year's record attendance at Royal Birkdale by forty-five thousand.

One thing more. Watson, who won the British Open at Carnoustie in 1975, at Turnberry in 1977, at Muirfield in 1980, and at Troon in 1982, will have another chance to see if he can win it at St. Andrews and so complete a grand slam of victories over the five Scottish courses on which the Open has been held since 1925, when Prestwick was taken off the rota because of its insufficient length and its lack of space for spectators. There is some talk these days that Carnoustie may be taken off the rota, but, whether it is or not, in six or seven years St. Andrews should again be the venue of the championship. In 1991, say, Watson will be only forty-one, and, all things being equal, he might still have a good shot at winning on the Old Course. We shall see.

(1984)